CALIFORNIA

THE POLITICS OF DIVERSITY

TENTH EDITION

DAVID G. LAWRENCE

Emeritus Professor, Westmont College

JEFFREY CUMMINS

Professor, California State University, Fresno

ROWMAN & LITTLEFIELD

Lanham • Boulder • New York • London

Jeff dedicates this edition to Coach Don Johnson (Cypress College), who passed away during the writing of this book. If not for his influence, this textbook partnership with David would not have been possible.

Executive Editor: Traci Crowell
Editorial Assistant: Deni Remsberg
Executive Marketing Manager: Amy Whitaker
Interior Designer: Rosanne Schloss

Credits and acknowledgments for material borrowed from other sources, and reproduced with permission, appear on the appropriate page within the text.

Published by Rowman & Littlefield
An imprint of The Rowman & Littlefield Publishing Group, Inc.
4501 Forbes Boulevard, Suite 200, Lanham, Maryland 20706
www.rowman.com

6 Tinworth Street, London SE11 5AL, United Kingdom

British Library Cataloguing in Publication Information Available

Library of Congress Cataloging-in-Publication Data
Names: Lawrence, David G., 1944- author. | Cummins, Jeff, 1975- author.
Title: California : the politics of diversity / David G. Lawrence, Westmont College,
    Jeff Cummins, California State University, Fresno.
Description: Tenth Edition. | Lanham : ROWMAN & LITTLEFIELD, [2019] |
    Previous edition published by Cengage in 2017. | Includes bibliographical
    references and index.
Identifiers: LCCN 2019018941 (print) | LCCN 2019020115 (ebook) |
    ISBN 9781538129302 (ebook) | ISBN 9781538132593 | ISBN 9781538132593
    (cloth : alk. paper) | ISBN 9781538129296 (paperback : alk. paper)
Subjects: LCSH: Cultural pluralism—California. | California—Politics and government.
Classification: LCC JK274 (ebook) | LCC JK274 .L46 2019 (print) |
    DDC 320.9794—dc23
LC record available at https://lccn.loc.gov/2019018941

♾™ The paper used in this publication meets the minimum requirements of American National Standard for Information Sciences—Permanence of Paper for Printed Library Materials, ANSI/NISO Z39.48-1992.

Brief Contents

★ ★ ★

Contents

Illustrations and Tables

★ ★ ★

FIGURES

CARTOONS

PHOTOS

TABLES

Preface

In revising *California: The Politics of Diversity* for its tenth edition, the political environment engulfing California politics has once again changed from that of the previous edition. One significant change taking place at the top of the executive branch is that the longest-serving governor in California history, Jerry Brown, departed office in 2019, leaving behind what he hopes to be a positive legacy for his successors. Perhaps his largest accomplishment is his fiscal stewardship. Unlike his two predecessors, and his own first stint in the governor's office, Jerry Brown will hand over to his successor a state budget that is on solid fiscal ground. Confronting a $25 billion deficit upon assuming office in 2011, he leaves the governorship with a budget surplus and the largest rainy-day reserve in state history. Despite this short-term turnaround in the state's financial condition, Governor Brown's fiscal legacy may be tarnished by looming pension and retiree healthcare spending obligations.

Another significant development in the state's political environment since the last edition is the election of Donald Trump as president and California's response to his administration's policies. Dubbed the "state of resistance," California's political leaders, most notably Governor Brown and Attorney General Xavier Becerra, vociferously opposed President Trump's immigration and climate change policies. After the Trump administration took a more proactive approach to deporting undocumented immigrants, Brown signed a "sanctuary state" law that limited the ability of state and local law enforcement to assist federal agents with immigration enforcement. The Trump administration sued the state and the feud is now pending in the federal court system. In a similar vein, when the president withdrew the United States from the Paris Climate Accord, an international agreement to limit worldwide carbon emissions, Governor Brown announced that California and other like-minded states would uphold the agreement and pursue immediate actions to reduce global temperatures.

Brown's departure also means that the state will have new leadership in the governor's office. After a relatively easy victory in the 2018 gubernatorial race, Gavin Newsom signaled that he intended to continue Brown's restrained fiscal policy by building up the state's rainy-day fund in order to prepare the budget for the next economic downturn. Newsom also indicated that he intended to depart from his predecessor in big ways. In his early days in office, he announced that he would pursue scaled-down versions of the state's high-speed rail system and the twin-tunnels plan to divert water around the Sacramento–San Joaquin Delta. Both were pet projects for Brown and major factors in his potential legacy.

From the legacy of Jerry Brown to the federal-state feud between President Trump and the state of resistance to the early developments in the new governor's administration, all of these and more permeate the new tenth edition of *California: The Politics of Diversity*.

TEXT FEATURES

While this new edition includes key political developments over the last few years, California politics remains affected by the diverse and hyperpluralistic nature of the state itself, particularly its people and the groups to which they belong. Although political leadership is central to governing, we continue to explain California politics through the dual lenses of diversity and a variant of pluralism we call *hyperpluralism*. In all nine editions, we have tried to show two things: (1) how demographic, cultural, economic, geographic, and political diversity affect how politics actually works in California and (2) how the exceedingly pluralistic nature of the state results in a highly competitive tug-of-war between ideologies, institutions, policymakers, political parties, interest groups, and voters. Both themes have been readily apparent in the last few years. Despite California's trend toward a more Democratic state, some local jurisdictions, siding with the Trump administration, have expressed their opposition to the state's new sanctuary law, illustrating both the diversity of ideologies in the state, particularly in certain geographic areas, and the fragmented political structure characteristic of hyperpluralism.

PEDAGOGICAL FEATURES

Along with these dual themes, the tenth edition continues to incorporate the latest research in political science and on California politics. In the last edition, we introduced a new feature on "How California Compares," which showcased how California is both similar and different to other states, and we are expanding this popular feature in the tenth edition. We continue to offer numerous pedagogical features that help students learn, including:

- Student Learning Outcomes that inform students what they should take away from each chapter
- Chapter conclusions that revisit key points and tie them to book themes
- Boldfaced key terms that are referenced by page number
- Study questions that help students review and apply chapter content
- Extensive endnotes that provide opportunities for further reading and research
- Updated charts, tables, photos, quotes, boxes, and cartoons designed to amplify key points
- A complete glossary at the end of the book for easy reference

REVISION HIGHLIGHTS

In terms of substance, the tenth edition involves cover-to-cover revisions that reflect the latest developments in California politics. They include the following:

- Analysis of state results for the 2018 elections, including the governor's race and ballot propositions
- Coverage of the last years of the Brown administration and his potential legacy
- Insight into the early days of the Newsom administration
- Summary of the #MeToo movement in the state capital
- New evidence of the trends in state partisanship
- Discussion of the 2016 presidential election and the Trump administration's impact on California, including trade and immigration
- Changes in voter registration procedures, including the new motor voter law
- Revised coverage of the housing crisis, water policy, and transportation
- Updated coverage of high-speed rail construction and its future

ONLINE SUPPLEMENTS

Instructor's Manual/Test Bank for Lawrence/Cummins' *California: The Politics of Diversity, 10th Edition*, https://textbooks.rowman.com/california10e.

Jeff Cummins has provided a revised instructor's manual and test bank that offer suggestions for class discussions, writing assignments, Internet and research projects, and exam questions.

ACKNOWLEDGMENTS

After a long and successful partnership with Cengage Learning, this is the first edition with the textbook's new home at Rowman & Littlefield. We are very excited about this new partnership and grateful to Traci Crowell, executive editor, for taking on our project. We wish to thank her for the enthusiasm, guidance, and smooth transition that she provided to us as new Rowman authors. We also wish to thank Charlotte Gosnell for her patient management of textbook production and responding to all our inquiries about the process.

We are also indebted to many people who helped educate and inform us about California politics. From our own years in and around state and local politics, we must credit the many practitioners who have shared their political insights with us—former city council and Legislative Analyst's Office colleagues, internship supervisors, classroom speakers, journalists, and countless Sacramento Legislative Seminar panelists. We would also like to thank our wives, Carolyn (David) and Natasha (Jeff), for their encouragement and support on our work on this and previous editions. Jeff Cummins authored the instructor's manual and test bank.

We also need to acknowledge and thank the political scientists who reviewed all or some of *California* along the way. They include the following: Theodore J. Anagnoson (California State University, Los Angeles), Jodi Balma (Fullerton College), Antoine Clerc (College of the Desert), Michele Colborn Harris (College of the Canyons), John H. Culver (California Polytechnic State University, San Luis Obispo), Robert L. Delorme (California State University, Long Beach), Scott A. Frisch (California State University, Channel Islands), Lawrence L. Giventer (California State University, Stanislaus), Herbert E. Gooch (California Lutheran University), Jack Hames (Butte College), Drake C. Hawkins (Glendale Community College), Peter H. Howse (American River College), Wesley Hussey (California State University, Sacramento), William W. Lammers (University of Southern California), Dianne Long (California Polytechnic State University, San Luis Obispo), Marilyn J. Loufek (Long Beach City College), Edward S. Malecki (California State University, Los Angeles), Donald J. Matthewson (California State University, Fullerton), Charles H. McCall (California State University, Bakersfield), John Mercurio (San Diego State University), Steve Monsma (Pepperdine University), Stanley W. Moore (Pepperdine University), Gerhard Peters (Citrus College), Eugene Price (California State University, Northridge), Donald Ranish (Antelope Valley College), John F. Roche III (Palomar College), Maria Sampanis (California State University, Sacramento), Mark Smith (University of California, Davis), Alvin D. Sokolow (University of California, Davis), Charles C. Turner (California State University, Chico), Richard S. Unruh (Fresno Pacific University), Linda O. Valenty (San Jose State University), JoAnn Victor (California State University, Long Beach), and Alan J. Wyner (University of California, Santa Barbara).

As helpful as these veteran colleagues were, we take full responsibility for the end product.

David G. Lawrence
Professor Emeritus of Political Science
Westmont College

Jeff Cummins
Professor of Political Science
California State University, Fresno

About the Authors

★ ★ ★

David G. Lawrence is professor emeritus of political science at Westmont College in Santa Barbara. As a teacher, scholar, and former public official, he has applied theory and practice to California politics. He served on a city council as mayor pro tem, chaired a regional planning agency, and is former president of the California Association of Councils of Governments (CALCOG). He currently serves on the Measure a Citizens Oversight Committee, a group that advises the Santa Barbara County Association of Governments on the expenditure of sales tax revenues earmarked for transportation (an estimated $1 billion over 30 years). He is also former president of the California Center for Education in Public Affairs, a consortium of colleges and universities dedicated to helping students better understand California politics through Sacramento seminars and post-election briefings.

Jeff Cummins is professor of political science at California State University, Fresno. He previously worked for the Legislative Analyst's Office (LAO) in Sacramento where he advised the legislature on budgetary and policy issues. He also worked for the California State Auditor, performing audits of various state agencies. He teaches several courses on California government, including California Politics and Public Budgeting. He is the author of *Boom and Bust: The Politics of the California Budget* and his publications on state politics and policy have appeared in such journals as *State Politics and Policy Quarterly*, *Social Science Quarterly*, *State and Local Government Review* and *American Politics Research*. He frequently provides commentary to news media and has been interviewed by National Public Radio (NPR) affiliates, the *New York Times*, *The Economist*, the *National Journal*, the *Sacramento Bee*, the *Los Angeles Times*, and the *Fresno Bee*.

1
Explaining California Politics

LEARNING OUTCOMES

Students will be able to:

★ Describe how California's diversity is reflected in its land, regions, resources, people, and economy.

★ Identify which events and historical developments brought different demographic groups to California.

★ Explain the five factors that characterize the state's economy and how the economy relates to diversity.

★ Assess the extent to which democratic theory, elite theory, and pluralist theory explain California politics.

★ Summarize the central components of hyperpluralism and how they apply to California politics.

IN BRIEF

In this introductory chapter, we survey the big picture of California politics. Many observers claim the Golden State is no longer the land of milk and honey, yet it continues to draw newcomers from the four corners of the earth. Why the differences in perception? The answer is in the diversity of California and how it is governed. This chapter covers these two subjects.

THE STATE'S DIVERSITY has been its strength. The land varies from temperate coastal plains to rugged mountain ranges, from lush agricultural valleys to barren deserts. People divide California into several regions, but these divisions seem to be a matter of perception. Some divide the state into north and south; others see multiple and diverse regions. California is rich in resources, especially water and desirable climate. Moving the state's water supply around has increased the usability of the land. Throughout its history, California has seen waves of people moving to and around the state seeking a better life. These factors have resulted in a diverse economy—one of the world's largest.

How political scientists explain U.S. politics in general helps us understand California politics in particular. To answer the question, "Who governs?" four theories have emerged. Democratic theory says the people do, usually through elected representatives. Elite theory claims that the upper classes exercise power and influence beyond their numbers. Pluralist theory contends that groups compete for power and policy advantage. Hyperpluralism, an emerging theory, contends that so many groups now compete and the political system is so complex that governing can become most difficult.

Although these theories seem incompatible, each helps to explain aspects of California politics. Evidence of hyperpluralism in California is growing. The outcome is a state of many paradoxes.

INTRODUCTION

At the end of Jerry Brown's first stint as governor in 1983, he saddled his successor, George Deukmejian, with a large budget deficit amid growing public hostility toward elected officials and government more generally. Fast-forward to the end of Brown's second stint as governor and the political environment he left behind in 2019 could not have been more different for his successor, Gavin Newsom. Buoyed by a surging economy, Governor Brown presided over a dramatic turnaround in the state's financial stability, converting a $20 billion deficit at the beginning of his term into a $20 billion surplus upon his departure. Students of California history, however, know that the state's fortunes can take a turn for the worse relatively quickly and with it public sentiment for its elected leaders.

In some ways, California could be likened to theme park roller coasters. People flock to both—enduring congestion in the process and experiencing the exhilaration of both ups and downs. In the Golden State, the highs include better jobs, economic opportunities, and living conditions that people could only have imagined about back home, whether they are from Missouri or Mexico. People envision California as a place where these dreams can come true. The lows include periodic recessions, occasional droughts, smog, crime, crowded freeways, and unaffordable housing.

Some Californians endure the lows to appreciate the highs, but others find California, like the roller coaster, a bit too much. They flee the state for Washington, Oregon, Nevada, Colorado, and beyond. Or they move within the state, seeking a calmer ride. As a whole, Californians' confidence in the future of the state can vary remarkably from year to year (see figure 1.1).

Although the overall outlook for Californians has become more positive in recent years, it obscures the deeply entrenched political divide that permeates state and national politics. When we further examine Californians' views of the state by party affiliation and region of residence, we find much greater variation in the confidence in the state's future. Republicans in inland California are much more likely to reject the direction of the state than Democrats in the highly populated coastal cities. Donald Trump's election as president in 2016 and subsequent policies toward immigrants and health care intensified these political fissures. State leaders responded by declaring the state as the head of the "resistance" against the Trump administration and invoking the importance of California in guiding the future direction of the nation. Newly elected governor Gavin Newsom captured this sentiment in his 2019 inaugural speech: "California has always helped write America's future. . . . But what we do today is even more consequential because of what's happening in the country. People's lives, freedom, security, the

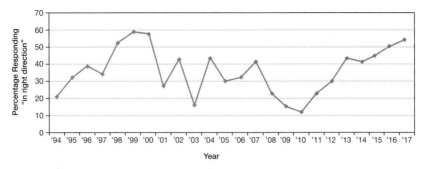

Figure 1.1 How Californians View California
When Pollsters Ask If California Is Going in the Right or Wrong Direction, Californians' Responses Have Varied Significantly over the Years

Question: In your opinion, to what extent do these data affect perceptions of governmental institutions and policymakers?

Notes: Results are based on representative statewide samples of about 1,000 California adults. The sampling error ranges from 3.2 to 4.5 percentage points.

Source: Successive surveys of The Field Poll (http://ucdata.berkeley.edu/data_record.php?recid=3) and Berkeley IGS Poll (https://igs.berkeley.edu/igs-poll/berkeley-igs-poll).

water we drink, the air we breathe—they all hang in the balance. The country is watching us. The world is waiting on us. And the future depends on us."[1]

These idealistic visions of California's promise are nothing new. In the 1500s, Spaniards desired to find and explore a mythical island of *California*. Writer Garci Ordóñez de Montalvo described this place as rich in "gold and precious stones"; its people were "robust of body, with strong and passionate hearts and great virtues." As for government, the queen "had ambitions to execute nobler actions than had been performed by any other ruler."[2] Wealth and good intentions—what a combination! No wonder California has been called not only a state but also a state of mind.

Centuries later, California's official state motto captures that mythic search: "Eureka" (I Have Found It). The motto itself refers to the real gold that many sought and some actually found. Symbolically, it refers to a host of images emanating from California: perpetually sunny days (advertised every year by Pasadena's Rose Parade), hope and opportunity, and a chance to start over, plus gorgeous scenery and people to match (says Hollywood). However, for an increasing number of Californians, that myth does not match reality.

Chapter 1 introduces two approaches to understanding California politics. The first is the state's remarkable diversity. The second is a set of theories that political scientists use to explain aspects of American politics generally. These two broad approaches (diversity and theory) are revisited throughout the book.

HOW DIVERSITY EXPLAINS CALIFORNIA POLITICS

California always has been a compelling place. Few observers write about it without describing its physical diversity, and fewer still ignore its politics. To understand this huge state, one must understand how its public sector works.

Political scientist David Easton defined **politics** as "the authoritative allocation of values for a society as a whole."[3] Politics occurs within the context of a **political system.** In our federal arrangement, there are 50 state systems and one national political system. These systems reflect ongoing patterns of human behavior involving control, influence, power, and authority. The process of making public policy, deciding "who gets what, when and how,"[4] exists within the context of a larger environment. The **political environment** is a set of social, cultural, economic, and physical attributes that inform and limit how politics is done. To begin this study of California politics, we must examine California's diverse environment—the land and regions of the state and its resources, people, and economy.

Land

Diverse is truly the only word to describe the physical geography of California. The state's diversity is made possible in part by its sheer size. California's length covers the distance between New York City and Jacksonville, Florida. As the nation's third-largest state in square miles (behind Alaska and Texas), California supports a rich variety of terrain.

Coastal communities enjoy moderate, semiarid Mediterranean weather in the south and wetter, cooler weather in the far north. Thick forests, including giant redwoods, are found in the North. In fact, 40 percent of the state is forested. The naturally barren south has been made less so over the years by farmers and gardeners alike. Numerous mountain ranges crisscross the state. The defining north/south range is the Sierra Nevada. Admired by naturalist John Muir, this magnificent mountain range is home to world-famous Yosemite National Park and giant sequoia trees. Farmers and urban residents to the west and south of the mountains depend on the Sierra's snowpack for year-round water supplies, the lifeblood of any arid state. Less-imposing coastal ranges help define the attractive but expensive environments around such places as Santa Barbara, Carmel, and Santa Cruz.

The transverse ranges, those mountains that lie in an east/west direction, were once defined by the limits of urbanization and, to some people's minds, serve as the boundary between Northern and Southern California. The Los Angeles Basin (surrounded by the Sierra Madre, Tehachapi, Santa Ana, San Gabriel, and San Jacinto ranges) once kept its poor air quality to itself. But urban growth and automobile proliferation have spread smog over the mountains to communities on the other side (e.g., Palm Springs and Lancaster) and locales as far away as the Grand Canyon in Arizona. The smoggy Central Valley supports some of the most productive agriculture in the world.

Below the observable land lie two massive tectonic plates, the North American and the Pacific. The grinding of these plates results in long-term geologic features such as mountains and the short-term terror of potentially destructive earthquakes.

Regions

The configuration of the land influences how people settle on and use it, leading to regional differences. These differences are partly a matter of perception. Consider the idea of Northern and Southern California, the most familiar division of the state. People know Northern California for San Francisco (called simply "The City"), wineries, redwoods, heavy water-consuming crops such as rice, and mountain resorts such as Lake Tahoe. They identify Southern California with its warm days, wide beaches, automobile culture, show business, Latino roots, and, of course, smog. Some suggest that these two regions are actually two states divided by water. The north has it, the south wants it, and the north knows it. These north/south differences are deeply rooted. In 1859, less than a decade after statehood, the legislature voted to split the state in two, but the U.S. Congress disallowed it. Occasional efforts to divide California have surfaced ever since. The latest effort by Silicon Valley venture capitalist Tim Draper would have divided California into three states, but the California Supreme Court removed it from the November 2018 ballot. These efforts seem motivated not only by classic regional differences but also by the mounting problems faced by a unified California—economic uncertainty, budget woes, population growth, and demographic diversity. Although these efforts are doomed to failure, they do exemplify intense regional divisions in the state. Pundits have long since divided California from north to south into Logland, Fogland, and Smogland.

Perceptions aside, California is a state of many regions. Different observers have divided the state into anywhere from 4 to 14 distinct regions. Each is markedly different from the others based on geography, economy, populations, political behavior, and public attitudes.[5] Public opinion surveys and election analyses of the four most populous regions—Los Angeles County, the San Francisco Bay area, the Central Valley, and the Orange County/Inland Empire region—document a number of differences (see figure 1.2). In general, coastal Californians are more liberal and Democratic and those who live inland are more conservative and Republican. This plays out in legislative elections, initiative results, and views on public policy.[6] As a consequence, according to analyst and pollster Mark Baldassare, these regional differences make it difficult for Californians to unify and see themselves as members of one state (see cartoon 1.1). Indeed, "the major regions are drifting further apart at a time when there is a need to reach a statewide consensus on social, environmental, land use, and infrastructure issues."[7]

Resources

In addition to regional perceptions, a state's natural resources affect its politics. Ironically, California's most important resource is its most precious—water. One simply cannot underestimate what the availability and redistribution of water have meant for the Golden State. As writer Carey McWilliams once noted, "the history of Southern California is the record of its eternal quest for water, and more water, and still more water."[8] The entire state has been called a "hydraulic society," and it is easy to see why. Water has transformed parched land into the nation's salad bowl and fruit basket. Water has enabled imaginative people in a semiarid climate to control vast amounts of land or merely turn their yards into tropical and subtropical gardens. And most important, dams, canals, and aqueducts have channeled water from the north to the south, allowing millions of people to live where nature alone could support very few. However, as indicated by the state's recent drought, from time to time, rain patterns remind residents of what a precious resource water is to California.

California's overall climate is itself a resource and has directly and indirectly caused the state's phenomenal growth. Americans have always been lured to

Figure 1.2 California's Regions

Note: The highlighted areas of California are the regions most used by the Public Policy Institute of California pollsters to document differing views of Californians based on geography.

Source: Public Policy Institute of California.

California because of its weather. Years ago, winter exports of citrus fruit and newspaper ads in the Midwest created a "Garden of Eden" image, which served as a magnet. Asked why he charged $200 an acre for seemingly worthless land, flamboyant speculator Lucky Baldwin retorted: "Hell! We're giving away the land. We're selling the climate."[9] Doctors would recommend California's milder climate to patients suffering from respiratory and arthritic ailments.

California's climate also has fostered elements of California's economy. Early movie producers found weather predictability helpful in shooting outdoor scenes. The films themselves became subtle advertisements for the Golden State. Farmers discovered that, given enough water, several harvests per year were

Cartoon 1.1 The Right Direction in California?

Question: Why are there different opinions about whether California is heading in the right direction?

possible. Developers and contractors found they could get away with cheaper, less-weather-resistant construction. Employers concerned with working conditions and living conditions for themselves found California an inviting destination. California's climate also fostered recreation-oriented "live for the weekend" lifestyles. Much leisure time can be spent outdoors—beach activities, snow skiing, fishing, water sports, camping, biking, hiking—the list is endless. Even at home, many Californians create their own micro-lifestyles, replete with expansive patios, pools, spas, barbecues, and gardens.

All this has resulted in a subtle attitude found in the Golden State. Just as people thought they could change their destiny by moving to California in the first place, many believe they can engineer their destiny once they arrive. Californians seek what they call the "good life" despite hindrances of all sorts. They expect their state and local governments to deliver policies fostering and protecting a certain quality of life. They become disillusioned and angry when policymakers fail to meet such expectations. They give policymakers low marks in public opinion surveys, oust them from office if possible, or pass initiatives designed to sidestep policy processes.

People

California's resources have encouraged waves of human settlement. In short, diversity and growth characterize the demographics of California. As in the past, the state attracts immigrants from all over the world. Furthermore, they are settling throughout the state. Mexicans were never limited solely to Los Angeles barrios or the Chinese to their Chinatowns. But the ethnic and geographic diversity of today's Californians is astounding. Iranians, Indians, Sri Lankans, Haitians, Koreans, Salvadorans, Vietnamese, and others are moving to and throughout California in large numbers. By 2000, no racial group or ethnic group constituted a majority of Californians. In fact, a decade later, more than 20 percent of

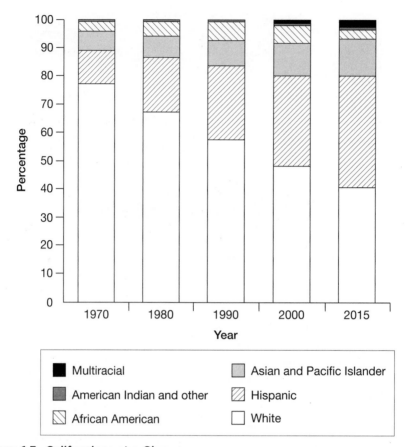

Figure 1.3   Californians at a Glance

Question: California is now a "minority majority" state. To what extent is this phenomenon evident where you live and work?

Source: Hans Johnson, "Just the Facts: California's Population" (San Francisco: Public Policy Institute of California, March 2017), https://www.ppic.org/publication/californias-population.

the nation's nonwhite population lived in California. California's population currently is growing at a rate of nearly 1,000 per day. In 2018, the state's population stood at 40 million. The change in ethnic diversity can be seen in figure 1.3.

Native Americans. California's first dwellers were widely dispersed Native Americans living off the land in small communities. By 1823, there were about 400,000 tribal members living in California. As peaceful peoples, they were no match for the succession of more aggressive Spanish, Mexican, and Anglo-American settlers. Due primarily to disease imported from these settlers, they and their cultures were driven to near extinction. Today, Native Americans constitute less than 1 percent (145,000) of its population and are discussed further in chapters 2 and 3. As a rule, they defy broad-brush generalizations. Some tribes remain poor whereas others have discovered newfound wealth and political influence by way of lucrative casino development and large-scale gaming.

Latinxs. By the time of Mexican independence from Spain in 1822, the remaining Native Americans plus a relative handful of Spaniards, Mexicans, and the offspring of mixed marriages between various groups populated the province of del norte. Like their predecessors, contemporary Mexicans and others from Latin America come to California seeking prosperity. Be they citizens, resident aliens, or undocumented workers, many Latinxs work in the agricultural, manufacturing, and service sectors of the state's economy. Due to continuing immigration and relatively high birth rates, they have become a sizable cultural and socioeconomic force in the state. They became the state's largest ethnic or racial group in 2015, surpassing whites for the first time. Geographically, they are well-represented in most of California's regions, and their political influence is on the rise. In one respect, Latinxs have been known for low voter turnout, in part, because many of them are not yet citizens or are too young to vote. Yet they are an increasing presence in elected public office throughout the state. In 2018, three out of the eight statewide officials elected are Latino. Population data and electoral returns suggest that Latino political influence will grow in the future and that the rather diverse Latino community might not behave as a monolithic political force.[10]

Non-Hispanic Whites. The Gold Rush of 1849 began what is known as the "American era." This provincial-sounding term refers to the successive waves of Euro-American citizens who moved to California from other parts of the United States. Within a year after gold was discovered at Sutter's Mill in 1848, roughly a third of the state's population was digging for gold in "them thar hills." Many with gold fever never intended to stay, but did. Others not only stayed but also sent for their families to join them. Population figures tell the story. In 1840, Californians numbered about 116,000, including 110,000 to 112,000 Native Americans. Two decades later, they numbered 380,000, including only 30,000 Native Americans.

A second population rush followed completion of the Transcontinental Railroad in 1869. That last spike, joining the Central Pacific and Union Pacific railroads in Utah, linked California both physically and symbolically with the rest of the nation. For urban Americans, the lure of open space "out West" actually made possible a newly emerging dream in the late 1800s—a single-family house on a single-family lot. But why California? For one thing, the Southern Pacific Railroad had received more than 10 million acres of Southern California land as a construction incentive. Through shameless hucksterism and discounted train tickets, developers and the railroads lured many Midwesterners to the Golden State. Later, the mass production of automobiles allowed others to bypass trains altogether on their way to sunny California.

In the 1900s, additional waves of Americans moved westward to seek various employment opportunities. Beginning with Summerland near Santa Barbara in 1920, the discovery and drilling of oil led to new jobs and still more land speculation. The Depression-era jobless and Dust Bowl refugees (many were called Okies and Arkies for their home states of Oklahoma and Arkansas, respectively) came to California in search of any opportunity they could find.

John Steinbeck's novel *The Grapes of Wrath* fictionalized the real misery of these migrants and what they hoped for in California (see box 1.1). World War II brought numerous Americans to California for training and war production efforts. Soldiers and sailors who had never been west of the Mississippi River were stationed briefly in California on their way to the Pacific theater. Many

> ### Box 1.1 ★ California Voices: Steinbeck on California
>
> "I like to think how nice it's gonna be, maybe, in California. Never cold. An' fruit ever'place, an' people just bein in the nicest places, little white houses in among the orange trees. I wonder—that is, if we all get jobs an' all work—maybe we can get one of them little white houses. An' the little fellas go out an' pick oranges right off the tree."
>
> **Question**: To what extent are today's visions of California like or unlike those of Steinbeck's Depression-ravaged characters?
>
> *Source:* John Steinbeck, *The Grapes of Wrath* (New York: Viking Press, 1939), 124.

of them vowed to return to California—for keeps—and they did. In 2018, white non-Hispanic Californians were less than 37 percent of the overall population. This percentage has been declining and will continue to do so in the future.

African Americans. The war effort in California provided unprecedented employment opportunities for African Americans, many of who migrated from the South. Their population in California grew 272 percent in the 1940s alone. In 2010, most of California's 2.3 million African Americans lived in the state's large metropolitan areas. As elsewhere, they have suffered racial discrimination, and many lag behind other groups in education and income. They have held prominent positions in state politics, including three Assembly speakerships (Willie Brown, Herb Wesson, and Karen Bass), as well as seats in Congress and the state legislature. According to the latest census figures, African Americans constitute less than 7 percent of California's overall population. Because of modest birth rates and some migration out of California, black political clout appears to be lessening; the number of black officeholders has steadily declined since the mid-1980s.

Asian Americans. A succession of other groups entered California over the years. Notable have been California's over 5 million Asian Americans (as of 2018), including those of Chinese, Japanese, Filipino, and Korean descent. Many Chinese were brought to the state during the Gold Rush or to work on railroad construction gangs. By 1870, nearly 150,000 of them were treated as virtual slaves by their employers. During economic downturns, they were considered as excess labor and had to retreat to their Chinatowns for protection and security.

Historically, Japanese Californians have also suffered oppression. Between 1900 and 1920 they increased in number from 10,000 to 72,000 and, to the dismay of whites, gained control of 11 percent of the state's farmland. Four years later, the U.S. Congress reacted by halting further Japanese immigration. After Japan attacked Pearl Harbor in 1941, Californians of Japanese descent, including American citizens, were moved to internment camps. Branded temporarily as "enemy aliens," Japanese Americans rose above this wholesale discrimination and economic dislocation to become successful both educationally and economically.

Filipino Californians, although sizable in number, do not command the economic influence of either the Chinese or the Japanese in California. The Vietnam

War resulted in an influx of Southeast Asians to California. Some have achieved material success in the Golden State, but others work at poverty wages in Southern California sweatshops.

Ethnic diversity in California also translates into language diversity. Census data indicate that about 44 percent of Californians speak a language other than English in the home; the national figure is a little over 21 percent. In general, children speak English more fluently than the adults in these homes.

What do all this racial and ethnic data tell us? Whereas other parts of America have historically thought of diversity in biracial (black and white) terms, describing the people of California is much more complex, given the state's many racial and ethnic groups. Some observers ask: Will this multiethnic and multiracial mix we find in California lead to divisive, Balkanized politics that emphasize difference over unity? It depends.

Aside from policies related to race or ethnicity such as affirmative action, services to undocumented immigrants, and bilingual education, polling data suggest that California's Asians, blacks, Latinos, and whites agree more often than not on a wide range of issues.[11] In the words of the nation's motto, there may well be more "unum" than "pluribus" on many issues. To the extent that diverse Californians view public life in similar terms, they embody what writer O. Henry once said of the state: "Californians are a race of people; not merely inhabitants of a state."[12] Furthermore, as you will see shortly, the "politics of diversity" in the Golden State is only in part a function of ethnic and racial diversity.

Economy

To the state's geographic and demographic diversity can be added economic diversity. To understand the politics of any state, knowing its economy is essential. Business and politics are closely intertwined. State and local policies can have an impact on economic growth, generally, particular economic sectors, and even individual businesses. The economy, in turn, provides the financial base for state and local policies. California's modern economy is large, postindustrial, diverse, driven by change, and affected by a tiered workforce.

1. *Size.* By any measure, California's economy is huge. If it were a nation-state, its gross state (domestic) product—in the range of $3 trillion—would make it the world's fifth-largest economy (see figure 1.4a). Compared to the other 49 states, California ranks first in a number of categories. Although agriculture constitutes a small fraction of the state's economic output, it outproduces all other states. Despite recent job losses, it also ranks first in manufacturing. Fifty-three Fortune 500 companies call California home, placing it third in the nation.

2. *Postindustrialism.* California has a **postindustrial economy**, meaning it is characterized by a large and growing service sector, economic interdependence, rapid change, innovation, and advanced technology. As a general rule, traditional manufacturing has lagged behind services and trade in numbers of workers. This is especially true with "off-shoring," the transfer of manufacturing jobs overseas. Today's postindustrial service economy includes technology, education, research, finance, insurance, and real

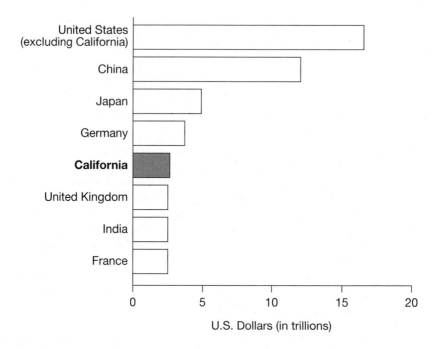

Figure 1.4a California: A Nation-Sized Economy

Source: Benjy Egel, "California Now World's Fifth-Largest Economy, Bigger Than Britain," *Sacramento Bee*, May 4, 2018, https://www.sacbee.com/news/business/article210466514.html.

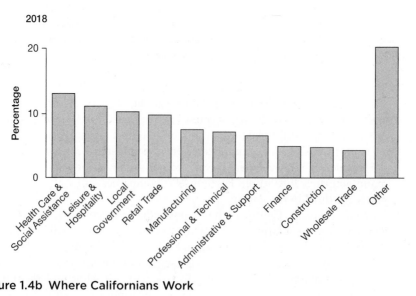

Figure 1.4b Where Californians Work

Source: Legislative Analyst's Office, "CalFacts 2018" (Sacramento: Legislative Analyst's Office, January 2019), https://lao.ca.gov/reports/2018/3905/calfacts-2018.pdf.

estate. It also includes both wholesale and retail sales of groceries, clothing, and a plethora of other consumer items. Taken together, the service sector includes both high-paying and low-paying jobs.[13]

3. *Change.* California's economic history has been one of constant change. The Gold Rush encouraged a "rush" of workers. The expansion of railroads (including the invention of refrigerated rolling stock), plus government-financed water projects, secured agriculture as an economic mainstay. The discovery of oil fueled the state's emerging automobile-oriented transportation system. World War II spawned a military-industrial complex, which anchored the state's manufacturing sector. Finally, the technological revolution laid the groundwork for the service-based economy described earlier. Economic change today is international in scope. The health of foreign economies affects trade from California and many jobs have been outsourced or "off-shored" to places such as India. Asian nations have become major competitors in numerous industries, and Mexico's border towns have lured U.S.- and foreign-owned assembly factories called maquiladoras. California's workers are changing too. The state's labor force is older, more ethnically diverse, and more female than it once was (see box 1.2).

4. *Diversity.* California's economy is richly diverse. As figure 1.4b portrays, California's employment base is highly diversified. In many ways, this helps California weather difficulties faced by other states that lean on a relative handful of economic sectors for their economic health. This diversity helped pulled the state out of the Great Recession with job growth that outpaced the nation as a whole.

5. *Multitiered Workforce.* Last, California's workforce or labor pool consists of multiple tiers. The upper tiers consist of highly educated, well-paid employees in high technology, knowledge-intensive businesses, and organizations. Included are the fields of education, medicine, communications, law, finance, real estate, transportation, and government. The lower tiers consist of those working in low-paying, low-status service jobs found in retail outlets, the tourism industry, agriculture, and marginal manufacturing concerns. The top tiers have enjoyed rising income in recent decades; the lower tiers have actually experienced a precipitous drop in income, especially among male workers, leading to growing income disparities among the tiers. California now ranks fourth among states with the highest income inequality, and this disparity is rising the second fastest of any state.

Box 1.2 ★ Did You Know . . . ?

From 2006 to 2016, 1.6 million more people moved to California from other countries than left to live abroad, while 1.2 million more people moved to other states than moved from those states. With the natural increase (births minus deaths), California's overall population still rose by 3.1 million people.

Question: Are these migration patterns likely to continue in the future?

Source: Hans Johnson, *Just the Facts: California's Population* (San Francisco: Public Policy Institute of California, March, 2017).

HOW POLITICAL THEORY EXPLAINS CALIFORNIA POLITICS

As important as it is, a state's political environment alone (land, regions, resources, people, and economy) does not explain its politics. Politics deals with complex sets of human relationships involving influence and power. To understand the complexity of politics, theories help explain who governs and why. But not all political scientists can agree on a single theory. As a result, alternative theories have emerged, which we will briefly explore and apply to California politics (see table 1.1 for an overview).

Democratic Theory

According to traditional **democratic theory**, the answer to "Who governs?" is "All of us," in a sense. Two forms of democracy exist. *Participatory democracy* envisions rule by the many as described by the ancient philosopher Aristotle. *Representative democracy* suggests rule by the few on behalf of the many—the people. In a representative democracy, policymakers may negotiate and compromise with each other but are influenced and ultimately controlled by the electorate. Political scientist Robert Dahl thought an ideal democratic process must meet five criteria relative to "the people": equality in voting, effective citizen participation, enlightened understanding, final control over government's agenda, and inclusion (the application of rights and laws to everyone).[14] The American Founders thought that the states would play dominant roles in making representative democracy work.

Democratic theory partly explains California politics, especially its political ideals. The preamble to the state's constitution reads: "*We, the People* of the State of California, grateful to Almighty God for our freedom, in order to secure and perpetuate its blessings, do establish this Constitution" (emphasis added). It contains the state's own "Bill of Rights" and establishes various institutions of government that, on paper, are responsible to the electorate. Furthermore, voters have the power to adopt their own legislation (initiatives), approve or disapprove

Table 1.1 The Governing Theories in Brief

Theory	Evidence in California
Democratic theory	Initiative process Frequent elections Elected legislative bodies (state and local)
Elite theory	Big Four Major campaign contributors Policy entrepreneurs Policies benefiting the relative few
Pluralism	Proliferation of interest groups Group competition Dueling initiatives Multicultural pluralism
Hyperpluralism	Individualistic approaches to public life Power by nonmajorities Diversity of interests and cultures Supermajority vote requirements Structural conflict and policy gridlock

various laws passed by the state legislature (referenda), and remove elected officials between elections (recall). They can do all this on a statewide basis and in their respective communities.

Traditional democratic theory advances political ideals better than it explains political reality. A representative democracy assumes greater citizen interest than often is the case. In California, the politically disinterested and economically weak are clearly disadvantaged. The political equality presumed by democratic thought is largely missing. The result in California is the emergence of a two-tier polity. Some observers perceive a political dominance by an "affluent, politically active over class using its position to protect its privileges against the larger but weaker underclass."[15] They ask, "Where is the 'common good' between the haves and the have-nots?" Democratic theory, then, needs to account for the relationship between government and wealth, the persistence of unequal subgroups in the polity, and what, if any, common ground exists between these unequal subgroups.

Elite Theory

Other theories also attempt to explain the origins and exercise of power. According to elite theorists, all societies naturally divide into two classes: the few who rule and the many who do not. Political power inevitably gravitates to the few out of necessity, what Robert Michels called an "iron law of oligarchy." As political scientist Harold Lasswell once put it, "Government is always government by the few, whether in the name of the few, the one, or the many."[16] Some elites consist of corporate owners and other wealthy persons who exercise political power directly or control those who do on their behalf.

As with democratic theory, elements of **elite and class politics** can be seen in California. Historically, one corporation, the Southern Pacific Railroad, wielded significant power. The "Big Four" (Leland Stanford, Collis Huntington, Charles Crocker, and Mark Hopkins) were successful businessmen. Controlling a virtual political machine, they shaped the state's early commerce, land development, and overall growth. Through his control of land and water, *Los Angeles Times* owner Harrison Gray Otis helped engineer Los Angeles's growth more profoundly than any city council could have. Elites are also evident in modern California. Some individuals continue to hold substantial power. For example, with little public notice, J. G. Boswell parlayed a Central Valley farm into a multinational agriculture-based empire through business savvy and political influence.[17] With that said, elites sometimes fail. One of the most notable examples is former eBay CEO Meg Whitman, who lost the 2010 gubernatorial race to Jerry Brown despite spending $150 million, much of it her own.

Furthermore, most elites today operate as groups. The state's media exercises considerable influence through major television stations and a small handful of newspaper chains. Among the most influential groups in Sacramento are large corporations or clusters of them, such as the California Manufacturers Association. The California legislature routinely provides tax incentives and other benefits to powerful economic interests and even single companies. Because they are frequently campaign contributors, when these groups speak, policymakers listen. Consider the 2014 election cycle. Compared to organized interest groups, individuals contributed only 25 percent of the $496 million spent on California candidates and ballot measures (followthemoney.org). Californians themselves sense the power of elites and distrust the results. According to a 2015 poll, 62 percent of respondents thought that the state government was "pretty much run by a few big interests looking out for themselves" instead of for the benefit of all Californians.[18]

As compelling as elite theory sounds, it, too, cannot fully explain California politics. The influence of the Big Four was ultimately broken in the Progressive Era. Today, many California businesses of all sizes compete for power—reducing the influence of any one business. Some initiatives remain downright populist, and the outcomes of others do not favor elite interests. For example, in November 2010, voters rejected business efforts to suspend the state's new global warming law (Proposition 23), whereas, in 2012, voters imposed higher taxes on multistate corporations (Proposition 39). In short, because elites exist in the political arena does not necessarily mean they win on, or even care about, all issues. California's elites tend to conserve their resources for issues they regard as most important.

Pluralist Theory

Pluralist theory tries to correct aspects of both democratic and elite theory. Electoral majorities, a cornerstone of democratic theory, are something of a myth, given voter apathy. According to Dahl, "On matters of specific policy, the majority rarely rules."[19] Pluralists admit that groups are controlled by elites but observe many groups having access to, competing for, and sharing power. No single group dominates all the time. In many ways, American politics *is* group politics—a fluid process of competing interests winning or losing, rising or falling, as they seek to influence transitory issues. Interest group politics is readily observable at all levels of our political system. Pluralism's critics, however, argue that the push and pull of pluralist politics do not explain the inherent and systemic inequalities that persist in American life. Furthermore, interests must be organized; some perfectly legitimate interests, such as children or the homeless, rarely organize.

Pluralism is an attractive option for students of California politics. If you google "associations advocacy Sacramento," you will be amazed at the breadth of interest groups in the state's capital. Group-inspired, lunch-hour rallies are a common sight on the Capitol steps. Proposition "wars" now feature dueling initiatives sponsored by opposing groups. Increasingly, ethnic groups are creating *multicultural pluralism* in California politics.

But not all politics in California can be labeled group politics. First, structural features of California's political system (its constitution and institutions) to some extent limit group power. Second, group competition alone does not explain the occasional rise of policy entrepreneurs—individuals who make a substantial difference, such as antitax crusader Howard Jarvis and, more recently, marijuana activist Richard Lee. Third, pluralism seems to suggest a satisfactory equilibrium among competing groups. But how does one explain policy indecision, delay, or paralysis—what is often called gridlock?

Hyperpluralism

Elements of truth in these three theories might suggest what Dahl calls an "American hybrid,"[20] but a nagging problem remains. All three presume that governing does, in fact, occur. Yet some observers claim that no one "rules" effectively anymore. State governments, California included, lurch from fiscal year to fiscal year. In a sense, California's history of budget crises serves to magnify the ongoing challenge of governing in the Golden State. In addition, initiatives sponsored by some organized interests, once passed, are challenged in court by other groups. Some political scientists call this state of affairs **hyperpluralism**. In this view, power is thinly scattered, not just widely or unevenly scattered as previous theories would suggest. The exercise of political power has become a highly competitive tug-of-war between institutions, policymakers, political parties, numerous interest groups, and voters.

Political scientists who hold this view are both describing a variant of pluralism and making a judgment about government's performance. They admit that the American system was intended to check power, not merely facilitate it. But they also believe checking power is different from preventing its exercise at all. Hyperpluralism seems increasingly helpful in explaining how aspects of American politics work. In explaining California politics, it is downright compelling. Let us consider it in more depth.

HOW HYPERPLURALISM EXPLAINS CALIFORNIA POLITICS

There is ample evidence of hyperpluralism in American politics, and in California politics in particular: individualism in political life, a growing diversity of group interests and cultures, the changing nature of majoritarian politics, and "built-in" or structural conflict. These **components of California hyperpluralism** are somewhat intertwined and dependent on each other.

The Constancy of Individualism

Individualism is a hallmark of American life, and it is nothing new. In the 1830s, French observer Alexis de Tocqueville correctly defined American individualism as "a calm and considered feeling which disposes each citizen to isolate himself from the mass of his fellows and withdraw into the circle of family and friends; with this little society formed to his taste, he gladly leaves the greater society to look after itself."[21] Recent scholars have observed the popularity of individualism among "middle Americans" and believe it exists at the expense of commitment to a larger community.[22] Individualism is a key tile in the mosaic of California politics. The proliferation of interest groups, the pursuit of leisure, gated communities, private security systems, solitary rush-hour commutes, and widespread gun ownership—a do-it-yourself law enforcement, of sorts—all suggest dependence on self rather than on society to fulfill both needs and wants. The increasing presence of social media only reinforces this individualism in a culture where political participation is considered optional and even unimportant. But individualism is not applied consistently. As writer Joan Didion reminds us, California's historic dependence on federal spending for water projects, highways, and defense contracts is "seemingly at odds with the [state's] emphasis on unfettered individualism that constitutes the local core belief."[23]

A Diversity of Interests and Cultures

One aspect of hyperpluralism is the range of interests that various groups bring to public life. The most fundamental interest is in civic life itself, what is called "civic engagement." Here the ethnic and racial diversity of California is not evident in voting or in other activities associated with public life—signing petitions, attending meetings, writing officials, making campaign contributions, attending rallies, and doing political party work. Research findings indicate that those Californians who are white, older, more affluent, homeowners, and more highly educated evidence the highest levels of civic engagement. Relative to their numbers in the population, whites are overrepresented in virtually every political activity we associate with civic engagement.[24] Politically speaking, those Californians who have the greatest say are not those who arguably have the greatest needs.

Of those groups that do engage in community and public life, many represent relatively narrow viewpoints or advocate relatively narrow agendas. Some even define themselves and behave politically in terms of one single issue—giving rise to what has been called *single-issue politics*. When public problems are viewed in such narrow terms, policy solutions seem obvious and clear-cut but only to the group espousing them. This leads such groups to hold their views with more determination and to communicate them with greater assertiveness. Some behave as grievance groups, out to correct negative treatment by the larger society. All this has increased group conflict in California and has decreased the potential for broader intergroup consensus. In the absence of a broader consensus, policymakers find that supporting certain groups has a price—the wrath of other groups.

Fading Majoritarianism

Another evidence of hyperpluralism is the changing nature of *majority rule*—a major principle of American politics. The nation's founders thought that, in a representative democracy, elected officials would seek the common good agreeable to a functioning majority. In California politics, a single public interest and a single majority seem to be endangered political species. In a sense, "minorities" already rule in the Golden State. On a statewide basis, a relatively small number of individuals and groups set legislative agendas and determine which issues make it to the ballot: a relatively small percentage of Californians who qualify to vote actually register to vote, an even smaller percentage turn out on Election Day, and only a *simple majority* of those determine election outcomes. In numerous California cities and now the state as a whole, there is no single ethnic majority. Ironically, while majority rule means less and less, some political ground rules in California require *supermajorities* to enact public policy. The state constitution requires a two-thirds majority of the legislature to raise taxes and a two-thirds popular vote to raise certain local taxes. Such numbers are often difficult to achieve.

Another aspect of fading majoritarianism is voter disinterest that leads to low voter turnout, at least in some elections. For example, of the more than 24 million eligible voters in California, only 18 million (73%) registered to vote for the 2014 general election. Only 42 percent of those actually voted, or 31 percent of those eligible. Of course, fewer still voted for any particular candidate or ballot measure. Aside from high-profile presidential races as we saw in 2008, election politics arguably can be viewed as a function of minority rule, not majoritarianism.

Structural Conflict

One reason why California voters decide issues directly is because interest groups that sponsor initiatives want to bypass a cumbersome policy process in Sacramento. Many Californians, ready to assess blame for the results of that process, choose to replace their elected officials or limit their terms of service. Term limits have been increasingly adopted at the local level and have been applied to state legislators and constitutional officers thanks to Proposition 140 (1990).

Are elected politicians to blame? Only in part. California's political structure itself invites political conflict. First, the state's constitution in effect predestines a horizontal power struggle between the executive, legislative, and judicial branches. While praised as a necessary "checks and balances" feature of our form of government, it does foster political and policy conflict. Second, by dictating certain roles for local government, it guarantees a vertical power struggle between the "locals" (cities, counties, and special districts) and the state itself. In a similar vein, the election of Donald Trump as president sparked a vertical clash with the federal government over immigration policy, health care, and climate change. Third, the initiative process allows voters to make policy and thereby circumvent and even contradict the very legislature they elect to make policy. According to journalist Peter Schrag, the result has been "an increasingly unmanageable and incomprehensible structure of state and local government that exacerbates the same public disaffection and alienation that brought it on."[25]

CALIFORNIA: THE IRONIES OF DIVERSITY

In this introductory chapter, we have surveyed California's rich **diversity**, the theories that help explain its politics, and the hyperpluralism that is increasingly evident. As California becomes more diverse and hyperpluralistic, several ironies have emerged. First, compared to other states, California has become both a policy innovator and a laggard. Over the years, it has "led the way" with such measures as Proposition 13 (which reduced property taxes), the legalization of marijuana for medical use, and, more recently, AB 32, the Global Warming Solutions Act. Years ago, its investment in freeways was the envy of other states. In recent decades, however, California's per capita spending on highways has declined considerably. In years past, other states imitated California's visionary 1961 master plan for higher education (which provided the structure for the state's community colleges and four-year universities). Yet, recent spending on education at all levels has lagged the state's growth.

Second, the policy generosity of California's electorate and its government is cyclical, contested, and occasionally ambivalent. Consider budgeting. As diverse as California's economy is, the state's dependence on inherently volatile sources of revenue such as the income tax can significantly alter budget priorities. When tax revenues from stock options and capital gains fluctuate, mirroring the fluctuations in the stock market and technology sectors, California's state budget can experience both record surpluses and record deficits—all within a few years. These revenue gyrations force difficult and contested budget decisions that highlight the public's ambivalence toward fiscal matters. Recent voter support for state tax increases (e.g., Proposition 55 in 2016) indicates the public's renewed interest in more policy generosity than was previously supported for a long stretch before that.

Third, while policy paralysis often grips Sacramento, policy progress can be found closer to home. The state's 482 cities have developed entrepreneurial ways to raise needed revenue. Numerous counties have increased sales taxes to pay for transportation projects once thought to be the state's responsibility. Those Californians who can afford it (the upper tier) are buying services their state or local government cannot afford or will not provide. Some have augmented meager public recreation programs with those of private groups like the YMCA. Some install their own security systems; others live in condominium or planned unit developments where neighborhood "quality of life" decisions are made by homeowner associations, not city councils. They transfer from troubled public schools to private ones, support their own public school with private fundraising efforts, or they resort to homeschooling. What does the bottom tier do? They rely on government programs despite the cuts, live by their wits, or simply do without.

The California portrayed in this chapter is of immense proportion. The challenges facing the most populous state in the Union are abundant to be sure, as they always have been. The capacity and potential for California governments to address these challenges is and always has been great. Its political system reflects a state "in which the best possibilities of the American experiment can be struggled for and sometimes achieved."[26] Political scientists search for theories to explain why California functions the way it does. While no single theory or approach will suffice, both the state's diversity and its hyperpluralistic political system seem useful in explaining California's current state of affairs.

As a subject of study, California politics is both fascinating and challenging. Because of term limits and demographic shifts, it is also ever-changing. As you read this book, you will discover why.

KEY TERMS

politics (p. 4)
political system (p. 4)
political environment (p. 4)
postindustrial economy (p. 11)
multitiered workforce (p. 13)
democratic theory (p. 14)
elite and class politics (p. 15)

pluralist theory (p. 16)
hyperpluralism (p. 17)
components of California
  hyperpluralism (p. 17)
diversity (p. 19)
ironies of diversity (p. 19)

REVIEW QUESTIONS

1. Identify the ways in which diversity explains California politics.
2. Describe the various regions of California.
3. How have water and climate affected the state's growth?
4. What demographic groups have come to California and why?
5. Describe the five keys to understanding the state's economy. What makes it two-tiered in nature?
6. Illustrate each theory with California examples.
7. In what ways does hyperpluralism seem particularly apt in describing California politics?
8. Discuss and illustrate California's ironies of diversity.

WEB RESOURCES

California Home Page

https://www.ca.gov

A good starting point, this site will take you in many different directions regarding life and politics in the Golden State.

California Department of Finance, Demographic Research Unit

http://www.dof.ca.gov/
Forecasting/Demographics

This "single official source of demographic data for state planning and budgeting" provides helpful information on population growth, change, and diversity in California.

U.S. Census Bureau

https://www.census.gov

You can find more census data on California by clicking "Population Finder" and "Quick Facts."

2
California's Political Development

LEARNING OUTCOMES

Students will be able to:

★ Describe the ideas of political culture and political development as they apply to the governing of California.

★ Explain the notable eras and events leading to statehood and the gradual unification of California.

★ Summarize the seminal events that constituted the modernization of California.

★ Discuss the factors including two key governorships that contributed to the politics of welfare in California.

★ Define the politics of abundance and analyze the challenge of maintaining it in today's California.

IN BRIEF

Chapter 2 focuses on the political culture and development of California. Understanding the variety of political subcultures found in California (traditionalistic, moralistic, and individualistic) helps put in context the political and policy challenges facing the state today. California's political history is a progression of developmental stages: unification, industrialization, welfare, and abundance. Historic events and a succession of political and economic leaders have shaped each stage.

IN THE UNIFICATION STAGE, Spanish and Mexican control gave way to what has been called an American era, which included statehood and the development of a constitution. The industrialization period featured the famous Gold Rush, the rise of the Southern Pacific Railroad, the development of water resources, the discovery of oil, and the impacts of World War II. The politics of welfare was noted for economic growth, progressive policies, and visionary leadership. During the politics of abundance period, growth and prosperity continue but mainly for those at the top of the income ladder while many below struggle with daily necessities. At the end of the chapter, we consider whether the politics of abundance will continue indefinitely into the future and how the politics of diversity affects these perceptions.

INTRODUCTION

How is California different from New York, besides its tendency to elect actors as governors? Both states have large, diverse populations, complex economies, megacities, huge state budgets, and geographic variety (seashore, mountains, farms, forests, etc.). Although Californians struggle to obtain water and New Yorkers do not, the similarities are there. Yet, Californians and New Yorkers know their states are different—and in profound ways. Political scientist Daniel Elazar called these variations the "geology of political culture."[1] A primary difference stems from how they grew and changed as political and cultural identities. This chapter surveys aspects of California's past that help explain its current political system. This process of growth and change is called "political development." Viewing California's history through the lens of political science is an essential prerequisite to understanding and contextualizing the state's politics today.

In 1949, the year of California's centennial, Carey McWilliams observed that the state, "the giant adolescent, has been outgrowing its governmental clothes, now, for a hundred years."[2] Today, he would likely underscore that point. This chapter helps us understand why that is the case.

The Idea of Political Culture

To understand the stages of political development found in California, we need to briefly examine the concept of political culture. **Political culture** is the product of historical events, migration and settlement patterns, and the presence of various social groups. It refers to the shared beliefs, values, customs, and symbols of a society that affect how the society governs itself. Political culture helps explain the policy choices made within political systems and why these choices vary between political systems.

Although, in many respects, the United States reflects one broad political culture, Elazar identified three distinct political subcultures: traditional, moralistic, and individualistic.[3] Although the descriptions of each subculture are largely impressionistic and difficult to prove, they do help explain why some states are so different from each other. The **traditionalistic** political subculture is characterized by the dominance of a small, self-perpetuating, paternalistic ruling elite and a large, compliant nonelite. Its goal is to maintain the established social and economic order rather than to provide wide access to the political system or initiate new policy. According to Elazar, this subculture had its historic roots in the preindustrial agrarian South.

The **moralistic** political subculture emphasizes a public-spirited citizenry dedicated to the common betterment of all its members. Widespread participation is both valued and expected. Dedicated, selfless, incorruptible public officials strive toward an assumed "general welfare." Politics is a high calling, not dirty work, and nonpartisanship is preferable to party politics. Government intervention in both the economy and society furthers the "public interest." Elazar believed this subculture grew out of the religious values of Puritan New England.

The **individualistic** political subculture emphasizes the goals, aspirations, and initiative of private individuals or groups. Government exists to serve and facilitate these interests. Policymaking is transactional, a process of bargaining between self-interested individuals and groups. Public officials represent not only these people but also their own personal interests. The private citizen's attitude toward government is "Stay out of my way, let me do my thing, or at least help me do it." Elazar traced this subculture to the mercantile centers of the Eastern Seaboard.

As more people immigrated to the United States and Americans already here migrated west, the features of these three subcultures moved and mingled as well. Historically, each of these three subcultures has played an important role in California's political development; elements of all three still exist. The *patron– client relationship* between California's Native Americans and the mission-era padres exemplified the traditionalistic subculture as do many immigrant relationships with the public sector today. Moralists moved into Southern California from the Midwest and brought with them pro-government values. They also came in such droves that the government had little choice but to accommodate their need for housing, schools, and other services. Individualists came from the East Coast to Northern California. Today, the individualistic impulse can be seen in the attributes of many Californians who favor tax cuts *and* tax-dependent public services or who oppose public services they do not need but others use. The blurring and stirring of these political subcultures help contribute to hyperpluralistic politics in California.

The Idea of Political Development

Political development refers to the growth and change that occur within political systems. It includes (1) government's increasing capacity to manage its own affairs, respond to demands placed on it, and do so in a stable manner; (2) an increase in democratic values, including the furthering of civil society, political participation, rule of law, and equality; and (3) an increase of economic specialization and complex social structures leading to group conflict and methods to resolve it.[4] Many political systems in the Western world have proceeded through distinct stages of political development—unification, modernization, welfare, and abundance.[5] These stages do not have neat beginnings and endings; they merge into each other.

Do states have their own stages of political development? To some extent. To be sure, the states together form a national political culture. Also, the nation's founding documents such as the U.S. Constitution have steered each state's political development in similar directions. Yet, the subsystems we call states entered the Union at different times and are distinctly different in terms of the people they attracted, the economies they established, and the political practices they developed.

California's political history from the viewpoint of its political development allows the student of California politics not only to understand the state's history but also to understand how the past informs the present. Larger than most nations, California has passed through all four stages of political development. To be sure, today's abundance does not affect all parts of the state and its people in equal measure. To analyze the present and anticipate the future, we must first make sense of the past—the goal of this chapter.

THE POLITICS OF UNIFICATION

During an early **unification** stage of political development, the primary function of government is making a society into a state. Government needs to establish its own central role, guard against early disunion, and develop a network of viable local economies. Early California from Native American times through the Gold Rush and statehood embodies this stage.

The West Coast has been a population magnet since prehistoric times. Archaeological evidence suggests that nomadic peoples from Asia once crossed a land bridge (now the Bering Strait) through Alaska and down the coast some 25,000 years ago. Native Californians were the eventual products of these early migration patterns. These first Californians were gatherers and coastal fishers who spoke 135 different languages. They were peaceable, nomadic, agrarian, and needed very little government. They resisted change, as early missionaries discovered, but were not resistant to the European diseases and violence that decimated their numbers.

The first nonnative visitors to California were European explorers who sailed California's coastal waters in the 1500s. They included Juan Rodriguez Cabrillo, Bartolome Ferrelo, and Sir Francis Drake. In 1579, Drake claimed the area north of modern-day San Francisco as Nova Albion (New England) 41 years *before* the Pilgrims touched shore at Plymouth.

Spanish "Rule"

Spain colonized Mexico in 1519 but did not extend its reach into Alta California until 1769. Governor Gaspar de Portola and Father Junipero Serra established a European settlement and Franciscan mission at San Diego. The missions (eventually numbering 21 and stretching from San Diego to Sonoma) were religious and evangelistic outposts intended to convert the Native Californians both to Christianity and to more "progressive" (read European) lifestyles. As a colonial power, Spain promptly built military bases (*presidios*). Nearby civilian towns (*pueblos*) accommodated modest population growth. Local economies and primitive local, albeit colonial, governments grew up around these settlements. At the height of their influence, the Spanish numbered no more than 3,000 people spread thinly along the California coast from San Diego to Sonoma. The relationship between the two groups was *patron–client* in nature: the ruled (Native Americans) supported or at least obeyed the rulers (military and church authorities) in exchange for relative security and safety. We should not exaggerate the governing influence of the missions: only 20,000 out of 400,000 Native Californians worked and lived under mission authority.

Colonial governments are extractive in nature, but Spain found little to extract from Alta California. Distant, sparsely populated settlements needed no unification. To the responsible viceroy in Mexico City, California was "out of sight, out of mind." This inattention allowed economic competition between the missions and the *presidios* and *pueblos* to spill into open conflict. Spain's "rule" of Alta California lasted only 58 years, during which time British, French, and Russian expeditions explored coastal lands. Despite these incursions, Spain's long-term legacy to modern California includes the continuing presence of her language, those iconic missions, countless place names, and some legal concepts such as communal water rights and community property.

Mexican "Control"

After years of Mexican frustration and Spanish inattention, Mexico obtained its independence from Spain in 1821. Ironically, the gold-hungry Spanish government abandoned Mexican California, unaware of the rich gold deposits to be discovered only a few decades later. California was now Mexico's colony—a distant and not too important province in Mexico's federal system. Concerned with solidifying its power base and unifying the rest of Mexico, the central government in Mexico City paid even less attention to California than had Spain. Feuds between the *presidios* and the missions and between the fledgling regions of California continued unabated during this Mexican era.

One act of unification during this time was to reduce the role of the church, which, in California, meant the vast mission enterprises developed under Spain. To do this, the Mexican government secularized the missions and distributed their massive landholdings to government loyalists.[6] Individuals could obtain 48,000-acre grants, and some influential families were able to accumulate *ranchos* as large as 250,000 acres. Many places familiar to Californians today derive their names from these *ranchos*.

Another development during this period had nothing to do with Mexican policy. A gradual but steady trickle of rugged Euro-Americans found their way to California. These intrepid individuals included whalers, fur trappers and traders called mountain men, and adventurers. Although some remained on the "wild side," others turned to farming and married into landholding Mexican families. Simply getting to California from the rest of the United States was a feat. After the adventurers proved it could be done (even the Donner party had survivors), more Americans arrived. Most of these travelers were peaceful. Not so with Lieutenant John C. Fremont, who favored westward expansion (by force if necessary) and led several military expeditions into California. In 1846, a "Bear Flag Revolt" ensued among Mexican authorities, their supporters among the *Californio* population (native-born, Spanish-speaking Californians), and the American settlers, aided and abetted by Fremont and his associates. The symbol was a flag portraying a grizzly bear with the inscription, "California Republic." A version of it remains the state flag today. Mexico's lax control of California ended in 1846 when American troops invaded Mexico and its northern holdings. In the Mexican–American War of 1848, an American sense of cultural and moral superiority over Mexico fueled the conduct of that war and the negotiations that followed Mexico's defeat.

What legacy did Mexico leave California after a mere 27 years of "control"? It did introduce several governing patterns that would become part of California's constitution, including a multitiered judicial system. Both Spain and Mexico left behind a traditionalistic political subculture. Vestiges of it remain today if one considers the relative powerlessness of California's newest immigrants, most of whom come from Mexico. Compared to Spain, Mexico's legacy has been ongoing. Spain retreated to Spain—a continent and an ocean away. Mexico retreated to the other side of a thin, porous, and contended border with California, as you will see in chapter 3.

Statehood

The unification stage of political development was completed with California's admission to the Union. To the Americans, California came to represent a logical stepping-stone in meeting the nation's "manifest destiny." The Mexican Cession turned over not only California but also Nevada, Utah, and portions of Wyoming, Colorado, New Mexico, and Arizona, reducing Mexico's land area by half. The $15 million price tag for this acquisition was not even paid by the United States but, rather, credited toward Mexico's war debt. Ironically, U.S. President James Polk had offered $40 million for California alone in 1846, but Mexico refused to accept the offer. The *1848 Treaty of Guadalupe Hidalgo* concluded the war and granted U.S. citizenship to the conquered peoples. Granting the rights that accompany citizenship in the new territory was more problematic. Accustomed to the 160-acre land grants under the Homestead Act, American settlers sought to acquire portions of the vast ranches still owned by the Californians. The results included title disputes and litigation, land squatting, and even officially sanctioned land transfers from the rancheros to the Americans (see box 2.1).

The United States, despite its euphoric westward expansion and sense of mission, did not bring unification to California instantly. The state's fragmented governance structure was based on a now-collapsed Spanish system of *presidios*. Furthermore, the bits of gold found by James Marshall on the American River only nine days before the treaty was signed would bring anything but peace to America's newest possession. The news of gold in the Sierra foothills first reached other Californians who quite literally dropped what they were doing to stake their claims. These reports spread like wildfire across the nation. Colonel Richard Mason, the military governor of California, reported the discovery to President James Polk, sending along 230 ounces to prove his point: "I have no hesitation in saying there is more gold in the country drained by the Sacramento and San Joaquin Rivers than will pay the cost of the war with Mexico a hundred times over."[7] Polk mentioned the discovery of abundant gold in his December 1848 annual message: "Now that this fine province is part of our country, all of the States of the Union . . . are deeply interested in the speedy development of its wealth and resources."[8] Ostensibly, he was trying to sell the Congress on locating a branch of the mint in California. What he sold was California itself. Professional advertisers could not have done a better job of it.

Box 2.1 ★ California Voices: The Cost of Conquest

The main issue in California was possession of land, but the proposed constitution was silent in this regard. The former Mexican citizens had to trust their fate to the courts and their interpretation of the Treaty of Guadalupe Hidalgo. Their trust was quickly betrayed as the U.S. government established complicated and lengthy procedures for verifying legitimate titles to the land. Thus, most *Californios* had to mortgage or sell their lands to pay for litigation costs. Within a generation, most *Californio* rancheros joined the impoverished ranks of their former vaqueros.

Source: Robert W. Cherny, Gretchen Lemke-Santangelo, and Richard Griswold del Castillo, *Competing Visions: A History of California* (New York: Houghton Mifflin, 2005), 121.

The 1849 Constitution

An important instrument in unifying a civil society is a *constitution*. This basic law provides general vision, establishes rights, creates political structures, and places limits on power and those who claim it. Theoretically, it is a contract between the government and the governed and a covenant among society's members.

California's first constitution was the result of a constitutional convention held in the fall of 1849. The process was a curious mixture of elitism and pluralism. All 48 delegates were relatively young men. Thirteen had lived in California for less than one year. The nonnative Californians came from 13 other states and five other nations.[9] The goal of unification remained a challenge. Differences between Northern and Southern California promptly emerged. Closer to their Mexican roots, Southern Californians preferred territorial status, thinking that would give them the best of both cultures. Northern Californians generally favored statehood, sent a majority of the delegates, and eventually controlled the convention.

The **Constitution of 1849** blended several theories of governing. The constitution began with a lofty, unifying preamble and a strong "bill of rights," reflecting democratic ideals. The idea of checks and balances (and the potential for structural gridlock) was found in a plural executive (a governor and several statewide officers) and a bicameral (two-house) legislature. Reflecting Mexican practice, it established a four-tier judicial system of elected judges. As elsewhere, suffrage (the right to vote) was limited to white males. Because of the *Californios*, the document was to be printed in both English and Spanish, as were all future official documents. The constitution won overwhelming voter approval in November 1849 and on September 9, 1850, Congress admitted California as the 31st state. California was to remain slave-free, a condition not applied to other ceded Mexican territories. At that moment, unification, to the extent California would ever experience it, was complete. The Mexican era ended; the North American era began.

In spite of its shortcomings (people demanded a new constitution only 30 years later), California's unifying document was considered a model worth imitating. Argentina's 1853 constitution was inspired by it. Argentinean Juan Bautista Alberti observed, "Without universities, without academies or law colleges, the newly organized people of California have drawn up a constitution full of foresight, of common sense and of opportunity."[10]

THE POLITICS OF MODERNIZATION

This sense of opportunity led to the **politics of modernization**, the next stage in the process of political development. This is a time when new political leaders emerge, a statewide economy is forged, and the political masses become fully incorporated—becoming the polity of the state. Government's purpose is to encourage economic modernization or industrialization. During this stage, California became a magnet of opportunity and a destination for those seeking jobs or simply a better way of life. Historic benchmarks during this stage were the Gold Rush, the rise of the Big Four, the industrialization of agriculture, and the consequences of World War II.

The Gold Rush

Discovery of gold created the mining frenzy we noted earlier. In retrospect, gold did not change California; the rush for it did. For a time, the population doubled every six months: from 9,000 in 1846 to 264,000 six years later. Seemingly overnight, a heavily Latinx California became 80 percent Euro-American. The newcomers were primarily young, single men from every state in the Union and from as far away as Europe and China. A spirit of entrepreneurialism mingled with hard labor and racism against African Americans, other non-Euro-Americans, and foreigners. For example, Chinese immigrants were allowed to mine the gold but not own rights to it. Policing the mining towns was a rough business. Committees of vigilance—*vigilantes*—often used violence to quell violence. A few miners found the gold they sought, but many more found unprecedented opportunities of other types. One luckless miner discovered that he could make more money selling pants to other miners—his name was Levi Strauss.

Those who stayed created a new base for California's emerging economy. In effect, the Gold Rush jump-started the state's second stage of development by adding instant diversity to California's population. It created numerous spillover effects (planned or unplanned consequences), such as heightened demand for goods and services. In turn, new demands for transportation improvements created still more opportunities for future entrepreneurs. The cultural change would be profound. According to writer J. H. Holliday: "In one astonishing year [1848–49] the place would be transformed from obscurity to world dominance . . . from a society of neighbors and families to one of strangers and transients; from an ox-cart economy based on hides and tallow to a complex economy based on gold; from Catholic to Protestant, from Latin to Anglo-Saxon."[11] Last, it created a worker base consisting of individuals with steely nerve to take a risk, not just on gold but also on California itself.

The Big Four

Four Sacramento merchants shared that steely nerve. Their actions furthered the economic growth of the state while making each of them very rich. As we noted, some Americans brought an individualistic political subculture to California; these men personified it. Their eventual political influence and abuse of it unleashed a political reform movement, which is still felt today. Mark Hopkins, Charles Crocker, Collis Huntington, and Leland Stanford responded to the post–Gold Rush demand for improved transportation by forming the Central Pacific Railroad in 1861. Huntington was well connected in Washington, D.C., and served as the group's lobbyist. His efforts paid off. Congress designated this company responsible for the western portion of the ambitious transcontinental railroad and gave it both land and loans to begin construction. However, that was not enough. Stanford became governor and, in a move that would likely violate conflict of interest laws today, obtained additional loans and subsidies from the state legislature.

Because California developed or industrialized so rapidly in contrast to the rest of the West, the Big Four anticipated demand for plenty of transportation within the state. They acquired small railroad companies throughout California. One such acquisition was the **Southern Pacific Railroad** (SPR), the future namesake for the entire system. Eventually, they controlled 85 percent of the state's rails. This elite became a monopoly and behaved accordingly. By varying freight rates, they rewarded their friends and punished their enemies. This was not just laissez-faire capitalism at work. Local governments, desiring rail service and all its economic blessings, donated right-of-way property in addition to cash (euphemistically called "subsidies"). The land grab was substantial. For every mile of track, SPR would receive up to 12,800 acres of adjacent land from the public domain. When San Bernardino refused its demands, the SPR sited its new depot in nearby Colton. If shippers tried to move their goods along the coast by steamship, the Big Four would simply buy the steamship line and reset rates. As with other monopolies, Southern Pacific rates were higher than necessary, angering growing numbers of Californians. Frank Norris's 1901 novel, *The Octopus*, was a chilling and transparent description of how the SPR operated in the state (see box 2.2).

Fearing that popular resentment might lead to state regulation, the Southern Pacific established a Political Bureau, a forerunner of the modern political action committee (PAC). Unlike today's PACs, which operate primarily in Sacramento, the Political Bureau was active at all levels of government. It controlled not only incumbent legislators but also party conventions and candidate nominations. In 1877, Stanford wrote Huntington, "The legislature elected I think is a good one and I apprehend less trouble [e.g., rate control legislation] from it than from any preceding legislature for the last 10 years—not a single unfriendly senator elected."[12]

As politically successful as the Big Four were, they could not cope with a national depression in the late 1800s that left many out of work. The unemployed blamed the railroads for importing poorly paid Chinese laborers who competed with whites for nonrailroad jobs. One such worker, the fiery Denis Kearney of San Francisco, helped found the radical Workingmen's Party. He was anti-Chinese and anti–Big Four. His incendiary rhetoric was prophetic given the reforms that would sweep the state in future decades: "The reign of bloated knaves is over. The people are about to take their own affairs into their own hands."[13]

Ironically, the same voters that elected a railroad-controlled state senate also authorized the calling of a constitutional convention—one noted for its antirailroad temperament. Original state constitutions seemed to need revision within

---

Box 2.2 ★ California Voices: Norris on the Southern Pacific

The clerk brought forward a folder of yellow paper and handed it to Dyke. It was inscribed at the top "Tariff Schedule No. 8," and underneath these words, in brackets, was a smaller inscription, "Supercedes No. 7 of Aug. 1." For a moment Dyke was confused. Then the matter swiftly became clear in his mind. The Railroad had raised the freight on hops from two cents to five. All his calculations as to a profit on his little investment he had were based on a freight rate of two cents a pound. He was under contract to deliver his crop. He could not draw back. The new rate ate up every cent of his gains. He stood there ruined. "Good Lord," he murmured, "good Lord! What will you people do next? Look here. What's your basis of applying freight rates anyhow?" he suddenly vociferated with furious sarcasm. "What's your rule? What are you guided by?" S. Behrman emphasized each word of his reply with a tap of one forefinger on the counter before him. "All—the—traffic—will—bear."

Source: Excerpted from Frank Norris, *The Octopus: A Story of California* (New York: Doubleday, Page and Co., 1904), 348–50.

several decades and California was no exception. In California's case, the 1878–79 convention coincided with economic troubles, antirailroad fervor, and worker radicalism. The revised constitution literally banned the employment of the Chinese—"aliens who are or may become vagrants, paupers, mendicants, criminals, or invalids with contagious or infectious diseases."[14] Numerous antirailroad regulations were embedded in the constitution to prevent their easy removal. The delegates established a railroad commission, thinking that such a regulatory body would be insulated from Big Four pressure. On the contrary, the commission proved no match for the power of the corporations and railroad interests. Furthermore, when there were occasional regulatory victories, they were often voided by economically conservative courts. A popular political cartoon of the day titled "The Curse of California" symbolized not only the power of the Big Four but also the elite theory of politics described in chapter 1 (see cartoon 2.1).

Changes in the larger political environment gradually lessened the influence of the Big Four and the massive company they left behind. Their political power was a house of cards based on a monopolistic rate structure and lack of

THE CURSE OF CALIFORNIA.

Pictorial Press Ltd/Alamy Stock Photo.

Cartoon 2.1 "The Curse of California"
This cartoon was published in *The Wasp* on August 19, 1882, and is regarded as the most influential political cartoon in California history. Keller employed the often-used octopus symbol to caricature the political and economic reach of the Big Four.

competition. But in the 1880s, when a competing southern transcontinental railroad emerged (the Santa Fe), ensuing rate wars ruined their monopoly. As more towns obtained railroad service, local rivalries waned, and company control was no longer necessary. Further industrialization of California would depend less on parochial, intrastate concerns and more on national and international forces. As new transportation routes crisscrossed the state, political subcultures gradually merged. The railroads helped both unify and industrialize the Golden State.

Water

A third factor in the modernization of California was water. This commodity affected both agriculture and urbanization in the state. A growing interstate network of railroad routes plus the advent of refrigerated rolling stock allowed the nation to enjoy an increasing variety of fruit and vegetables. The early padres, and later farmers, found that California's geography could accommodate at least some crops, anytime, anywhere in the state. This led not only to highly specialized farming but also a demand for adequate water. Specialty crops increased a farmer's return per acre, but only if there was a sufficient, continual supply of water. The state's endless cycles of wet and dry years produced a yo-yo economy from a grower's perspective.

The Great Drought during the 1860s spurred local irrigation efforts, especially in the great agricultural valleys of California. Instead of isolated farmsteads as found in the Midwest, California farmers settled in colonies. This allowed and, in fact, required them to cooperate on various water projects. These efforts included the diversion of water from the state's major river systems, rivers fed from a permanent snowpack in the Sierra Nevada.

The late 1800s and early 1900s witnessed numerous efforts to increase the volume and dependability of water. The Wright Act of 1887 authorized the formation of local water irrigation districts, precursors to modern-day water districts. From that point on, the agricultural sector, in partnership with the state and federal governments, pursued the construction of dams, wells, canals, reservoirs, catchment basins, and aqueducts to move water ever farther from its source. In 1908, Los Angeles engineer William Mulholland and business leaders Harrison Gray Otis and his son-in-law Harry Chandler (successive publishers of the *Los Angeles Times*) spearheaded an effort to construct an aqueduct from the Owens River, east of the Sierras, to the San Fernando Valley. This project eventually sucked dry a previously productive agricultural valley.

The federal government played a major role in later water projects. In 1933, Congress appropriated start-up funds to initiate the Central Valley Project after a $170 million state construction bond went unsold. This effort to conserve, divert, and redistribute the Sacramento and San Joaquin Rivers turned family farms into agribusinesses. Three years later, the federally financed Hoover Dam was completed, thereby creating Lake Mead. This massive effort to tame the mighty Colorado River garnered agricultural water for the Imperial Valley and still more water for Los Angeles. In addition, it produced huge amounts of electrical power, an additional prerequisite for urban growth in Southern California. Subsequent statewide water plans simply added to the patchwork of projects and confusing laws that constitute water policy in California. During this industrialization period, California would become one of the world's great "hydraulic societies," as Donald Worster put it.[15] Migrant workers during the Depression and later would provide the necessary labor required of industrialized agriculture. For more on water, see chapter 12.

Other Modernizing Factors

The impact of the Gold Rush and visionary water planning were only two features of California's modernization. Several others deserve mention.

Oil. **Black gold** was discovered in various parts of Southern California between 1900 and 1940, creating new economic opportunities. Unlike California's farmers and their crops, the oil companies faced tremendous obstacles shipping crude to distant out-of-state markets. They became vulnerable to overproduction and the vagaries of local demand within California. Despite logistical challenges of drilling and shipping oil, this activity helped diversify California's mushrooming economy. New interest groups emerged, as well as calls for the regulation of oil production, transit, and pricing. Like yellow gold, early discoveries of black gold produced ripple effects—land speculation and further population growth. It became still another magnet drawing both job seekers and environmentalists concerned about oil-generated pollution. Finally, it gave major oil companies a significant and permanent stake in California politics.

World War II. A second event that propelled California's industrialization was World War II. The Great Depression drove people hoping for a better life to California. The nation's war effort, though, dwarfed Depression-era migration. Nearly 2 million people (including African Americans and whites from the South and Midwest) came to or through California to work in defense plants, neighboring communities, or military bases. A transportation network (thanks to the railroads) and plenty of water (thanks to the water visionaries) made wartime growth possible. California's location on the Pacific Rim during a war with Japan made wartime growth inevitable.

Although military spending on aircraft predated World War II, the war itself helped the state to both grow and urbanize. During the 1940s, the state grew by 53 percent; more than 1 million people migrated to California just between July 1945 and July 1947. The thirst for defense contracts, call it **federal gold**, continued during the Cold War (1950s–80s) and helped forge an alliance between big business and big labor. Political moderates of both parties were elected to continue economic growth brought on by the war. Remnants of wartime California remain visible today, including numerous World War II–era military bases that never closed.[16]

THE POLITICS OF WELFARE

The third stage in political development is the **politics of welfare**. In this stage, government's task is to shield the citizenry from hardship, manage a well-functioning economy, improve standards of living, and assist the less fortunate. It takes an industrial base to afford these activities. In California, several factors influenced this stage of development: the Progressive Movement, the Depression, and the leadership of two governors, Earl Warren and Edmund G. (Pat) Brown. Combined, they represented the state's moralistic political subculture on a grand scale.

The Progressive Movement

Although California's role as a modern welfare state came after World War II, the foundation for welfare politics was built earlier. California's version of the nationwide **Progressive Movement,** led by Governor Hiram Johnson (1911–17), eliminated the overbearing political influence of the SPR and stressed political individualism and nonpartisanship (see chapter 4). Progressive reforms weakened political parties by requiring many officeholders to run as nonpartisans. The result was a nonpartisan public spirit to accomplish shared policy goals.

Economic growth heightened people's economic expectations, soon to be dashed by the Depression. The Progressives, in effect, created a leadership vacuum by allowing voters to make decisions previously reserved for elected representatives. Indirectly, they fostered an *expectation* of greater participation by the masses. This, in turn, fueled large-scale demand for more services and greater benefits.

The Great Depression

The Depression itself accelerated demands for public assistance to those crushed by economic hardship. In 1934, novelist and socialist Upton Sinclair became the Democratic nominee for governor. His platform, End Poverty in California, combined the goals of tax reform and public employment. Some voters, especially senior citizens, became Sinclair enthusiasts; big business labeled him a radical, a crackpot, and even a communist. He lost to Republican Frank Merriam. Four years later, the same year that *The Grapes of Wrath* was published, Democrat Culbert L. Olson won the governorship. Although he served only one term, he, too, developed ambitious policies to aid those untouched by progress in California.[17] What really helped California was the New Deal, which converted good intentions into actual assistance. The Works Progress Administration funded projects from Shasta Dam and the Golden Gate Bridge to lesser-scale schools, libraries, and hospitals. Through what Kevin Starr calls the "therapy of public works," California seemingly built itself out of the Depression.[18] The experiences of this era suggested that Californians would support an array of policies to improve living conditions *if* those policies were proposed by competent, moderate, progressive leaders. Wartime California produced those leaders.

Earl Warren

World War II expedited the welfare era by pumping even more federal expenditures into the state's economy. Politically, it helped produce a coalition of business and labor dedicated to one common goal: a healthy economic future for California. Elected in 1942, Governor Earl Warren was just the leader this coalition needed. During the campaign, Warren, a progressive Republican, rejected incumbent Governor Olson's partisan pleas: "I am, as you know, a Republican. But, I shall make no appeal to blind partisanship, or follow any other divisive tactics."[19] Thanks to his popularity and a Progressive Era reform called cross-filing, he was nominated for reelection in 1946 by three parties—Republicans, Democrats, and Progressives. He won a third consecutive term in 1950, the only California governor ever to do so, and was a contender for the Republican presidential nomination in 1952. He resigned in 1953 when U.S. President Dwight D. Eisenhower appointed him chief justice of the U.S. Supreme Court.

Dorothea Lange/Library of Congress Prints and Photographs Division [LC-DIG-fsa-8b29516]

This 1936 photo of migrant pea-picker Florence Owens Thompson and her children outside Nipomo, California, became a famous symbol of the Depression nationwide.

During Warren's tenure as governor, California made great strides in education and various social programs. In some respects, Warren continued a moralistic political subculture advanced by the Progressives. His social reforms included improvements to old-age pensions, unemployment benefits, medical care, labor law, prisons, and mental hospitals. A massive freeway-building program was launched in 1947, financed through increased gasoline taxes. Mind you, he pushed these policies through a Republican-controlled legislature. No wonder U.S. President Harry Truman once said of Warren, "He's a Democrat—and doesn't know it."[20] His one major legislative defeat—compulsory health insurance—would resurface decades later.

Growing state services in the Warren years meant a growing bureaucracy. State employees swelled from 24,000 in 1943 to 56,000 a decade later. An expanding economy made this growth affordable, and a 50 percent population increase made it necessary. In the spirit of Progressivism, Warren hired experts rather than political cronies to run these growing state agencies and appointed nonpartisan "committees of experts" to render policy advice. Historian Robert Glass Cleland credited the state's economy for all this policy vigor: "The war and postwar booms gave Warren only problems of prosperity to solve."[21] In fact, Warren was able to spend liberally *and* maintain a "rainy day" fund.

Lieutenant Governor Goodwin Knight succeeded Warren. Although more conservative than Warren, he adopted many of his predecessor's policies.

California had become a relatively generous social welfare state, the populace supported that development, and politicians of both parties knew it. An implicit social contract was in place. California was to represent continual prosperity and government was to be a guarantor of it. This political consensus would last for several decades.

Edmund G. (Pat) Brown

In 1958, Democratic votes finally caught up with Democratic registration trends and Pat Brown succeeded Knight as governor. Like Warren, Brown had been state attorney general and had avoided overly partisan election campaigns. He too avoided close ties with his own party. Under Brown's leadership, the state's Water Project was funded, providing the infrastructure to move vast amounts of water from the mountains to the growing Bay Area and Southern California cities. School and university enrollments mushroomed, as did requisite school construction, reflecting the state's continued growth.

Brown called for a master plan for higher education in 1959. This plan allocated different tasks to the University of California, the state colleges, and the junior colleges (as they were called then). Access to higher education by all Californians became part of the state's implicit social contract. Brown continued Warren's progressive welfare policies—an agenda he called **responsible liberalism**. Regarding civil rights, he pushed through the legislature various antidiscrimination measures and a Fair Employment Practices Commission to enforce them. Regarding infrastructure, Brown oversaw massive public construction projects including new college campuses, public schools, and a thousand miles of additional freeways. Brown was fortunate in that the freeways were largely funded by the *Federal Interstate Highway Act of 1956*. The state also became the regulator of air quality and the consumer's protector.[22] Responding to population and economic growth, public officials could not have imagined future growth that later Californians would no longer be willing to accommodate.

By 1966, unrestrained population growth, increased taxes, urban congestion, growing pollution, university campus unrest, farmworker strikes, and the 1965 Watts riot took their toll on Governor Brown. According to journalist and biographer Lou Cannon, "Many Californians who had previously voted Democratic blamed their grievances on government and no longer believed that they lived in the Golden State of their dreams and memories." California was a state "hungering for reform and a new sense of direction."[23]

Brown's successor was actor, liberal-turned-conservative, citizen politician Ronald Reagan. He spelled out his sense of direction in his January 1967 inaugural address: "The cost of California's government is too high. It adversely affects our business climate. We are going to squeeze and cut and trim until we reduce the cost of government."[24] Reagan soon learned that his "cut and trim" rhetoric was difficult, if not impossible, to implement. Most state spending was the product of legislative statutes or federal regulations, not gubernatorial wishes. Promising to cut government waste and "clean up the mess at Berkeley" (where student protests were commonplace), Reagan did make substantial cuts in welfare, mental health, and higher education. Nevertheless, the overall state budget doubled (from $5 billion to $10.2 billion) during his two terms as governor. He even signed into law a major tax increase when a revenue shortfall necessitated it and the state's first-ever income-tax withholding plan. This pragmatic conservatism also marked his years as American president (1981–89).

THE POLITICS OF ABUNDANCE AND BEYOND

Ironically, responsible liberalism can produce negative reactions, even by those it helps. True, the standard of living had increased in California through both public and private spending. The state had moved into the **politics of abundance**. A growing economy provided the taxes to fund a social welfare state and a plethora of services Californians had come to expect. In nature, these were **majoritarian policies**: the majority both paid for them and received their benefits. For instance, low-cost public higher education was available to every resident regardless of need. These policies not only were widely supported; they also attracted still more people to the Golden State.

But when does growth become too much of a good thing? By the 1960s, many Californians were asking that question. Growth had funded programs they supported but had also replaced orange groves with endless housing tracts and fueled freeway congestion, air pollution, and overcrowded parks and schools (see cartoon 2.2). Although many effects of growth are privately generated, Californians sensed that "politics as usual" was somehow to blame. Responsible liberalism apparently had become irresponsible. A succession of governors, including Reagan, would try to reverse at least some of the governmental growth that had characterized the state's history. California entered an era of lowered expectations. Reagan's successor and Pat Brown's son, Jerry Brown (1975–83

Tom Meyer

Cartoon 2.2 California's Seasons
California is well known for its climate, but certain times of the year are better than others. Wildfires have increasingly impacted all of California.

Question: Are the seasons depicted in this cartoon evident where you live?

and 2011–19), declared "small is beautiful" and claimed Californians were living in an **era of limits**, hardly the language his father would have used. George Deukmejian succeeded Brown (1983–91). As Reagan did, Deukmejian championed free enterprise; claimed government was the problem, not the solution; and rejected most tax and spending increases.

Political leaders in the 1970s and 1980s heeded Californians' pleas to preserve the "abundant state." If government was the problem, cut off its lifeblood—in a word, taxes. Elected officials imposed some of these tax limits in the annual budget process. Voters imposed others, such as Proposition 13 (which drastically cut property taxes). Buffeted by raging inflation and tax increases in the 1970s, they sincerely believed government revenue could be cut without reducing the services they enjoyed.

While governmental growth slowed, the state's population growth did not. By the dawn of a new century, observers were conflicted over the future of Abundant California. Given the constant drumbeat of population growth (up to 1,000 per day!), would there continue to be enough abundance to go around? This was a fundamental policy dilemma for Deukmejian's successor Pete Wilson (1991–98) and subsequent governors, Gray Davis (1999–2003) and Arnold Schwarzenegger (2003–11). In 2006, Schwarzenegger rode to reelection on a successful package of infrastructure bonds, but the Great Recession of 2008 soon derailed further efforts to accommodate the infrastructure needs pushed by population growth.

As noted in the last chapter, Jerry Brown's administration ended more than a decade of budget crises and placed the state's financial condition on firm ground. Incoming Governor Gavin Newsom found himself in an enviable position at the beginning of his administration in 2019: for the first time in 20 years, spanning two different governors, an incoming governor had a large surplus to work with. While the budget largesse gave the impression of abundance, intractable social problems were simmering, if not boiling, below the surface. Newsom conceded as much in his 2019 inaugural address:

> Even in a booming economy, there is a disquieting sense that things are not as predictable as they once were. That we all must now run faster just to stay in place. Stagnant wages. Costs that keep rising—rent, utilities, visiting the doctor—the basics are increasingly out of reach. We face a gulf between the rich and everyone else—and it's not just inequality of wealth, it's inequality of opportunity. We have a homeless epidemic that should keep each and every one of us up at night. An achievement gap in our schools and a readiness gap that holds back millions of our kids. And too many children know the ache of chronic hunger.[25]

The problems remain challenging in large part due to the widening income gap that Newsom alludes to and mentioned in the previous chapter. For those at the top, the California Dream is very much a reality. For those in the middle and below, they are a long way from living the dream, and the changing economy makes it harder to make up ground.

To be sure, every period of California's political development has carried its own set of governing challenges. Decades from now, what will historians write of this period? What stage of political development will they be describing? Will a politics of abundance be replaced by a version of post-abundance, at least for some Californians, or will abundance and its successor live side by side in this diverse state? Or will contemporary Californians of all backgrounds unite behind the promise that California held for generations past and be willing to invest or reinvest in its future? As you read the balance of this book, consider these questions.

KEY TERMS

political culture (p. 23)
traditionalistic (p. 23)
moralistic (p. 23)
individualistic (pp. 24)
political development (p. 24)
unification (p. 25)
Constitution of 1849 (p. 28)
politics of modernization (p. 28)
Southern Pacific Railroad (p. 29)

black gold (p. 39)
federal gold (p. 33)
politics of welfare (p. 33)
Progressive Movement (p. 34)
responsible liberalism (p. 36)
politics of abundance (p. 37)
majoritarian policies (p. 37)
era of limits (p. 38)

REVIEW QUESTIONS

1. Describe Elazar's three political subcultures and their application to California.
2. Describe political history as a process of political development. Define the four stages of political development used in this chapter.
3. Why are Spanish "rule" and Mexican "control" in quotes?
4. Describe the long-term impact of the Gold Rush
5. Why were the Big Four so powerful and so resented?
6. How did California become a great "hydraulic society"?
7. What effects did the discovery of oil and World War II have on California's political development?
8. How do the governorships of Earl Warren and Pat Brown compare to modern California politics?
9. Describe the politics of abundance and assess its future.
10. What do you think will be the next stage of California's political development and why?

WEB RESOURCES

California Historical Society
https://www.californiahistorical society.org

The Golden State's official historical society provides historical data and numerous links to statewide and local resources. Included is another history time line.

Bancroft Library

http://www.lib.berkeley.edu/
libraries/bancroft-library

Short of a visit to UC Berkeley's Bancroft Library and its vast California collection, check out its digital collection on various California topics.

California State Library

http://www.governors.library.
ca.gov

At the Governors' Gallery, locate several governors' inaugural speeches and consider how they reflect the state's political development at that time.

3

Constitutionalism and Federalism: The Perimeters of California Politics

★ ★ ★

LEARNING OUTCOMES

Students will be able to:

★ Explain the salient features of California's two constitutions.

★ Describe the stages of American federalism as they apply to California.

★ Discuss how California's Native Americans alter our common understanding of American federalism.

★ Analyze the factors behind California's clout or lack thereof in Washington, D.C.

★ Explain how the politics of fences in California apply to both immigration and world trade.

IN BRIEF

California is a nation unto itself. The most populous state in the Union, its economy dwarfs those of all other states and most nations. The state's political development is checkered with unique individuals, groups, and circumstances both historical and contemporary. Yet, when California became the 31st state, it joined a preexisting nation, one with its own constitution and emerging political institutions and traditions. Ever since, California has affected and been affected by the nation as a whole. In recent years, it has been increasingly affected by its neighbors, especially Mexico.

★ ★ ★

IN CHAPTER 3, we focus on several perimeters or outer limits that affect California politics. First, we examine California's constitution as a rulebook to which policymakers, institutions, and voters must conform. California's constitutional development helps explain why its core document or rulebook is similar to or different from that of other states. It also helps to explain why some political fragmentation is essentially structural in nature. Second, we discuss California's role in affecting national affairs and public policy. In doing so, we examine the successive stages of federalism as they relate to California and how Californians attempt to exercise influence in Washington. The chapter concludes by surveying how California's borders create policy challenges not faced by most states.

INTRODUCTION: RULES AND BOUNDARIES

Western democracies place certain limits on governments. Some of these limitations may be rules that dictate how and under what circumstances power can be exercised, policy made, and by whom. State constitutions and local governing charters contain such rules. Other limitations take the form of boundaries that demarcate territorial jurisdiction. These are legal borders beyond which influence wanes and power means little. National and state borders and city, county, and special district lines mark off the legal reach of most public policy efforts. From a state perspective, constitutions and federalism are the **perimeters of politics**—the outer limits that in effect contain the scope of political power.

Political scientists call the idea of limited government—government operating within certain rules—**constitutionalism**. American constitutionalism is derived in part from English political theorist John Locke (1632–1704). He believed that rights of the people and limits on those who govern them should be spelled out in a "social contract." Natural rights and rules governing the relationship between the people and government would occupy higher legal ground than ordinary laws (statutes passed by legislatures). In fact, the validity of these laws would be measured against the constitution. Accordingly, changing a constitution should be more difficult than changing an ordinary law. Furthermore, any such change should be made by the people themselves.

Locke's views on governance (including the idea of separation of powers) deeply influenced the framers of the U.S. Constitution. They were largely successful in limiting the document to basic fundamental law. (The original was only 4,600 words long and is only 8,700 words long today.) It would be the "Supreme Law of the Land," superseding the Articles of Confederation. With revisions, the colonial constitutions became state constitutions in 1789. Despite their regard for Locke, the framers rejected his idea of constitutional change by "the People." They believed in a republican form of government where only qualified voters would choose their representatives and only those representatives would make public policy. Ordinary citizens never voted on the original document and have never directly ratified its amendments.

America's constitutional history actually predates the U.S. Constitution. The 13 original colonies possessed extensive governing charters reflecting their respective political cultures. Later states brought with them comparable experiences and traditions. Because the founding elites in each new state generally understood what limited government and civil liberties meant, and what basic institutions were necessary to govern, state constitutions were destined to look alike in many respects. Yet they were never intended to be clones of the federal document. For better or for worse, they would reflect not only the beliefs shared by American society as a whole but also the culture, traditions, and unique attributes of each state.

Over the years, some reformers have viewed state constitutions as jumbles of unnecessary trivia. They have sought to both strengthen governmental power and to eliminate what they consider needless clutter. In their view, a state constitution should contain only basic, fundamental law and represent a governing consensus. A contrary view holds that constitutions are political documents—living, breathing expressions of policy conflict, not policy consensus. As such, constitutional language can advantage some groups over others and determine policy winners and losers.

CALIFORNIA'S CONSTITUTION

California's current constitution is eight times longer than the U.S. Constitution and has been amended more than 500 times, second in frequency only to Alabama. Some of the document's most interesting provisions are certain amendments that will be discussed shortly. Yet, the basic framework for California's government was established in the 1800s by two separate conventions producing two distinct constitutions.

The **Constitution of 1849** provided the basic structure of the state government and a 16-section Declaration of Rights. Slavery was banned. Married women were granted separate property rights, the first such guarantee found in any state (see figure 3.1). Certain policy directions were also set in this constitution. Provisions for public education were specified in some detail, and income from selected state lands was set aside for a future state university. Public debt of any magnitude was disallowed. This constitution lasted 30 years, longer than many observers thought it would. The voters repeatedly rejected legislative calls for a second constitutional convention, despite pleas that the state was "lawless, penniless and powerless."[1] Finally, a second one was held in 1878 amid rapid

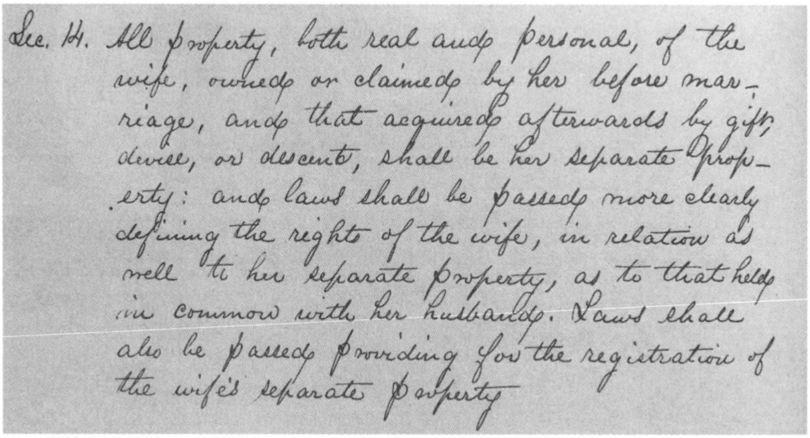

Sec. 14. All property, both real and personal, of the wife, owned or claimed by her before marriage, and that acquired afterwards by gift, devise, or descent, shall be her separate property: and laws shall be passed more clearly defining the rights of the wife, in relation as well to her separate property, as to that held in common with her husband. Laws shall also be passed providing for the registration of the wife's separate property

Figure 3.1 Women and the Constitution of 1849
At a time in American history when women were considered legally subservient to their husbands, California's first constitution suggested otherwise. Consider Section 14 of Article 11 (Miscellaneous Provisions) as it appeared in the original document.

Source: The Original Constitution of the State of California, 1849: The Engrossed Copy with the Official Spanish Translation (Sacramento: Telefact Foundation, 1965), 94.

population growth, feuds between farmers and the railroads, and the rise of the militant and reactionary Workingmen's Party. Many Californians thought constitutional reform would solve these problems.

The delegates to the 1878 convention generally represented three opposing interest groups: large financial interests (banks, corporations, and large landowners), farmers (opposed to the Southern Pacific Railroad and the tax system), and urban workers (alienated by both big business and the influx of Chinese workers). After months of hard bargaining, they adopted the document on a 120–15 vote; on May 7, 1879, California voters ratified it.

The **Constitution of 1879** was nearly twice as long as the old one and much more detailed. It was also viscerally anti-Chinese, containing provisions barring their immigration to California and disallowing the employment of those already in the state. Meant to check the power and influence of the Southern Pacific Railroad, the new railroad commission was quickly captured by the Southern Pacific itself, not only rendering it powerless but also converting it into a new bureaucratic tool of the railroad. Contemporary analysts Joe Mathews and Mark Paul called the new document a civic disaster. "Much of the next half-century of political reform efforts in California would be devoted to undoing its worst provisions."[2]

Over the years, California's constitution has continued to grow just as the state has. Today, it is eight times as long as the U.S. Constitution. Over the years, many original provisions have survived intact and others have been slightly revised. Entire new sections have been added, and other sections have been reorganized.

What It Contains

California's constitution illustrates features common to all state constitutions.

Duties of Government. It reflects the particular obligations of state government overall and necessary institutions such as the governor, legislature, and judiciary. Because local governments are subdivisions of the state, the constitution must spell out their duties and powers. Therefore, extensive sections of California's constitution deal with cities, counties, special districts, and school districts.

Mistrust of Politicians. California's constitution, like those of other states, has reflected historic mistrust of elected officials. This mistrust has been aimed at legislators as well as at governors. In the 1800s, the state legislature was considered so corrupt it was called the Legislature of 1,000 Drinks and the Legislature of 1,000 Steals. As a result, its powers were sharply delineated. In fact, the 1879 document actually *prohibited* the legislature from passing a variety of laws. Governors have not been spared either. California's constitution requires the governor to share power with separately elected executive officers—the lieutenant governor, attorney general, secretary of state, treasurer, controller, insurance commissioner, and school superintendent plus numerous boards and commissions. In some respects, term limits for the legislature and statewide officers reveal a mistrust of both "career" politicians *and* the voters who continually reelect them.

Group Benefits. Typical of other state constitutions, California has conferred particular advantages or imposed various regulations on interest groups. Numerous provisions specifically address financial institutions, the legal profession, the alcoholic beverage industry, churches, contractors, utility companies, the fishing industry, farmers, realtors, and transportation providers. One recent example is an Article 4, Section 19 provision guaranteeing gaming rights of California's Native American tribes. Although the constitution does not exactly mirror hyperpluralism as we use the term, any group with requisite political power can use it to garner benefits for themselves or deny them to others.

Money. California's constitution addresses taxation and finance in detail. Tax policies embedded in this document are used to benefit a plethora of interests and causes: charitable groups, orchards and vineyards, historic preservation, nonprofit hospitals, the elderly, renters, homeowners, museums, and veterans. Unlike the federal government, state constitutions usually limit the amount of debt states and their subdivisions can incur. In California, the 1879 state limit of $300,000 remains, but the wording of Article 16 provides ample room for policymakers to borrow considerably more.

Clutter and Trivia. Like other states, California's constitution is filled with clutter and trivia. This minutia must have seemed important at the time it was enacted. For instance, today's public school teachers can be grateful that the state's constitution prevents their annual salaries from dipping below $2,400.[3] In the early 1900s, the length of boxing matches and rounds was specified (12 rounds and three minutes, respectively). An 1849 ban on dueling remained in the constitution until 1970. A symbol of Cold War America is found in Article 20, Section 3. This 1952 provision requires virtually all public employees in the state to sign a loyalty oath (see box 3.1). Occasionally, the voters eliminate such provisions, but others remain simply because they are politically irrelevant. More important, some constitutional trivia remains because trivia is relative in a pluralistic society; what is undue clutter to one group might be economic survival to another. Even trivia represents hard-fought political conflict, winners and losers, and historical events in the life of a state. In a sense, it is pluralism at work.

Box 3.1 ★ California's Oath of Office

Sometimes called a loyalty oath, this oath of office dates from 1952 and is found in Article XX of the California Constitution:

> I do solemnly swear (or affirm) that I will support and defend the Constitution of the United States and the Constitution of the State of California against all enemies, foreign and domestic; that I will bear true faith and allegiance to the Constitution of the United States and the Constitution of the State of California; that I take this obligation freely, without any mental reservation or purpose of evasion; and that I will well and faithfully discharge the duties upon which I am about to enter.
>
> And I do further swear (or affirm) that I do not advocate, nor am I a member of any party or organization, political or otherwise, that advocates the overthrow of the Government of the United States or of the State of California by force or violence or other unlawful means.

Question: In recent years, several California teachers and professors have resisted signing this oath, and some have been fired as a result. Is this oath an outdated Cold War relic, or should it still apply given the nation's war on terror?

Change. California, like other states, allows its basic document to change. Three methods are available. First is a **constitutional convention**. The legislature, by a two-thirds vote, may call for a constitutional convention. The last such convention was in 1878. California has not used this method as frequently or recently as other states. In fact, voters have turned down such convention proposals on four occasions. In the 1960s, the legislature modified this method by appointing a "blue ribbon" constitutional revision commission to study the document and recommend changes for legislative approval and voter ratification. Overall, the revisions that survived voter approval resulted in a briefer, more streamlined document, at least by state constitution standards. In the mid-1990s, a 23-member Constitutional Revision Commission studied potential changes to the constitution. After two years of hearings and reports, it proposed a package of constitutional amendments to overhaul and streamline state and local government, but each of them died in the legislature. Groups such as California Forward continue to advocate for constitutional reform, but the prospect of comprehensive change is dim.

A second method is change by **legislative proposal**, a method common in all states. Individual members of the California Assembly and Senate propose legislative constitutional amendments and process them as bills. If two-thirds of their colleagues agree, measures are placed on the ballot for voter consideration. "Housekeeping" changes and more significant policy proposals have resulted from this method. For instance, in 2010 voters approved a legislatively referred constitutional amendment allowing the top two primary vote-getters to appear on the general election ballot regardless of party affiliation. A third method is the **initiative**, a product of the Progressive Era. The initiative allows individuals and groups to bypass the legislature entirely by placing proposed statutes or constitutional amendments on the ballot. Proponents of an initiative constitutional amendment must gather valid signatures equal to 8 percent of the total votes cast for governor in the most recent gubernatorial election (997,139 during the period 2019–2023). To be enacted, initiative constitutional amendments require only a simple majority of votes cast. Eighteen states allow this method, but no state uses it more than California. Chapter 4 discusses the initiative process in depth.

What Makes It Distinctive

As we have seen, newer states leaned on the older constitutions for framework and language. Structurally, all state constitutions resemble the U.S. Constitution. However, state constitutions invariably reflect their regional context, dominant political subcultures, historical experience, and subsequent political trends. At this point, we briefly spotlight several provisions in California's constitution that are quintessentially "Californian."

Power to the People. As noted earlier, one significant result of California's Progressive movement, under Governor Hiram Johnson's leadership, was the addition of initiatives, referenda, and recall. None of these is provided for in the U.S. Constitution. The **initiative**, allowing voters to directly place constitutional amendments and statutory proposals on the ballot, was approved in 1911. The **referendum** allows voters to approve or reject statutes already passed by the legislature. In the 2019–2023 period, initiative statutes and referenda required

623,212 valid signatures to be placed on a California ballot (5 percent of the total votes cast for governor in the 2018 election). The **recall** allows the electorate to remove elective officials between elections. This provision applies to all elective officials at both the state and local levels, including judges. Once thought impossible to accomplish at the statewide level (it takes the signatures of 20 percent of the votes cast in the last gubernatorial election), Governor Gray Davis was recalled in a 2003 special election. For more on power to the people, see chapter 4.

The Right of Privacy. Only 10 state constitutions contain an explicit right of privacy, and California is one of them. Even though it is not specifically mentioned in the U.S. Constitution, the U.S. Supreme Court in *Roe v. Wade* (1973) established a right of privacy relative to reproductive choice.[4] California's original "Declaration of Rights" in 1849 did not include privacy. It read: "All men are by nature free and independent, and have certain inalienable rights, among which are those of enjoying and defending life and liberty; acquiring, possessing, and protecting property; and pursuing and obtaining safety and happiness."[5] In 1974, the year after *Roe v. Wade*, California voters replaced *men* with *people* and added *privacy* after *happiness*. Although the emerging abortion controversy was not a key issue in its passage, this rewording has been used to support a pro-choice policy in California.

Water. Many states take water for granted, but not those in the West. California's history of drought, coupled with its agricultural potential, virtually required the government's attention from the start. Over the years, much water policy has made its way into the constitution itself. A separate article is simply titled "Water" (Article X). Overall, these provisions encompass water development and regulation, water rates, riparian rights (rights of those who live next to a body of water); the water policy role of the state; protection of fish, wildlife, and scenic rivers; and needs of specific areas such as the Sacramento–San Joaquin Delta.

English Only. The original 1849 Constitution was clear: "All laws, decrees, regulations, and provisions, which, from their nature, require publication, shall be published in English and Spanish."[6] The constitution itself was handwritten in both languages, reflecting California's two dominant cultures. Possibly due to the influx of Euro-Americans during the Gold Rush, that bilingual requirement was eliminated in the 1879 Constitution. Californians have struggled with this issue ever since. By the 1980s, California's bicultural identity was rapidly becoming bipolar (two cultures in conflict and poles apart). In some communities, the influx of immigrants from Asia and elsewhere suggested a multipolar state. Many white Californians were increasingly uncomfortable with the pluralism around them and the bilingual policies that resulted from it. In 1986, voters overwhelmingly approved Proposition 63, which declared English as the official language of the state. In 1998, they also rejected bilingual education in the public schools by approving Proposition 227. But in 2016, voters approved a legislative referendum that repealed Proposition 227, reversing a decades-long trend toward "English only" policies. The new policy placed discretion over bilingual education programs in the hands of local school districts, further adding to the ways that California already addresses a multilingual society. Multilingual ballots are commonplace and California's court interpreters are available for over 50 languages.

Proposition 13. In June 1978, California voters approved Proposition 13, a property-tax-cutting measure that fundamentally altered the relationship between the state and its local governments. The media widely portrayed its passage as the opening volley of a national tax revolt. Careful analysis suggests that the revolt was most successful in Western states with initiative provisions, such as California.[7] It had a more subtle effect: it paved the way for former Governor Ronald Reagan's national antitax message two years later as he ran for the presidency. Although other states have adopted their own tax cuts in the intervening years, Proposition 13 captured the nation's attention like no other.

From a governing perspective, California's constitution has fostered fragmentation and gridlock in state politics and policymaking, key elements in hyperpluralism. The state's governors must share their power with other elected executives. Legislative prerogatives are curtailed or limited. Protections for powerful interest groups are sprinkled throughout the document. The initiative process allows well-funded interest groups and individuals, via the electorate, to share legislative power. California's constitutional clutter actually encourages litigation, as groups seek to clarify what particular provisions really mean. This increases the policy role of the courts relative to the other branches.

California's constitution reflects all three political subcultures. Constitutional policies fostering education, water development, and other infrastructure investments, plus checks on corruption, connote a noble view of government characteristic of a moralistic political subculture. The individualistic political subculture (a more negative view of government) seems evident in efforts to curb political power and elevate individual rights. The traditionalistic political subculture (placing the powerful over the powerless) may be evident in a few scattered provisions such as public housing limits (Article 34) and sales taxes that impact the poor households more than rich ones.

CALIFORNIA AND THE NATION:
THE BOUNDARIES OF FEDERALISM

California's relationship with the national government, as with other states, has depended on both constitutional language and political practice. As times have changed, so has this relationship. The Tenth Amendment to the U.S. Constitution defines the general relationship that was supposed to exist between all the states and the national government: "The powers not delegated to the United States by the constitution, nor prohibited by it to the states, are reserved to the states respectively, or to the people."

The Founders assumed that the national government would defer to the states in domestic matters. As James Madison put it, "The State governments may be regarded as constituent and essential parts of the federal government; whilst the latter is nowise essential to the operation or organization of the former."[8] Alexander Hamilton considered citizens' loyalties to be primarily local; they would control any encroachments by their federal representatives.

To modern-day Americans and Californians, these arguments seem both idealistic and unrealistic. The Founders simply could not have anticipated the profound changes that would take place in the federal system. In a sense, there has been no single federalism but, rather, multiple "federalisms" reflecting different historical eras, public demands, and alternative visions of who does what in our political system. Political scientists have grouped these federalisms into five historical periods.

Dual Federalism

This is the original pattern of which Madison and Hamilton wrote. From the founding to about 1913, the national government largely limited itself to activities specifically mentioned in the U.S. Constitution, such as national defense, foreign affairs, coining money, issuing tariffs, and maintaining a post office. The states were expected to make policy on domestic matters such as education, welfare, health, and law enforcement. Political scientists called this division of labor **dual federalism**; one compared it to a layer cake.[9] California achieved statehood during this dual federalism period. With few exceptions, such as aid for the transcontinental railroad, the federal presence in California politics was minimal and indirect.

Cooperative Federalism

As American society became more complex and the Industrial Revolution produced a national economy, the division of labor between the federal and state levels blurred. From 1913 to 1964, a **cooperative federalism** pattern emerged. A national income tax, two world wars, and the Great Depression combined to make both levels active policy partners concerned with health, welfare, transportation, education, crime, and other issues. Political scientists considered the marble cake with its intermingling of layers a better analogy to describe the relationship during those years. During this period, California benefited greatly from federal spending on water projects, New Deal programs, high highway construction, and defense contracts.

Centralized Federalism

"He who pays the piper calls the tune," claims the adage. As the federal government's capacity to tax and spend grew, it also became more than simply a cooperative partner in policymaking. The "feds" (as state and local officials call national-level policymakers) gradually established their own goals. U.S. President Lyndon Johnson's Great Society legislation in the 1960s epitomized the next stage, **centralized federalism**.

The rationale was simple: if policy problems are national in *scope*, they must be national in *nature*—requiring a centralized response. People assumed that states could not or would not provide policy leadership or needed funding. During this period, the Tenth Amendment lost so much of its meaning that political scientists were now describing federalism as a pineapple upside-down cake. Three methods used to centralize policymaking included preemptions, partial preemptions, and mandates. *Preemptions* are when federal policies supersede the authority of subnational governments (e.g., immigration). *Partial preemptions* occur when the federal government takes over a policy area but allows states to impose higher standards (e.g., some environmental regulations). *Mandates* are when the federal government imposes certain duties on subnational governments (e.g., housing undocumented prisoners). During this period, federal aid was commonplace. California followed the national pattern—seeking and relying on federal grants for everything from highways to health care while resenting the federal conditions ("strings") that accompanied such funding. Increasingly, California officials had to lobby Washington, not just Sacramento, to get more funds and to avoid more strings.

The New Federalism

U.S. President Richard Nixon used the term **New Federalism** to describe his program that would share federal revenues with subnational governments with few conditions or strings attached. His General Revenue Sharing program delighted state and local officials in California and around the nation. The 1980s and the "Reagan revolution" continued this New Federalism in part. Building on his experience as California's governor, President Reagan sought to end centralized federalism and decrease the national government's overall role vis-à-vis state and local government. Targets were revenue sharing, various grants, and assorted federal programs. Some of his efforts were more rhetorical than real, such as threats to abolish the U.S. Department of Education. During this period, federal controls never disappeared and sometimes grew. But overall, California policymakers learned to develop their own programs and revenue sources independent of federal policy.

Pragmatic Federalism

Today, the relationship between the federal government and subnational governments, including California, has been called **pragmatic federalism**—"a constantly evolving, problem solving attempt to work out solutions to major problems on an issue by issue basis."[10] By pragmatic, we simply mean that there is a certain level of political opportunism at work here. Pragmatic federalism expresses itself in two ways. First, the federal government (relative to the states) and states (relative to their local governments) use coercion in lieu of funding to achieve policy objectives (see table 3.1). That is, public officials at each level do what they can to solve a particular problem while shifting the burdensome costs of doing so down the governmental chain. For example, Congress continues to preempt state and local authority over such issues as bankruptcy, environmental policy, transportation, water, and cable television regulation. It also requires states and local governments to implement federal policies through a complex mix of incentives, penalties, and mandates, only some of which are fully or even partially funded. These requirements may also be a function of U.S. Supreme Court decisions.

Although complaining of federal coercion, California state officials often require local governments to provide various services (e.g., general assistance welfare), adopt various policies without providing requisite funding (e.g., recycling requirements), or preempt local action entirely (e.g., gun control). What do local governments do to respond to coercive state tactics? Located on the lowest rung of the intergovernmental ladder, local officials have little choice but to increase user fees and local development fees, privatize some services such as trash collection, or encourage "do it yourself" governments such as homeowners associations that maintain streets within their limited jurisdictions.

Table 3.1 Examples of Federal Policy Impacts on California

Federal Action	California's Response
Federal Every Student Succeeds Act requires states to use Title 1 federal funds to assist low-performing schools in improving student performance	Use the California School Dashboard to measure performance and set aside $135 million for the task
Federal government disputes $1.4 billion in federal reimbursements for the state's Medi-Cal program, which provides insurance to low-income residents	The state must return $1.4 billion to the federal government and backfill that lost revenue with state general fund money
Requires state to use electronic visit verification system for Medicaid-funded In-Home Supportive Services program, which provides personal care to elderly and disabled residents	Sets aside $600,000 to plan for mandated verification system
Authorized funding support for six urban levee improvement projects to prevent flooding	Allocated $170 million to meet the state's share of funding for the levee projects and to match local and federal funding
Imposes new federal standards for driver licenses and ID cards, referred to as REAL IDs	Provides $21 million to reduce customer wait lines at Department of Motor Vehicles field offices to issue new ID cards; allows Director of Finance to increase funding up to $16.6 million as necessary

Source: "The 2018–19 Budget: California Spending Plan" (Sacramento: Legislative Analyst's Office, 2018), https://lao.ca.gov/Publications/Report/3870.

Second, due to federal government inaction on what states consider pressing issues, states have resorted to what some call "progressive federalism." Once a conservative argument intended to hamper governmental action in the days of dual federalism, political liberals have rediscovered "states rights" in order to address issues of health care, environmental regulation, medical marijuana, same-sex marriage, stem cell research, greater homeland security funding, immigration, and minimum wage increases. California's more progressive policymakers have sought to pass legislation in virtually all of these areas in response to what they consider policy gridlock, ideological opposition, or a lack of policy innovation in the nation's capital.[11]

FEDERALISM AND CALIFORNIA'S NATIVE AMERICANS

A commonly neglected aspect of federalism in California is the presence of California's Native Americans. How do these semi-sovereign tribal governments fit into the federalism mix? As you read in chapter 2, California's Native Americans were subjected to abuse, disease, violence, and premature death in pre-statehood California. Relegated to relatively remote, small-acreage reservations, their numbers and cultural influence dwindled. Their political influence was nonexistent. Until recently, they were among the state's poorest residents.

Legally speaking, the federal government confers nationhood on recognized American tribes, including inherent powers of local self-government. However, these principles have been compromised repeatedly. The federal government often disregarded treaties and viewed the tribes as domestic dependent nations in need of federal guardianship. Native Americans achieved full American citizenship and voting rights in 1924.

Today, California's 109 tribes relate to all three levels of our political system—federal, state, and local. At the federal level, the Bureau of Indian Affairs (BIA) provides various services to Native Americans and oversees the management of lands held in trust for 573 federally recognized tribes. The federal government holds legal title to the land, but the tribes hold it communally and exercise authority over its use. Some California tribes have sought to add nonreservation land to expand housing opportunities or for other purposes. To do so, they must first seek BIA approval to add it to their jurisdiction. Once added, it is taken off local tax rolls and is largely exempt from typical local government land use regulations and processes.

At the state level, both federal and state initiatives have led to the growth of casinos in California. In 1987, the U.S. Supreme Court in *California v. Cabazon Band of Mission Indians* recognized the right of tribal governments to offer gaming on their own lands. One year later, Congress enacted the *Indian Gaming Regulatory Act*, a law specifying and restricting gaming practices. One requirement of the law was that tribal governments must enter gaming compacts with state governments in order to offer casino-style gambling. In 1999, Governor Gray Davis signed the first of several state gaming compacts with 61 of California's 109 tribes. It provided for the operation of slot machines, lottery games, and various card games. Regulations addressed revenue-sharing with the state and with nongaming tribes, environmental protections, and labor matters. Proposition 1A ratified the compact's provisions in 2000 and locked them into the state constitution. Currently, 63 tribal governments own 63 casinos in 28 California counties. Fifteen are full-service resorts offering dining opportunities, spa treatments, and concert venues, much like Las Vegas. The remaining tribes offer no gaming whatsoever. Their reservations may be too remote to support profitable casino operations.

At the local level, California's cities, counties, and special districts have little power over the tribes and therefore must seek voluntary cooperation and compliance with various local ordinances. Newly proposed casinos and expansion of existing casinos are usually met with resistance from local communities, but the latter have little input in these projects. Gaming tribes do share some of their profits with local governments to help mitigate local impacts from casino activities. Tribal governments have also sought to spread political "goodwill" through campaign donations. In 2018, they contributed $6.2 million to state elected officials.[12]

The growth and popularity of Indian gaming in California have created needed jobs and bolstered local economies throughout the state.[13] Although the public has generally supported tribal self-sufficiency, including gaming on tribal lands, casino expansion has spawned a number of political controversies. These controversies raise puzzling questions for policymakers and students of federalism. For example, because tribes need not pay traditional taxes, to what extent should they make "in lieu" payments to the State of California and the local

Indian casinos, such as the Morongo Casino and Resort, have become lucrative businesses.

jurisdictions where casinos are located? To what extent should tribes voluntarily abide by the same land use regulations required of their neighbors? Should Native American sovereignty extend to any nonreservation land a tribe might acquire? These questions suggest that federalism, as it relates to Native Americans in California, is somewhat enigmatic. Whereas pragmatic federalism may characterize intergovernmental relations generally in America and the states, the presence, sovereignty, and the newfound power of California's gaming tribes suggest the presence of a hybrid form of federalism. In this form, semi-sovereign tribes exercise a variety of rights and powers. The federal government acts as benefactor, service provider (in some remote locations), and trustee of tribal lands. The state manages the regulation of casinos and is party to tribal compacts outlining casino activities, limits, and responsibilities. Local governments accept voluntary "in lieu" payments from casino-owning tribes, provide law enforcement via contracts, and continually lobby for a greater voice in tribal matters.

CALIFORNIA IN WASHINGTON

As with the other 49 states, California seeks to maximize its influence on federal policymaking, a process called intergovernmental lobbying. Compared to less diverse or smaller states, representing California in Washington is more challenging than size alone would suggest. In one notorious case, California's lack of clout once resulted in Congress awarding a federal earthquake research center to New York State rather than to earthquake-prone California.

One measure of a state's clout is the extent to which it receives more in federal spending than it sends to Washington in taxes. Federal spending in California includes everything from Social Security, Medicare, and Medicaid payments to military wages, college financial aid, and highway construction. How does California fare? Historically, California has been a so-called donor state. This is partially due to California's higher-than-average personal incomes (resulting in higher taxes paid), a comparatively young population (resulting in fewer Social Security payments), and recent cuts in defense spending (resulting in fewer government contracts). Also, as we noted earlier, some federal programs do not adequately cover state costs associated with illegal immigration and Medicaid. At times, these trends work in reverse. During the recent Great Recession, California incomes (and taxes) dropped whereas federal stimulus policies boosted federal spending in California, if only temporarily.

The reasons for California's relative lack of influence in Washington are numerous and complex. First, the rules of the federalism game have shifted in the last two decades. Earlier, lobbyists in Washington worked routinely with executive branch bureaucrats who controlled the distribution of grant monies. As both funding and federal programs were reduced in the 1980s, some grant decision-making shifted from anonymous bureaucrats to members of Congress. As a result, California lobbyists found they had to influence the content of legislation, not just "touch base" with grant administrators. This trend put a conflict-prone state at the mercy of a conflict-ridden Congress.

Second, California may lack clout because of its distance both geographically and politically. Members of Congress may resent the state's sheer size and its role as a competitor for federal dollars. Washington veterans call this attitude the "Anywhere but California" Syndrome.

Third, California's congressional delegation (two senators and 53 House members) is by far the nation's largest and most diverse. It faces both structural and ideological challenges. Structurally speaking, mega-states such as California are outnumbered in the U.S. Senate, where each state, regardless of size, gets two senators and, accordingly, two votes. California's influence in Washington can also wax and wane depending on whether members of its delegation are in Congressional leadership positions. For instance, Democrat Nancy Pelosi (San Francisco) became Speaker of the House, the most powerful position in the chamber, in 2007 and again in 2019, while Republican Kevin McCarthy (Bakersfield) has served in several leadership positions during his tenure. However, partisan differences can reduce the impact of these influential positions when party loyalty supersedes state interests. In addition, California's diverse political geography (north/south, coastal/inland, and urban/rural) creates diverse agendas within the delegation. Although the challenge of uniting this diverse delegation has been likened to herding cats, cooperation is possible, as has been seen on such issues as disaster insurance, skilled worker visas, and water issues.

Given California's diversity of interests in Washington, several strategies have been employed to maximize the state's political effectiveness. First, growing numbers of the state's public and private interest groups now saturate the federal government with lobbying activity. Dozens of California counties, cities, special districts, and state agencies (including the legislature) are represented in Washington. All three public higher education systems (the community colleges, the California State University, and the University of California) employ registered lobbyists. Such activity can be costly. In 2013, one drought-plagued Central

Valley water district spent $600,000 on federal-level lobbying and another $1 million on "outreach and awareness."[14]

Second, California's congressional delegation and California-based organizations seek to frame their needs in broader terms and look outside of California for support. That is, they build coalitions. The broadest coalitions involve well-established associations such as the National Governors' Association, the Council of State Governments, or the National League of Cities. Narrower ones might involve regional allies (e.g., the Western States Recycling Coalition). Because many issues come and go, California lobbyists must constantly build new coalitions to deal with new policy challenges. Third, California policymakers have found it beneficial to downplay California's interests or embed them in vague bill language. State agencies have been known to quietly support or oppose a bill in Congress without actually acknowledging its impact on California.

CALIFORNIA AND THE WORLD: THE POLITICS OF FENCES

Just as federalism delineates the relationships between California and the national government, it is important to delineate the relationships between California and nation-states beyond its borders. According to former California Assembly Speaker Robert M. Hertzberg, "In no other era in the history of California have local interests been more directly tied to international concerns."[15] In fact, some analysts agree that California needs and deserves its own foreign policy.

International pressures on the Golden State are primarily twofold. First, California is by far the most popular destination for both authorized and unauthorized immigrants (those with and without currently valid visas). What made the state attractive to early immigrants continues to make it attractive today. Second, California's colossal economy—one of the world's largest—is increasingly dependent on international trade. As the nation's largest exporter, the state relies on the ability to trade freely with Canada, Mexico, Europe, and its largest trading partner, Asia. Much of California's "foreign policy" is related to immigration and trade. Here, the perimeters of California power are likened to literal and figurative fences. In general, policymakers have sought to heighten fences relative to immigration and lower them relative to trade.

Immigration

One gets the impression there are few fences between California and the world, and immigration data bear this out. As figure 3.2 portrays, this is not a new phenomenon. According to the U.S. Census Bureau, the foreign-born now account for over a quarter of California residents, the highest proportion in the nation. The leading countries of origin have been Mexico, China, and the Philippines. Although precise figures are elusive, experts believe that more than 11 million undocumented immigrants reside in the United States and that about 2.5 million of those live in California.[16]

Movement across California's border with Mexico is nothing new. Historically, the nation's approach toward Mexican workers, one shared in California, has been called the **flower petal policy**: "I need you, I need you not, I need you. . . ."[17] That is, immigrants are welcome depending on whether the American workforce needs them. For instance, California welcomed Mexican immigrants after the

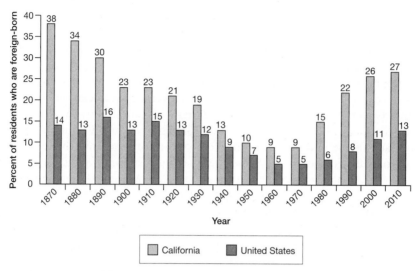

Figure 3.2 How California Compares: The Foreign-Born in California and the Nation

Source: Hans P. Johnson and Sergio Sanchez, "Just the Facts: Immigrants in California" (San Francisco: Public Policy Institute of California, May 2018), https://www.ppic.org.

Mexican Revolution of 1910 when Japanese and Chinese workers were unwelcome. During the Depression, people thought Mexicans were taking "American" jobs. But World War II resulted in another labor shortage, and Mexican laborers were welcomed once again. Renewed deportation efforts occurred in the 1950s and early in the 1980s. Although the "I need you not" rhetoric has been common in recent years, in reality, immigrant labor has been essential to numerous California industries, including agriculture, garment, furniture, and electronics manufacturing, food processing, and tourism.

The attraction of California is understandable. The state's minimum wage is far more than prevailing wages in many "sending" countries. In fact, job-hungry immigrants are as likely to be in the state's civilian workforce as U.S.-born residents. Some make enough to send excess income to family left behind; others occupy low-skill and low-wage jobs.[18]

Federal immigration policy has focused on shoring up the fence, that is, on border enforcement. First, Congress passed the **Immigration Reform and Control Act of 1986 (IRCA)**. This law created an amnesty program leading to legal residency for more than 3 million foreigners, half of whom lived in California. One purpose was to unite family members divided only by national boundaries. In reaction to the continued flow into California of unauthorized immigrants, the Immigration and Naturalization Service (INS; now called U.S. Citizenship and Immigration Services), launched "Operation Gatekeeper" in 1994 along the San Diego–Tijuana border—the busiest land-border crossing in the world.

In 1996, Congress followed up with the **Illegal Immigration Reform and Immigrant Responsibility Act**. This law increased criminal penalties for immigration-related offenses and authorized the INS to hire more border patrol agents, construct new fencing, and employ new underground sensors and night-vision equipment. Furthermore, the law made deportations easier and increased penalties for those unlawfully present in the United States. Fearing such penalties, many otherwise eligible unauthorized immigrants were discouraged from pursuing lawful admission. Congress also authorized the construction of a 700-mile fence along portions of the 1,951-mile U.S.–Mexico border, much of it east of California. But comprehensive immigration reforms have eluded congressional action, despite the dire need for it.

In 2017, the need for immigration reform boiled over during the first year of the Trump administration. Immigration policy took center stage soon after Trump was sworn in as president, after running on an anti-immigrant agenda that stressed the need for building a wall at the U.S.–Mexico border and referred to undocumented Mexican immigrants as "rapists." His initial actions included issuing an executive order that banned immigrants from predominantly Muslim countries and reversing executive orders from the Obama administration that granted temporary legal status to undocumented immigrants brought into the country as children (Deferred Action for Childhood Arrivals program). These policies led to a loud outcry from pro-immigration advocates and were modified in subsequent federal court challenges. California's elected officials, Governor Brown among them, were some of the most vociferous opponents of the new immigration policies: "And let me be clear: we will defend everybody—every man, woman, and child—who has come here for a better life and has contributed to the well-being of our state."[19]

In response to the Trump administration, Governor Brown and the legislature enacted "sanctuary state" laws that sought to make it more difficult for federal agents to apprehend and deport undocumented immigrants (see cartoon 3.1). The main piece of legislation was SB 54, which prohibited state

Cartoon 3.1 Immigration and the California Border
California officials and the Trump administration have feuded over immigration policy.

and local law enforcement from assisting federal agents in apprehending undoc-umented immigrants. More than a dozen cities and counties, mainly conservative jurisdictions, responded by passing resolutions opposing the laws and, with the Trump administration, filed lawsuits challenging them. In 2018, a federal court dismissed a large part of these legal challenges, leaving in place SB 54.[20]

Recent state efforts to protect undocumented immigrants reinforce steps that California policymakers had already taken in recent years to emphasize assimila-tion over rigid enforcement. In fact, the California Supreme Court in 2010 unan-imously ruled that undocumented students may receive in-state tuition rates at California's public universities if they attended and graduated from a California high school.[21] This ruling affected an estimated 25,000 undocumented students. In 2015, a number of California laws took effect allowing unauthorized immigrants to obtain specially marked drivers' licenses, qualify for low-cost auto insurance, and apply for state-funded college loans.

In many of these policy debates, immigration issues and Mexico are closely linked. But what about immigration to California from Asia? Asian immigrants to California now surpass those coming from Latin America, but this trend seems less controversial. The reasons may be several. First, many Americans and their elected officials believe the border with Mexico is identifiable and securable—even fence-able. Entries into California from Asia and elsewhere are more dif-ficult to identify, monitor, and enforce. Second, many Asian immigrants bring high-level job skills desired by many California employers. As a result, Asian immigrants receive more employment preferences and necessary visas than do less-educated or lower-skilled immigrants from elsewhere.

At times, resourceful California businesses bypass immigration hurdles entirely and outsource certain tasks to nations with cheaper labor pools (such as India). Where feasible, they also have learned to replace higher paid workers at home with lesser paid immigrants.

World Trade

The impact of international trade on California is immense. California exports over $172 billion in goods to about 229 foreign markets, (nations, economies, and locales in 2017). Such trade employs a million California workers. And like immigration policy, trade largely depends on the federal government's approach. Up until the Trump administration, the approach of California and the federal government to world trade has been to *lower* economic fences. In 1993, Congress passed the **North American Free Trade Agreement (NAFTA)** to encourage trade between Canada, the United States, and Mexico. Over time, it would eliminate tariffs completely and remove many nontariff barriers to trade such as import licenses. By 2004, it became the world's largest free trade zone, and the United States is Mexico's largest trading partner. NAFTA's specific impact has been mixed depending on company size, economic sector, and locale. Some California man-ufacturers have benefited from their proximity to low-wage, assembly-line labor in Mexico's border towns while some growers have been hurt due to lower-priced commodities from abroad. In short, NAFTA has promised more than it has deliv-ered, especially for workers.[22]

In 2017, after calling NAFTA "the worst trade deal ever made" and imposing tariffs (import taxes) on Canada and Mexico for steel and aluminum, President

Trump began negotiations to revise the agreement to grant the United States more favorable terms. The leaders of the three nations signed a new deal in late 2018 that, among other things, set new minimum wages for auto parts workers and opened Canada's dairy market to U.S. farmers. The fate of NAFTA 2.0 awaited final approval in Congress in 2019.[23]

California's trade policy has been, at best, a work in progress. In the 1980s, it established a California World Trade Commission with offices in numerous foreign capitals. In 2003, these offices and the rest of the Technology, Trade, and Commerce Agency were closed for being ineffective. In a reversal of sorts, a 2012 state law made the Governor's Office of Business and Economic Development (Go-Biz) the lead agency for international trade and investment. This included the creation of several trade offices; the first was in Shanghai, China. Before leaving office, Jerry Brown signed international agreements with eight nations, including China and Mexico, to foster economic cooperation across borders. Yet many observers agree that economic conditions, federal policies, and public policies in other nations, from Mexico to the outer reaches of the Pacific Rim, will more likely affect the politics of borders and fences than Sacramento-based efforts.

CONCLUSION

California's position relative to the nation as a whole is most interesting. Its political development has resulted in constitutional provisions both similar and dissimilar to constitutions in other states. California's diversity is mirrored both in its constitution and in the variety of representatives it sends to Congress. Its sheer size makes it the focal point of media attention when voters dramatically alter their constitution. As a result, California can give birth to national political movements through such changes (e.g., Proposition 13 and the "taxpayers' revolt").

California's constitutional development reflects American political theory. The state constitution provides the basic elements of representative government—the cornerstone of American political thought. Political elites dominated California's two constitutional conventions and greatly influenced much of its language. Well-organized interests are amply provided for in the document. Yet the constitution allows for widespread group participation and has been partly responsible for the state's political pluralism. It also planted the seeds of hyperpluralism by dividing political responsibility, limiting some governmental powers, and, through the initiative process, compromising the notion of representative government.

California's size and diversity have affected its intergovernmental relationships. The state is both the automatic recipient of large amounts of federal spending and the source of resentment at the money being spent. But California's interests are so diffuse and its congressional delegation so diverse that the state rarely speaks with one voice, even when doing so would be in its own best interest. In its own midst, the growing power of California's gaming tribes has raised numerous questions of governance. Finally, California's relationships with the rest of the world present an ongoing challenge and reflect the politics of diversity. A solid black line on maps, California's border is, in reality, a porous screen door through which flow workers, families, jobs, and dollars. Despite recent federal efforts to impose new barriers on immigration and trade, California policymakers have largely sought to embrace their international neighbors, both near and far.

KEY TERMS

perimeters of politics (p. 42)
constitutionalism (p. 42)
Constitution of 1849 (p. 28)
Constitution of 1879 (p. 44)
constitutional convention (p. 46)
legislative proposal (p. 46)
initiative (p. 46)
referendum (p. 46)
recall (p. 47)
dual federalism (p. 49)
cooperative federalism (p. 49)

centralized federalism (p. 49)
New Federalism (p. 49)
pragmatic federalism (p. 50)
flower petal policy (p. 55)
Immigration Reform and Control
    Act of 1986 (IRCA) (p. 56)
Illegal Immigration Reform and
    Immigrant Responsibility
    Act (p. 56)
North American Free Trade
    Agreement (NAFTA) (p. 58)

REVIEW QUESTIONS

1. Describe the concept of constitutionalism and illustrate that concept from California's constitution.
2. Contrast California's 1848 and 1879 constitutions.
3. In what ways is California's constitution similar to and unique from those of other states?
4. California's constitution both planted the seeds of hyperpluralism and over time mirrored the political subcultures of the state. Illustrate this statement.
5. How did the various stages of American federalism manifest themselves in California?
6. How do California's tribal governments fit into American federalism?
7. How do Californians represent their interests in the nation's capital?
8. In what ways are California politics affected by the state's proximity to Mexico and the Pacific Rim?

WEB RESOURCES

The California Constitution
http://leginfo.legislature.ca.gov/faces/codes.xhtml

The Legislative Counsel of California maintains this website, which contains a fully searchable copy of the state constitution. Contrast it to the U.S. Constitution.

Federation for American Immigration Reform
http://www.fairus.org

FAIR is an anti-immigration group that features some straightforward immigration data in California, both statewide and by county.

National Immigration Law Center
https://www.nilc.org

The National Immigration Law Center focuses on the rights of immigrants already in the United States and California.

4

Direct Democracy in a Hyperpluralistic Age

★ ★ ★

LEARNING OUTCOMES

Students will be able to:

★ Explain how Progressivism altered California politics.

★ Illustrate how statewide initiatives work using chapter case studies.

★ Analyze why some observers consider the state's initiative process to be a governing mess.

★ Describe other tools of direct democracy including the referendum and recall.

★ Discuss how direct democracy is a paradoxical phenomenon in California politics.

IN BRIEF

In a mature representative democracy, voters play a key role in governing. In a real sense, the "people" are sovereign, yet they do not behave in a political vacuum. Just as the public officials they elect, the voters themselves are influenced by profound social, economic, and political forces they do not fully understand. Consider these questions: Why does the electorate vote so often in California? How can voters throw out elected politicians without waiting for the next election? What empowers them to directly legislate on policy issues about which they know little or nothing? The average Californian is probably unable to give cogent answers to these questions. Yet, that same person would heartily defend all those electoral powers as necessary in a democracy.

★ ★ ★

IN CHAPTER 4, these questions are addressed first by unraveling the various layers of history that shroud the origins of the typical contemporary California voter. Beginning with political corruption and emerging urban problems during the "politics of modernization," we trace the rise of the Progressive movement in California; describe its continuing presence in modern politics; and examine the hyperpluralistic election system that has resulted. In the end, what emerges is something of a paradox in the Progressive legacy: the same reforms that gave voters ultimate power also have contributed to the policy and political gridlock we observe in California today.

INTRODUCTION: THE IMPACT OF PROGRESSIVISM

It seems Californians are perennially voting, thinking about the next election, or recovering from the last one. They are inundated with more candidate and policy choices than most Americans could imagine. In some respects, Progressive reforms predestined this state of affairs. **Progressivism** was a turn-of-the-century political movement that sought to rid politics of corrupting influences, return power to "the people," and make government more business-like. The movement both benefited and departed from a populist strain in American politics that distrusted political and economic elites.

The era from about 1900 to 1920 was one of social upheaval and intense political competition among social classes in the United States. The Progressive reformers were in the middle of this upheaval. Across the nation, these reformers were appalled by the political dark side of the Industrial Revolution. From coast to coast, new immigrant voters were routinely bribed by members of urban political machines. Unelected bosses of both parties easily controlled many city halls and statehouses. Rather than being above the dirt, political parties were rolling around in it.

Preoccupied with the demands of both machine bosses and corporate moguls, local and state legislators neglected the mounting problems faced by cities in the late 1800s and early 1900s: labor unrest, unemployment, poverty, and urban crowding. Political corruption was only part of the story. As urban problems mounted, the machine bosses were poorly equipped to manage the increasingly complex affairs of city hall. Urban professionals, intellectuals, and muckraking journalists joined to expose the incapacity of the machines to govern effectively. The differences between these warring groups were profound. To the typical machine boss, politics was individualistic, the essence of good personal relations. To the Progressives, politics was a moral obligation to efficiently manage public resources for a larger public good.[1] They assumed that there was one public and one public good achievable through consensus. Californians easily equate the Progressive Era with the introduction of the initiative, referendum, and recall. Yet across the nation as well as in California, an entire set of other **Progressive reforms** was enacted to inhibit the influence of political machines. They included the following:

- *Direct primaries:* Boss-controlled nominating conventions were replaced by direct primaries, allowing voters to bypass party organizations and directly elect nominees to compete in general elections.
- *At-large elections:* Local elections were revised so that candidates would run citywide rather than from a specific district or ward. This would minimize machine control of individual votes and encourage officeholders to adopt citywide policy perspectives.
- *Nonpartisan elections:* Another reform removed party designations next to candidates' names on ballots. In California, this applied to all local and judicial offices requiring an election. Reformers thought that machine influence

would thereby lessen and that endorsements by "good government" groups would gain importance.

- *Merit systems and short ballots:* Under new civil service systems, government workers would be hired on the basis of merit—experience, training—not politics. Also, voters would directly elect fewer officials at the local level; in turn, these officials would hire civil servants to carry out the routines of government.
- *Professional management:* Related to the idea of merit, this reform created positions such as city manager, a professional administrator who would ideally be above and apart from politics. Today, most California cities have city managers or city administrators; counties and special districts have comparable positions.

PROGRESSIVISM: CALIFORNIA STYLE

California was a major center of Progressive-era activity. By the turn of the century, its politics exhibited many of the problems detested by the reformers. Analogous to the urban political machines elsewhere in the nation, California had its own statewide machine, the Southern Pacific Railroad (SPR). Its brazen and arrogant exercise of power became an easy target for the Progressives. Elsewhere in the United States, economic problems and social turbulence were blamed on new immigrants from Europe. In California, comparable problems were blamed on Chinese laborers and the railroad that originally employed them.

California Progressivism possessed five characteristics in common with the movement nationwide. First, it represented to some extent both the individualistic and moralistic political subcultures in California. On one hand, progressive reformers wanted to pursue their own agendas, unencumbered by big business monopolies or selfish labor union influence. On the other hand, they possessed a moral sense. As historian George E. Mowry noted, the California Progressive "pictured himself as a complete individual wholly divorced from particular economic as well as class interests. Ready to do justice in the name of the common good, he was, in his own estimation, something akin to Plato's guardians, above and beyond the reach of corrupting material forces."[2]

Second, Progressivism was white and middle class. Yet Progressives were not just middle class; they were anti–upper class and anti–lower class. As the progressive *California Weekly* editorialized in 1908, "Nearly all the problems which vex society have their sources above or below the middle-class man. From above come the problems of predatory wealth. From below come the problems of poverty and of pigheaded brutish criminality."[3]

Third, as with the rest of the nation, it was urban in nature. Although California Progressivism capitalized on agrarian unrest, its roots were in the state's emerging coastal cities. By 1910, 60 percent of California's population was urban; almost half lived in San Francisco, Alameda, and Los Angeles Counties. In these places, the Progressives waged war with organized labor, the Southern Pacific, and in San Francisco, a political machine controlled by Abe Ruef, a boss in the mold of New York City's legendary Boss Tweed.

Fourth, California Progressivism was nonradical. The movement's leaders were small business owners, lawyers, real estate operators, doctors, and journalists. As members of an upwardly mobile middle class, they sought to reduce the influence of one corporation, not to destroy the corporate idea. They rejected the socialist leanings of the labor unions, not labor itself. The Progressives sought to clean up government, not completely restructure it. Sensing even then a splintering of the state into diverse, hyperpluralistic groups, California's progressives sought to blunt the rising power of groups unlike themselves.

Fifth, California's Progressives depended on entrepreneurial leadership—those dynamic individuals who could rally relatively unorganized interests against entrenched power structures. For instance, through the influence of wealthy physician John Randolph Haynes, Los Angeles was one of the first cities in the nation to adopt local versions of the initiative, referendum, and recall. Other cities in the state rapidly followed suit. Los Angeles was ripe for this reform. Collis Huntington of the SPR tried to control harbor facilities near Los Angeles and had made numerous enemies in the process.

Another leader was Hiram Johnson, a prosperous San Francisco attorney who had helped prosecute local political corruption. One target was San Francisco's Union Labor Party headed by "Boss" Ruef, who controlled numerous local officials and was eventually convicted of political graft. Another target was William F. Herrin, chief counsel of the SPR and head of its Political Bureau. Herrin had showered legislators with free railroad tickets and even bribed newspaper editors to receive positive coverage, a rare commodity for the SPR. A statewide reform group, the Lincoln–Roosevelt League, talked Johnson into running for governor in 1910. In a style reminiscent of Theodore Roosevelt, Johnson campaigned throughout the state by automobile (he boycotted trains for obvious reasons), promising at every stop to boot the SPR out of politics. Johnson and other Lincoln–Roosevelt candidates ran as progressive Republicans and won huge election victories that November.

Courtesy of the California History Room, California State Library, Sacramento, California

Progressive reformer Hiram Johnson speaks at a political rally.

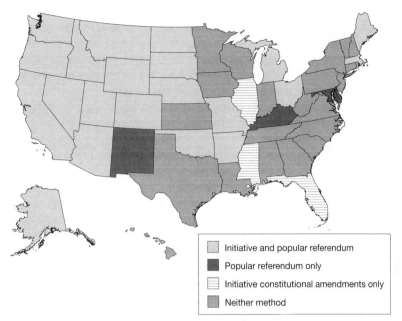

Figure 4.1 How California Compares: Direct Democracy across the States
California is one of twenty-four states that has an initiative process for statutes or constitutional amendments or both.

Source: National Conference of State Legislatures, http://www.ncsl.org/research/elections-and-campaigns/chart-of-the-initiative-states.aspx.

At the height of their success, the Progressives in California energized state government and institutionalized all the reforms associated with the era. In some ways, modern reform-minded groups such as Common Cause, the League of Women Voters, and the Public Interest Research Group have continued the Progressive tradition. They view their policy agendas as equally enlightened and have used the old reforms such as the initiative process to enact their goals. Over the years, 24 states, including many in the West, adopted the initiative (see figure 4.1). Arguably, California uses it more than most.[4]

SELECTED INITIATIVE BATTLES IN CALIFORNIA

Progressive Era reforms are so familiar that modern Californians take them for granted. The reform that has become most familiar to voters is the initiative. In theory, the initiative would empower ordinary people to fight entrenched special interests. In reality, it quickly evolved into a weapon readily available to any group willing and able to use it. Reflecting the state's individualist political subculture, individuals and groups quickly discovered how valuable the initiative process could be. For example, in 1924—13 short years after its advent—Artie Samish, then employed by the Motor Carriers Association, used an initiative to stabilize taxes on bus companies (he later became an infamous lobbyist). By 1939, well-financed interest groups were initiating measures more often than ad hoc reform groups. Today, instead of using the initiative process as the occasional

---

Box 4.1 ★ How an Initiative Becomes a Law

According to California law, any policy idea considered the proper subject of legislation can become an initiative measure. Here are the steps that groups and individuals must complete for an idea to become a law via that process:

1. Write the text of the proposed law (the Legislative Counsel's Office provides assistance upon the request of 25 electors).
2. Pay the $2,000 filing fee and request that the attorney general provide a title and a brief summary of the chief purpose and points of the measure.
3. Upon completion of step 2, the secretary of state prepares a calendar of filing deadlines. For example, proponents are allowed 150 days to circulate petitions and collect signatures (initiatives must qualify 131 days before the next statewide election).
4. Proponents circulate petitions and gather signatures, again within certain rules and detailed procedures. The petitions themselves must conform to a certain format and other specifications.
5. Proponents file completed petitions with the appropriate county election offices; they, in turn, submit signature totals to the secretary of state. If the list meets the minimum number of signatures required to qualify the measure, county officials use a random sampling technique to verify signature validity. If less than 95 percent of the sample is valid, the measure fails to qualify; if the submitted signatures are greater than 110 percent of the total number necessary, the measure automatically qualifies. If the random sample suggests that the number of valid signatures is between 95 and 110 percent, county elections officials must verify every signature—a so-called full check. Results are submitted to the secretary of state.
6. The secretary of state deems an initiative qualified and notifies counties and proponents accordingly. The state legislature holds hearings on the measure but cannot alter it or prevent it from appearing on the ballot.
7. The initiative appears on the next statewide ballot and, if approved, becomes law immediately, unless the measure states otherwise. If the provisions of two initiative measures conflict, those of the measure receiving the most affirmative votes prevails. The legislature may amend or repeal an initiative statute but voters must agree to such changes (unless the measure provides otherwise).

Source: Summarized from the California Secretary of State, https://www.sos.ca.gov/elections/ballot-measures/how-qualify-initiative/initiative-guide.

---

safety valve it was intended to be, interest groups *and* politicians use it regularly to bypass the legislature. A brief survey of several recent initiatives demonstrates the evolving role the initiative has played in California's electoral politics. Each of these has followed the steps noted in box 4.1.

Proposition 13: Give the Money Back

The first of these initiatives, **Proposition 13**, is a classic measure rooted in California's real estate market. In the 1970s, California home prices skyrocketed and so did property taxes because they were pegged to those rising values. Legislators and Jerry Brown, whose first stint as governor was from 1975 to 1983, could not agree on how to best provide tax relief. Homeowner frustration mounted. Los Angeles real estate developer and apartment owner Howard Jarvis proposed cutting property taxes by half and curbing their subsequent growth. He formed the populist-sounding United Organization of Taxpayers, which gathered a record 1.2 million signatures to qualify this historic tax reduction measure for the June 1978 ballot. Its provisions did the following: (1) rolled back assessed property values to those of 1975, (2) capped the tax at only 1 percent of assessed value, (3) limited tax growth to 2 percent per year, (4) limited future assessment increases to changes in ownership, and (5) required two-thirds voter approval for future tax increases (see box 4.2).

Despite the dire predictions about its potential consequences, Proposition 13 passed with 64 percent of the statewide vote. Nearly every electoral group measured by political scientists supported it. The consequences *were* dire and numerous. First, with property taxes cut by 57 percent, local services were slashed severely. As a result, local governments, especially counties and school districts, appealed to Sacramento for help and became increasingly dependent on state funding to fill in revenue shortfalls. These "bailouts" became an annual feature of the state budget, and in the process, local government lost a measure of its autonomy. Eventually, the state eliminated the bailout and redirected billions of dollars in local property taxes to the state for education spending.

Second, the measure fostered tax inequity. As real estate values continued to rise, the property tax paid by two neighbors living in identical houses could vary substantially over time depending on when the homes were purchased. Due to more frequent turnover, this phenomenon affected residential more than commercial real estate. In 1992, the U.S. Supreme Court, in *Nordlinger v. Hahn*, upheld Proposition 13, including this unequal treatment of property owners.

Third, Proposition 13's two-thirds voter approval requirement made it exceedingly difficult to raise most ad valorem or property-based taxes. In 2000, voters approved one modest exception: they lowered the two-thirds threshold to 55 percent for only local school bond measures (Proposition 39).

Fourth, for cities and counties, the supermajority restrictions encouraged local officials to seek revenue elsewhere, including the adoption of myriad fees and the approval of land use projects that generated sales taxes not constrained by Proposition 13 (see chapter 12).[5]

Box 4.2 ★ California Voices: A Governor on Initiatives

Appearing outside a Burbank COSTCO store to support workers gathering signatures for a workers' compensation measure, Governor Schwarzenegger proclaimed: "I'm a hands on governor. I'm out here with a pen. I'm out here with a paper, saying, sign here. I'm not one to sit around in Sacramento and do nothing."

Source: Quoted in David M. Drucker and Dana Bartholomew, "Schwarzenegger Stumps for Workers' Comp Reform," *Los Angeles Daily News*, April 12, 2004.

Propositions 22 and 8: Limits on Same-Sex Marriage

"Only marriage between a man and a woman is valid or recognized in California" was the only provision of **Proposition 22**, a controversial measure on the March 7, 2000, ballot. Those 14 words galvanized both supporters and opponents of gay rights and gay marriage in California. Although the proposition seemed simple enough, the issue it addressed was quite complex.

In an effort to seek societal recognition and fight discrimination, LGBT (lesbian, gay, bisexual, transgender) activists had demanded that same-sex marriages be given the same legal footing as heterosexual marriages. If they could achieve that in one state, the U.S. Constitution's Article IV, Section 1 would presumably require such marriages be recognized in all states. Section 1 reads: "Full Faith and Credit shall be given in each State to the public acts, Records, and judicial Proceedings of every other State." Concerned about that possibility, Congress passed and President Bill Clinton signed the *Defense of Marriage Act* in 1996. This law permitted states to not recognize gay marriages performed in other states. By early 2000, 30 states had passed similar laws.

The concerns of the LGBT community extended beyond the legal recognition of same-sex marriages. They feared that nonrecognition would result in the denial of various rights, including hospital visitations, inheritance, and dependent health insurance.

Prior to Proposition 22, California disallowed the marriage of same-sex couples but customarily recognized as legally valid all marriages occurring outside the state under Article IV. The proponents of Proposition 22 had become alarmed because Hawaii had come close to recognizing gay marriages and Vermont was on the verge of doing so (it legalized gay marriages in May 2000).

The impetus for Proposition 22 came from California State Senator William "Pete" Knight (R-Palmdale), who had unsuccessfully sought similar limits in the state legislature. For Knight, it was personal—his own son was gay, and his gay brother had died of AIDS. Lining up to support the measure were conservative religious groups (including the Mormon Church and the California Catholic Conference of Bishops), the state Republican Party, and the Hispanic Business Roundtable. Opposed were various gay-rights organizations and sympathizers: the American Civil Liberties Union, a number of labor unions, the California Democratic Party, and still other religious leaders. By the end of the campaign, Proposition 22's supporters outspent its opponents by a wide margin—$9.5 million versus $5 million. As usual, much of this money was spent on television advertising.

In the end, Proposition 22 passed with 61 percent of the vote. The only region to oppose it was the Bay Area, where fully 69 percent of voters rejected it. Analysts speculated that large numbers of conservatives turned out statewide because of a competitive Republican presidential primary election on the same ballot and effective get-out-the-vote efforts by pro-22 forces.

Gay-rights advocates were disheartened by the results but resolved to press on through more initiatives and legislation. They had reason to hope. For one thing, Californians had become somewhat more accepting of gay rights in general. Polls at the time suggested that fully 81 percent of Californians opposed discrimination based on sexual orientation and that 54 percent thought that homophobia was morally wrong. In addition, it appeared that younger voters were more concerned about discrimination against gays than were older voters.[6] Gay-rights activists also became newly energized in early 2004 when, contrary to Proposition 22, San Francisco Mayor (and future governor) Gavin Newsom declared same-sex unions to be valid in his city. Same-sex weddings commenced in that city immediately.

In reaction, same-sex marriage opponents vowed to wage still another initiative campaign—this time, placing the exact wording of Proposition 22 into the state constitution. They began circulating such a measure in late 2007. Why they believed they needed a constitutional amendment became clear when the California Supreme Court declared that same-sex couples have the same fundamental "right to marry" as do heterosexual couples.[7] This broadly worded decision appeared to invalidate any law that would discriminate based on sexual orientation. By the time this decision was announced in May 2008, **Proposition 8** indeed had qualified for the November 2008 ballot.

The fall campaign was vocal, emotional, and costly; campaign spending on both sides surpassed $73 million. The pro side argued that the defeat of Proposition 8 would endanger the position of traditional marriage in society and would require schools to teach the acceptance of homosexuality. The con side argued that same-sex unions are an important additional step on the road toward civil rights for all Americans. In the end, Proposition 8 passed by a 52.5 to 47.5 percent margin.

But, as often occurs, the battle continued in the courts. In 2009, the California Supreme Court ruled that Proposition 8 was a limited but valid exception to the state's equal protection clause.[8] Opponents of "8" promptly filed a suit in federal court, claiming that the measure violated the U.S. Constitution's Due Process and Equal Protection Clauses of the Fourteenth Amendment. In 2013, the U.S. Supreme Court dismissed that suit, ruling on narrow, procedural grounds that Proposition 8's supporters lacked standing to defend it in court. (Believing it was unconstitutional, state officials had declined to argue on its behalf.)[9] Days later, same-sex marriages resumed in California after the Ninth Circuit lifted a stay on such marriages put in place while the case was being litigated. In 2015, the U.S. Supreme Court heard four cases challenging same-sex marriage bans in four other states. In a sweeping 6–3 majority opinion, Justice Anthony Kennedy declared that "the right to marry is a fundamental right inherent in the liberty of the person, and under the Due Process and Equal Protection Clauses of the Fourteenth Amendment couples of the same sex may not be deprived of that right and that liberty." Accordingly, all states must recognize same-sex marriage.[10]

Propositions 215 and 64: Legalizing Marijuana

A few weeks before California's 1996 general election, U.S. Senator Dianne Feinstein expressed concerns over **Proposition 215**, the Compassionate Use Act. This initiative statute proposed to legalize the possession and use of marijuana (*Cannabis sativa*) for medical purposes, including serious illnesses and for relief of pain. Feinstein thought the measure was so badly worded that "you'll be able to drive a truck load of marijuana through the holes in it. Although it seems simple, the devil is in the details, or in this particular bill, the lack of details." Unconvinced, voters passed it with nearly 56 percent of the vote. Six years later, Governor Gray Davis signed SB 420, the Medical Marijuana Protection Act, which established an identification card system for medical marijuana patients.

Presumably, this would enable such patients to avoid arrest by local police on the lookout for recreational users.

In contrast, federal law continued to ban the use of marijuana for any purpose, medical or recreational, and two U.S. Supreme Court cases from California affirmed that position. In *U.S. v. Oakland Cannabis Buyer's Group* (2001), the court agreed that federal Controlled Substances Act does not provide a medical exception because Congress, at the time, concluded that cannabis has no "currently accepted medical use." In 2005, the court further ruled in *Gonzales v. Raich* that even if persons are cultivating, possessing, or distributing cannabis under state-approved medical marijuana programs, they remain in violation of federal law and subject to federal prosecution.[11] While not endorsing its use, U.S. Attorney General Eric Holder announced in 2009 that prosecuting individual users of marijuana for medical purposes would not be a Justice Department priority.

Proposition 215's goal of providing access to marijuana for medical uses has been highly successful, to say the least. It has provided pain relief to more than 1 million Californians and has encouraged the creation of cannabis cooperatives and dispensaries. Although some physicians refused to prescribe it, others have done so for a wide variety of serious and not so serious disorders. In subsequent years, local officials have had to create their own ordinances and regulations in response to the growth in dispensaries.

Given the cost of and frustration over the national war on drugs and public ambivalence about the harmfulness of marijuana, it was only a matter of time before an initiative would seek to decriminalize it altogether. It did so in November 2010 in the form of Proposition 19, which would have allowed anyone over 21 years of age to possess, cultivate, or transport marijuana for recreational or personal use. Although local governments could regulate and tax the distribution of marijuana, the drug would remain illegal on school grounds. Marijuana-impaired driving would be prosecutable just as drunk driving always has been. Despite outspending opponents $2.8 million to $212,000, Proposition 19 was defeated 54 to 46 percent.

The mantra "if at first you don't succeed, try, try again" applies to many initiative efforts, and marijuana legalization is no exception. Proponents retooled their arguments, addressing some of the concerns expressed by opponents of Proposition 19, and placed a new measure, **Proposition 64**, on the November 8, 2016, ballot. The new measure was nearly identical to the old one: for anyone 21 or older, it legalized the use, possession, growth, and sharing of cannabis. Supporters and opponents recycled many of their arguments from the previous campaign. Supporters argued that marijuana was already everywhere, criminalization of it was not working, and regulation of the industry would squeeze the black market, generating significant revenue for state and local government to fund afterschool programs, drug prevention and treatment, and crackdowns on impaired driving. Opponents pointed out that marijuana-related car crashes would increase, TV ads could promote marijuana smoking, and the black market could flourish. Celebrity endorsements and campaign donations lined up on both sides of the issue. Sean Parker, founder of Napster and onetime president of Facebook, donated $8.6 million to the yes side and joined forces with hip hop artists Jay-Z and Common, actor Danny Glover, and former NBA player Al

Cartoon 4.1 California Has Gone to Pot
How has your local community approached the legalization of marijuana?

Harrington. Many Republican and some Democratic elected officials opposed the measure, including Senator Dianne Feinstein. The biggest donation for the No side, $1.4 million, came from Julie Schauer. Who, might you ask, is Julie Schauer? She is an anti-marijuana activist and retired college professor from the East Coast who oversees a Pennsylvania trust fund.

Once again, the yes side outspent the no side, but this time it was a 12–1 margin: $25.1 million to $2.1 million. Preelection polling showed support for the measure hovering close to 60 percent, which was spot-on. Proposition 64 passed 57 to 43 percent. [12] Many of the details still needed to be worked out by state regulators and local jurisdictions (see cartoon 4.1). The California Highway Patrol was tasked with identifying a driving-under-the-influence standard and cities and counties retain discretion over local retail businesses. On January 1, 2018, around 100 dispensaries were licensed to sell marijuana throughout the state.[13] A *Time* magazine article summarized the passage of the measure this way: "the basic idea was simple: a majority of people in America's most populous state believe that adults should be able to consume marijuana if they feel like, like a glass of wine at 5 o'clock."[14]

THE INITIATIVE MESS

The stories behind the preceding initiatives are typical of many others, and they point to some disturbing trends. Media titles give you a clue: "Initiatives: Too Much of a Good Thing," "Hiram's Folly?" "California Initiatives: Out of Control," "California: The State That Tied Its Own Hands," and "Is Direct Democracy Killing California?" Veteran journalist Peter Schrag believes today's initiative process has caused a "seismic shift in the state's political center of gravity."[15]

What has happened to this ultimate tool of the sovereign voter? To answer this question, one must think in terms of democratic theory and two faulty assumptions stemming from it. Before the initiative was instituted, there was *misplaced confidence in legislators as competent representatives*. In truth, legislators often dodge tough policy choices and favor the views of special interests over those of relatively uninformed constituents. Consider this question: Are legislators primarily trustees using their own best judgment to represent the broad interests of their constituents or delegates following every constituent preference? The classic debate between trustee and delegate functions of legislators usually assumes constituents are voters back home, not the interest groups and lobbyists with whom contemporary legislators have much more contact.[16]

After the initiative process was established in California, there was *misplaced confidence in the voters as competent legislators*. Admittedly, political scientists do not always agree on this point. Years ago, Lester Milbrath did not expect ordinary voters "to give a lot of attention to, and be active in resolving issues of public policy. Nor should we expect [them] to stand up and be counted on every issue that comes along."[17] Thomas Cronin has taken a more generous view. He suggested that voters approach initiatives cautiously and vote against measures unless they see a direct personal or public benefit. "Voters who do vote on ballot measures do so more responsibly and intelligently than we have any right to expect." He further concluded that bad legislation is just as likely to come from the legislature as from the initiative process.[18] As you examine table 4.1, a list of the November 2018 propositions, ask yourself how many voters would be as competent as legislators in making those decisions.

Many observers blame the state's initiative mess largely on the ease with which direct democracy can be used. A parade of reforms made this possible. In the 1960s, the same constitution revision commission that recommended professionalizing the state legislature also opened the initiative process to amateur policymakers—the voters—in some profound ways. First, it recommended ending the "indirect initiative," where the legislature could vote on a citizen initiative before it headed to the ballot. Second, it lowered the signature threshold for initiative statutes from 8 to 5 percent of the votes cast for governor in the most recent gubernatorial election. In doing so, an effort to discourage the proliferation of unwise, voter-initiated constitutional amendments made signature gathering easier for all statutory initiatives. Third, after voters approved these reforms, the legislature liberalized the process further by permitting initiatives to appear on primary election ballots in addition to general election ballots. The lower turnouts typical of primary elections made initiatives easier to pass. Fourth, the legislature also ended the requirement that voters list their exact precinct number on petition forms. Can you name yours? This saved signature campaigns the time and effort it took to verify such data. Fifth, the California Supreme Court ruled in 1979 that shopping malls were not just private property but also the functional equivalent of town squares. To petition circulators, this decision was the functional equivalent of a welcome mat. Working individually or in pairs, they could amass huge numbers of signatures in a single day; 80 an hour became commonplace.[19]

These changes in initiative rules and methods moved policymaking well beyond Sacramento and into every California community. Writer Carey McWilliams once called the state capital the "marketplace of California" where competing groups "bid for allotments of state power."[20] Today, the initiative

Table 4.1 Propositions on the November 2018 Ballot in California

Proposition	Subject	% For	% Against
1	Authorizes $4 billion in bond funding for specified housing assistance programs. Legislative Statute.	56.2	43.8
2	Authorizes $2 billion in bond funding for housing programs for those with mental illnesses. Legislative Statute.	63.4	36.6
3	Authorizes $9 billion bond funding for water supply and quality projects. Initiative Statute.	49.3	50.7
4	Authorizes $1.5 billion in bond funding for construction of children's hospitals. Initiative Statute.	62.7	37.3
5	Changes requirements for certain property owners to transfer their property tax base to a replacement property (tax reduction). Initiative Constitutional Amendment and Statute.	40.2	59.8
6	Eliminates fuel and vehicle taxes to pay for road repair and transportation infrastructure. Requires certain fees and taxes to be approved by the electorate. Initiative Constitutional Amendment.	43.2	56.8
7	Changes California daylight saving time to conform with federal law and allows the legislature to change daylight-savings-time period. Legislative Statute.	59.7	40.3
8	Regulates the amount of money that kidney dialysis clinics charge for dialysis treatment. Initiative Statute.	40.1	59.9
9	Would split California into three states. Removed from the ballot by the California Supreme Court.	—	—
10	Allows local governments to enact rent control on residential property. Initiative Statute.	40.6	59.4
11	Requires private-sector emergency ambulance employees to remain on-call during work breaks. Initiative Statute.	59.6	40.4
12	Establishes new standards for confinement of specified farm animals. Initiative Statute.	62.7	37.3

Source: California Secretary of State, https://www.sos.ca.gov/elections/ballot-measures/qualified-ballot-measures.

process itself has become California's new marketplace where multiple groups employ the initiative to achieve or defeat various policy outcomes. As political scientist Elizabeth R. Gerber observed, citizen groups tend to use direct legislation to bring about policy change whereas economic and business groups tend to use it to block policy change.[21] Furthermore, the Progressive Era assumption that initiatives would bypass political parties has proved to be untrue. In fact, California's political parties themselves encourage ballot measures to promote their own policy views, damage opposing parties, and rally voter turnout. Initiative backers also rely on political parties and their supporters for endorsements and campaign contributions. In particular, Republicans have successfully used the initiative process to enact anti-tax and other conservative measures otherwise unachievable in a legislature controlled by Democrats.[22]

Widespread access to and use of the initiative process has had numerous consequences, some of which have been unintended:

1. *Big money can trump good ideas.* A significant feature of the initiative process today is the increased amount of money spent to affect the outcome. In fact, in recent election cycles, more money has been raised and spent on ballot measures than on state legislative races. For example, in the 2018 election cycle, California's 100 state legislative campaigns raised over $165.1 million, while only 12 ballot measures attracted $379.3 million.[23] The difference is typical—Californians spend far more on direct democracy than on representative democracy (www.followthemoney.org/). True, many ballot measures require large financial resources, but this does not mean that business groups invariably have the upper hand. Consumer, environmental, and public interest groups find considerable expenditures well spent if a favored regulation or bond issue is approved. To be sure, not all initiative campaigns require heavy spending, and heavy spending does not always ensure victory. For example, in 2018, Proposition 5 would have allowed seniors to transfer their current property tax assessment to a new home even if the new home's value was much larger than their previous one. Proponents spent over $13 million (and nearly all of that from the California Association of Realtors). Opponents spent only $3.4 million but were victorious nonetheless. Also, some ballot measures never attain the visibility of higher-profile measures and candidates. When voters know little about them, they often vote no.

2. *Unelected persons can rival the power of elected policy makers, including governors.* Some Californians have become **initiative entrepreneurs**, known for the measures they have supported or opposed: Howard Jarvis and Paul Gann (property tax cuts), Harvey Rosenfield (auto insurance reform), Mike Reynolds (three-strikes sentencing reform), Ward Connerly (affirmative action), Ron Unz (bilingual education), and Robert Klein (stem cell research). The process itself has spawned something of an initiative industrial complex. It takes $2,000 to file an initiative with the secretary of state, but that fee is refunded if the measure qualifies for the ballot. However, gathering 1 million or more signatures to qualify it for the ballot is no job for amateurs. The vast majority of initiatives require professional assistance. Major for-profit firms such as National Petition Management, Kimball Petition Management, CTA Petition Management, and Arno Political Consulting hire independent subcontractors who in turn employ solicitors to collect signatures. What are they paid? According to Michael Arno, the going rate varies depending on deadlines, the subject matter, the time of year, and competition in California and other states. Signature gatherers can earn several dollars per signature for an initiative statute and even more for an initiative constitutional amendment. "How much time proponents have to collect the signatures is the key driver of costs."[24] For example, the plastic bag industry qualified a 2016 veto

referendum to overturn the state's new ban on single-use plastic bags by gathering 800,000 signatures within the required 90 days at a cost of over $3 million—or roughly $6.00 per required signature. Signature-gathering specialists are joined by the standard assortment of campaign consultants, media buyers, and public relations firms.

3. *Television becomes unduly important.* California's television stations do a remarkably poor job of covering the policy process in a representative democracy (see chapter 6). Complicated, inside-the-capitol issues do not lend themselves to short, visually entertaining stories. Much legislative activity takes place behind closed doors and beyond the cameras. But direct democracy is different. With well-funded ballot measures, television ads can saturate the airwaves months before voters receive their official voter information guides in the mail. Even if they were so inclined to do further homework—the 2018 general election official voter information guide ran 96 pages—prolific, negative, and misleading ads often frame issues in the minds of voters long before Election Day.

4. *Elected officials use it too.* Criticized as damaging representative government, the initiative has actually become another tool of representative government. Statewide officeholders—even governors—and legislators alike see it as a new route to public policy and electoral popularity. Policy gridlock in Sacramento has driven some policymakers to bypass their own process. The initiative serves a variety of motives. Depending on the situation, it can be an opportunity for minority party members to go around majority party leaders; it can also be a policy vehicle for legislative mavericks or outsiders, a platform for higher office, or one more bargaining chip relative to pending legislation. Even governors rely on it (see box 4.3). In 2012, a temporary tax increase on the wealthy became synonymous with Governor Jerry Brown, who had tied his budget plans to its passage. Local officials rarely attempt statewide initiatives, but in 2010 a coalition of them sponsored an initiative constitutional amendment that prohibited the state from borrowing or taking funds destined for transportation, redevelopment, or local government projects and services. It won with 61 percent of the vote.

5. *Successful initiatives expand government's workload.* To work at all, many measures require the legislature to fill in the missing details or enact implementing language. For instance, Proposition 20, the coastal protection initiative in 1972, required the appointment, staffing, and funding of a State Coastal Commission and several regional coastal commissions. The State Coastal Commission remains to this day. Proposition 71 (2004) created a

---

Box 4.3 ★ Did You Know . . . ?

All nine pages of Article XIII Section A in the California State Constitution are devoted to Proposition 13 and voter-approved revisions of it. This is about the same length as Article I in the U.S. Constitution detailing the powers of Congress.

stem cell research institute and Proposition 11 (2008) created a Citizens Redistricting Commission; both these required subsequent staffing and funding. However, researchers have found that the losing side of initiatives can thwart the intent of initiatives in their implementation and through legal challenges.[25]

6. *Citizen initiatives enhance judicial power.* Students of American government know that courts interpret constitutions and review legislation accordingly. Because initiative statutes are voter-approved legislation, they present similar opportunities. Many are often poorly drafted, vaguely worded, or patently unconstitutional. A lawsuit is so likely that initiative drafters usually insert severability clauses; if the courts find one section unconstitutional, the balance of the measure survives. In our dual judicial system, initiatives can be challenged in state or federal courts. Where the challenge is filed (court shopping) affects the outcome. California courts are more likely to uphold initiatives than are federal courts. As we noted earlier, the California Supreme Court upheld Proposition 8 that limited marriage only to heterosexual couples only one year after it ruled same-sex unions are constitutionally protected. The difference? According to the court, with Proposition 8, the voters had used their "precious right" of the initiative to alter the state's constitution.[26] When courts at either level choose to review initiatives, they may invalidate entire measures or only those provisions they find to be unconstitutional. In recent years, the conservative majority of the U.S. Supreme Court has attempted to defer to the states where possible. It did so, for example, in 2003 when it upheld California's Three Strikes Law, enacted as Proposition 184. In *Ewing v. California*, the court majority argued that "selecting sentencing rationales is generally a policy choice to be made by state legislatures, not federal courts."[27]

Clearly, state and federal courts play important roles in the initiative process. Although they may infuriate initiative zealots, the courts can modify, rewrite, overturn, or uphold challenged initiatives. In effect, they repair faulty provisions or put the brakes on what they consider unconstitutional ones.

REFORMING THE INITIATIVE

What we have called the initiative mess would be messier still if voters were less selective. The history of initiatives in California suggests that the vast majority of them never qualify for the ballot. Those that make it to the ballot face greater scrutiny than was the case with earlier signature campaigns. As table 4.1 indicates, more than half of all recent ballot measures failed. The failure rate during special elections is substantially higher. Nonetheless, reformers are concerned about the growing reliance on initiatives by citizens and policymakers alike and the problems caused by the troublesome measures that do pass (see table 4.2 for a historical snapshot of initiatives).

In the mid-1990s, the California Constitution Revision Commission made three modest recommendations: (1) allow the legislature to rewrite an initiative before it is submitted to the voters, (2) limit initiative constitutional amendments to November elections when voter turnout is higher, and (3) permit the legislature,

Table 4.2 California Initiatives, 1912–2017

Initiatives circulated for the ballot	1,996	
Initiatives withdrawn from circulation	113	6%
Qualified for the ballot	376	19%
Failed to qualify for the ballot	1,483	75%
Initiatives that qualified for the ballot that were approved	132	35%
Initiatives that qualified for the ballot that were rejected	241	64%
Initiatives removed from the ballot by court order	3	<1%

Source: California Secretary of State, https://www.sos.ca.gov/elections/ballot-measures/resources-and-historical-information/history-california-initiatives.

with the governor's approval, to amend statutory initiatives after they have been in effect for six years. While the legislature has not enacted those reforms, it did enact some new rules governing the process in recent years. In 2011, a new rule required initiatives to only appear on general election ballots. As part of a package of reforms adopted in 2014, the attorney general was authorized to open a 30-day review period before approving an initiative for circulation. During that time, the public could comment on it and supporters could alter it in response. Another change required the legislature to hold a joint public hearing on a proposed initiative after 25 percent of the required signatures were collected. Furthermore, initiative backers would be able to withdraw an initiative much closer to the ballot printing deadline. These changes were intended to improve the wording of initiatives and avoid legal pitfalls.

Ordinary Californians appear to be ambivalent regarding the initiative process. Polls suggest they are relatively aware of its shortcomings as described in this chapter. They also admit that many initiatives are confusingly worded, unnecessarily complicated, and often represent the concerns of special interests, not the state as a whole. Regardless of party affiliation, most support various reform ideas. Yet, a large majority of them cherish the idea of citizen initiatives and believe that they result in better decisions than those made by the legislature and the governor.[28]

PROGRESSIVE COUSINS: REFERENDUM AND RECALL

In contrast to the initiative, two other Progressive-era reforms, referendum and recall, are much less used. For example, the referendum—sometimes called the veto referendum—gives voters the power to approve or reject legislative statutes. There are two kinds: a **petition referendum** and a **compulsory referendum**. The petition version is relatively rare but has been used recently. As with legislation, a referendum "yes" vote approves an already enacted law; a "no" vote repeals it. For example, in 2014, voters vetoed or rejected Proposition 48, two Indian gaming compacts negotiated by Governor Jerry Brown and approved by the legislature. These two compacts would have allowed two Indian tribes (the North Fork Rancheria of Mono Indians near Yosemite and the Wiyot Tribe near Humboldt Bay) to operate a casino resort on nonreservation land in the Central Valley's Madera County.

The compulsory referendum, where voters must approve a legislative action for it to take effect, is more common. All constitutional amendments initiated by the legislature and all bond issues over $300,000 require voter approval. In recent years, bond issues have appeared on many ballots as legislators seek additional revenue for schools, prisons, and transportation systems without raising taxes.

The mechanics of the referendum are simple enough. Compulsory referenda are placed on the ballot by the legislature. The petition referendum is another matter. Within three months of a law's passage, opponents may gather a requisite number of signatures to place the matter on the next regularly scheduled statewide ballot. Certain categories of legislation are exempt: calls for special elections, tax levies, urgency measures, and spending bills. To be successful, referendum advocates must gather 623,212 valid signatures within a scant 90 days of a bill's enactment. Initiative backers have 150 days to gather the same number of signatures.

State-Level Recalls

The **recall** allows voters to remove from office state or local elected officials before the end of their terms. California is one of 19 states allowing statewide recall; of many attempts nationwide, the 2003 recall of Governor Gray Davis was the only successful one in modern times. The only other one was North Dakota's Lynn Frazier in 1921. The hurdles to any statewide recall in California are substantial. To place a recall on the ballot, people must gather signatures equal to 12 percent of the votes cast in the previous election for that office (20 percent in the case of a state legislator). Signatures for a statewide recall must come from at least five counties (to prevent undue influence by mega-counties such as Los Angeles).

The Recall of Gray Davis. The historic recall of Governor Davis is instructive not only because it happened but also because of how it happened. Davis's troubles began in his first term (1999–2002) when the economic downturn of the early 2000s and a 2001 energy crisis left voters feeling anxious, pessimistic, and angry. Davis became the most visible culprit. Although voters reelected him in 2002, they did so with a meager 5 percent margin against Republican businessman and political neophyte Bill Simon. Lost in the campaign noise that year was an emerging budget crisis. His proposed January 2003 budget was balanced (as all state budgets must be) with higher taxes, deep spending cuts, plus the usual accounting gimmicks, but Californians were unprepared for such budget pain. Davis was rapidly becoming the center of the closest thing to "The Perfect Storm" one finds in politics.

In early 2003, anti-tax gadfly Ted Costa pushed the idea of recalling Davis for "gross mismanagement of California's finances" and other misdeeds. When his drive to collect nearly 900,000 signatures in 160 days began to falter, U.S. Representative Darrell Issa, a wealthy car alarm magnate and former U.S. Senate candidate, came to the rescue. He poured roughly $1.7 million into the recall drive. Paid petition gatherers blanketed the state, turning in a whopping 2.1 million signatures by the deadline.

Democratic lieutenant governor Cruz Bustamante had no choice but to set a fall election date. So, the question, "Shall Gray Davis be recalled (removed) from the office of governor?" would be on an October 7, 2003, special election ballot. As was the custom in lower-level recall elections, replacement candidates would appear on the same ballot. Comparatively low entry requirements—65 signatures and a $3,500 filing fee—encouraged 135 candidates to file, including a porn star, a porn publisher, and underemployed actor Gary Coleman (of *Different Strokes* fame). No wonder the British newspaper *The Guardian* called the recall "a circus fit for the fruit and nut state." But media and public attention quickly narrowed to a handful of candidates, and by Election Day, the most viable candidates were Bustamante, Republican State Senator Tom McClintock, and movie star Arnold Schwarzenegger, who announced his candidacy on Jay Leno's *Tonight Show*. Early polls and media reports presumed Davis would be recalled and attention quickly shifted to his potential replacements.

The entrance of candidate Schwarzenegger essentially altered the dynamics of this truncated 77-day campaign. The television media, in particular, covered his campaign to the virtual exclusion of other major candidates. Many aspects of the campaign were framed or reframed around him. Did *he* have the stuff to govern? Would *he* divide moderate and conservative Republicans? Would *he* debate his recall opponents? If so, would *he* measure up? Would *he* accept special interest campaign contributions? Would *he* discuss issues in more detail? The actual recall campaign was smothered in the process.

In the end, more than 55 percent of voters chose to recall Davis, and more than 48 percent chose Schwarzenegger to replace him, an impressive plurality number given the field of other candidates. Although Schwarzenegger commanded the state's attention in his years as governor, do remember that the election itself was as much or more about recalling Davis as it was about electing Schwarzenegger. Given the confluence of events and the entry of a media-savvy celebrity candidate, the 2003 gubernatorial recall will likely remain a stunning, if rare, example of how a statewide recall election works.[29]

Other State-Level Recalls. Only a handful of other state-level officials have been recalled in California, including a few legislators. Two legislators were ousted in the mid-1990s when they agreed to support or cooperate with Democrat Willie Brown's continuance as Assembly Speaker. In one notable case, state senator David Roberti, who was about to be termed out of the legislature and was planning a bid for state treasurer, handily survived a 1994 recall election engineered by gun control opponents, but his $800,000 recall defense campaign drained resources from his state treasurer campaign; in the end, he lost that race.

In a more recent recall election, Democrat Josh Newman lost his state senate seat in Orange County when 58 percent of voters supported his recall in June 2018. Republicans had targeted his historically Republican seat after Newman cast a vote in favor of new gas taxes. The seat was pivotal because it meant that Democrats would lose their two-thirds majority in the Senate, which gives them additional powers (see chapter 7). Democrats recaptured their two-thirds majority in both chambers several months later.

Local-Level Recalls

Recall is much more common at the local level (as is defeating incumbents at regular elections). A relatively small number of qualifying signatures make it quite feasible indeed. Such recall efforts are often characterized by bitter conflict. What angers local voters enough to recall an official? Most controversies involve unpopular policy decisions, personnel controversies, outrageous behavior, alleged corruption, or general voter anger. Supporters of losing candidates sometimes want a "do-over" of the last election. In 2018, there were more than 30 such recall efforts in California aimed at elected officials in cities, special districts, and school districts. Six of these campaigns were targeted at more than one member of a city council or board of supervisors at one time. For instance, marijuana proved to be a contentious issue in the city of Corona. One city councilmember was targeted for supporting the commercial cultivation of cannabis, while two other members were targeted for voting to *ban* cannabis. None of the recall petitions qualified for the ballot.

Sometimes, voter anger even targets an entire governing board. More than 70 percent of voters in the Big Flat-Oak Unified School District recalled the whole school board after it fired a popular high school math teacher. The entire city council of Bell, California, was recalled amid a scandal involving exorbitant pay for themselves and several administrators (see chapter 10 for more on Bell). Because recalls are by definition mandatory, stand-alone elections, they can strain local budgets. The February 2010 recall of a Mission Viejo mayor cost the city $288,000 to administer; he would have been up for reelection the following November.[30]

CONCLUSION: THE LEGACY AND THE PARADOX

The legacy of the Progressive Era cannot be overemphasized. In fact, it has fostered hyperpluralism. By kicking one group—the SPR—out of politics, Californians invited many other groups into politics. Numerous reforms at both the state and local levels were implemented in those early years. We take many of them for granted today, such as nonpartisan local elections and city managers. Some reforms, such as the referendum, have proved to be rather unworkable. Others, such as the local recall, have truly become the safety valve they were meant to be. The initiative gets the most attention and with good reason. Savvy individuals with enough money can qualify almost any pet policy or project for the ballot. But historically, most California initiatives have resulted from interest group activity and, more recently, major policymakers. Progressives defeated one powerful interest group and limited what they considered the negative influence of political parties, as chapter 6 will attest. Inadvertently, they also strengthened the long-term role of California's interest groups for generations to come.

The process now appears to be a function of hyperpluralism in a technological age. As a result, some have called California a "hybrid democracy."[31] Interest groups participate via initiatives, not just statehouse bills. Truly revolutionary policy can result from this process, but so can policy paralysis. An initiative victory can be whittled away or substantially revised in its implementation. A stunning initiative victory or defeat can actually inhibit further discussion on the policy involved as with Proposition 13. The process has produced more choices and information about them than typical voters can handle. At the same time, it has produced media-centered campaigns that often insult voters' intelligence. Yet, for all its faults and abuses, contemporary Californians resist efforts to tamper with the system they have inherited. Voters may well realize that if they do not understand an issue, in spite of or due to an information blitz on it, they can simply vote "No."

The initiative process is analogous to true-or-false tests. What voters face at the polls are highly technical issues with uncertain and far-reaching ramifications. Wise policy alternatives come in shades of gray, not black or white. Yet the voters are examined on these complex subjects with up or down decisions. No multiple-choice, fill-ins, or essay questions are allowed. The requirements of direct democracy are such that only the well-educated and homework-inclined can vote wisely. But a growing number of Californians do not fit that description. As we will see in chapter 5, all Californians are affected by the state's policies, but a much smaller number actually participate in the system that produces those policies.

KEY TERMS

Progressivism (p. 62)
Progressive reforms (p. 62)
California progressivism (p. 63)
Proposition 13 (p. 66)
Proposition 22 (p. 68)
Proposition 8 (p. 69)

Proposition 215 (p. 69)
Proposition 64 (p. 70)
initiative entrepreneurs (p. 74)
petition referendum (p. 77)
compulsory referendum (p. 77)
recall (statewide and local) (p. 78)

REVIEW QUESTIONS

1. What gave rise to Progressivism nationwide? In California?
2. Who were the Progressives, and what were their goals in California?
3. Describe and illustrate the initiative, petition referendum, compulsory referendum, and recall.
4. How do the initiative cases described here illustrate the pros and cons of the initiative process?
5. What have been the consequences, intended and unintended, of the initiative in California?
6. To what extent does the initiative process need reform? What recommendations would you make?
7. Do you think recalls (statewide and local) are a good idea? Why or why not?
8. What larger issues of California politics does direct democracy illustrate?

WEB RESOURCES

Initiative and Referendum Institute
http://www.iandrinstitute.org

As you will see from this site, California is not alone or unique in allowing voters to legislate.

California Secretary of State
https://www.sos.ca.gov

Go to the elections area for progress reports on initiatives currently in circulation. If you want to circulate your own, complete how-to instructions are available.

National Institute on Money in State Politics
https://www.followthemoney.org
Click the national overview map, then California, for a plethora of campaign data including spending by and contributions to ballot measure committees.

Ballotpedia
https://www.ballotpedia.org
This wiki-platform-based site is a good starting point when researching California's state and local ballot measures, including recalls.

5

How Californians Participate

LEARNING OUTCOMES

Students will be able to:

- ★ Describe civic engagement and the various forms of political participation.
- ★ Analyze and illustrate the exit and protest forms of political participation.
- ★ Define public opinion and discuss its presence in California politics.
- ★ Explain how California elections work, including the role of campaign professionals and money.
- ★ Describe the various electoral gaps in California and their consequences for governing.

IN BRIEF

Despite the image of a politically involved citizenry, Californians' political behavior generally mirrors that of other Americans. Political scientists have categorized the political participation levels of Americans and Californians along a range from uninvolvement to voting and active campaigning. Chapter 5 surveys the diversity of conventional forms of participation and two nonconventional ones—exiting the political system altogether and political protest. All these forms are commonplace in California.

SHORT OF FORMAL POLITICAL PARTICIPATION, Californians hold various opinions on politics and public policy—opinions that can sway policy-makers. Pollsters survey and monitor these opinions using both scientific and unscientific methods. The traits of California voters are discussed, as are the reasons some Californians cannot vote and why qualified voters choose not to vote. Traditionally, Americans have identified with the major political parties, but they do so with a greater diversity of motives than once thought. In California, these party identification patterns vary from region to region. Differences emerge between Northern and Southern California and between coastal and inland

California. Emerging patterns of political behavior statewide suggest gaps among different groups of Californian voters and nonvoters—a sign of growing hyperpluralism in the state. Voters express themselves in numerous elections, including presidential primary, state primary, general, and special elections. Aiding both voters and candidates are a plethora of campaign professionals and various state laws governing the conduct of these elections.

In that context, a steady parade of candidates and policy issues vie for the attention of Californians. Yet, despite the political demands placed on them, Californians are much like other Americans in their political activity. Only a few are very involved, a larger number vote, and still others choose not to participate in any meaningful way. Specific groups of Californians differ from each other in their political behavior. Generalizing about voting behavior is a challenge. Voting is an individual, private act, and it is also a continuous activity. Electoral attitudes and behavior change and the motivations of voters and nonvoters are mixed. Also, voting is only one political behavior among many to measure and analyze. First, we consider the larger idea of political participation.

INTRODUCTION: FORMS OF PARTICIPATION IN A DEMOCRACY

How ordinary citizens participate in a representative democracy has always intrigued political scientists. In recent years, they have identified and categorized the political activities of Americans. **Political participation** consists of individual or group activity intended to exercise influence in the political system. Methods used to exercise such influence are either conventional or unconventional in nature, that is, inside or outside the norms considered acceptable by the larger society. We briefly explore these channels of influence.

Civic Engagement and Conventional Participation

Political scientists have identified a wide range of civic activities engaged in by Americans. National surveys suggest that, in addition to voting, the most frequently listed activities (in 2018) include expressing support for a campaign on social media (29 percent); contacting a public official (23 percent); contributing money to a political candidate, party, or cause (14 percent); attending a political rally or event (11 percent); attending a local government meeting (10 percent); and working or volunteering for a campaign (5 percent).[1] However, political participation is only one measure of community life. Many people participate in voluntary associations that political scientists call "civil societies." These include service organizations (Rotary, Lions, Soroptimists), youth clubs (Boys and Girls Clubs, Girls Inc.), and churches, mosques, or synagogues. Many parents are deeply involved in their children's schooling and sports activities. Yet, there is growing evidence that many Americans are becoming less engaged in civic life. Many do charity work but remain largely uninvolved in national, state, local, or neighborhood issues.

California lags the nation in terms of nonelectoral civic engagement. The numbers are low indeed. One study revealed that only 8 percent of Californians report working with neighbors to solve a problem. Only 9 percent attend town hall meetings or similar events.[2] Who "engages," and who does not? Demographics are the key. In general, whites are more engaged than blacks, Hispanics, and Asians. Citizens born in the United States are more active than are citizens born elsewhere and noncitizens. According to James E. Prieger and Kelly M. Faltis, "The fact that California has more Hispanics, Asians, naturalized citizens, and noncitizens than the rest of the U.S., appears to go a long way toward explaining the lower level of civic engagement in the state."[3]

The very meaning of civic engagement is gradually changing. Increasingly, the use of social media for political purposes is regarded as engagement or at least a form of political speech. In fact, Facebook argues that clicking "like" is the 21st-century equivalent of a front-yard campaign sign. Obviously, obtaining an actual campaign yard sign, pounding it into one's lawn, and displaying it to neighbors and strangers alike requires more investment than a click.

The Exit Option

Thus far, we have emphasized voting and other forms of civic participation. But what about those Californians who move from one community to another because of policy dissatisfaction? Such concerns may relate to traffic conges- tion, gang violence, school issues, or various quality of life issues. Arguably, this opting-out behavior also is a form of political participation, what we call the **exit option**.[4] For example, this form of participation applies to urban Californians who are fed up with crime, smog, and congestion. Given the chance, some may move elsewhere in California or anywhere that is more affordable (equity refugees), or they pull their children out of ethnically diverse public schools and send them to less-diverse, private ones (ethnic refugees). Some parents seek out charter schools, public schools that operate indepen- dent of local school boards and are designed to provide alternative educational experiences. Or they may homeschool their children—the ultimate educational exit option. Parents who choose to exempt their children from school-required vaccinations (e.g., measles) are opting out of what many consider a reasonable public health policy.

How people and businesses respond to political dissatisfaction depends on how invested they are in their communities. Those who are relatively sat- isfied with a local political system behave constructively—they speak up or express system loyalty in other ways, such as voting. Their level of invest- ment in the community (homeownership, a job, or children in school) makes a difference. Low investors more easily opt for political neglect (such as not voting), exiting the system, or even protest or violence. Also, the availability of viable alternatives to the status quo determines what dissatisfied people do. For instance, for people to exit an unsatisfactory public school, feasible alternatives need to be either nearby (a neighboring jurisdiction) or affordable (alternative schools).

The Protest Option

Extreme levels of community dissatisfaction may result in the use of protest activities—the **protest option**. Sporadic political protest, both violent and non- violent, has always been a part of America's political heritage. Historically, California has had its fair share. Most of the well-publicized incidents of protest and violence in California have been ethnic in nature. Consider the anti-Chinese

An anti-Trump rally in downtown Los Angeles. The election of President Trump sparked many rallies across the state and country over inflammatory comments he made about immigrants and others.

demonstrations in San Francisco inspired by the Workingmen's Party (1877), union strikes and the union-inspired bombing of the *Los Angeles Times* building (early 1900s), the "zoot suit" riots in Los Angeles (1943), the Watts riot in Los Angeles following a controversial police arrest (1965), and the Los Angeles riot following the acquittal of four Los Angeles police officers accused of beating motorist Rodney King (1992). In 2017, an estimated one million people in 50 different cities in California participated in the Women's March to protest the inauguration of President Donald Trump, after misogynist and denigrating comments he made about his opponent Hillary Clinton and women during the campaign.

As forms of political behavior, political protest and violence are difficult to study. Developing a direct cause-and-effect relationship between arson or looting and some conscious political message can be rather speculative. To be sure, protest is a form of political behavior used by groups who lack more conventional resources. These groups, however, might not be able to articulate their motives clearly or even accurately. One study of the Watts riots in the 1960s found that rioters were not only expressing antiwhite hostility but also anger over their own status in the larger society.[5] In many instances, though, mob behavior lacks any civic purpose—it is simply mob behavior. Vandalism after a sporting event comes to mind. It is fair to say that the connection between protest and violence is tenuous, albeit related. Not all protest is violent, and not all violence is protest.

THE ROLE OF PUBLIC OPINION

In a representative democracy, the opinions of the people matter—or at least they should. Strongly held opinions lead to political action, and even weakly held opinions affect how people vote and relate to each other. As with the nation, the diverse opinions held by Californians contribute to the politics of diversity. On some issues, the state's political leaders have little or no direction from the public. On others, the views of the public are so conflicted; taking any position is bound to alienate some people. Holding an opinion may not qualify as political participation in an active sense. But it does provide the motivation for more active forms of participation such as voting, campaigning, demonstrating, joining a political party, and working through interest groups.

What Is Public Opinion?

Public opinion consists of the collective beliefs, attitudes, and values held by the citizenry. Political scientists consider public opinion to be what people think about politics, public policy, and those aspects of life that affect politics and policy—"those opinions that governments find it prudent to heed."[6] At any given time, state and local officials believe they know what the public is thinking on a host of issues both large and small. Those officials may choose to ignore public opinion, follow it, or simply take it under advisement, but they do pay attention. In California's hybrid democracy, where voters use the initiative process to make public policy, their opinions can take shape as policy decisions, not just policy perceptions.

California's Major Pollsters

Given California's size, polling organizations find it worthwhile to survey its citizens. Two of the state's major polling organizations are the Public Policy Institute of California and the Institute of Governmental Studies (IGS) at University of California, Berkeley. The Public Policy Institute of California is an endowed public-policy think tank headquartered in San Francisco. Its frequent statewide surveys provide policymakers, the media, and California residents with objective information on the opinions, perceptions, and policy preferences of the state's residents. The IGS poll is relatively new after it became the successor of the now defunct Field Poll, which was originally established by Mervin Field in 1947. The Field Poll and now IGS have a national reputation for accurately predicting the results of California elections. Both these polling organizations repeat similar questions having to do with the general mood of Californians over time. For example, "Is California moving in the right direction?" is a polling question repeated from year to year, as we saw in chapter 1. Whether the public mood is optimistic or pessimistic over the long term affects the ability of policymakers to make decisions requiring public support.

How They Measure Public Opinion

Finding out what Californians think is no easy task but polling is an attempt to do just that. There are two types of polls: straw polls and scientific polls. **Straw polls** are educated guesses as to what the public in general or a particular group of people is thinking. Various media organizations conduct such polls (person-on-the-street interviews or website-based surveys) in order to gauge public support for or opposition to a particular policy. State political party conventions may conduct straw polls among the attendees to measure support for particular gubernatorial candidates or even presidential candidates. Some straw polls are done with focus groups. These relatively small gatherings of people may be questioned in order to construct a larger opinion survey or to obtain feedback on political commercials.

In contrast, **scientific polls** use a number of techniques to increase the likelihood that their results more nearly reflect the actual views of the larger population. First, scientific polls survey relatively large numbers of people. The larger polling organizations in California may sample 1,400 to 2,400 adults, substantially more than many straw polls would. Second, these polls do random sampling in order to give every potential respondent the same chance of being chosen. They may select key precincts, control for various ethnic groups, or randomly survey every 10th or 100th household. In order to predict election outcomes, pollsters seek out those most likely to vote, not just those registered to vote. They also employ computer-aided random-digit dialing to include those with unlisted numbers or cell phones. Third, scientific polling also seeks to reduce or at least admit to sampling error—the fact that a sample cannot accurately mirror the views of an entire population as if it had been polled. For example, a margin of error of 3.6 percent means that the true result would be within 3.6 points of what would be the case if all likely voters were surveyed. Margins of error are even higher for smaller subgroups (likely voters, women, etc.).[7]

Fourth, pollsters try to ask the right questions. Wittingly or unwittingly, bias can creep into surveys, so scientific surveys attempt to avoid wording that directs respondents to specific answers. Also, simple agree/disagree or approve/disapprove answers rarely ascertain the intensity of opinion so pollsters often provide more than two options, as figure 5.1 portrays. Specifically, this IGS poll asked respondents about their support for California's sanctuary state policy.

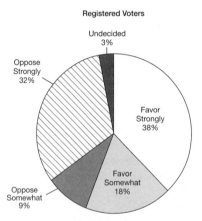

Figure 5.1 Californians' Views on the State's Sanctuary State Law

Note: The question asked, "Last year California passed a state law that provides sanctuary to undocumented immigrants living in the country and limits cooperation with federal immigration officials who are attempting to deport these immigrants. Generally speaking, do you favor or oppose this law?"

Source: Mark DiCamillo, "While the Statewide Law Providing Sanctuary to Undocumented Immigrants Is Supported by a Majority of California Voters, the Issue Is Highly Divisive," IGS Poll, Release #2018-05 (Berkeley: Institute of Government Studies, April 2018), https://escholarship.org/uc/item/443790rm.

VOTERS AND NONVOTERS IN CALIFORNIA

Of all the forms of political participation and expression, suffrage—the right to vote—is considered sacred. To better understand this central tenet of American democracy, political scientists examine voters (those who show up at the polls on Election Day or vote absentee), nonvoters (those who cannot or will not vote), and the electoral system in which voting takes place. The process before Election Day is analogous to a funnel that continually narrows the number of people until actual voters appear. Those who are eligible are considered to be the **voting age population (VAP)** or the electorate. For instance, in the 2018 statewide general election, California's voting age population numbered more than 25 million people, and more than 78 percent of those were registered to vote. The next level down the funnel is the number of officially registered voters for any particular election. The narrowest portion connotes **voter turnout**—those registered voters who actually vote in any particular election, whether in person or by mail. In the 2018 election, 65 percent of those Californians registered to vote actually did so, while 50 percent of those *eligible* to vote did so. Both these figures were marked improvements over the 2014 election, which saw the lowest turnout in state history.

Who Votes in California?

Political scientists want to know not only how many people vote but also who votes and what those voters are like. The Public Policy Institute of California surveys likely voters and infrequent voters on a regular basis. What characterizes the state's likely voters? Closely examine Table 5.1, which provides data from a series of statewide polls. Some highlights include the following: Women outnumber men, and the largest age group to vote is 55 and older. White voters constitute 59 percent of likely voters, a significantly larger percentage than their portion of the overall population. A majority of likely voters have gone to or completed college. Democrats outnumber Republicans, while liberals slightly outnumber conservatives. Moderates or middle-of-the-roaders constitute 28 percent of California's likely voters. About 44 percent of them have household incomes over $80,000, and the vast majority are homeowners. An impressive 52 percent reside in Southern California, including Los Angeles County. We will discuss the contrast between likely voters and California's population shortly.

Those Who Cannot Vote

The health of representative democracy depends on voting. However, California and other states have experienced rather high levels of nonparticipation, especially at the ballot box. Nonparticipation takes two forms: **structural nonvoting** (those disenfranchised by the rules) and **preferential nonvoting** (those disenfranchised by their own behavior and attitudes). We will explore both forms.

In our federal system, states administer all elections. "Universal suffrage" does not mean all people get to vote. In fact, states often establish barriers to voting, and California is no exception. As we noted, only 25.2 of about 40 million Californians were legally eligible to vote in 2018. The other nearly 15 million included people in the following categories:

- Those under 18 years of age
- Noncitizens (documented and undocumented)

Table 5.1 California's Likely Voters: A Snapshot

Gender

46%	Male
54%	Female

Age

18%	18–34
34%	35–54
48%	55 and older

Race/Ethnicity

59%	White
6%	Black
21%	Latino
11%	Asian
3%	Others

Education

19%	No college
42%	Some college
39%	College graduate

Party Registration

47%	Democrat
21%	Independent
28%	Republican
4%	Other

Ideology

38%	Liberal
28%	Middle of the road
34%	Conservative

Own/Rent

67%	Own
33%	Rent

Annual Family Income

29%	Under $40,000
27%	$40,000 to under $80,000
44%	$80,000 or more

Region

26%	Los Angeles
23%	SF Bay Area
16%	Central Valley
17%	Orange/San Diego
9%	Inland Empire
9%	Other

Note: These figures represent the combined results of several PPIC Surveys conducted between September 2017 and July 2018. More than 13,000 people were questioned, including likely voters, infrequent voters, and unregistered adults.

Source: Public Policy Institute of California, "Just the Facts: California's Likely Voters" (San Francisco: Public Policy Institute of California, August, 2018).

- Those who have moved to or within California within 15 days of an election
- Current prisoners and parolees (former prisoners regain their voting rights; those serving jail time for misdemeanor convictions may vote, by absentee ballot, of course!)
- The mentally incompetent (as determined by a court)

Surmounting these barriers is not enough. Individuals must proactively register to vote either online or by filing a brief registration form with the appropriate county office (usually a registrar of voters or the county clerk's office). Originally designed to inhibit voter fraud, registration requirements effectively inhibit many Californians from voting. Because one must reregister after every move, highly mobile groups (such as agricultural employees, some construction workers, and college students) find they are unregistered on Election Day.

That said, registering to vote is now easier than ever. The 1993 National Voter Registration Act (called the motor voter law) required states to lower registration hurdles, for instance, by allowing people to register at motor vehicle or welfare offices. Due to recently enacted changes, California voters can now register online at the secretary of state's website (https://register tovote.ca.gov) or even register on Election Day as a conditional registered voter. Voters are also *automatically* registered at the California Department of Motor Vehicles when they renew their driver's license. Unlike 35 other states, California does not have a voter identification (ID) requirement (see figure 5.2) where voters must show some form of ID such as a driver's license

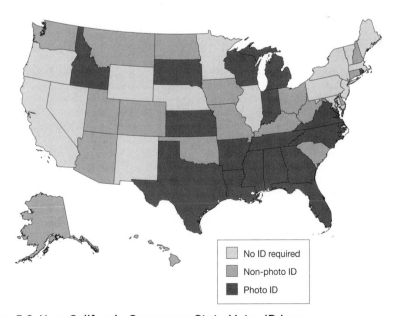

No ID required
Non-photo ID
Photo ID

Figure 5.2 How California Compares: State Voter ID Laws
Thirty-five states have some type of voter identification law, but California does not.

Source: "Voter Identification Laws by State," Ballotpedia, https://ballotpedia.org/Voter_identification_laws_by_state.

to cast their ballot. Some research has shown that these voter ID requirements can suppress turnout.[8]

Those Who Will Not Vote

When political scientists, media pundits, and election officials bemoan low voter turnout, particularly in state and local elections, they refer to either eligible voters or registered voters who choose not to vote—preferential nonvoters. Why do otherwise qualified voters choose not to vote? The reasons can be divided into personal factors and structural factors.

Personal Factors

For many Californians, voting is a daunting task and not worth the trouble. A 2015 statewide survey by the Public Policy Institute of California identifies some of the primary reasons why people do not always vote:

1. Too busy/no time: 29 percent
2. Lack of interest in the issues/particular election: 12 percent
3. Don't know enough about the choices or issues: 9 percent
4. Not interested in politics: 8 percent
5. Voting doesn't change things/my vote doesn't matter: 6 percent[9]

Indeed, going to the polls on Election Day is only the temporary end of a long, information-laden campaign—replete with official voter pamphlets, constant television commercials, political "junk mail," door hangers, and precinct walkers. Many elections, especially those with multiple propositions, create information overload for average voters. For some, the cost of voting (including the homework involved) is not worth the trouble, especially if the benefit is not clear. Even those who turn out may not vote on every ballot item, a phenomenon called undervoting, or ballot roll-off. For example, in 2018, nearly 2 million California voters who voted for the governor did not vote in the race for superintendent of public instruction.

Another way Californians themselves make it easier to vote is to become absentee voters. The only expense is a first-class stamp, although even that is not required. In the 2018 general election, more than 65 percent of all voters did so by mail—a threefold increase in only 20 years.[10] As we shall see, this affects how today's campaigns are waged.

The personal factor of age also affects voter turnout. Younger voters, aged 18 to 34, are 33 percent of all adults, but only 18 percent of likely voters. In contrast, voters who are 55 or older represent 32 percent of the adult population but are nearly half (48 percent) of likely voters. Although younger adults express little interest in politics compared to their older counterparts, basic demographics are at work here as well. Many younger Californians are also members of low propensity voter groups as well, such as Latinxs.[11]

Structural Factors

The way the election system is structured also affects voting frequency. Primary elections, general elections, special elections, off-year elections, advisory elections—if it is Tuesday it must be Election Day, or so it seems. Accordingly, many

Californians pick and choose elections in which to vote. In general, they view higher-level elections to be more important than lower-level ones. Voter turnout drops successively from presidential to state to local elections. General elections witness higher turnouts than primary elections and presidential primaries are higher than primaries involving only state offices (see figure 5.3). After dismal turnout in the 2014 primary, turnout among registered voters was up to 38 percent in the 2018 primary—still only 28 percent of those eligible. The turnout in separately scheduled local elections is lower still. Turnout in the 2015 city council election in Los Angeles, California's largest city, was less than 10 percent.[12]

Other factors also affect voting numbers. Turnout drops in state legislative races where incumbents run unopposed or in special elections to fill a single legislative vacancy. When Californians have a chance to vote directly on well-publicized, easy-to-understand issues (initiatives and referenda), voter interest and motivation to turn out appear to increase. For example, the 2003 gubernatorial recall election combined voter anger (at incumbent Gray Davis), a celebrity replacement candidate (Arnold Schwarzenegger), and extraordinary media coverage, resulting in a 61 percent voter turnout—on par with regularly scheduled gubernatorial general elections.

Political scientists also believe that voter turnout tends to increase where candidate races are reasonably competitive and either side has a chance to win. But voter turnout research in California's majority-minority congressional districts—where various minority groups constitute a majority of the voting population—alters somewhat this generalization. One study suggested that when Latinxs or blacks are voting majorities, their respective turnouts increase significantly compared to their turnouts in Anglo-majority districts. Turnout among Latinxs was particularly high in Latinx-majority districts with Latinx Congress members.[13]

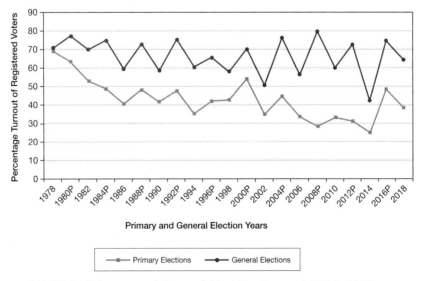

Figure 5.3 State Primary and General Election Turnout, 1978-2018

Source: California Secretary of State, https://elections.cdn.sos.ca.gov/sov/2018-general/sov/04-historical-voter-reg-participation.pdf.

Partisan Factors

The conventional wisdom among political scientists is that Republicans have somewhat higher turnouts than Democrats, but that historic advantage may be disappearing in California. Groups that benefit Republicans, such as older, white voters, are a shrinking portion of the overall electorate. In addition, ethnic voters, especially younger ones, are voting in greater numbers and these voters tend to support Democratic candidates and issues. In 2018, Democrats captured their largest majority in the state legislature in recent memory and once again retained all the statewide offices, which led to some calling into question the future viability of the Grand Old Party (GOP).

Regional Factors

All these general explanations apply to California as a whole but not to all parts of the state. Dramatic differences exist between the state's 58 counties. For the 2018 election, tiny Alpine County had the highest turnout among registered voters at 83 percent, but they only had 758 voters. Imperial County on the southern California border had the lowest with 49 percent. Of those simply *eligible* to vote, Marin had the highest turnout at 73 percent, while Imperial again had the lowest with 33 percent. Why these intercounty differences? One explanation is that counties with high numbers of Latinxs, immigrants, and other low-propensity voters tend to experience lower turnouts than those with lower concentrations of such groups.

What are the long-term trends in California? Even though presidential elections generate a great deal of voter interest and comparatively high voter turnout, the long-term trend in state elections has been declining turnout. Still lower turnouts in local-only elections, where democracy is closest to "The People," concerns many observers. Many local jurisdictions have consolidated their elections to boost turnout but find their issues and candidates being subsumed by state and national contests.

ELECTIONS AND CAMPAIGNS IN CALIFORNIA

H. G. Wells once said, "Democracy's ceremonial, its feast, its great function is the election." And so it is in California. Elections link average citizens to their government in profound ways. Public officials are to be held accountable periodically for what they do and say. Elections are important to policymakers, too, because they provide some measure of government legitimacy. In other words, voters grant the officials they choose credibility and authority to act on their behalf. Policymakers occasionally misinterpret their election victories as mandates to do something in particular, especially if they win by wide margins. Aware of the complex factors that determine election outcomes, political scientists tend to discount the mandates so often claimed by election winners.

California's Elections

Californians are peppered with elections. Partisan elections for federal and state offices are scheduled in even-numbered years. State **primary elections** are where voters choose party nominees to run for Congress, the state legislature, and statewide offices. Primary ballots also include judicial candidates, some local offices, and ballot propositions. In California, primaries occur on the Tuesday after the first Monday in June of even-numbered years. Thanks to Proposition 14 (2010), partisan candidates now run on a single ballot list and the two top vote-getters, regardless of party, compete in the general election. These **general elections** occur on the Tuesday after the first Monday in November. In some nonpartisan races where candidates did not receive the required simple majority of the vote to win in June (e.g., county supervisors), the general election serves as a runoff election between the top two candidates. Since 2011, all voter initiatives appear only on general election ballots; the November 2012 election featured 11 of them. Occasionally, the governor and legislature may call statewide **special elections** to consider certain propositions. Local governments (cities, counties, special districts, and school districts) may schedule elections for June, November, or other times of their own choosing.

Presidential primaries, in which many delegates are chosen to attend national party nominating conventions, occur every four years and are a special case in California. Historically, the state has moved its primary earlier and later in different presidential years seeking to maximize its influence over party nominees. After a late June primary in 2016, the state moved it to March 3 for 2020. With the state's early voting period, voters could cast ballots by mail or drop them off at voting centers a month before that date, allowing California's election to effectively compete with the Iowa caucuses.

Given the frequency of California elections, the prolific use of citizen initiatives, and the sheer size of the state, it should not surprise us that even willing, able, and qualified voters find the "great feast" difficult to manage. Election campaigns and the people who work in them link candidates and ballot measure activists to the voters whose support they seek.

California's Campaign Professionals

Campaigning for many offices in California is challenging and arduous, and therefore, candidates and ballot measure committees rely on political consultants to provide advice and actually run campaigns. California's first political consultants were Clem Whitaker and his wife, Leona Baxter, who established Whitaker and Baxter in the early 1930s. These two conservatives had close ties to the state's 700 newspaper publishers, and they helped defeat Upton Sinclair's bid for governor in 1934. One observer believes this particular campaign gave birth to the modern media-centered, professionally managed campaign.[14] Contemporary California is home to all manner of campaign professionals—large and small, liberal and conservative, general and specialized. These people call California the "Golden State" for the campaign gold that can be mined there. For example, the so-called "ho-hum" election of 2014 (with very low turnout) saw nearly $300 million go to hundreds of campaign professionals, including specialists in Internet and social media advertising.[15]

To run a candidate or proposition campaign in California requires a variety of consultants: campaign managers, fund-raisers, media experts, lawyers, accountants, web masters, and other technology specialists. General campaign managers range from solo practitioners (found in smaller communities) to large firms located in Sacramento, San Francisco, Los Angeles, or even out of state. They advise candidates on all aspects of campaigning, coordinate the use of specialists, and control the technology used in the campaign. Given the cost of campaigning in California, public relations firms adept at fund-raising are a must. They do direct mail or stage expensive dinners featuring "drawing card" celebrities, such as movie stars or recording artists.

Traditional media specialists divide California into media markets, not electoral districts. They work with candidates and initiative campaigns to produce newspaper advertisements and broadcast commercials. All these media are tailored to specific markets and audiences. Because San Francisco voters are different than San Bernardino voters, appeals are customized based on geographic, demographic, and ideological differences. Candidates use television ads, not only to hype their own qualifications but also to criticize opponents. Some are simple "comparison" ads; others are full-blown attack ads featuring ominous, insinuating voice-overs, and unflattering photos. Today, over half of California voters vote by mail, often weeks before Election Day. As a result, campaigns have been forced to spend earlier than was once the case; a last-minute ad blitz might be too little, too late.

The complex world of campaign finance also requires expertise no matter the scale of the campaign. State regulations require candidates to report campaign spending and to disclose personal income, which, in turn, requires legal analysis and meticulous bookkeeping, especially in the larger races. Increasingly, computer software allows campaigns of any size to manage the overall effort; maintain lists of voters, volunteers, and donors; generate correspondence; and compile reports required by California's Fair Political Practices Commission.

Polling specialists ask voters what they think about issues and candidates. The most helpful are those hired by particular campaigns. For example, initial benchmark polls tell a campaign what issues are important and measure early candidate support. Tracking polls, taken during the course of the campaign, reveal to what extent particular strategies are working. Small focus groups test voter reactions to commercials and other political stimuli. All these techniques help pollsters measure the intensity of voter feelings and the impact of campaign messages.

Do election professionals make a difference in elections? Candidates and proposition campaigners seem to think so. But other factors such as incumbency, political party strength, policy issues, candidate personality, and media coverage often water down the impact of big money. Win or lose, consultants appear to contribute to escalating campaign costs. In addition to retainer fees, consultants also often charge a percentage of whatever is spent so there is little incentive to economize unless contributions fall short.

The Role of Money

Given the scope of election campaigns in California, raising the funds to compete electorally also raises concerns about the role of money itself. Former Assembly Speaker and state treasurer Jesse Unruh once said, "Money is the mother's milk of politics." After assessing the modern role of money in election campaigns, he revised his adage: "Money has become clabber in the mouth of the body politic." Candidates and officeholders complain about escalating campaign costs but seem ready to raise and spend whatever it takes to win. Furthermore, fund-raising does not take a vacation once a candidate is elected. It becomes an ongoing task alongside governing. Candidates and officeholders remind us that advertising of all sorts is costly, old campaign debts must be retired, and future election challengers must be anticipated. But how much campaign fundraising is enough? No amount seems sufficient. Regardless of the amount raised, there are ways to spend or allocate every dime. Given the ready availability of campaign contributions and the prevalence of safe legislative seats, some candidates generate surplus funds to spend on behalf of other candidates or to bank for future campaigns (see box 5.1).

Where do candidates obtain the funds necessary to run? First, wealthy candidates are allowed to spend unlimited amounts of their own money. But wealth does not ensure victory and can even be a hindrance. Meg Whitman's record personal expenditure of $141 million in a losing bid to become California's governor in 2010 illustrates the problem. Wealthy, self-funded candidates are tempted to bypass or ignore the vast network of personal and party relationships necessary to win modern campaigns. Second, candidates use direct mail and the Internet, including social media, to attract small "grassroots" contributions. Although the amounts may be modest, these contributions signal broad-based support.

Third, to bring in larger contributions, candidates seek contributions from the state's **political action committees** (PACs). The election arms of interest groups, PACs are the largest source of campaign funds for legislative and statewide races. Claiming that they simply want access, PACs commonly contribute to incumbents and to those legislators who control legislation of interest to them. In open seat elections, they may contribute to both sides, assuring some access regardless of who wins. Contributions often come by way of expensive Sacramento dinners, receptions, or other events such as golf outings or concerts; legislators routinely ask at least $1,000 per ticket. Many of these events coincide with the late-summer end of a legislative session when hundreds of bills of interest to these groups are scheduled for votes. Why Sacramento rather than the legislative districts where voters live? The capital is where full-time legislators spend much of their time and where lobbyists are situated. In fact, these mutually convenient capital fund-raisers are called "Third House events."

Contributions to candidate campaigns are strictly monitored in California. The **Political Reform Act of 1974 (Proposition 9)** requires disclosure of campaign contributions and expenditures, regulates the organization of campaign committees, limits entertaining by lobbyists, and prohibits conflict of interest by local officials. The **Fair Political Practices Commission (FPPC)** was established to implement this law. Its staff monitors all nonfederal elections, issues advisory opinions, and conducts random audits. It also investigates charges

Box 5.1 ★ Did You Know . . . ?

In the 2018 election cycle, all California candidates and ballot measure committees raised $979 million. The total for the 2014 cycle topped $556 million.

Source: The National Institute on Money in State Politics, https://www.followthemoney.org/tools/election-overview?s=CA&y=2018.

of wrongdoing and fines candidates for missing filing deadlines, submitting inaccurate reports, sending deceptive mailers, and laundering contributions. For example, in 2012, it filed a lawsuit against Americans for Responsible Leadership for hiding the true source of $11 million in contributions aimed at defeating Propositions 30 and 32. Most FPPC fines are small, but one state senator was fined a record $350,000 for illegally using surplus campaign funds.

In 2000, voters amended the 1974 act by passing Proposition 34, which established contribution limits and voluntary expenditure ceilings for state candidates. It allowed the FPPC to adjust these limits and ceilings to reflect changes in the Consumer Price Index. The FPPC website lists current contribution limits for individuals and committees (www.fppc.ca.gov/). There are no limits on political parties. Their "soft money" spending is supposed to be used for party building and get-out-the-vote efforts. In fact, they are also used to attack opposing parties, candidates, and views. To get around Proposition 34 limits, individuals and interest groups now form "independent expenditure committees." These committees can raise and spend unlimited amounts of money on a particular candidate as long as they do not consult, cooperate, or coordinate their efforts with the relevant campaign or measure. What do loopholes like independent expenditure committees teach us? Like water running downhill, campaign money seems to flow around any reform obstacle in its path.

In short, meaningful election reform of any sort faces numerous obstacles. Incumbents are loath to create a level playing field and the courts think spending limits curtail free speech. Voters repeatedly reject using tax dollars for campaigning, as they did with Proposition 15 in June 2010. Some reformers once recommended so-called Clean Money systems found in several other states. Under such systems, participating candidates raise small contributions, agree to limit overall spending, and obtain state funds to match those of privately financed opponents. But in 2011, the U.S. Supreme Court found that those matching fund provisions violated free-speech rights of those not accepting public financing. In general, California candidates compete in a system that favors large contributions or personal wealth.

The Role of National Politics

California is not an island and its elections do not exist in a vacuum. Increasingly, they play an important role in national politics. Four factors help explain this presence:

1. As was noted earlier, voter-approved initiatives often engender similar efforts in other states. Proposition 13 (1978) spawned similar tax-cutting efforts elsewhere. California's rejection of affirmative action in public programs (Proposition 209) encouraged such efforts in several other states. Ron Unz, the primary backer of a successful antibilingual education measure (Proposition 227), and Ward Connerly, sponsor of 209, traveled widely to advise policy activists in other states.
2. California is a significant source of campaign contributions sought by out-of-state candidates regardless of party, especially those running for

president. During the 2016 presidential election, presidential candidates raised more than $152 million from California donors, making it the top donor state. Hillary Clinton's campaign garnered $132.1 million and Donald Trump's over $20 million.[16]

3. California candidates are compelling recipients of out-of-state campaign funds. National PACs join their in-state counterparts and numbers of individual donors join in to swell campaign coffers. Consider U.S. Senator Kamala Harris. During the period from 2013 to 2018, about 26 percent of reportable contributions (those over $200) came from out-of-state sources. Of the top metropolitan areas contributing to her reelection effort—in or out of state—the New York area came in fourth.

4. California's role in the selection of presidential nominees and in the election of presidents is anomalous. Because the state is the source of many convention delegates and by far the largest number of Electoral College votes—55 out of 270 needed to win—one might think candidates would need to devote considerable resources here. Think again! As we noted earlier, California tried to frontload its presidential primary for 2020 by moving it up to March 3 in order to draw more interest to the state from presidential candidates.

Beyond calendar considerations and party rules, California is a daunting place to wage a presidential primary campaign. The state is too large to meet many voters in person and its expensive TV markets can quickly drain advertising budgets. Even cash-rich campaigns find it profitable to spend media funds elsewhere. The California anomaly continues into the general election period. In recent presidential campaigns, both public opinion polls and election results have indicated consistent support in the Golden State for Democratic nominees since 1992. Presuming a loss in California, Republican candidates spend their time and campaign resources in states with winning potential. Presuming victory in California, Democratic candidates shift their resources to competitive swing or "battleground" states where such efforts could tip the balance.

Of course, the Electoral College determines who becomes president. In the last presidential election cycle, several groups sought to alter how California's 55 electoral votes would be allocated. Some Republicans sponsored a statewide initiative—The Presidential Election Reform Act—that would allocate California's electoral votes by the popular vote results in each congressional district (as is done in Maine and Nebraska). Such a change would give the Republican candidate a better chance of winning and, at minimum, would require Democratic presidential candidates to spend precious time and money in California. However, the effort never made it to the ballot. Another group, the California-based National Popular Vote, has proposed a novel reform wherein states would commit to allocate their electoral votes to the national popular vote winner. Obviously, it would take enough states totaling 270 electoral votes to participate in this interstate compact. Eleven states including California have thus far joined in this effort.

CALIFORNIA'S ELECTORAL GAPS

The political participation patterns we have described must be viewed against a larger backdrop: recent demographic trends affecting both California and the nation. From a political behavior perspective, we see the emergence of two Californias—the state's richly diverse population on the one hand and the state's much less diverse electorate on the other. This two-California idea can be expressed in terms of a number of gaps.

Voter/Nonvoter Gap

The most profound gap is between *voters* and *nonvoters*. As California's population has grown, this gap has also grown because the segments of the population that are increasing the most are reflected in the electorate the least. This trend is occurring across the nation, but according to pollster Mark Baldassare, the trend "could be more problematic for California—a state that calls on its voters not only to elect representatives but to make so much policy through ballot initiatives."[17]

Consider the contrasting views of the two groups:

Typical Nonvoters	*Typical Likely Voters*
Want more active government	Want less active government
Favor more social spending	Favor less social spending
Support higher taxes	Oppose higher taxes
Oppose initiatives that limit government	Support initiatives that limit government

Although it could be argued that nonvoters do not count because they do not participate, they do receive a variety of public services and pay taxes like voters; they do have a stake in the political system. Because many nonvoters are the most vulnerable Californians, this gap should be of concern to the state's voters.

Race/Ethnicity Gap

A second gap that reflects two different Californias is the *race/ethnicity gap*. This gap is expressed in figure 5.4. Most tellingly, Latinos make up 39 percent of the state's overall population but constitute only 21 percent of likely voters. In contrast, white voters are disproportionately represented on Election Day. Experts expect this gap to persist well into the future. That said, California's overall electorate is proportionately more diverse than the U.S. electorate and much more so than many other states.

The Age Gap

Embedded in the voter—nonvoter gap is the *age gap*. This refers to the fact that, compared to older voters, younger voters express less interest in politics, register to vote at lower rates, are less likely to vote, and are less likely to identify with the major parties. The 2018 general election was a glaring example. Only 8 percent of all voters were in the youngest age category (18–24), while more than three times that number (27 percent) were in the oldest category, 65 and up. Not only is there a disparity in the age composition of the electorate, but one also exists

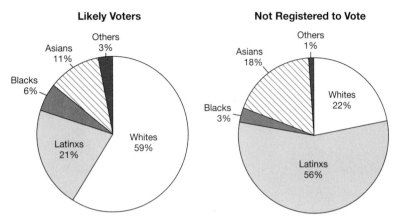

Figure 5.4 California's Nondiverse Electorate

Source: Public Policy Institute of California, "Just the Facts: California's Likely Voters" (San Francisco: Public Policy Institute of California, August 2018).

in the candidates each supports. Seventy-two percent of young voters supported Democrat Gavin Newsom in the gubernatorial election, whereas 57 percent of those 65 and older did.[18]

The Partisan Gap
Recent elections have exposed a growing *partisan* divide in the United States. Various surveys of Californians also reveal sizable gaps in the views of California Republicans and Democrats. Partisan differences were pronounced in the poll featured in figure 5.1. Fully 83 percent of registered Democrats favored California's sanctuary state laws; *only 11 percent* of registered Republicans did. Partisan differences can be found on a host of other issues as well like taxes, health care, and welfare.[19] Given this ideological divide between the major parties, it is understandable that hyperpartisanship would be reflected in the state legislature.

The Gender Gap
A subtler gap not reflected in this chapter's data is the *gender gap*—the margin of difference between the opinions and votes of men and women. In many elections, women side with the Democratic Party and their candidates in greater numbers than men do. For example, take the 2018 gubernatorial election. An impressive 64 percent of women supported Newsom whereas only 55 percent of male voters did—a 9-point gap. Does marital status help narrow the gap? Apparently not. Instead, it grows by 3 percent; 65 percent of married females supported Newsom, whereas 53 percent of married males did.[20]

Some observers fear that these gaps have led to voter apathy, citizen alienation, and political dysfunction. Although the gaps indeed have consequences for today, some of these fears may well subside over time. First, the portion of the electorate that is white is gradually declining. The Latinx population is now a plurality in California for the first time since statehood. A growing number of California cities are also nonmajority—no ethnic or racial group constitutes more than 50 percent of the population. Second, whereas the proportion of white voters is declining, the educational and income levels of voters remain relatively high. As more ethnic and racial minorities assimilate and enter the middle class, they will to some extent vote as breadwinners and taxpayers, not just as Latinxs, African Americans, or Asians. This will also influence party politics. Although Latinxs often align themselves with the Democratic Party (60 percent do), only 36 percent consider themselves to be liberal. Another 31 percent of them identify as moderates, while 33 percent lean conservative.[21] Neither Democrats nor Republicans can afford to take for granted this growing group.

CONCLUSION: DIVIDED BY DIVERSITY

Once again, diversity helps explain how Californians participate in their political system. We see it in generalized forms of participation—varying degrees of civic engagement, from attending meetings to leaving communities altogether or being involved in political protest. We see it in the wide spectrum of public opinions held by Californians on a host of political and policy issues. Various socioeconomic factors explain whether Californians can vote or indeed do vote. Campaign professionals must work with the state's plethora of elections and election rules in order to sort, sift, and attract California's electorate—or, more accurately, its diverse subelectorates.

Whether the electoral gaps noted in this chapter are regional or based on race and ethnicity, age, partisanship, or gender, California's policymakers must cope with the biggest gap of all—the enduring difference between California's overall population and the composition of its electorate. The importance of this gap for California politics cannot be emphasized enough. To the extent today's underrepresented groups choose to become part of the political process, profound changes could well occur in the future.

KEY TERMS

political participation (p. 84)
exit option (p. 85)
protest option (p. 85)
public opinion (p. 87)
straw polls (p. 87)
scientific polls (p. 88)
voting age population (VAP) (p. 89)
voter turnout (p. 89)
structural nonvoting (p. 89)
preferential nonvoting (p. 89)
primary elections (p. 94)
general elections (p. 95)

special elections (p. 95)
political action committees (p. 97)
Political Reform Act of 1974 (p. 97)
Fair Political Practices Commission (p. 97)
electoral gaps (p. 100)
voter/nonvoter gap (p. 100)
racial/ethnic gap (p. 100)
gender gap (p. 101)
age gap (p. 100)
partisan gap (p. 101)

REVIEW QUESTIONS

1. Survey the various forms of political participation. Which forms most aptly describe your participation in the political system?

2. Describe and illustrate the exit and protest options evident in California. What would cause you to consider these options?
3. How are the opinions of Californians expressed and measured?
4. Why do otherwise qualified adults not register to vote? Why do registered voters neglect to vote?
5. Describe the various types of elections in California.
6. Why are campaign professionals so important in California's electoral process?
7. How do recent election results demonstrate trends in voter demographics, turnout, and behavior?
8. Describe the various electoral gaps in California. What do you think is the long-term significance of these gaps?

WEB RESOURCES

The IGS Poll

https://igs.berkeley.edu/igs-poll/berkeley-igs-poll

Public Policy Institute of California

https://www.ppic.org

These sites feature statewide polling data including the policy views, general attitudes, electoral preferences, and demographic attributes of California's electorate.

California Voter Foundation

https://www.calvoter.org

This site features numerous reports and election aids with the voter in mind.

California Secretary of State

https://www.sos.ca.gov

Click on "Elections" to locate registration forms, voter registration statistics, turnout data, and past election results.

Fair Political Practices Commission

http://www.fppc.ca.gov

This site contains a wealth of information on campaign finance from a regulatory perspective.

6

Linking People and Policymakers: Media, Parties, and Interest Groups

★ ★ ★

LEARNING OUTCOMES

Students will be able to:

★ Describe the roles of the media, political parties, and interest groups in linking Californians with their government.

★ Identify the changing media trends and explain how different mediums influence the information the public receives about its government.

★ Assess the strength of the party system in California and the role it plays in elections.

★ Explain the tactics and tools interest groups use to influence public policy.

★ Analyze how linkage institutions compete for consumers and the attention of voters and policymakers.

IN BRIEF

Chapter 6 examines various links between ordinary Californians and the policy institutions profiled in the next four chapters. In a representative democracy, these linkage efforts provide channels of access and influence for ordinary citizens; this input helps make the political system viable and legitimate to these citizens.

★ ★ ★

THE MASS MEDIA LINKS Californians with policy processes primarily through television, newspapers, and now the Internet. Newspapers provide substantial amounts of political news and guide public opinion by means of editorials and endorsements. Television has limits unique to the medium but reaches a huge audience in California. Increasingly, the Internet and social media are displacing printed newspapers as a source of news. Thanks to the Progressives, political parties are weak in California, their powers limited either by law or practice.

But thanks to the endurance of the two-party system, they remain important to many voters. Interest groups might well be the driving force in California politics. Groups represent every conceivable interest in the state and use a variety of resources to express their members' policy preferences to policymakers.

INTRODUCTION

Chapter 5 examined the political behavior of Californians acting as individuals and groups. We analyzed how they participate in civil society and in politics, how they form opinions, and how they vote or not vote. Subsequent chapters examine the formal governing institutions found in California's political system: the executive, legislative, and judicial branches of state government plus numerous local governments. Chapter 6 addresses these linkage activities and processes that connect individual Californians to those officials and institutions that make policy—what people think of as "the government." In a representative democracy, such linkage institutions provide channels through which citizens have input in the political system.[1] They help inform ordinary citizens (the media), frame their political choices (political parties), and voice their policy preferences to the government (through interest groups). To be clear, direct democracy in California is its own channel of access and influence; it is so important to the state's politics both past and present that we treated it separately in chapter 4. In this chapter, we will use linkages and channels of access and influence interchangeably.

In a representative democracy (where the people are sovereign, but delegate decision-making is done by a relative few), these channels are essential. Power residing in "the people" is only latent (potential but unused) power until people have ways to express it. In California's evolving, complex, and pluralistic society, these channels are the only practical way ordinary citizens can speak or relate to those making policy on their behalf.

Scholars of American politics commonly focus on elections (discussed in chapter 5), the media, political parties, and interest groups. At times these linkages work smoothly. Both the people and policymakers, respectively, get what they want and need. Indeed, democratic theory would suggest the two agendas agree much of the time. At other times, however, these linkage institutions might not serve their intended purpose, or they lose meaning to average citizens. When this happens, the ability to govern is affected. Some believe this is the condition of modern California politics. The media might not adequately inform the state's residents. Political parties and interest groups increasingly compete with one another, usually at the expense of the parties. Even during elections, the media and interest groups appear to exercise more power than do parties. These developments affect the relationship between those who govern and those who are governed. This chapter describes and evaluates each of these linkages and the role they play in connecting California's diverse citizenry and its government.

MASS MEDIA

A primary linkage or channel of influence in national and California state politics is the mass media. The **mass media** funnels information, opinion, and user-friendly analysis to large numbers of people without direct, face-to-face contact. This consists primarily of print media (newspapers and magazines), electronic media (radio and television), and new media (the Internet). Citizens and public officials alike depend on the media to send and receive messages. Their resulting power is enormous. When he was Assembly Speaker (one of the most powerful offices in the state), Willie Brown said, "The press has as much influence on public policy as I have."[2] To reinforce his point, consider that media organizations are the only businesses (yes, businesses) constitutionally protected as a check on the government.

In addition to mass media, various **elite media** (those catering to select groups) thrive in California. For decades, the now-defunct *California Journal* covered state politics, personalities, and issues for an influential but small readership. Numerous print and Internet political newsletters (including *Capitol Weekly*, *Fox and Hounds Daily*, *Around the Capitol*, and *Calbuzz*) provide timely inside news and gossip, but their readership is small. Journalists specializing in California politics increasingly offer blogs alongside stories and columns.

So, on which of these news sources do Californians most rely? In one statewide survey, television was the most cited source of political news, followed closely by the Internet, and further down the list were newspapers and radio. In the last decade, the Internet has surpassed newspapers as a primary source of news. Combined, these media warrant particular attention.

Newspapers

The rise of California's newspapers parallels the state's political development. Wealthy individuals and families managed the earliest newspapers. One example was James McClatchy of the *Sacramento Bee*, who in the late 1800s worked his way up to editor while gradually purchasing shares in the paper. His heirs gained control of the *Bee* and still own a portion of it. He fought for land reform (dividing huge landholdings that had survived statehood) and the transcontinental railroad; he also fought against monopolies and environmentally destructive hydraulic mining. The McClatchy Company is now publicly traded and owns media properties across the nation.

The *Los Angeles Times* was decidedly more conservative than McClatchy's *Bee*. Harrison Gray Otis bought the *Los Angeles Times* shortly after a Southern California railroad project linked Los Angeles to points east. He preached pro-business, antiunion sermons in editorials while hyping the Los Angeles land boom in which he himself had invested. He cooperated with the Big Four, who shared his desire for economic growth, personal power, and enormous income. On the other hand, William Randolph Hearst's *San Francisco Examiner* was decidedly anti-railroad and friendly to Progressive reforms. During much of this period, newspapers from San Diego to San Francisco were owned by Republicans and espoused conservative values.

Today, California's newspapers have undergone substantial change since those early crusading years. Many have merged to create "one newspaper" towns or have been acquired by out-of-town media chains, conglomerates, or wealthy individuals. Nowadays, concerns over profitability and even survivability trump the traditional community and public service functions of newspapers. For example, the *Los Angeles Times*, the state's largest newspaper, has undergone ownership changes in recent years and is now owned by a biotech billionaire. The *Times* and other once-thick weekday metropolitan dailies have thinned considerably as rounds of layoffs decimate newsroom staffs.

Large corporations may dominate the newspaper scene, but California is also home to many ethnic minority newspapers. For example, *La Opinion* is the largest Spanish language newspaper in the nation with a circulation of over 115,000. In Los Angeles, only the *Los Angeles Times* has higher circulation (about 650,000). The media association New America Media lists roughly 800 California-based media outlets including print, radio, broadcast, and online versions that serve groups including African Americans, Arabs, Armenians, Cambodians, Chinese, Hispanics, and Koreans. Many of these outlets operate below the radar of other Californians and the state's public officials. To the extent that they reinforce subgroup identities, issues, and concerns, they may also reinforce the hyperpluralistic nature of California politics.

Despite readership declines, many Californians still depend on newspapers for state and local government news, but the quality and the quantity of the news they receive varies. The *Sacramento Bee*, whose daily circulation is over 279,000, reports state politics heavily because its readers include not only elected officials but also thousands of state employees. Sacramento is, after all, a "company town." Only a small handful of large newspapers can afford to staff a Sacramento bureau; smaller newspapers have either combined forces or abandoned the capital entirely. Instead of traditional investigative reporting, they rely on wire services (Associated Press) and direct government sources (press releases).

Coverage of local politics is just as problematic. On one hand, the large, metropolitan dailies (presumably read by California's urban majority) are too large to cover public affairs in the hundreds of communities that comprise their circulation areas.

On the other hand, smaller, more localized newspapers often lack the resources, regularity (many are published weekly), or the desire to cover political issues on a frequent basis, especially those that reach beyond their circulation base.

Are there any bright spots in this assessment of newspapers as channels of influence and access? Ironically, one bright spot might be technology. Although it is portrayed as the major enemy of traditional print journalism, technology has actually made newspaper reading easier and more widely accessible. All major newspapers have web versions. Many of those are accessible at no charge to the reader, although increasingly newspapers are imposing limitations on the number of free articles before a fee is required. Furthermore, stories run throughout the day; one need not wait until tomorrow to see how the *Los Angeles Times* or the *San Francisco Chronicle* covers today's breaking story. Also, the website "Rough & Tumble" (www.rtumble.com) provides a daily compilation of California newspaper stories on state politics and public policy. Although the long-term future of California's print newspapers may be bleak, for now, more of them are more accessible than ever before.

Television

The popularity of television has diminished the political influence of newspapers, especially among certain groups. As figure 6.1 portrays, when asked where Californians get most of their news about the governor and the legislature, 38 percent of all respondents cited television; for Latino respondents, this figure jumped to 51 percent.[3] Given its pervasiveness in much of California's political

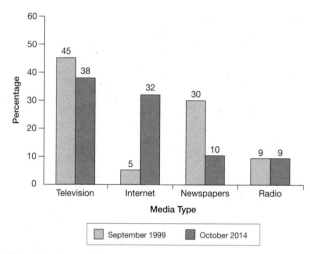

Figure 6.1 Political Information Sources in California

Question: What mix of media do you use to keep up with California politics?

Note: Survey question asks the following: Do you get most of your information about what is going on in politics today from television, Internet, newspapers, or radio sources?

life, television falls far short of its potential as a channel of access and influence. The reasons are several.

A Visual Medium. Compared to other media, television focuses on the visual. To a news producer, a political story is not inherently interesting unless it is visually interesting. As one television producer admitted, his colleagues are interested in "slash, flash, and trash. They want the [story] to bleed, scream and yell."[4] In response, public officials deliberately employ symbols, stunts, or pseudo-events to make their messages visually interesting. Celebrity witnesses virtually guarantee media coverage of committee hearings that might otherwise go unnoticed. In 2014, Governor Jerry Brown issued playing cards to the media with his dog, Sutter, prominently displayed on them uttering aphorisms about prudent budgeting. In their defense, legislators claim they must resort to such measures to inform their constituents and shed light on the state's problems.

Media Bias. Many Americans claim the media is biased and that they treat the news in a partial, unfair manner. Some see an **ideological bias** where the media tends to favor Republicans or Democrats, conservatives or liberals. California journalists think this might be in the eye of the beholder. People want to see a story reported in a predetermined way and find fault if it is not. *Los Angeles Times* columnist George Skelton was asked about his partisan leanings to which he responded, "What am I? *I* don't know what I am." A recent study of two California newspapers found that the news coverage of the state legislature was mostly neutral, despite one paper endorsing Republican candidates and the other endorsing Democrats.[5]

California reporters do examine what policymakers say and do and compare the differences. According to journalist Steve Scott, "We have a low threshold for hypocrisy." The media also seems to be attracted to inconsistency and the ironies that abound in politics. For example, during the 2010 gubernatorial campaign, billionaire Republican candidate Meg Whitman faced accusations that she retained a Latina housekeeper after finding out she had forged her immigration documents. Whitman's behavior seemed inconsistent for a candidate who had taken hard-line anti-immigration positions during the primary race. The story ran for weeks and dogged the balance of her fall campaign.

Television, in particular, exhibits a **structural bias**. As a business, television structures news to minimize coverage of government and politics. It tends to focus less on politics and more on human-interest stories: entertainment, crime, sports, and weather—anything but politics.

Reflecting on that dismal coverage, television columnist Howard Rosenberg suggested that the only way to attract media attention would be to "have the four leading candidates chase each other on a freeway."[6] Structural bias takes place in the context of fierce competition among stations for ratings and "market share." In addition, television's use of pictures—its primary product—can lead to false impressions. For instance, one study revealed that crime reports by Southern California stations followed a predictable narrative with two elements: crime is violent and perpetrators are nonwhite males.[7]

Sparse Coverage. When television does cover public affairs, the coverage tends to be sparse and shallow. News stories themselves tend to be brief—very brief—due to the inherent limitations of commercial television. The result is a lack of analysis—why events, political or otherwise, happen. For example, one study of California television news showed that violence dominated local news coverage. Furthermore, the emphasis was on the specifics of particular crimes, not on the underlying social conditions that contribute to violence.[8] Coverage of state politics has a similar quality to it, to the extent it is covered at all. Many stations neglect live coverage of the governor's State of the State speech but, rather, refer interested viewers to streaming video of the event on their own websites.

Another measure of television news coverage in California is how stations assign reporters. Sacramento-based news coverage had declined significantly from its zenith in the Reagan years—a phenomenon shared with other state capitals.[9] Local Sacramento stations still cover state politics and, on occasion, send footage to their network affiliates in Los Angeles and San Francisco. The Northern California News Satellite sells its state politics stories to client stations. Furthermore, the California Channel, the state's version of C-SPAN, provides live and archived cable broadcasts and web casts of legislative floor sessions, committee hearings, news conferences, and other related programming.

Given its limitations, why does television news still hold promise as a linkage institution in California politics? In a word, size. The state has more than 90 local stations and more cable subscribers than any other state. Ninety-five percent of the state's households own television sets. More important, more than 85 percent of them live in only four media markets: greater Los Angeles, the San Francisco Bay Area, Sacramento, and San Diego. Access to these markets is a precious, costly commodity for public officials, election candidates, and interest groups. The sheer size of the Los Angeles television market (it reaches more than 50 percent of the state's voters) gives statewide candidates from Southern California built-in advantages over competitors from elsewhere in the state, especially if they have had prior media exposure.

In addition, television plays an important linkage role covering elections and crises. They do so through straight news reporting and through the airing of campaign commercials. Political advertising is prolific because it is the only realistic way candidates can reach voters. As a result, candidates often inundate newscast commercial time with messages unmediated by editors, reporters, and producers. The messages get through. Focus group research suggests that Californians are more likely to remember a candidate's television commercials than straight news about the candidate.[10] In covering crises, television has no peer; it has the capacity to provide nonstop news coverage of terrorist attacks, earthquakes, fires, and riots. Regular programming and much commercial time are suspended during such events. Crises in the nation's largest state often attract network attention.

Radio

As any reader will already know, most of California's radio stations are commercial enterprises featuring a variety of music formats. There are about 15 stations that use an all-news/talk format and about 30 public radio stations, some of which include state and local news in their programming. One of the most public affairs–oriented of these is San Francisco's KQED. It hosts daily reports and a weekly program called the *California Report* with extensive coverage of state issues, a program carried by other public radio stations across the state. Radio has something of a captive audience during commute times, and much public affairs programming is scheduled for those rush-hour times. Talk radio is tailored to those listeners and can be hard-hitting and abrasive in tone. Many former elected officials have used their own talk radio shows to stay relevant among their partisan brethren. This group includes former governor Jerry Brown, Governor Gavin Newsom, former assembly Speaker Willie Brown, former assemblyman Tim Donnelly, and Attorney General Dan Lungren. Assemblyman Jim Patterson, a station owner in California and Idaho, captured the appeal for conservative talk show hosts in particular: "Quite frankly, we have a tool generally in California where the talk stations provide a forum for our side to be heard and our side to be in front of very large audiences."[11]

Although most California voters, regardless of ethnicity, use mainstream media outlets to consume political news, ethnic media outlets are a secondary source of political news for voters from different ethnic groups. For instance, about one-third of Latinx, black, and Asian voters use ethnic radio as a source of political information.[12]

THE INTERNET AND SOCIAL MEDIA

Arguably, the growth of the Internet is revolutionizing U.S. and California politics. As we saw in figure 6.1, Internet use in California has grown rapidly in the last decade. In fact, it has overtaken television as a news source for younger adults, upper-income residents, independents, and college graduates. Eighty-six percent of Californians use the Internet, about the same as the population nationwide.[13] Media websites are ubiquitous, and both blogs and online political newsletters are within reach of most Californians.

Although the Internet provides additional news options for California's news consumers, it is simply a *must* for the state's political elites including legislators, government workers, lobbyists, and the news media themselves. Online communication moves in two directions. According to one survey of these elites, receiving political information online (via websites, email, blogs, or podcasts) is on the rise, often at the expense of television usage.[14] In terms of disseminating information, the Internet is equally essential for these elites. Some ballot initiatives have relied heavily on the Internet to jump-start the campaign process. Rarely are candidates or issues without their own websites. Not only is the Internet an increasingly effective way to raise funds—Visa or MasterCard will do just fine—it communicates its own symbolic message.

How politically important is the Internet? The answer depends on the user. So far, the Internet seems to have attracted already-well-informed Californians and political activists. But as a tool of persuasion, it tends to reinforce user views rather than convert undecided voters. According to Dan Schnur, "The Internet is a proactive medium. With television, you have to make a proactive decision to not watch the commercial. But with the Internet, you have to make an active decision to click, to participate. Base voters of each party are much more likely to do that than the undecided."[15] What about the Californians who are not yet wired, who for economic or other reasons do not communicate or consume information online? Will there eventually be a technological version of a second-class citizen? Surveys by the Public Policy Institute of California suggest such a digital divide. Latinxs, older residents, and the disabled have lower rates of broadband access and Internet use than other groups, but the gap has narrowed in recent years.[16] According to Kassy Perry of the Perry Communications Group, "as more legislators, staff, and agency officials move online, many constituents who don't have access to the technology will find it harder to communicate with their elected and appointed officials."[17]

In terms of political access, will Californians ever be able to vote online? The state took a big step forward on this path in the November 2012 election. For the first time in California, potential voters registered to vote completely online at the secretary of state's website. About 60 percent of the nearly 1 million newly registered voters did so online. Nearly half of those online registrants were between the ages of 18 and 29, indicating how the Internet can serve as a tool for stoking political participation among younger voters. The influx of younger voters was one major reason Proposition 30 passed, which raised income and sales taxes and dedicated most of the revenues to education. This puts California voters one step closer to casting ballots online; however, some critics fear vote tampering with this new method. Of course, this was a concern for online registration, but so far it has been deemed a success.

Another important trend in the use of the Internet has been the rise of social media, such as Facebook, Twitter, and YouTube. Most, if not all, candidate and ballot measure campaigns use one or all of these venues to announce their latest policy positions or release new advertisements. Candidates with little financial backing find these outlets are inexpensive ways to draw attention to their campaigns. In the 2014 gubernatorial race, both Republican candidates, Tim Donnelly and Neil Kashkari, used YouTube extensively to reach voters. In one instance that generated widespread attention from mass media outlets, including newspapers and television, Kashkari spent a week as a homeless person in Fresno and posted a video chronicle of it on YouTube.

But what, if any, is the impact of social media on California politics? As of late 2010, there were more than 15 million voting-age Facebookers in California—a sizable pool of potential voters and supporters of various causes. As indicated by the increasing use of social media to reach voters, campaign managers seem to view it as a necessity. The state of California itself has encouraged the use of social media among its departments and agencies and issued guidelines for managing information released and posted on these sites.[18] Some initial research on the impact of social media on political participation is encouraging, although it does not seem to increase voters' political knowledge despite the greater access to information. One study showed that belonging to political groups on Facebook can "provide many of the benefits that we have known face-to-face groups to provide for decades, such as information, motivation for political action, and a forum for discussion and communicative exchanges."[19]

Although social media can provide these positive information-sharing benefits, there is some concern that these websites may convey seemingly neutral opinions when in fact they are campaign materials targeting voters. To provide more disclosure on the sources of these postings, the Fair Political Practices Commission (FPPC) issued new regulations in 2013. Campaign committees are now required to report who they paid to post materials on social media sites and blogs and list the names of the websites where they appeared. Opponents of the new regulations complained that this would only result in more paperwork and not prevent the tactic.[20] Still, overall, the early indications are that social media is not likely to drastically change election outcomes, but it may displace some of the older ways candidates, campaigns, and government officials communicate and receive information from voters.

POLITICAL PARTIES

In addition to the media, **political parties** also link citizens to their government. Parties are organized groups that (1) possess certain labels, (2) espouse policy preferences, (3) both nominate and work to elect candidates for public office, and (4) help frame government's postelection policy agenda. In American politics, they are found at all levels—federal, state, and local—although not in equal measure. Political parties come in three forms.[21] The **party in the electorate** refers to voters who hold partisan affiliations. The **party in government** refers to partisan elected officials and institutions, such as the legislature, that organize around party labels. These leaders (primarily governors and legislators) translate party positions into policy and personify the party in the minds of many voters. The **party organization** means the formal party apparatus: its structure, staff, budget, rules, and processes for achieving its goals. Here, we will discuss partisanship and its alternatives in California as well as how political parties are organized.

Partisanship in California

A political party is a relatively permanent coalition that exists to win public offices for its candidates, promote policy positions, and serve as a primary frame of reference for voters. **Party identification** is the extent to which citizens affiliate with, relate to, or support a specific political party. Identifiers believe support for a party makes their vote more meaningful. Unlike many multiparty systems elsewhere, the American two-party system presents relatively few choices. Voters respond to that lack by shading or qualifying their partisan loyalties. Common categories are (1) strong Democrat, (2) weak Democrat, (3) independent-leaning Democrat, (4) independent, (5) independent-leaning Republican, (6) weak Republican, and (7) strong Republican. In general, the two major parties have been losing identification, a process called dealignment, and independent voters have been increasing (see figure 6.2).

In California, both Republicans and Democrats have lost their share of registered voters. Since 1994, the percentage share of independents (those who check "Decline to State" on their registration forms) has grown from about 10 percent to more than 27 percent in 2018. If these trends continue, independents could outnumber Democrats and Republicans by 2025—making California what some call an "unparty state." In the parlance of televised electoral maps (where red is Republican and blue is Democratic), California is gradually moving from blue to purple.[22]

What do we know about these independent voters? How independent are they? While there are "pure" independents, they tend to be more apolitical than leaners, tend to be less knowledgeable, and tend to vote less frequently. Of those who are more likely to vote, 43 percent lean Democratic and 29 percent lean Republican. Even the leaners can be unpredictable. More than Republicans and Democrats, independents think that California needs a viable third party. On some issues like health care, independents side slightly more with Democrats, but on issues of immigration and climate change, they overwhelmingly fall in line with Democrats rather than with Republicans.

California independents span the demographic spectrum. According to polls of likely voters (those who habitually vote), 20 percent of Latinxs, 19 percent of whites, 17 percent of blacks, and 28 percent of Asian Californians consider

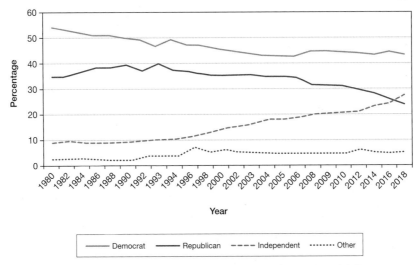

Figure 6.2 Party Registration in California, November 1980–2018

Question: What rule changes could improve the success of minor parties in California? What do the major parties need to do to regain those registered voters who now call themselves "Independents" or "Decline to State"?

Source: California Secretary of State's Office, https://www.sos.ca.gov.

themselves to be independents. Still, recent election results have seen an alignment of most Latinx voters with the Democratic Party. Some observers credit Latinxs' recent voting behavior to Republican Party support for Proposition 187 (an anti-immigration measure) and Proposition 209 (an anti-affirmative action measure). These two measures, in particular, were voting motivators, especially for newly naturalized Latinxs.[23] Whether or not they officially register as Democrats, Latinxs have been voting for Democratic candidates in impressive numbers. Their choices for president have been consistently Democratic. Bill Clinton won 63 percent of their votes in 1992, while Al Gore won 75 percent in 2000. More recently, Barack Obama won 72 percent in 2012 and Hillary Clinton 71 percent in 2016. Whether Latinx influence increases in the future depends on whether their citizenship and participation rates match their population growth.[24]

The Partisan Geography of California

Generalizations about party affiliation in California can be understood only in the context of the state's diverse geographical regions. These regions have different voting habits and partisan loyalties. Pollsters often identify five distinct voting regions of California—Los Angeles County, the rest of Southern California, the San Francisco Bay Area, the rest of Northern California, and the Central Valley. Here we utilize presidential election data because turnouts are so much higher than in state elections.

At one time, with the exception of Los Angeles County, Southern California voted predominantly for Republican presidential candidates. Demographic changes slowly converted much of this region to the Democratic side, although Orange County remained a Republican stronghold through the 2012 election. In that year, Republican Mitt Romney beat Democrat Barack Obama by 8 points. By 2016, however, the region had fully converted to the Democratic candidate; every county south of Kern County supported Democrat Hillary Clinton over Republican Donald Trump. This time, Clinton even won Orange County by 8 points, reversing the outcome of the previous election in 2012. Los Angeles County, once a Democratic island in a larger conservative region, registered the highest support for Clinton, with 72 percent voting in her favor, but it was no longer alone. Clinton won rather comfortably in Riverside County (5-point margin), San Bernardino County (8-point margin), and San Diego County (20-point margin). Meanwhile, in the Bay Area in Northern California, another dense voter region, it continued its longtime support of Democratic candidates, with Clinton receiving 79 percent of the votes. These results showed that the traditional north/south divide in support of presidential candidates was broken. The weakening support for the Republican presidential candidate reinforced other trends, signaling increasing Democratic dominance in the state.

In recent years, as the north/south split has waned, analysts have noticed an east/west contrast between coastal and inland California. Note the contrasts portrayed in figure 6.3. This map shows which 2016 presidential candidates won pluralities in each county. Most coastal Californians—and that means most Californians—preferred Clinton over Trump. Reflecting a region-level realignment, voters in portions of the Central Valley and the mountain regions preferred

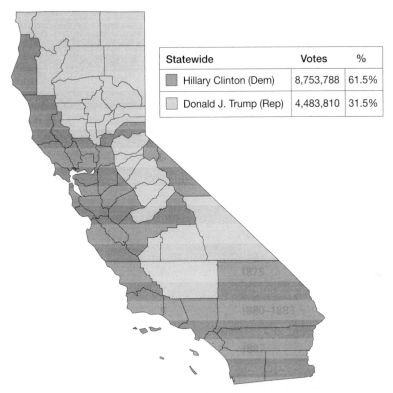

Statewide	Votes	%
▨ Hillary Clinton (Dem)	8,753,788	61.5%
▢ Donald J. Trump (Rep)	4,483,810	31.5%

Figure 6.3 California's Presidential Preferences by County, 2016

Source: New York Times, https://www.nytimes.com/elections/2016/results/california.

Trump by varying margins. An east/west contrast is also evident in political ideologies. Various surveys suggest that Central Valley residents are more politically conservative and more Republican than other Californians. While there are pockets of Democratic strength in inland California, Frederick Douzet and Kenneth P. Miller observe that the state's "coastal region politically resembles New York state while the interior looks like Texas."[25]

Political Parties: California Style

Like the United States as a whole, California has a two-party system. Democrats and Republicans dominate partisan elections. But California's system is one of weak parties. To curb machine bosses, such as San Francisco's Abe Ruef, and corporate elites, such as the Big Four, the Progressives established elements of a weak party system. *Direct primaries* allowed voters themselves to nominate candidates; *cross-filing* allowed the candidates themselves to run as Democrats, Republicans, or, on occasion, both; and *nonpartisan elections* blurred affiliations of judges and disallowed parties from endorsing or assisting local officeholders.

Many voters seem to prefer weak parties. Over the objections of party leaders in 1996, they approved an Open Primary Law (Proposition 198). It created a blanket primary that allowed voters to cross party lines and vote for any candidate, regardless of party label (that is, a registered Republican could vote for a Democratic candidate and vice versa). This innovation enabled more than 1.7 million "Decline to State" voters a chance to vote for partisan candidates. The blanket primary was employed for the June 1998 primary election and the March 2000 presidential primary. But in late June 2000, the U.S. Supreme Court overturned the law on a 7–2 vote, claiming that it forced parties to associate with those who do not necessarily support them, in violation of the First Amendment.[26] In reaction, a new election law established a "modified" closed primary that permits unaffiliated ("Decline to State") voters to participate in a partisan primary if party rules permit it. The Democratic, Republican, and American Independent parties revised their rules accordingly. (In a notable exception, the Republicans disallowed independents from voting in their 2008, 2012, and 2016 presidential primaries.)

As noted in chapter 5, voters tweaked the system still further with Proposition 14 (2010). Since 2011, there has been a single ballot for primary elections for congressional and state elective offices. In this **top-two primary**, the two candidates for each office with the most votes, regardless of party, advance to compete in the general election. In heavily Republican or Democratic districts, both nominees can be of the same party. Partisan primaries still exist for presidential elections and party offices. Defenders of this reform believe more moderates will be elected because candidates have to appeal to a broader electorate. Critics believe the reform will increase campaign costs and decimate minor parties.

California has had four election cycles (2012–18) under the new top-two system, and most observers believe that the impact has been mixed. First, under the new system, the number of competitive races has increased, but oftentimes, these are same-party races, where two candidates from the same party run against one another in the general election. In 2018, the races for lieutenant governor and for U.S. Senator had two Democrats running, but there was a sizable drop-off in the number of voters in those contests, presumably Republicans. The impact on campaign spending has been mixed, as average House and state senate candidates spent more than previous elections, while Assembly candidates spent less.[27] One of the more closely watched questions is whether the top-two leads to the election of more moderate legislators. On this front, initial research found some limited support for moderation among Democratic state legislators, but it may be a decade or longer before we can draw more definitive conclusions about the effects of the top-two primary on legislative behavior.[28]

In California's weak party system, Democrats and Republicans control major offices in Sacramento. The rise of these independent voters we discussed earlier has not given rise to many officeholders with an "I" next to their name. Based on how successful the parties were in electing governors and legislators, political scientists long regarded California as either "two-party competitive" or "modified one-party Democratic." During the 2000s, the label returned to two-party competitive.[29] After Progressive Era reforms, Republicans dominated state politics from 1924 to 1957. Both parties were relatively competitive from 1958 to 1973, and Democrats dominated from 1974 to 1982. Aside from brief Republican control of the Assembly in 1996, Democrats continued to dominate the legislature throughout the 1980s and into the late 1990s, while Republicans occupied the governor's office.

In recent years, with the exception of the Schwarzenegger administration in the 2000s, Democrats have dominated statewide offices and maintained a strong majority in the legislature. In 2012, Democrats accomplished a feat that had not been done since the 1930s: they gained two-thirds majorities in the Assembly and the Senate. This important threshold bestowed considerable powers on legislative Democrats, who were now able to pass tax increases on their own, place bond measures on the ballot, and even override vetoes of their fellow co-partisan governor, Jerry Brown (if they chose to). Due to vacancies and criminal charges against some legislators, Democrats' two-thirds majority waxed and waned (losing and regaining it several times) until 2018 when they secured strong supermajorities with votes to spare. In addition, Democrats once again swept all statewide offices. The ongoing Democratic dominance has led some Republicans to wonder if their party is still viable. Former Assembly Republican leader Kristin Olsen put it this way: "The California Republican Party isn't salvageable at this time. The Grand Old Party is dead—partly because it has failed to separate itself from today's toxic, national brand of Republican politics."[30] Unless state Republicans can broaden their appeal to more voters, Democrats will remain the dominant party for the near future.

Minor or third parties widen voter choice at least for some voters. How does a third party qualify to be included on a California ballot? Two routes are possible: (1) signing up about 65,000 registered voters (0.33 percent of voters registered) or (2) getting nearly 1.2 million registered voters to sign a petition seeking party qualification (10 percent of the total votes cast in the previous gubernatorial election). The first option is relatively easy; the second has never succeeded. To remain qualified, registration figures must remain above one-fifteenth of 1 percent of total state registration. The Natural Law Party failed this test and was disqualified in 2006. In addition to the Democrats and the Republicans, California's officially recognized third or minor parties include the American Independent Party, the Green Party, the Libertarian Party, and the Peace and Freedom Party. These minor parties represent the lowest line of the graph shown in figure 6.2.

How the Parties Are Organized

Because the state elections code dictates how California parties are organized, party structures look very similar. California parties do not have precinct-level organizations common in "strong party" states. Therefore, the lowest level is the **county central committee.** Most voters elect these committee members in primary elections without really knowing who they are. These local committees do not "run" local party affairs and must compete for influence with elected officials and unofficial party clubs. However, their role in elections has been raised in recent years as they have come to serve as "middlemen" between donors and candidates. Wealthy donors give large chunks of money to county committees, who, in turn, send it to party candidates in competitive races.

The **state central committee** is the key organizational unit for both Republicans and Democrats. Numbering in the hundreds, its membership is a hodgepodge of party leaders, elected officials, and appointees from the ranks of activist party members. Every year, state central committee members meet to discuss policy issues, select party leaders, hear elected officials and major candidates speak, "network" with each other, and rally the party faithful. Historically, the Republicans have been more cohesive than the Democrats, who divide into multiple caucuses representing the disabled, women, labor, LGBT (lesbian, gay, bisexual, transgender), and seemingly every racial/ethnic group in the state. This devotion to group-specific interests has given the party a hyperpluralistic outlook. These party gatherings showcase, for better or worse, the current diversity that exists within both major parties. In the Democratic Party, liberals, moderates, and caucus groups fight among themselves. In the past, Republican Party conventions tended to pit fiscal conservatives against social issue conservatives and pragmatists against ideologues. Some intraparty differences also occur due to the state's geographic diversity. Many party activists from interior California have little in common with those from coastal and metropolitan areas apart from sharing party labels. As a general rule, party activists regardless of party tend to be more doctrinaire than the public at large. Many are ideologically brittle and lack the ability, willingness, and skill to compromise—traits that are expected of elected officials. During state party conventions, these activists may boo or shout down high-profile candidates who are perceived as not being liberal or conservative enough to please "the base."

In addition to the state and county committee structures, the political parties in California send representatives to the national committees. Full-time party chairpersons are selected to staff the state central committees. These positions often attract wealthy hyper-activists desiring to rub elbows with elected officials and party donors. Most are unknown to average voters. In 2018, Eric Bauman, the first openly gay Democratic Party chairperson, became swept up in the #MeToo movement, which encouraged victims of sexual harassment and assault to publicly report their offenses. After allegations surfaced that Bauman had assaulted several people, growing public pressure and a request from incoming Governor Gavin Newsom led him to resign.

"Independent" Groups

In addition to the formal party organizations, independent groups, who are frequently affiliated with the parties, have become powerful forces in election campaigns. These groups were unleashed by the U.S. Supreme Court's *Citizens United* decision, which allowed them to raise and spend unlimited amounts of money for or against candidates, as long as they do not coordinate with a candidate's campaign. Minimally staffed with only a treasurer and political consultant, their sole purpose is to make independent expenditures (IEs) on behalf of their donors. They usually support one party's candidates and receive their funding from major businesses, labor unions, or a small group of wealthy donors, all of whom normally give to candidates' campaigns as well. In some races, the independent groups spend more than the candidates themselves. These independent committees, as they are also known, adopt patriotic or high-minded names that obscure the donors behind them. For example, the Spirit of Democracy, a Republican-leaning group funded by Charles Munger, Jr., spent $5.9 million on candidate campaigns in 2014.[31] The influence of independent groups on elections is only likely to grow in the future.

Endorsement Politics

Arguably the most important test of a strong political party organization is its ability to control the selection of nominees for public office. Short of handpicking nominees, parties should be able to at least endorse them. In their quest for nonpartisanship, California's Progressives banned that practice in 1913. Through legislation and party practice, the ban was even strengthened to disallow parties from supporting or opposing preprimary candidates. In the 1980s, the U.S. Supreme Court intervened in California's party affairs by declaring the state ban on party endorsements unconstitutional. In a case involving San Francisco Democrats, the court majority argued that such bans violated the parties' rights to spread their views and the voters' rights to inform themselves about candidates and issues.[32]

With the advent of the top-two primary, endorsement politics is evolving for each party. Republicans usually do not endorse anybody in the primary when more than one Republican is running but changed that rule in 2018 for the gubernatorial race in hopes of coalescing the party around one candidate. On the other hand, the Democratic Party does endorse candidates with more than one of their own in a race. In a high-profile snub in 2018, the party endorsed Kevin De León over longtime incumbent Dianne Feinstein for U.S. Senate when the two Democrats moved on to the general election. Party endorsements have a mixed record of success. The Republican Party–endorsed John Cox won his party's primary in the 2018 gubernatorial race, while the Democratic Party–endorsed De León lost to Feinstein in the general election. Party endorsements seem to matter more in lower-level races. In 2014, for example, the party-endorsed candidates won 15 out of the 18 elections, or 83 percent of the time.[33]

Whether parties endorse or not, another option is available, namely the use of **slate mailers**—large postcards listing "endorsed" candidates and propositions. Note the quotation marks. In many cases, distributors of these mailers are actually campaign-oriented businesses. While contributors are not disclosed, tiny asterisks reveal who paid to be included. These colorful mailers may sound official with titles like "Voter Information Guide." They may emphasize a particular theme (Official Non-Partisan Voter Guide) or tailor their messages to particular groups of voters. But many are flatly misleading. For example, in 2010, the "Voting Guide for Republicans" recommended reelection of Democrat Bill Lockyer as state treasurer. It turns out he paid $60,000 to be listed in that mailer.[34] Some candidates feel pressured to pay for such "endorsements" or even blackmailed into doing so if the outfit threatens to "endorse" opposing candidates.

Although they appear to be unregulated, and they largely are, slate mailer organizations must file with the California secretary of state. In the 2018 cycle, 88 of them were listed as active. As long as parties remain weak and propositions remain popular, slate mailers will likely remain a dubious, yet attractive, electoral tool.

INTEREST GROUPS

Interest groups are a significant force in national and state politics. It would be difficult to overemphasize their power and influence in California politics, both state and local. An **interest group** is a body of individuals who share similar goals and organize to influence public policy around those goals. Their development in U.S. politics was early and immediate. Founder James Madison considered the potential problem of "factions" in America (his term for both groups and political parties) but thought the new republic could control them. By the 1830s,

Frenchman Alexis de Tocqueville observed, "In no country in the world has the principle of association been more successfully used or applied to a greater multitude of objects than in America."[35] By the 1950s, political scientists considered the activity of interest groups central to politics. Legislatures basically referee group struggles; victories come in the form of statutes—passed or defeated. The job of government in a pluralistic society is to manage conflict among groups.

State-level interest group politics does not lend itself to easy generalization. The interest group environment varies from state to state. Because political parties are relatively weak in California, one would expect interest groups to be rather strong—and they are. One illustration of their power comes from the *Capitol Weekly* publication, which is a news source for government workers and the Sacramento political community. Each year, the outlet compiles its list of the top 100 most influential people working in and around the state capitol. In 2018, about half of the top 100 worked for interest groups as lobbyists or executive staff. But due to the size of the state and the scope of its government, interest group power is not concentrated among a few dominant interests. Depending on the issue, many groups not only actively participate but also actively compete on opposing sides of the same issue.

For ordinary citizens, interest groups provide still another important link to the political system. Multiple memberships are common. For instance, a local homebuilder is likely to be a member of a local builders group and the chamber of commerce plus several statewide groups, the Building Industry Association, and the Associated Contractors of California. These statewide groups provide the contractor with political access while furthering the broad interests of the building industry: environmental regulations, building code matters, land-use controls, and growth policies. But builders are not just builders. They may also be members of churches, health insurance groups, automobile associations, and sporting groups. These interests are also organized at the state level to push their own public policy preferences.

Interest groups have an enormous impact on California politics and clearly contribute to its hyperpluralistic character. The secretary of state's official online lobbying directory runs more than 900 pages and is divided into individual registered lobbyists, lobbying firms, and lobbyist employers (http://cal-access.ss.ca.gov/Lobbying). Other groups, including local chapters of statewide groups, operate below the state level to sway county governments, cities, special districts, and school districts. For example, local chambers of commerce often have government relations offices that monitor and influence local government decision-making from a pro-business perspective.

The development and growth of interest groups paralleled the political development of the Golden State. By winning the war against the Southern Pacific Railroad, the Progressives in effect invited other interest groups to participate in California politics. Furthermore, the development of the state's political system coincided with the industrial revolution, the rise of corporate California, and the development of a complex economy. Private-sector interest groups multiplied as a result. As the scope of government enlarged, so did the number of government employees. They formed their own interest groups (such as the American Federation of State, County, and Municipal Employees; the AFL-CIO). By the end of the twentieth century, an increasingly active state government, spurred by new policy demands and a shrinking federal role, required constant vigilance by an ever-growing corps of interest groups.

California Groups: Who Are They?

In contemporary California, interest groups are as diverse as the state itself. Together, they resemble the interest group system in the nation's capital. This hyperpluralistic maze of groups can be divided into five categories based on primary interest or motivation:

1. *Economic Groups.* These groups are primarily motivated by money—income, profits, better salaries, or the economic health of a company or trade. In their view, business regulations, tax policies, labor/management issues, access to markets, occupational safety, and environmental rules can mean financial gain or loss. They range from individual companies to trade associations to employee groups. Some of the biggest, measured in lobbyist spending, include the Association of California Insurance Companies, the Western State Petroleum Association, the California Manufacturers and Technology Association, ARCO, and Chevron.

2. *Professional Groups.* Professionally motivated groups both provide member services and represent group interests in the policy process. They possess economic interests, to be sure, but are also concerned about the regulation of their particular professions. It is common for the state to both regulate entry into certain professions and oversee their conduct. Notable California examples include the California Teachers Association, the California Medical Association, the California Bar Association, and the California Trial Lawyers Association.

3. *Public Agency Groups.* These groups represent various units of government at the state and local level. Representatives are the following: the League of California Cities, the California State Association of Counties, the California Special Districts Association, the Association of California Water Agencies, and the California District Attorneys Association. At least 85 separate cities hire their own lobbyists. As sovereign governments, California's gaming tribes lobby individually and collectively via the California Nations Indian Gaming Association. The state even lobbies itself; executive branch agencies routinely defend their own interests at legislative hearings.

4. *Crosscutting Groups.* These groups do not fit neatly into other categories even though they share some overlapping interests. Cross cutting groups attract members from other groups due to social, ethnic, ideological, religious, or emotional ties. Illustrative are California Church Impact, the Coalition to Abolish Slavery and Trafficking, the Sierra Club, and the Drug Policy Alliance Network. Scholars and policymakers alike call some of these groups "public interest" groups (or PIGs) because their policy goals are not solely economic or professional in nature. Such groups regard themselves as public interest groups because *they* believe their causes serve a larger public interest or an underrepresented group.

5. *Miscellaneous.* This catchall category simply means that some California groups defy reasonable classification. Where do you place the Americans

for Nonsmokers' Rights, the California State Numismatic (coins and medals) Association, the California Thoroughbred Breeders Association, or California Trout, Inc.? Some groups are ad hoc or single issue in nature: they temporarily organize around a "hot" issue or legislative bill or an initiative. When the issue dies, so do they.

6. *Local Groups*. We should not ignore the many interest groups at the local level in California. Of course, some are local chapters of statewide groups such as the Sierra Club, the Chamber of Commerce, and local teachers union affiliates. They provide "on the ground" support for statewide policy positions and are available to lobby legislators during frequent district visits. Others are purely local, focusing on issues of local or regional interest. For example, the San Francisco Bay Area interest groups focusing on mass transit issues have included the Bay Area Transportation and Land Use Coalition, Rescue Muni, Train Riders Association of California, and the San Francisco Bicycle Coalition.

As is the case in national politics, the power of California interest groups ebbs and flows depending on economic trends, and whether their interests match the interests of those in power. For example, members of the California Chamber of Commerce had extraordinary access to Governor Schwarzenegger because they endorsed him and shared his pro-business agenda. The power of labor unions largely depends on the health of the sectors they represent. The clout of unions representing traditional blue-collar trades has fallen as manufacturing jobs have declined in numbers or moved out of state. Today, the power of public-sector unions (schoolteachers, various state employees, law enforcement officers, and health care workers) reflects the growth of these sectors and their claim on public budgets. No wonder public-sector unions now contribute more to political candidates and ballot measures than do traditional trade unions.[36]

People often confuse interest groups with lobbyists. **Lobbyists** are those individuals who represent interest groups in the policy process. In California, they prefer to be called "legislative advocates." All in all, more than 1,700 groups or individuals actually lobby the state government (and are duly registered as lobbyists with the secretary of state). There are so many of them that they have their own group—the Institute of Governmental Advocates (http://californiaiga.org).

How Interest Groups Organize

Interest groups in California have found there is no best method of organizing to function as linkage institutions. The following patterns are common.

In-House Lobbyists. Because policymaking greatly affects their interests, some businesses find that hiring their own in-house lobbyists is the most effective route to adequate representation. For instance, ARCO, Chevron, Allstate Insurance Company, Ford Motor Company, and United Airlines represent themselves in the political process. Some public-sector agencies, such as the City and County of Los Angeles, also have offices in Sacramento. For good measure, many of these interests hire contract lobbying firms to augment their own employees.

Associations. Many individual entities join together around common goals. One can almost fill in the blank: the California Association of Nurserymen, nonprofits, health maintenance organizations (HMOs), winegrape growers, or suburban school districts. These are only a handful of the myriad associations found in the capital. Such groups link members to the policy process through numerous meetings, legislative briefings, and newsletters. The larger ones command substantial resources for lobbying and campaign activity. Because policy priorities are established only at periodic meetings, some associations find it difficult to respond quickly to changing policy developments. Relatively small associations find it economical to contract out even their own management functions.

Contract Lobbyists. Known as "hired guns" in the lobbying world, contract lobbying firms represent multiple clients often in the same general subject area such as education, health, or insurance. Examples of large firms include KP Public Affairs, California Advocates, A-K Associates, Advocation Inc., and California Strategies and Advocacy. KP is regarded as one of the largest, employing 13 lobbyists and serving more than 70 clients ranging from Hertz and Google to the Barona Band of Mission Indians. Some contract lobbyists are former legislators, legislative staff members, and administration officials who apply their knowledge of the process and the policymakers involved. State law requires a cooling-off or waiting period of one year before former legislators can lobby their former colleagues.

"Brown Bag" Advocates. These modestly funded groups may be associations or individuals. Their lack of financial resources sets them apart from the lobbying firms and associations. Large campaign contributions and lavish receptions—tools of the trade for large groups and big firms—are out of the question for groups such as the interfaith group JERICO: A Voice for Justice. Instead, these groups rely on networks of intense believers. For instance, the Children's Defense Fund champions the needs of poor children and relies on a combination of grassroots activism, a telephone network, and "white hat" issues to provide what clout they have. The availability of email and social networking helps groups like these mobilize their members over particular issues.

What Interest Groups Do

When interest groups come to mind, the image is of lobbying—testifying at committee hearings or entertaining legislators. But interest group representation is more complex than that. Several tactics are employed to link group members to the political system.

Public Relations. Interest groups want the general public to know that their respective goals are similar. For instance, subtle and not-so-subtle television commercials equate an oil company with a venerated public television series or as protector of the state's wildlife. Numerous companies have "adopted" public school classrooms to further their image in the community and throughout the state. Many interests now rely on Sacramento-based public relations firms to help craft and sell their messages to the media and other attentive publics. For example, Perry Communications Group offers its clients expertise in these areas: public affairs, issues management, media relations, event planning, advocacy and coalition building, multicultural communication, social marketing, and (even) reputation management.[37]

Electioneering. Once regarded as risky business, interest groups now work both to elect their friends and to defeat their enemies, and they do so both directly and indirectly. The development of political action committees has allowed all manner of groups to contribute directly to legislative campaigns through essentially paper organizations registered with the FPPC. Some cannot afford to contribute much (the brown baggers) or legally cannot (government groups, such as the League of California Cities). To hedge their bets, some political action committees (PACs) contribute to both sides, especially in open-seat elections where no incumbent is running. As noted earlier, PACs feel obligated to attend pricey Sacramento testimonial dinners and "legislative briefings." The money pours in continually whether or not it is an election year. As a result, incumbents often amass huge campaign war chests even before they announce their reelection plans. In recent years, the largest campaign contributors have been a revolving door of casino interests, energy companies, utilities, candidate committees, and both public sector and trade unions (see figure 6.4).

If interest groups wish to fund a campaign unencumbered by contribution limits or onerous reporting, they can make indirect contributions through "independent expenditure committees." Because candidates do not control the raising or spending of those funds, these efforts are outside the authority of the FPPC. Anyone or any group can give any amount. According to the National Institute on Money in State Politics, "independent expenditures are the single largest loophole contributors use to circumvent state limits on direct campaign contributions."[38] Many observers believe that this presumed divorce between contributions and candidates is an artificial one at best. Officeholders are invariably aware of those interests that helped elect them and will be mindful of them when making policy decisions.

Influencing Propositions. As noted earlier, interest groups can sponsor, support, or oppose various statewide ballot measures. Of course, this is a form of electioneering, but it avoids the normal legislative process in most respects. Some of these efforts combine altruism with traditional self-interest and pit major interests against one another. For instance, the California Association of Realtors

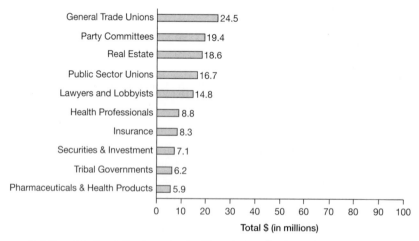

Figure 6.4 Top 10 Contributors to California Campaigns by Sector, 2018

Note: The presence and order of groups on these lists vary depending on the nature of elections that particular year and the presence of certain ballot measures.

Source: National Institute on Money in State Politics, https://www.followthemoney.org.

sponsored Proposition 5 in 2018, which would have reduced property taxes for seniors and the disabled who moved to more expensive homes. Had the initiative passed, it would have increased residential home sales and business for realtors. The association contributed over $10 million to the campaign. On the other side, a liberal coalition of groups including social justice organizations, labor unions, and the Democratic party made numerous small contributions to the No side totaling about $3 million. The measure was defeated by a margin of 60 to 40 percent.

Money and clout do not always persuade voters. In another example from the 2010 primary election, the utility giant PG&E contributed nearly all the $46 million spent in support of Proposition 16. This measure would have required a two-thirds popular vote for public jurisdictions to enter the energy business, such as generating and selling electricity. It lost to a campaign that raised only $136,000.

Political consultants aid interest groups in this process and sometimes even initiate initiatives. Some have been known to "test market" issues to see whether direct mail would be a profitable tactic. If so, these consultants shop around for interest groups to back them. Fellow political consultant Joe Cerrell once observed that these people propose initiatives "so they can make money. It's become a straight business."[39]

Lobbying. **Lobbying** is what interest groups do to influence policymakers. It includes monitoring legislation, drafting bills for legislators to introduce (see box 6.1), testifying at public hearings, and contacting individual members and/or their staffs (see figure 6.5). Lobbyists also pay attention to the executive branch, where agencies issue rules and otherwise implement legislation. Their most important asset is credible, albeit one-sided, information on how a legislative bill or an agency decision will affect their group. According to Patrick McCallum, a Sacramento lobbyist who specializes in higher education, "Much of what we do to be effective lobbyists requires being very analytical. Having a

---

Box 6.1 ★ Case in Point: Who Writes the Bills?

It is not uncommon for a legislator to carry a bill that was proposed, or sponsored, by an interest group lobbyist. A *Sacramento Bee* analysis found that 27 percent of the 4,800 bills introduced in the 2011–12 legislative session indicated a sponsor. However, the actual rate of sponsorship was probably higher because either the legislator did not want to be linked to the sponsoring group or the bill was subsequently rewritten. Sponsorship of a bill can vary from suggested language to be included in a bill to a bill completely written by the lobbyist and handed to the legislator. California, like many states, does not require disclosure of sponsors so the public may not know who is behind a given bill. In some cases, the bill author will refer media inquiries to the sponsoring group. Sponsorship appears to be mutually beneficial to legislators and lobbyists alike; about 60 percent of sponsored bills became law, more than double the passage rate of bills without a sponsor.

Source: Laurel Rosenhall, "California Legislation Often 'Sponsored'—or Even Written—by Interest Groups," *Sacramento Bee*, April 28, 2013.

	AB 748	AB 2119	AB 2601	AB 3080	AB 3131	SB 244	SB 320	SB 607	SB 822	SB 923	SB 1194	SB 1393	SB 1421
TOTAL SCORE %													
GOVERNOR													
Brown (D) — 69.2%	✓	✓	✓	X	X	✓	X	X	✓	✓	✓	✓	✓
SENATOR													
Allen, B (D) — 100%	✓	✓	✓	✓	✓	✓	✓	✓	✓	✓	✓	✓	✓
Anderson (R) — 7.7%	X	X	X	X	X	X	X	X	X	✓	X	X	X
Atkins (R) — 100%	✓	✓	✓	✓	✓	✓	✓	✓	✓	✓	✓	✓	✓
Bates (R) — 0%	X	X	X	X	X	X	X	X	X	X	X	X	X
Beall (D) — 100%	✓	✓	✓	✓	✓	✓	✓	✓	✓	✓	✓	✓	✓
Berryhill (R) — 33.3%	-	-	-	-	-	-	-	-	X	✓	-	X	-
Bradford (D) — 100%	✓	✓	✓	✓	✓	✓	✓	✓	✓	✓	✓	✓	✓
Cannella (R) — 23.1%	X	X	X	X	X	X	X	✓	X	✓	✓	X	X
Chang (R) — 0%	X	X	X	X	X	X	X	X	-	-	X	-	X

Figure 6.5 ACLU 2018 California Legislative Scorecard

Note: The scorecard shows how each legislator and the governor voted on bills important to the ACLU and the percentage of the time that they voted in support of the ACLU's position.

Source: American Civil Liberties Union (ACLU), https://www.aclunc.org/article/2018-california-legislative-scorecard.

technical understanding of why the regulation was created in the first place, why it's there, and its potential impact on your client. Taking a formulaic regulation or statute and 'tweaking' it, using this technical knowledge to legally recreate the regulation in a way that's advantageous to the client, protecting and supporting the client's best interests."[40] Because a large part of what lobbyists do relies on the trust of legislators, developing and maintaining relationships with legislators and their staff are essential. This is why many lobbyists are former legislators or staff, who already have a lengthy contacts list. Because lobbyists are often called the third house of the legislature, we discuss them further in chapter 7.

Influencing Appointments. California's executive branch not only presents lobbying opportunities; it also offers interest groups a place at the table via appointments to several hundred boards and commissions. Some boards regulate or oversee particular professions or businesses (such as the California Architects Board and the California Board of Accountancy), so it behooves professional associations to make sure the "right" members are appointed. To an interest group, the right appointment may be someone with professional expertise and a sympathetic ear. To a governor, it may be an old friend, a long-time supporter, or a termed-out legislative ally. The governor nominates most board and commission members, subject to confirmation by the state senate. With a few exceptions like the California Air Resources Board, most boards and commissions operate well outside public view or media coverage unless they render a controversial decision or the governor attempts a controversial appointment.

Litigation. Interest groups often find the courts making policy through interpreting the state constitution, legislative statutes, and administrative rulings. Therefore, in many situations, the most effective method of participation by an interest group is to litigate. Increasingly, this is the case over budget matters. For instance, the California firefighters' union sued the state over legislation that stripped members of a retirement perk in the CalPERS pension system that allowed them to increase their service years and thus their pension payments. Governor Jerry Brown and the legislature had included the provision in 2012 legislation that sought to boost the solvency of the state's pension funds. Member organizations of CalPERS (e.g., state, cities, and counties) are concerned that the rising costs of the pension systems are displacing funding for other services the agencies provide and that it is unsustainable. Representing the state's cities, the League of California Cities joined Brown's defense of the legislation. In some cases, California is merely a convenient venue to file high-profile suits. For example, a Sacramento mother, aided by the Center for Science in the Public Interest, filed a class action lawsuit against McDonald's, claiming that the chain used toys to lure children into consuming nutritionally unhealthy Happy Meals.

If interest groups do not qualify as litigants, they can file *amicus curiae* (friend of the court) briefs to explain their position in court cases. These legal arguments provide information or advocate a particular result. This is done at every level of California's legal system. For example, the recent initiatives seeking to ban same-sex marriage and the ensuing court cases stemming from those initiatives fostered dozens of amicus briefs on every side of the issue.

CONCLUSION: COMPETING FOR INFLUENCE

California's linkage institutions, indeed, connect Californians with their policy-makers. They essentially compete with each other based on different priorities. *The media competes for consumers.* The media is the daily conduit of political and governmental news, if readers, listeners, and viewers bother to pay attention. During election campaigns, California's television stations link candidates and issue campaigns to voters through paid political advertising. The Internet and social media are increasingly replacing television and newspapers as the key link between Californians and the public square.

Political parties compete for voter attention—unsuccessfully it seems. They face competition from the media, public officials who owe them little, and the variety of constraints—legal and otherwise—placed on parties in California. Parties are augmented by independent groups, for-profit "endorsers," and campaign professionals working for both candidates and causes.

The most formidable competitors to California's political parties are a plethora of interest groups. *Interest groups compete for policymaker attention;* at this they have been highly successful. Theodore Lowi once called this "interest group liberalism," where "the most important difference between liberals and conservatives, Republicans and Democrats, is to be found in the interest groups they identify with."[41] These groups seemingly represent every agenda, population segment, economic interest, social value, or walk of life in the state. In California, where voters commonly make policy via citizen initiatives, interest groups compete for their attention as well. Increasingly, the size, scope, complexity, and diversity of the Golden State are mirrored in and represented by these groups. In a sense, California politics today is a hyperpluralistic mix of interest groups clamoring for access, influence, and power.

KEY TERMS

mass media (p. 105)

elite media (p. 106)

ideological bias (p. 108)

structural bias (p. 109)

political parties (p. 112)

party in the electorate (p. 112)

party in government (p. 112)

party organization (p. 112)

party identification (p. 112)

top-two primary (p. 116)

minor or third parties (p. 117)

county central committees (p. 117)

state central committees (p. 118)

independent groups (p. 118)

slate mailers (p. 119)

interest group (p. 119)

lobbyists (p. 122)

lobbying (p. 122)

REVIEW QUESTIONS

1. Illustrate the concept of linkage with each institution in California politics.
2. How did newspapers evolve in California?

3. What are television's shortcomings as a linkage institution in California politics?
4. How are the Internet and social media changing the way that Californians access political information?
5. How are the major parties organized in California, and why are they so weak?
6. The Democrats captured a two-thirds majority in the legislature in the 2012 election. Why was this a significant development?
7. Trace the rise of interest groups in California and describe the means they use to exercise political influence.
8. To what extent do interest groups mirror the diversity of the state and contribute to hyperpluralism?

WEB RESOURCES

Political Parties

California Democratic Party
https://www.cadem.org

California Republican Party
https://www.cagop.org

These are the chief party websites in California's version of our two-party system. They include party descriptions, news, events, and platforms.

Rough & Tumble

https://www.rtumble.com

Updated daily, this site links you to California newspaper articles and columns dealing with state and local government and politics.

Secretary of State

https://www.sos.ca.gov

Extensive data on political party qualifications as well as interest group spending on elections and lobbying.

National Institute on Money in State Politics

https://www.followthemoney.org

Locate California to access election data including interest group contributions to candidates, ballot measures, and party committees.

7
Legislative Politics

★ ★ ★

LEARNING OUTCOMES

Students will be able to:

★ Describe key developments in California's legislative history.

★ Explain the functions of the legislature.

★ Discuss how representatives are recruited and the benefits once they are there.

★ Identify the organizational structure of the legislature and the role of leadership.

★ Explain how a bill becomes law and the role of interest groups in that process.

IN BRIEF

California's legislature illustrates many of the challenges facing California politics. Increasingly, the legislature also represents the diversity of the Golden State. Once dominated by rural interests and the Southern Pacific Railroad (SPR), its powers were tightly drawn by the Progressives in the early 1900s. After decades of stagnation, the legislature became more professional in the 1960s and, through reapportionment, more reflective of the state's urban growth. Since the 1970s, the legislature has gradually become more partisan and increasingly deadlocked—reflecting the state's growing diversity of interests. Furthermore, once challenged by the term limits imposed by Proposition 140, new looser term limits are expected to strengthen the policy role of a once-envied institution.

THE CALIFORNIA LEGISLATURE performs a variety of functions: policy-making, representation, executive oversight, and civic education. Most legislators attain office through a combination of personal initiative and sponsorship by legislative and party leaders. Although the career trajectories have been altered by term limits, it still offers opportunities for advancement from one house to another, to statewide offices and Congress, and to influential lobbying positions.

In doing its business, the legislature relies heavily on a handful of leaders, including the Assembly Speaker and the Senate president pro tempore. A combination of committees and leadership positions provide structure for the legislative process, one that seems simple on paper but that actually boils with internal politics. Lobbyists provide essential information to members and committees while representing a diversity of interests in California.

Nowadays, the California legislature faces a variety of challenges: a growing number of conflicting interests, social change, economic turmoil, and a restive public dissatisfied with the legislature's performance.

INTRODUCTION: THE ROAD TO PROFESSIONALISM AND DYSFUNCTIONALITY

The California state legislature is an anomaly. It makes statutory policy for the largest state in the Union, incubates political leaders, and is an enviable place to act on behalf of the public interest. It was once regarded as the most professional of all state legislatures and, in many ways, it still is. But today's challenges are sobering. Campaigns are exorbitantly expensive, independent groups routinely exert their influence in high-profile legislative races, and the policy stakes are higher than ever in a $3 trillion economy. The legislature is an easy target of criticism. In fact, no matter who occupies the governor's office, the legislature usually fares far worse in job approval surveys. Believers in representative democracy placed great confidence in legislatures.

Although admitting the executive would share lawmaking power, political philosopher John Locke viewed legislative power as supreme. American colonial legislatures viewed themselves as mini-parliaments. The framers assumed Congress would be first among the three federal branches. In the early 1800s, state legislatures were modeled after the Congress and were considered superior to Congress as policymaking bodies. After all, states had larger policy responsibilities. But by the late 1800s, state legislatures had fallen into disrepute. British observer James Bryce summed up a prevailing attitude: "If [the legislature] meets, it will pass bad laws. Let us therefore prevent it from meeting."[1] By the 1980s, state legislatures had become much more professionalized institutions capable of making effective public policy. Larger staffs, higher salaries, and longer sessions marked this "institutionalization." But by the early 1990s, these trends had backfired. The public began losing confidence in their legislatures as policymaking bodies. Today, state legislatures are undergoing a process of "deinstitutionalization." That is, they are affected more now than ever before by outside forces beyond the control of legislative bodies— public opinion, the media, voter-imposed term limits, and interest groups.[2]

Many of these outside forces contributed to the perception of the legislature as dysfunctional. In response to this dysfunction, and a decade of budget crises, California voters adopted a number of reforms in recent years that have left the institution in flux. Each reform was intended to address problems that have plagued the legislature for decades. The new top-two primary and redistricting process were intended to increase competition in elections and reduce partisanship. The new term-limits law was intended to increase the knowledge and experience of legislators and encourage long-term perspectives. All these reforms have led to questions about whether the intended effects will come to fruition.

Some early indicators point in that direction, such as legislators assuming longer tenures, but we will not have firm answers for a decade or longer. To understand where the legislature is headed, knowing how it has evolved over time is helpful.

California's Legislative History

Criticism of the California legislature is as old as statehood. In fact, the institution has always reflected the state's different political eras. Its history includes the early years, the Progressive Era, stagnation amid change, reform, the golden years, and life during the term-limits era.

The Early Years. In the mid-1800s, the state legislature was an amateur body dominated by farmers and beholden to the SPR. People considered the members of the legislature to be dishonest drunks—the legislature of "1,000 steals" or "1,000 drinks." In 1849, it consisted of 16 senators and 36 assemblymen. By the second constitutional convention in 1878, it had grown to its current size, 40 senators serving four-year terms and 80 assembly members serving two-year terms. The combination of frequent elections, part-time politicians, and domination by the SPR's Political Bureau led to a corrupt "political machine" atmosphere and fueled the rise of the Progressives.

The Progressive Era. Under the righteous indignation of the Progressives, Hiram Johnson assumed the governorship in 1911. That same year, voters approved constitutional amendments limiting what the legislature could do, plus how and when it could do it. They even specified the number of days the legislature could meet. More important, they approved the initiative, a reform that would eventually compete with the legislature for policymaking power. Yet the voters did not support every anti-legislature proposal. Between 1913 and 1925, they rejected six referenda to create a unicameral (one-house) legislature—an idea some Californians still favor. During this period, the legislature lost an important political role in appointing U.S. senators due to the passage of the Seventeenth Amendment to the U.S. Constitution in 1913. It required direct election of senators.

Stagnation amid Change. From the 1920s to the 1960s, California experienced tremendous growth and change. Urban and suburban populations surged, as did the economy. The Depression and World War II brought federal programs and dollars to California. The legislature did not fully reflect these changes; in fact, it resisted them. Like the Congress, representation in the lower house (the Assembly) was based on population; in the upper house (the State Senate), it was based on area. No county could have more than one senator (the so-called **Federal plan**). The result was skewed representation. In fact, as late as the 1960s, San Diego, Los Angeles, and Alameda Counties claimed half the state's population but sent to Sacramento only one senator each. As a result, rural interests predominated and policymaking was fractionalized more by region than by partisanship.[3] Meanwhile, interest groups grew in number as the state's economy became more complex. In the process, individual lobbyists, such as the colorful Artie Samish, gained enormous influence and power.

Reform. In the 1960s, two events led to substantial legislative reforms. First, a legislatively appointed Constitution Revision Commission recommended a series of constitutional amendments allowing the legislature to govern most of its affairs (such as setting salaries and determining calendars). In 1966, voters approved Proposition 1A by a 3–1 margin. Spearheading this effort was Assembly Speaker

Jesse Unruh, who became something of a nationwide guru for legislative professionalization. Under his leadership, the legislature aggressively pursued a policy agenda apart from the governor's. To this day, an unoccupied desk remains on the Assembly floor to memorialize Unruh's legacy. Second, federal courts ruled against California's "Federal plan" in 1965. Both houses in a state legislature would have to be reapportioned based on "one person, one vote."[4] The post-reapportionment election of 1966 produced immediate change. Compared to the old guard, many new legislators were younger, were better educated, possessed more professional backgrounds, and represented more minorities. They also seemed more partisan in their dealings with each other.

The Golden Years. The 1960s and 1970s ushered in still more reforms such as the two-year session adopted in 1972. This allowed bills to remain alive longer, avoided time-consuming reintroductions, and gave bills greater chance of passage. A robust economy allowed the legislature to spend generously on both public policy and on itself. Staffs and salaries grew steadily. Among the 50 states, the California legislature was rated number one by the Citizens' Conference on State Legislatures in 1973.[5] All was not well, however. Proposition 9 (1974) addressed what the public considered an all-too-cozy relationship between legislators and lobbyists. It limited campaign finances and lobbying practices and disallowed campaign work by state-paid legislative staff. Those elected after Proposition 13, passed in 1978, seemed more rigidly conservative than their veteran colleagues. The breakup of the postwar bipartisan consensus (favoring active government and greater spending) appeared complete.

The First Term-Limits Era. Angry Californians passed Proposition 140 in November 1990, which had far-ranging impacts on the legislature, including its members, their staff, and the inner workings of the institution. The measure limited Assembly members to three two-year terms and senators to two four-year terms and severely cut its operating budget. Voter approval of term limits was the culmination of several developments. First, divided government (Republicans controlling the governor's office; Democrats, the legislature) became routine and led to well-publicized policy gridlock. Second, the initiative process increasingly supplanted the legislature as the driving policy force in California. Third, although some voters were gradually "dealigning" from their respective parties (considering themselves to be independents), legislators were becoming *more* partisan in their dealings with each other. Fourth, the media began spotlighting how campaign funds were raised and spent. Then Assembly Speaker Willie Brown doled out excess campaign funds of his own to loyal colleagues.[6] Brown engendered both grudging respect and fear on the part of colleagues. Some observers believe that the primary motivation for 140 was to remove Brown from office. Although the African American Speaker was a source of enmity, other members added to the public's growing frustration with the legislature. They readily sought out service on so-called **juice committees** because industries most interested in those committees would contribute to the committee members' political campaigns.[7] The whole business looked tawdry to ordinary voters. After several well-publicized bribery scandals, the public's general regard for the legislature plummeted.

The Second Term-Limits Era. By the late 1990s, California had experienced a 100 percent turnover in its legislature, and Proposition 140 had profoundly affected the legislature in one area after another. Post-140 legislators were younger, more diverse, and more female than their pre-140 predecessors. Member turn-over meant higher staff turnover and less experience—some say competence—all around. Many observers believed that power shifted to lobbyists and the execu-tive branch, both of which had more experience and institutional memory than their legislative counterparts. Term limits were not the only culprit in the increas-ingly dysfunctional legislature. An ideological divide between Republicans and Democrats had been growing for decades in California, just as it had in the rest of the country, and reached an all-time high in the 2000s. This hyperpartisanship, coupled with a two-thirds vote requirement to pass the budget each year, resulted in frequent budget stalemates that brought state government to a virtual stand-still. By 2012, voters had endured enough and approved a new term-limits law, Proposition 28, which allows members to serve a total of 12 years in the legisla-ture, regardless of the chamber. Early signs point to a more stable legislative envi-ronment. Legislative leaders and committee chairs can now serve longer stints in their posts and develop valuable experience and expertise. Members also seem to be adopting longer-term perspectives, realizing that they have more time in each chamber to reach their policy goals. Unlike their 140 predecessors, post-28 legis-lators do not have to constantly seek electoral opportunities for different offices.

WHAT THE LEGISLATURE DOES

Amid all this change, the California legislature still remains at the core of politics in the Golden State. As with all legislatures, its functions are varied. We discuss four broad and overlapping ones: policymaking, representation, executive over-sight, and civic education.

Policymaking

The first function of a legislature is policymaking. California's legislature addresses a stunning variety of policy issues each year. Among the more than 1,000 laws that took effect in 2019 were bills that did the following:

- Require overtime pay for farmworkers who work longer than 9.5 hours in a day or 55 hours in a week at farms with more than 25 employees
- Ban nondisclosure agreements in sexual misconduct cases that were signed after January 1, 2019
- Require the release of video footage from police body cameras within 45 days of a police shooting
- Allow law enforcement officers to confiscate guns and ammunition when serving gun-violence restraining orders
- Allow Californians to designate their gender as "nonbinary" on official state documents, including driver's licenses[8]

In California, there are three types of legislation: bills, constitutional amend-ments, and resolutions. **Bills** are proposed statutes (laws at the state level) and can be introduced only by legislators. Even the governor's budget (itself a bill) must have a legislator's name on it.[9] **Constitutional amendments** originating in the leg-islature require a two-thirds vote of the members and a concurrence of a majority of voters at a subsequent election. **Resolutions** are merely statements representing the collective opinion of one house or both on miscellaneous subjects. They may commend individual Californians, praise a champion sports team, or express a popular opinion on some fleeting issue. The most important bill, and most important set of policies, the legislature adopts each year is the state budget (see figure 7.1).

Representation

A second legislative function, *representation*, sounds simple enough. In a representative democracy, legislators ideally reflect or act on the wishes of those who elect them. In reality, representation is complex and operates on a variety of levels. This is especially true in a diverse and hyperpluralistic state like California.

Geographic Representation. The first level of representation is geographic. Forty senators and 80 assembly members represent the particular interests of their home districts (see figures 7.2a and 7.2b). Given the state's diversity, from densely urban districts near the coast to sparsely populated districts in the interior, a

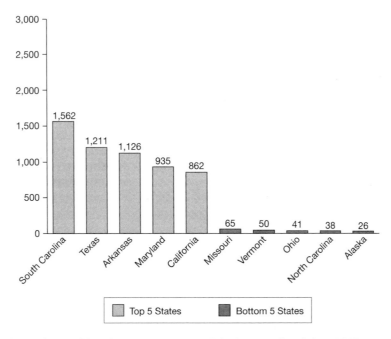

Figure 7.1 How California Compares: Legislative Productivity, 2017
The figure shows the number of bills that each state legislature enacted in the 2017 legislative session. California adopted the fifth-highest number. Many legislatures are "part time" and have much shorter sessions than California.

Source: The Book of the States: Bills and Resolution Introductions and Enactments (The Council of State Governments, 2018), http://knowledgecenter.csg.org/kc/system/files/3.19.2018_0.pdf.

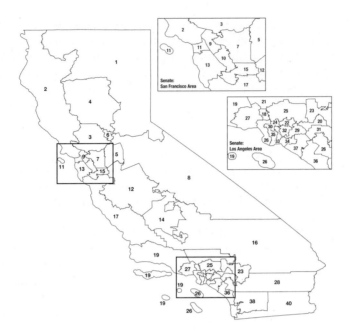

Figure 7.2a California's Senate Districts

Source: California Citizens Redistricting Commission.

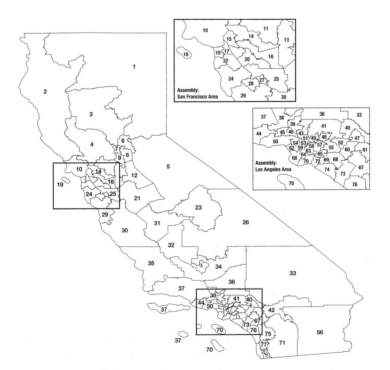

Figure 7.2b California's Assembly Districts

Source: California Citizens Redistricting Commission.

multitude of geographic perspectives translate into a multitude of policy perspectives and priorities. Sometimes these differences are manifest in *local bills* that affect only one district. For instance, a bill adopted in 2014 expedited the environmental review process for building a new NFL stadium in downtown Los Angeles. Legislators may also form coalitions with like-minded members based on common geographic interests, as coastal lawmakers do on offshore oil drilling or Bay Area members do on transportation issues.

Social and Cultural Representation. At another level, legislators often represent the characteristics of constituents back home. Overall, legislators usually approximate their districts in terms of race, religion, or ethnicity, although statewide Latinxs and Asians are underrepresented (see figure 7.3). In recent years, there has been a surge of Latinx and female legislators. In fact, in 2015 California ranked fourth among the 50 states in the percentage of Latinx legislators at 19 percent; New Mexico easily ranked first with 37 percent. As of 2019, 29 percent of California legislators were female, which is about the average for all states.[10] Although legislators arguably seek out the good of California as a whole, they also desire to "represent" their racial, ethnic, or other affinity group. For example, several caucuses (Latino, Black Caucus, Asian, and LGBT [lesbian, gay, bisexual, and transgendered]) are organized around this motivation. California's female legislators are sensitive to family and health issues and consider themselves uniquely qualified to deal with them.[11] Their bipartisan caucus also seeks to increase the participation and representation of women in state government. Sometimes, social representation is highly personal. Four legislators once formed

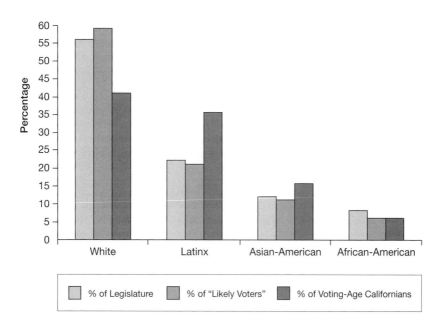

Figure 7.3 Comparing the Demographics of the Legislature with the Electorate

Source: Matt Levin, Elizabeth Castillo, and John Osborn D'Agostino, "Finding Yourself in the California Legislature—Or Not," CalMatters, https://calmatters.org/articles/california-legislature-diversity-demographics. 2017 American Community Survey; Public Policy Institute of California.

a "family caucus" to support and defend state programs for the mentally disabled; their reason quite simply was that each has a family member in need of such programs.

Specific Representation. Individual constituents sometimes need specific representation, that is, individual attention. Constituent service, called "casework," is the vehicle through which this function takes place. For instance, many constituents seek help dealing with assorted state bureaucracies such as the Department of Motor Vehicles. Casework often involves little more than researching pending bills or listening to callers vent their frustrations over the telephone. District office staffers, including college and university interns, do the bulk of this work.

Functional Representation. Functional representation refers to the specific policy interests and preferences that legislators bring to Sacramento. Former teachers, farmers, or city officials might logically gravitate to education, agriculture, or local government committees. Other members might wish to represent key industries in their districts, such as computer technology. As table 7.1

Table 7.1 California's Standing Legislative Committees

Assembly (32)	*Senate (23)*
Accountability and Administrative Review	Agriculture
Aging and Long-Term Care	Appropriations
Agriculture	Banking and Financial Institutions
Appropriations	Budget and Fiscal Review
Arts, Entertainment, Sports, Tourism, and Internet Media	Business, Professions, and Economic Development
Banking and Finance	Education
Budget	Elections and Constitutional Amendments
Business and Professions	Energy, Utilities, and Communications
Education	Environmental Quality
Elections and Redistricting	Governance and Finance
Environmental Safety and Toxic Materials	Governmental Organization
Governmental Organization	Health
Health	Human Services
Higher Education	Housing
Housing and Community Development	Insurance
Human Services	Judiciary
Insurance	Natural Resources and Water
Jobs, Economic Development, and the Economy	Public Safety
Judiciary	Rules
Labor and Employment	Transportation and Housing
Local Government	Veterans Affairs
Natural Resources	
Privacy and Consumer Protection	
Public Employment and Retirement	
Public Safety	
Revenue and Taxation	

Assembly (32)	Senate (23)
Rules	
Transportation	
Utilities and Energy	
Veterans Affairs	
Water, Parks, and Wildlife	

Source: California State Assembly and Senate.

portrays, the legislature's policy committees are organized around a rich diversity of functional interests. Although constituents may not routinely think in these functional terms, interest groups do. Each committee is monitored by a familiar assortment of interest groups (such as the Aging and Long-Term Care Committee by senior groups).

Perceptual Representation. Legislators themselves perceive their representational roles in different ways. British philosopher and member of Parliament Edmund Burke once distinguished between trustee roles and delegate roles. **Trustees** rely primarily on their own best judgment when voting on legislation rather than the wishes (fleeting wishes, thought Burke) of their constituents who elected them. **Delegates** lean primarily on those constituent wishes and deliberately seek them out. Modern political scientists have added the politico role. **Politicos** combine the two roles depending on how controversial specific issues are locally.[12] For instance, even though he harbored personal reservations about several "Three Strikes" bills, which imposed long sentences on repeat criminal offenders, then state senator Leroy Greene concluded he would nonetheless support them. "I'm going to vote for these turkeys because my constituents want me to." These perceptions are not static. One study of the California Assembly suggested that, over time, legislators change their role perceptions. Why? It could be that legislators vote inconsistently or do not think about whether they are trustees, delegates, or politicos.[13]

Executive Oversight

A third function of California's legislature is **executive branch oversight**. The state constitution mandates some of these oversight activities. For instance, the Senate must confirm various gubernatorial appointments to commissions (such as Fish and Game, and the University of California Regents). Both the Senate and the Assembly confirm gubernatorial appointments to fill vacancies in constitutional offices. Like Congress, the legislature can remove statewide officeholders and judges through a rarely used impeachment process. The Joint Legislative Audit Committee works with the Bureau of State Audits to assess the financial and operational activities of various state agencies and programs. Such investigations may uncover various spending abuses by state employees.

A routinely used oversight tool is the "power of the purse." This phrase actually refers to several processes. In the **authorization process**, the legislature gives authority for an agency program to exist. In the **appropriation process**, the legislature creates spending authority, thereby allowing the agency to implement the program. When the legislature considers the annual budget, budget committees in each chamber perform both functions under one track. Outside the budget process, any bill authorizing spending must be heard by the appropriations committees, usually in addition to the policy committees. In doing this work, legislative committees hear from executive branch officials as much as from private-sector lobbyists.

Civic Education

The final function involves the *civic education* of constituents. Legislators are expected to educate people about the legislative process and California politics generally. In Sacramento, they meet with district constituents, students, professional lobbyists, and many interest group members who visit the capitol. Legislators explain their version of how the process works and why favored legislation is so difficult to pass or afford. Back in the districts, legislators speak to service clubs and community gatherings, issue press releases, hold "office hours," and confer with local chapters of statewide groups. Each activity provides an opportunity for them to explain the process and their views on policy. In many ways, the members' websites serve the same function.

These four legislative functions commingle constantly. A constituent complaint about the Department of Motor Vehicles might lead to a member inquiry about how the department operates. Urban and rural legislators sit side by side on committees, learning to appreciate the geographic diversity they bring to their work. Historically underrepresented groups in the legislature, such as African Americans and Latinxs, form their own bicameral caucuses to make social representation more visible and deliberate in the eyes of colleagues. Those more theoretical roles also intermingle. Legislators who think they are "trustees" relative to their districts often behave like "delegates," not of their constituents but of interest groups with whom they more routinely work.

GETTING THERE AND STAYING THERE

Why people seek *any* public office is an interesting question to political scientists. Joining a legislature often means giving up one's privacy, normal family life, career continuity, and, for some people, substantial income. What motivates California candidates are especially fascinating. Because being a legislator is a full-time job (and then some, legislators would argue), a member must maintain two residences, even if one is a small Sacramento apartment. Family dislocation (Where do you put the kids in school? What about a working spouse?) and frequent travel to the district create stresses most Californians can only imagine. Yet, the price is worth it to many members who attempt to convert their beliefs into public policy.

Recruitment

The initial decision to run for the legislature is determined by both personal desire and requests by others. Three patterns of candidate recruitment have emerged in California.

Self-Starters. Some individuals run for the legislature because they desire to implement policy preferences or begin political careers. They talk themselves into it. Some come from local offices such as school boards, city councils, and county boards of supervisors. They figure they can do as good a job as the legislators they meet coping with state policies and legislative mandates. Other aspiring legislators become interested in the impact of state policy on their own professions. Farmers, doctors, and members of "brokerage" occupations (law, real estate, and insurance) often fit this category. Some gain valuable policy and political experience as staff members in Sacramento or in district offices. Others spend large sums of their own wealth to run for office, claiming independence from special interests.

Sponsorship. Some legislative candidates are sponsored by or recruited to run by others. In California, sponsorship comes not so much from local party officials but from legislative leaders and state party officials in Sacramento. In recent years, the Assembly Speaker, Senate president pro tempore, and partisan caucus staffs have provided both encouragement and campaign funding to promising candidates. In 2018, there was a considerable effort made to recruit more female candidates, propelled by the Women's March and the #MeToo movement, which helped increase the percentage of female legislators. What do these legislative leaders look for in potential candidates? They generally seek candidates who will be good legislators *and* who will support them in future leadership battles. The ability to win always helps.

Combination Pattern. In recent years, many legislative races have featured a combination of self-starting and sponsorship. Given the entrepreneurial nature of California politics and the historically weak local political parties, many candidates need self-starter qualities, such as a burning ambition to run and win. Yet, these people alone cannot marshal the resources needed to win. Remember, compared to many states, California's legislature is relatively small: 40 senators and 80 assembly members who represent more than 40 million people. That translates into huge districts—roughly 1 million people per Senate district and 500,000 people per Assembly district. No other state legislature has near these per-district populations. Face-to-face voter contact in some districts necessarily gives way to political advertising. Media costs, the largest chunk of any modern campaign budget, are expensive in California. Unless a candidate is wealthy, outside help is essential. Once they are nominated, legislative candidates may be showered with resources including endorsements, party assistance, funding from legislative leaders, PAC contributions, and soft money expenditures.

The Power of Incumbency. Once elected, incumbents enjoy tremendous advantages when running for reelection. They attract the vast majority of PAC contributions, can "draft" staffers as campaign aides, command media attention, and benefit from districtwide name recognition. Interestingly, in the case of presumably competitive open-seat primaries—where incumbents are vacating office voluntarily or due to term limits—one candidate per office per party is commonplace. This suggests considerable candidate sorting even before candidates file nomination papers. The best indicator of the power of incumbency is the reelection rate. In 2016, 93 percent of incumbents who sought office were reelected to the California legislature.

Why They Stay: Rewards of Office

Given the frustrations of the legislative life in California (hyperpartisanship, gridlock, incessant travel, and family pressures), one might wonder why legislators want to stay and hate to leave. What drives them to remain? For instance, why do they run for the Senate when their Assembly terms expire? The reasons are several.

Policy Achievement. Given the problems and challenges facing California, finding solutions and crafting statewide policy are primary goals for many legislators. These members have genuine public service goals, and they operate in Sacramento and back home with those goals in mind. Serving on just the right committees and moving into leadership positions on those committees are paramount to policy achievers. In the first term limits era, members brought a sense of policy urgency because they faced a short time in office. Under Proposition 28, legislators' time horizon for policy achievement has lengthened, giving them more time to attain their goals.

Material Benefits. Many state legislatures provide poor salaries and working conditions. Not in California, however, where an independent citizens compensation commission sets members' annual salaries. In 2018, a legislator's salary was $110,459, the nation's highest. Legislative leaders such as the Assembly Speaker and the Senate president pro tempore earn somewhat more. On top of that, out-of-town legislators receive a tax-free $142 stipend for unvouchered living expenses each day their house is "in session," a figure which can be upward of $30,000 in largely tax-free compensation annually.[14] As a result, brief "check-in" sessions are commonplace, even when there is little business to conduct. Additional benefits include a cell phone, health insurance, and funds to hire staff and rent office space. After several high-profile arrests for drunk driving, in 2015, the Senate even hired drivers to provide a 24-hour dial-a-ride service for senators who may become too intoxicated to drive.

Psychic Satisfaction. If legislators do not bring big egos to Sacramento, they acquire them there. They have many staff members to help with policy, research, personal, party, and leadership responsibilities. Deference is paid to them constantly. Yet, although the psychic rewards of working on the state's most pressing problems are typically highlighted by legislators and their staff, the working environment in and around the capitol has long been likened to a college fraternity, fraught with sexism and misogyny. This was brought to light in 2017 when about 150 women working in the capital, including several female legislators, signed a letter attesting to these conditions (see box 7.1). In response, the legislature took a number of steps, including the creation of a sexual harassment investigation unit, to improve the working environment.

Careerism, Then and Now. Careerism and political ambition are related. According to political scientists, political ambitions may be discrete (short-term service with a return to private life), static (making a long-run career out of a particular office), or progressive (using an office as a stepping stone to still higher office).[15] Until Proposition 140, the California legislature had become known as a hothouse for political careers. The power of incumbency and relatively safe districts assured some job security. By state legislative standards, the pay and perks were good and needed to be because the work was increasingly full-time. Considered a dead end in many other states, legislative service in California allowed rapid advancement and rewarded political ambition and policy entrepreneurship.

With the new term-limits law in effect, the direction of careerism is unclear. Under Proposition 140, two distinct patterns arose over time. For some, it

---

Box 7.1 ★ California Voices: We're Done with This

In October 2017, more than 140 women working in the state capital, including legislative staff, lobbyists, legislators, and public relations professionals penned an open letter to the *Los Angeles Times* that the culture of intimidation, sexism, and sexual harassment was no longer tolerable. Here is an excerpt of that letter calling for fundamental changes to the working conditions and culture of the political world in Sacramento:

> Each of us has endured, or witnessed or worked with women who have experienced some form of dehumanizing behavior by men with power in our workplaces. Men have groped and touched us without our consent, made inappropriate comments about our bodies and our abilities. . . . Men have made promises, or threats, about our jobs in exchange for our compliance, or our silence. They have leveraged their power and positions to treat us however they would like. Why didn't we speak up? Sometimes out of fear. Sometimes out of shame. Often these men hold our professional fates in their hands. They are bosses, gatekeepers, and contacts. Our relationships with them are crucial to our personal success. . . . We have felt powerless to stop the cycle. We're done with this. Each of us who signed this op-ed will no longer tolerate the perpetrators or enablers who do.

Source: "Read the Letter: Women in Politics Call Out 'Pervasive' Culture of Sexual Harassment," *Los Angeles Times*, October 16, 2017, http://documents.latimes.com/women-california-politics-call-out-pervasive-culture-sexual-harassment.

---

effectively aborted a long-term career as an elected official. For others, it altered the stepping-stone process. In what has been called the term-limits shuffle, legislators constantly cast about for other offices—federal, state, and even local—to extend their public careers. Some landed appointments to head executive branch agencies or sit on relatively obscure but well-paid boards and commissions. In recent years, politicians have extended their careers in local elected offices, especially in big cities, waiting for a crack at a more prestigious seat, such as the House of Representatives. Now able to spend 12 years in one chamber, legislators are likely to stay put in one office for longer, or at least until a permanent seat (i.e., without term limits) opens at the federal or the local level. Initial evidence indicates that legislative turnover is slightly down since Proposition 28 took effect.

In addition to changes brought by Proposition 28, other recent reforms are likely to alter legislative ambitions still further. First, when voters turned the redistricting process over to an independent citizen commission, it prevented the legislature from drawing district boundary lines that benefit incumbents or the major political parties. This has produced more competitive districts that make current officeholders' electoral future more uncertain, especially every 10 years following the new reapportionment process. Second, similar to the new redistricting process, the top-two primary is expected to increase electoral competition, which should make incumbents more vulnerable in the future. Although these reforms may help knock off a few incumbent legislators, the power of incumbency is likely to remain strong.

How They Stay: Reapportionment Politics

To understand reapportionment, you must understand the motives of legislators. Willingness to stay in office is not the same as staying; ask any incumbent who loses a reelection bid. But incumbents generally know what it takes to get elected time and time again. More than challengers, they can afford the campaign techniques described in chapter 5. Also, they fully understand that campaigning is territorial: the boundaries of a legislative district can spell victory or defeat. How are these boundaries drawn? After each decade, the U.S. Census Bureau counts the population and gathers other demographic data. Historically, **reapportionment** involved the legislature redrawing district lines for the U.S. House of Representatives, the state Assembly, and the state senate to reflect population growth and movement within the state. As with other bills, the governor would need to sign any reapportionment plan. The California Constitution requires that any plan consider, to the extent possible, the "geographic integrity" of existing city and county boundaries.

In reality, the legislature rarely followed that constitutional guideline because population shifts and communities of interest are not the only factors in redrawing district boundaries. Reapportioning districts for partisan or other advantage is called **gerrymandering**. There are three types: (1) **Partisan gerrymandering** means either "splintering" a district (dividing either Republicans or Democrats among several districts to dilute their strength) or "packing" a district (say, concentrating Democrats into one district to enhance election chances for Republicans in other districts). (2) **Incumbent gerrymandering** protects incumbents regardless of party. Often called "sweetheart" gerrymandering, this type is sometimes found under divided government conditions. That incumbents protect each other should hardly be surprising. (3) **Racial gerrymandering** has historically been used in the United States to dilute the strength of racial minorities. In recent years, it has been used, often in the South, to concentrate minority voting strength—often ensuring victory for minority candidates. Although this goal may be laudable, the U.S. Supreme Court has rejected the most obvious racial gerrymanders as a violation of the Fourteenth Amendment's equal protection clause.

When California legislators faced the task of redistricting, previous reapportionment efforts colored their efforts. In the 1980s, redistricting maps drawn by Democrats favored their party, triggering a bitter dispute with Republicans that was eventually resolved by the state Supreme Court. By the 1990s, the redistricting process became more complicated as minority groups sought more districts that would represent their interests. They were aided by the *Voting Rights Act of 1965* (as amended in 1982 and interpreted by the courts), which required state legislatures to *create* racial and ethnic majority voting districts if at all feasible. Political scientist Bruce Cain called this form of racial gerrymandering the "affirmative action gerrymander."[16]

In 1991, after a prolonged redistricting stalemate between Republican governor Pete Wilson and legislative Democrats, the state Supreme Court appointed a panel of "masters" (retired judges) to redraw the districts presumably from scratch, taking into account those legal mandates. The resulting 1992 reapportionment plan dealt a stunning blow to many incumbents—forcing some into retirement, others into campaigns against colleagues, and still others into premature stepping-stone races. Following Proposition 140, that reapportionment was truly a bitter pill for California's legislature.

The 2001 reapportionment was an altogether different experience. With little or no debate, the state senate approved the new maps on two votes: 38 to 2 and 40 to 0. The Assembly approved the maps on a bipartisan 58–10 vote. What happened to the rancor of earlier battles? First, sizable voting majorities in the Assembly and the Senate (50–30 and 26–14, respectively) gave Democrats a substantial advantage in redrawing the maps; Republicans were at their mercy. Just retaining current Republican districts would be something of a victory for them. Second, although California's ethnic minorities had been growing in the 1990s, eking out still more "majority-minority" districts was unlikely. In the end, the 2001 reapportionment process was a classic incumbent protection effort. As a result, it locked in (to the extent redistricting can) Democratic majorities and prior gains made by the state's minorities.

The 2011 Reapportionment

The 2001 reapportionment angered both reform groups and voters. Only a handful of legislative seats changed parties during the 2000s, plausibly reducing voter turnout because election outcomes were foregone conclusions (see box 7.2).[17] Other analysts traced the ideological extremes in the California legislature (more conservative Republicans and more liberal Democrats than in the past) and the policy gridlock that ensued to safe districts gerrymandered by incumbents.[18]

Although angry voters rejected a Schwarzenegger-backed measure to transfer redistricting power from the legislature to a panel of retired judges, they did approve a ground-breaking reform in 2008. **Proposition 11** was an initiative constitutional amendment and statute granting remapping authority over legislative districts and the five-member Board of Equalization (BOA) to a 14-member independent Citizen Redistricting Commission. In 2010, an initial group of 30,000 interested individuals was winnowed down to 4,500 applicants and eventually 14 commissioners by a complex and laborious selection process. In November 2010, voters added to the commission's purview California's 53 congressional districts that had been exempted under Proposition 11. The transfer was complete. The voters had removed all redistricting authority from the state legislature for the first time in California's history.

What would be different this time? Seemingly everything. The commission itself was made up of five Democrats, five Republicans, and four others, but none were seasoned politicos or even related to them. In addition to meeting various federal requirements (one person, one vote), district boundaries had to (1) maintain the geographic integrity of cities, counties, neighborhoods, and "communities of interest"; (2) be geographically compact; and (3) nest two Assembly districts into one Senate district and 10 Senate districts within one BOA district. Furthermore, the commission could *not* favor particular incumbents, political candidates, or political parties. Muddying these uncharted waters were the initial census results. The Latinx population had grown substantially in the 2000s as had inland California. The final maps approved by the commission in August 2011 made many state legislative and congressional districts more competitive and viewed incumbents neutrally.[19]

Although the new reapportionment commission was designed to be as nonpolitical as possible, it was not immune from partisan attacks. Republicans criticized the selection of technical experts who drew the actual maps, alleging that

Box 7.2 ★ How California Compares: Electoral Competition

One of the reasons for the adoption of the Citizen Redistricting Commission was the lack of electoral competition in legislative districts. But is California an outlier when it comes to this level of competition? Political scientists use numerous ways to compare electoral competition between states. One way is to look at the percentage of people in a state who live in legislative districts where the winner won with *10 percent or less* of the vote. In California's 2012 and 2014 elections, only *18 percent* of Californians lived in these competitive districts. California is not the worst by this measure when compared with other states. Georgia was the lowest with 2 percent, followed by Hawaii, Texas, Mississippi, and Utah at 4 percent. West Virginia (36 percent), Maine (35 percent), and Minnesota (31 percent) were the highest. In California, this low competition level is also an indicator of how Democrats are increasing their dominance in the state.

Source: Keith E. Hamm and Nancy Martorano Miller, "Legislative Politics in the States," in *Politics in the American States*, eds. Virginia Gray, Russell L. Hanson, and Thad Kousser (Washington, DC: CQ Press, 2018), 199.

the firm chosen had partisan leanings that favored Democrats. Dueling opinion pieces in state newspapers from partisan supporters either critiqued the process or defended it, in the case of Democrats. Once drawn, Republicans feared that a two-thirds majority—a critical threshold for legislative powers—was within reach of the Democrats. Republicans successfully placed a referendum on the ballot to overturn the Senate maps, claiming they violated legal requirements and diluted Latinx influence, normally a concern for Democrats. After a state Supreme Court ruling kept the maps intact for the 2012 elections, Republicans dropped their referendum effort (Proposition 40), leaving it on the ballot with no funding or support behind it.

California is now one of only five states that have an independent commission that draws district boundaries. The rest allow the process to be controlled by the legislature in one form or another. The authority of independent commissions was challenged in an Arizona lawsuit that reached the U.S. Supreme Court in 2015. Commission opponents argued that the federal Constitution gives exclusive authority to state legislatures to draw district maps. A ruling against the commissions would have potentially threatened the authority of California's independent commission to draw congressional district boundaries but not state legislative boundaries. However, the court ruled in favor of independent commissions, keeping the powers of California's independent commission intact.

ORGANIZING TO LEGISLATE

No matter who redraws legislative districts, making laws is still the legislature's primary task. Thousands of bills may be introduced during each two-year session of the California legislature. When the great jurist Oliver Wendell Holmes observed that "every opinion tends to become a law," one might have thought he was commenting on California's legislature. On paper, the process of making a law seems straightforward enough. In reality, it is complex and fraught with intrigue and, particularly at the end of sessions, chaos.

The California Constitution requires a bicameral legislature, consisting of a lower house (an 80-member Assembly) and an upper house (a 40-member Senate). Assembly members serve two-year terms; senators, four-year terms. Under the new term-limits law (Proposition 28), legislators can serve up to 12 years in either chamber. Although both houses behave similarly in many respects, there are differences. The state Senate is more prestigious due to its smaller size and longer terms. Senators tend to be more politically experienced; many gained that experience in the Assembly. Senators can seek still higher office in the middle of their terms without losing their seats—a "free ride." Compared to the Speaker-dominated Assembly, senators are more independent. Each finds publicity easier to attain. As a body, the Senate can more easily challenge a governor by not confirming gubernatorial appointments that require Senate confirmation. Also, the Senate seems quieter and more deliberative than the rough-and-tumble Assembly.

How does the legislature itself organize to do its work? The process in both houses leans heavily on leadership, a committee system, and professional staffs.

The Role of Leadership

Groups large and small need leaders to manage what they do. Legislatures are no different. In his study of state legislative politics, Alan Rosenthal listed six different leadership tasks: organizing for work, processing legislation, negotiating agreements, dispensing benefits, handling the press, and maintaining the institution.[20] California's legislative leaders perform each of these tasks. The key positions are discussed in this section.

Assembly Speaker. One of the most fascinating offices in California politics is the Assembly Speaker, the pinnacle of what used to be called a "self-inflicted dictatorship." Once elected by the entire Assembly, the majority party caucus has chosen recent Speakers. A *party's caucus* is its total membership in the chamber when gathered to do business. Speakers balance power and policy—perpetuating their own power while using it to achieve policy goals. In part, this is done by controlling committees: determining the number and titles of committees, assigning all members to committees (with the exception of the Rules Committee), controlling the selection of other leadership positions within the Speaker's party, managing floor action, enforcing Assembly customs, and assigning office space and some staff. When asked why he had assigned a newly elected critic of his a smelly, windowless broom closet of an office, then Speaker Willie Brown replied, "I didn't have anything smaller." No wonder he nicknamed himself the "ayatollah of the legislature."

Jesse Unruh was the first Assembly Speaker to buttress the role of the office. Under his leadership in the 1960s, the Assembly became a powerful policymaking force in state government. Brown occupied the post from 1980 to 1996. He was the first African American to hold the post and served longer than any predecessor. His lengthy tenure provided leadership, stability, and operational predictability. His policy expertise, ability to craft legislative deals, and fundraising prowess kept his post secure.

The old term-limits law (Proposition 140) had a mixed impact on this powerful office. On one hand, it resulted in a number of firsts for the position. Cruz

Bustamante became the first Latino Speaker and others followed, including Antonio Villaraigosa, Fabian Nunez, and, most recently, John Perez. Karen Bass also became the first African American woman in the nation to head a legislative body. On the other hand, term limits presented a conundrum for the majority party that selected the new Speaker. The party had to choose between a veteran legislator who would be termed out shortly or a relatively inexperienced colleague who could provide more continuity. In short, the new Speakers became power-limited lame ducks the moment they assumed the position.

After a brief stint with a Speaker from San Diego (Toni Atkins), the position returned to an Assembly member from the Los Angeles area, Anthony Rendon, in 2016. He is the first Speaker to fall under the new term limits law and could therefore serve until 2024. He was first elected in 2012.

Other Assembly Posts. Several other leadership posts round out the legislative elite in the assembly. The *Speaker pro tempore* is a member of the Speaker's party and exercises the powers of the Speaker in the latter's absence. Although this individual is technically chosen by the entire Assembly, the Speaker's choice gets the nod. The Speaker pro tempore usually presides during floor sessions, allowing the Speaker to mingle with other members. The *assembly majority* and *minority leaders* are selected from their respective party caucuses. They represent caucus interests on the Assembly floor; the latter communicates minority wishes to the Speaker. Several whips monitor legislation and secure floor votes from caucus members.

Senate President Pro Tempore. In the U.S. Senate, the vice president can preside and vote in case of a tie but rarely performs either function. In the California Senate, the lieutenant governor has comparable powers but rarely uses them. Day-to-day leadership is in the hands of the **president pro tempore** (pro tem for short). Although the entire Senate votes to fill this post, the majority party invariably chooses one of its own. In the 1990s and into the 2000s, there was an implicit understanding between the Assembly and Senate that the leader of the Senate would hail from the Bay Area and the Assembly Speaker would come from the Los Angeles area. These regions both had the numbers (i.e., voting members) to make this happen. In the Senate, this pattern began with the selection of Bill Lockyer (D, Oakland) in 1994. He was followed by two consecutive pro tempores from the Bay Area until Darrell Steinberg (D-Sacramento) broke this tradition in 2008. This pattern was further disrupted in 2014 when Kevin de León (D-Los Angeles) was elected to the post. He became the first Latino to hold the position in state history. Toni Atkins (D-San Diego) succeeded de León in 2018. She became the first woman and first openly gay member to serve as pro tempore. She also became the first person in 150 years to serve as both Speaker and pro tempore.

On paper, the Senate pro tempore appears less powerful than the Assembly Speaker. However, under the old, stricter term limits, the pro tempore emerged as the more influential power broker because of constant turnover in the Assembly leadership and longer terms in the Senate. With looser term limits, the power may flow back to the Assembly Speaker. Much of the pro tempore's power stems from chairing a five-member *Rules Committee*. The other four members consist of two senators from each party caucus. Its powers are comparable to both the Assembly Speaker and the Assembly Rules Committee.

Senate President Pro Tempore Toni Atkins (left) on the floor of the Senate

Assembly Speaker Anthony Rendon speaking to college students

The Committee System

To carry out their policymaking responsibilities, modern legislatures must organize into committees—much as Congress does. The committee process recognizes that screening legislation takes specialization and division of labor. California's legislature is divided into numerous committees. Combined, they form a *committee system*: the web of relationships among a number of committees required to enact policy.

Several kinds of committees constitute the committee system in California's legislature. The job of permanent **standing committees** is to process legislation. In other words, they formulate public policy (see table 7.1 for a complete list of these committees). Members seek assignment to certain policy committees because of former occupations, current policy interests, or the possibility of receiving campaign contributions. Some women legislators have preferred to serve on committees dealing with human services issues such as children and welfare.[21]

Several other committees deserve mention. **Fiscal committees** handle bills that require the spending of money. Both houses have appropriations and budget committees devoted to this task. Members seeking power, prestige, or institutional importance covet these assignments. **Conference committees** are convened if the two houses produce different versions of the same bill; their job is to iron out the differences and send unified bills back to both houses for final passage. **Select committees** study various issues facing California with long-term solutions in mind. Both houses have dozens of them. They cover topics ranging from e-commerce, the Colorado River, and wine to California–Mexico relations, school safety, and mobile homes. Various **joint committees** include members from both houses. They consider matters of common concern such as fisheries, the arts, and homeland security.

Why all these seemingly extra committees? They can give needed visibility to emerging issues such as border conflicts and school safety. But they also create added chairmanships, opportunities to hire additional staff, and pools of potential campaign contributors. Not only are there more committees than in the past, many standing committees—the workhorses of the legislature—are larger than ever. For example, of its 80 members, fully 32 are on the Assembly Budget Committee. Scheduling conflicts are commonplace, and quorums are elusive as members juggle their time. According to Jim Knox, executive director of California Common Cause, "The idea of members listening to actual testimony at these hearings has become sort of quaint." As a result, committees are less deliberative than in the past.[22]

The Staff

One mark of a professional legislature is a professional staff. Before the California legislature became full-time in the 1960s, a few staff offices met its needs for information and analysis: the Legislative Counsel of California (created in 1913 to help draft bills), the California State Auditor (established in 1955 to provide fiscal oversight of state agencies), and the Legislative Analyst's Office (created in 1941 to give nonpartisan advice on fiscal and policy issues). The Analyst annually issues a series of reports that reviews the governor's budget and makes fiscal recommendations to the legislature. Over the years, it has developed a national reputation for expertise, solid analysis, and nonpartisanship.[23] In some ways, these offices have been islands of objectivity in a sea of subjective, partisan wrangling. That is, they serve the legislature as an institution and not the agendas of individual members.

As committees grew in number, so did committee staffs. In Sacramento, professional committee staffers are called "consultants." Given the many policy hats members must wear, the expertise these consultants provide is essential to the committee system. They may earn as much as or more than their elected bosses.[24] In addition to the consultants, each house maintains separate staff to analyze pending bills and to do long-range research. Leadership staffs assist the house officers for both parties. Party staffs assist the respective party caucuses. In addition to secretaries and clerks, both houses employ undergraduate- and graduate-level interns to perform a variety of tasks. Some interns land full-time jobs as a result. More than a few have eventually become legislators.

Proposition 140 affected the legislative staff system in direct and indirect ways. Historically known for their expertise and relative objectivity, many legislative staffers became more partisan. According to some critics, advocacy overshadowed analysis, and political operatives eclipsed policy experts. On the other hand, staff under 140 served as institutional memory for new members and provided a level of stability amid constant legislative turnover. Some observers felt that staff acquired too much power because inexperienced legislators looked to them for policy guidance. With longer stints in office for legislators as a result of Proposition 28, staff influence may subside a bit as new members gain more and more institutional memory and policy expertise.

THE LEGISLATIVE PROCESS

In truth, passing most legislation requires neither vision nor political courage. Constituents back home could hardly care less about many bills; most are minor changes to existing law, business regulations, and policies that affect the relative few. But all bills, large or small, must survive the same process. As figure 7.4 illustrates, the flow of legislation is quite simple—on paper. Internal deadlines impose additional structure on the process. For example, the last day to introduce a bill is in late February. The last day for bills to be passed out of a house of origin is in late May. August 31 is the last day for each house to pass bills. Fiscal committees impose and must meet additional deadlines. Beyond the deadlines and behind the scenes, informal processes work to speed up, slow down, pass, or defeat bills. When people quote German Chancellor Otto Von Bismarck—"Laws are like sausages, it is better not to see them being made"—they likely are referring to these informal processes.

Bill Introduction

An idea for a law can come from any number of sources, such as staff, lobbyists, executive agencies, constituents, and the member's experience (see box 7.1). For example, one legislator introduced a bill to electronically monitor perpetrators of domestic violence after a constituent suggested it. The Legislative Counsel's office takes that idea and drafts the necessary legal language. The legislator who formally submits a bill is its author and is expected to shepherd it through the process; coauthors or cosponsors lend their names as supporters but do

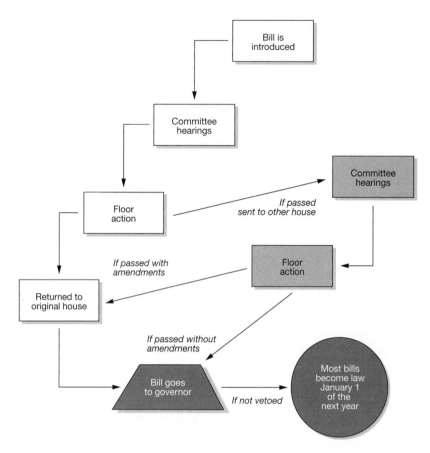

Figure 7.4 California Legislative Process in Brief

little else. Members must introduce bills by late February, but what if they are not ready by then? They can introduce "spot bills" containing nonsubstantive language that will be eventually replaced with substantive changes the author really wants.

Committee Consideration

In both houses, the respective Rules Committees assign bills to committees for hearings. The fate of a bill may hinge on which committee hears it. All spending bills must be heard by each house's appropriations committee. During a typical hearing, the committee hears testimony on the bill from its author, government agencies, and/or interest groups. Managing enough committee votes for a "do-pass" recommendation can be tricky business. A majority of all committee members is required whether or not they are in attendance when a vote is taken. Given multiple committee memberships, hectic schedules, and the sheer number of bills, simply getting supporters to be there at the right time is a challenge. Ways to kill a bill include assigning it to more than one committee or calling for a committee vote when supporters are absent. Given the plethora of bills each session, some committees are awash in bills, preventing careful analysis of each one during the hearing process.

It is not unusual for the appropriations committees in each chamber to consider over a hundred bills in one hearing at the end of the legislative session, killing many of them. For example, in 2014, the Senate Appropriations Committee shelved a bill that would have required adult film performers to wear condoms after reports that some had contracted HIV. Performers and public health professionals testified on both sides of the bill. It was the second consecutive year that it was defeated. Voters later rejected the bill as an initiative in 2016.

Floor Action and Conference Committee

On each house floor, garnering enough votes is equally challenging. Majorities of 41 in the Assembly and 21 in the Senate are required to pass legislation, even if there is only a bare quorum at the time.

A two-thirds vote is necessary for tax and emergency bills (those taking immediate effect). Yet, during floor debate, amendments to the bill may be offered and voted on by a simple majority *of those present*. Because it is so easy (numerically speaking) to amend a bill compared to passing it, floor amendments can be used to substantially modify a bill even to the point of killing it. The ultimate modification is called GANDA or "gut and amend." Here, the entire contents of a bill are stripped and replaced with new content, a practice that often occurs near the end of a legislative session. For instance, in 2014, SB 270 was introduced as a bill to combat the underground economy but later morphed into the controversial grocery store ban on single-use plastic bags that was enacted into law and subjected to a referendum. Although gut and amend appears to violate the legislature's own rules (amendments must be germane to the original bill) the rules are ignored as needed. Amendments aside, the generic process that began in the house of origin repeats itself in the second house. A conference committee resolves interhouse differences. If its members cannot agree with the conference report, the bill dies. Conferees have been known to rewrite bills well beyond original language.

The Governor and the Final Stages

If a bill passes through both houses, the governor may sign it (making it law), do nothing (making it law without a signature), or veto it. As in Congress, a vetoed bill then requires an extraordinary two-thirds vote of both the Assembly and the Senate for it to become law. The mere threat of a veto can halt a bill's progress or alter its content. Understandably, this is more commonplace when the governor and the legislature are of different parties or when personal relations between the governor and affected legislators are strained. The last time a governor's veto was overridden was during Jerry Brown's first stint in the late 1970s.

The pace of the legislature changes over the course of a legislative session. The beginning of a term moves rather slowly. By the end of a session (usually late summer), the pace becomes frenetic. At that point, the textbook process becomes fiction as legislators "hijack" and rewrite scores of bills and bypass what were once-essential committee hearings. During the closing days and weeks, some legislators try to slip through local bills (benefiting individual constituents or single groups). Numerous interest group—sponsored bills are considered during the day whereas fund-raisers targeting those same interests are scheduled at night. Upward of 1,500 bills may be considered during those final weeks.

As you reflect on the legislative process in California, remember that the job of the legislature is to both pass and *not pass* legislation. Bills fail for various reasons. Of course, a bill might lack widespread support or be unacceptable to the governor. But less-obvious reasons also exist. Some members may introduce bills but expend little effort on their behalf. Merely introducing bills (along with the requisite press releases) may placate some groups or constituents. Members may cast "yes" votes on relatively harmless legislation to appease legislative colleagues; this has been the nature of logrolling throughout legislative history. If a bill dies, especially a bad one, a legislator can breathe easier while blaming committees, the leadership, "special interests," a media blitz, the governor, or whomever for its defeat. In his last year in office, Jerry Brown signed 1,016 bills and vetoed 201.

THE THIRD HOUSE

In many ways, the legislative process requires lobbying by interest groups. In a representative democracy, interest groups would have to be invented if they did not already exist. Chapter 6 outlined the role of interest groups as linkage institutions in California politics. They organize in different ways to express their policy preferences and serve their members. The professionals they employ to affect the policy process are called *lobbyists*. Sacramento's lobbyists influence the legislative process in six distinct ways:

1. *Making Campaign Contributions.* Contributing to campaigns is not lobbying *per se*. But because so many fund-raisers occur in Sacramento, lobbyists are expected to attend. Legislators and lobbyists alike agree that this practice is more used to "buy" access rather than votes on specific bills. Because contributions are made on a year-round basis, lobbyists sometimes make them—and legislators sometimes solicit them—at the same time bills of interest to those lobbyists are being considered. This perceived "pay to play" atmosphere is particularly evident near the end of legislative sessions when fund-raising events multiply much like the bills awaiting action. The practice is unseemly even to some legislators. According to former Assembly member Nicole Parra, "It's happening while bills are moving and despite the fact that we're all professionals and you never talk about legislation, it's just too close—not illegal, just too close for comfort."[25] Some interest groups such as local governments are barred from making campaign contributions (they would be using tax revenues to do so), so they must rely all the more on lobbyists and former local officials who are now legislative allies.

2. *Simply Being There.* If a physical presence in Sacramento was optional, many groups would locate elsewhere. But because timing is so important in the legislative process, lobbyists need to be on hand to monitor or "watchdog" bills as they proceed through the legislative labyrinth. Being there also includes making friends and establishing numerous contacts with legislators and their staffs. Capitol hallways, elevators, the sixth-floor eatery, and members' offices all serve as contact opportunities. One part of the job is knowing how legislators will vote on a bill. To find out, a

veteran lobbyist noted, "We stalk members until they commit and tell us how they'll vote."

3. *Knowing the Process.* Simply being there is not enough. An intimate knowledge of the process and of the personality quirks of members and their staff is essential. Any legislature is a parliamentary labyrinth characterized by a host of written and unwritten rules. The written rules involve the intricacies of the legislative process discussed earlier. Unwritten rules might encompass everything from how members address each other to what they wear. This is why so many successful lobbyists have been former members or staffers (see box 7.3).

Box 7.3 ★ Case in Point: Tech Giants Battle over Consumer Privacy

In the same year that Facebook founder, Mark Zuckerberg, got grilled in congressional hearings over the manipulation of Facebook users' private information in the 2016 presidential election, the social network juggernaut, along with other tech giants, including Google, Amazon, Microsoft, Comcast, and AT&T, sought to kill, or at least water down, two legislative efforts in California to protect consumer privacy. Both efforts sought to give digital users more discretion over how their personal information is used by tech companies and hold those companies accountable for abuses. For instance, provisions would allow consumers to ask companies to delete their personal information and sue companies if there was an unauthorized breach of their personal data.

Illustrating the dual track legislative process made possible by the initiative process, a San Francisco real estate developer had qualified an initiative by June 2018 that would have severely cracked down on the sale of personal data. Gearing up for an initiative campaign that was expected to generate $100 million in campaign spending, Facebook gave $200,000 to the opposition campaign only to later withdraw its opposition to the initiative measure after it was revealed that British firm Cambridge Analytica had provided Donald Trump's campaign with illegal access to Facebook data. Meanwhile, Assembly Bill 375 wound its way through the legislative process and was intensely lobbied by TechNet, an advocacy organization for tech giants, including Facebook and Amazon. Eventually, compromise legislation was worked out between the tech industry and consumer advocacy groups and considered by the Senate Judiciary Committee. The committee chairwoman, Senator Hannah-Beth Jackson, captured the committee's choice: "Somebody stepped forward and now we are in a Hobson's choice. Either this goes to the ballot and is a hundred million dollars or more I'm told is likely to be spent. Or if the bill is killed we're back at ground zero." Governor Brown later signed AB 375 into law and left members of both camps unhappy—just another day in the legislative process.

Source: Lee Fang, "Google and Facebook Are Quietly Fighting California's Privacy Rights Initiative, Emails Reveal," *The Intercept*, June 26, 2018, https://theintercept.com/2018/06/26/google-and-facebook-are-quietly-fighting-californias-privacy-rights-initiative-emails-reveal; Bryan Anderson, "Sweeping California Consumer Privacy Bill Approved by Jerry Brown," *Sacramento Bee*, June 28, 2018, https://www.sacbee.com/news/politics-government/capitol-alert/article213993229.html.

4. *Providing Information.* The most important role a lobbyist can play is giving legislators, committees, and staff accurate, detailed information on a bill, especially its impact on their clients. Lobbyists should be and often are masters of the subject encompassed by a bill. Appealing to common sense and logic works especially well on minor bills where other pressures might be absent. On controversial matters, "winning on the merits" is less fruitful. A related technique is the use of a silver bullet—a piece of information that, if made public, would prove too damaging for a bill to survive. If there is opposition to a particular bill, groups often propose amendments to make a bill more acceptable or even harmless. Observers believe term limits have increased the informational power of lobbyists and interest groups, the new repositories of institutional memory.

5. *Coalition Building.* Many interest groups believe there is strength in numbers. Accordingly, they develop coalitions with each other to help craft policy or defeat policies injurious to their interests. Given the umbrella structure and generalized interests of the California Chamber of Commerce, the chamber hosts 24 such coalitions, addressing topics like Latin American trade and free trade. Holding large coalitions in place is not easy. Several environmentally oriented members left the AB32 Implementation Group after learning that other members, including some of the state's largest polluters, were working to water down the state's landmark global warming law.[26]

6. *Grassroots Lobbying.* An increasingly common lobbying technique is the use of **grassroots pressure**. Because legislators of necessity pay attention to constituents back home, grassroots efforts help mobilize them and connect them with their representatives on specific policy issues—even single bills. Modern technology and the presence of term limits makes "farming the membership" both feasible and effective. According to public relations executive Katherine MacDonald, "Grass-roots efforts work more now because new legislators tend to be more grass-roots based and less Sacramento based."[27] As a result, they respond to organized phone call, letter, fax, and email campaigns. A variant of grassroots lobbying is **crowd lobbying**. Here, interest group members gather in Sacramento for briefings and to play "lobbyist for a day," as they roam statehouse hallways. The more organized wear business attire, sport name tags, meet legislators and staff, and may even testify at a hearing. Others, sometimes busloads of them, rally on the capitol steps to voice their views. That said, not all constituents are equal or equally significant to legislators. Successful lobbyists know how to cultivate the constituents closest to legislators or how to help their clients become significant constituents worth listening to.[28]

In short, the lobbyists, or the third house, represent one point of a legislative triangle. The other two points are legislative committees (both members and staffs) and executive branch agencies (their legislative liaison offices). These triangles or issue networks exist on every subject of permanent interest in state government. They best portray the three-way communication and influence pattern that characterizes the legislative process.

CONCLUSION

California's legislature is the most professionalized in the nation. Its well-paid members work full time and can rely on ample resources to make informed public policy.[29] But this body has faced daunting challenges in recent years. Term limits diluted legislative competency, erased institutional memory, and transferred policy influence and expertise to the third house and the executive branch. In many ways, the initiative process has provided a viable alternative to the California legislature and the very notion of representative government for interest groups, individuals, and even public officials themselves.

Reapportionment practices have lessened electoral competition, hardened partisan views, and reduced bipartisan approaches to policymaking, in general, and the state budget, in particular. Future challenges might well include the state's growing diversity. Although legislatures are intended to represent the people of a state, representation in modern California is no easy matter. As noted, California is becoming increasingly diverse in every sense of the word—culturally, ethnically, socially, and economically. Pluralism is giving way to hyperpluralism. The legislature is increasingly a place where conflicts between diverse groups unfold. Historically, the legislature has best represented the social, economic, and political upper tiers of California—those who can afford to organize. Occasionally, it represents the problems faced by the relatively poor or powerless. In political theory, it is an institution designed potentially to represent pluralistic interests, but in reality, it most effectively represents the state's business and economic elites. As but one example, all 29 bills on the "job killer" list of the California Chamber of Commerce were defeated in 2018. Other groups will need to amass political power to match their growing numbers if they are to have comparable clout in the state capital.

California's legislature is also in the midst of considerable change as a result of significant reforms adopted in recent years. Longer expected tenures in office, the new redistricting process, and the top-two primary are likely to change the outlook and perspectives of incoming legislators. Similar to their predecessors in the 1960s and 1970s, new legislators, with longer time horizons, may be more willing to tackle some of the pressing long-term problems afflicting the state. Although interparty warfare was often the obstacle to grappling with the state's most severe problems in the past, new, larger Democratic supermajorities in both chambers may prove cumbersome in themselves. The adage "be careful what you wish for" may apply, as Democrats attempt to avoid political infighting that could derail progress on the state's major problems.

KEY TERMS

Federal plan (p. 132)
juice committees (p. 133)
bills (p. 134)
constitutional amendments (p. 134)
resolutions (p. 135)
trustees (p. 139)

delegates (p. 139)
politicos (p. 139)
executive branch oversight (p. 139)
authorization process (p. 139)
appropriation process (p. 139)
reapportionment (p. 144)

gerrymandering (p. 144)
partisan gerrymandering (p. 144)
incumbent gerrymandering (p. 144)
racial gerrymandering (p. 144)
Proposition 11 (p. 145)
party caucus (p. 147)
Assembly Speaker (p. 147)
Senate president pro tempore (p. 148)

standing committees (p. 150)
fiscal committees (p. 150)
conference committees (p. 150)
select committees (p. 150)
joint committees (p. 150)
grassroots pressure (p. 156)
crowd lobbying (p. 156)

REVIEW QUESTIONS

1. Briefly survey California's legislative history.
2. Describe the functions legislatures perform.
3. In what ways do legislators perceive their own roles?
4. How are legislative candidates recruited? Why and how do they manage to stay?
5. How is the new reapportionment process different than the previous way that legislative districts were drawn? What is the likely impact on elections?
6. Explain how the committee system represents both a diverse state and the ambitions of legislators.
7. If you were to redraw the legislation flow chart to reflect informal processes and rules, what would it look like?
8. As a lobbyist, how would you most effectively deal with today's legislature?

WEB RESOURCES

California Assembly and Senate

https://www.assembly.ca.gov and https://www.senate.ca.gov

These sites provide current schedules, district finders, member directories, links to legislation, various caucuses, and other California government websites.

Legislative Analyst's Office

https://lao.ca.gov

Here you have access to the same policy expertise available to the legislature.

Legislative Counsel of California

http://www.leginfo.ca.gov

This is an excellent gateway site leading you to bill information, state laws, legislative information, and related publications.

Calmatters

https://calmatters.org/articles/california-legislature-diversity-demographics

The nonprofit news organization website allows users to compare their own demographic characteristics to those of the California legislature.

8

Executive Politics

LEARNING OUTCOMES

Students will be able to:

★ Define the five gubernatorial leadership variables and how they relate to the behavior of recent governors.

★ Explain the major duties and powers of the governor.

★ Describe the governor's role in the legislative process and the tools available in that role.

★ Identify the other statewide executive offices and explain their functions.

★ Analyze the responsibilities of the bureaucracy and how its role in government relates to diversity.

IN BRIEF

Administering California's state government is the responsibility of the executive branch; administering that branch and providing overall political leadership for the entire state fall on the governor. In chapter 8, we survey the office of governor, other executive officers, plus a sizable bureaucracy—all of whom compete for power and leadership in the Golden State.

CALIFORNIA'S POST-STATEHOOD GOVERNORS have run the gamut in personality, governing styles, and political skills. Most have been forgotten by history, but others have provided uncommon leadership and made a mark on the state through policy entrepreneurship. Governors exercise a variety of duties and powers, including executive powers, budget leadership opportunities, and legislative and judicial power, plus roles such as the state's commander-in-chief and chief of state. They share power and leadership authority with several other separately elected leaders, the most powerful of whom is the attorney general.

In addition to these top posts, California's bureaucracy numbers more than 300,000. They exercise functions common to all bureaucracies and, in doing so, diffuse executive leadership and administration still further. Yet, they deliver state services and personify state government to many Californians. California's executive branch both mirrors and attempts to govern a diverse state. In the process, it is limited by political and organizational fragmentation that resists efforts to reform it.

INTRODUCTION

In January 2019, the longest-serving governor in California history, Jerry Brown, stepped down from office after serving 16 years overall. Unlike the first time he left the governorship in 1983, term limits prevented him from serving another term this time around. Thirty-six years had passed between the first time he left the governor's office and the second time he left office. The two stints in office were different in many ways. On his first watch, Brown governed at a time that some consider the start of the state's demise. Proposition 13, which drastically cut property tax revenue, passed in 1978, the same year Brown was reelected. He initially opposed the measure but then became a born-again tax-cutter when it passed overwhelmingly. The budgets of local governments and school districts, largely dependent on property tax revenue, were severely shaken. Brown stepped into backfill the lost revenue using a large state budget surplus. That rescue, coupled with an economic recession in 1981, sent the state budget into a hole that it would not consistently emerge from until 2013. After a failed attempt to run for president while still governor, Brown left office on a sour note: "I believe the people of California would like a respite from me, and in some ways I would like a respite from them."[1]

In the decades subsequent to Brown's first stint in office, California's financial situation remained volatile until the 2000s when it nearly reached the point of insolvency. Many performance indicators showed a state in distress. California ranked near the bottom of the 50 states in K–12 standardized test scores, infrastructure conditions, and traffic congestion. The U.S. Supreme Court took control of the state's prison system due to overcrowding and deplorable living conditions for inmates. Housing affordability and the cost of living more generally slowed population growth and turned some seekers of the California Dream away. Many started to question whether the state was governable. At the heart of this question are the two themes emphasized in this book. Could one person, the governor, effectively lead such a large, *diverse* population approaching 40 million people? And second, is the *hyperpluralistic* political structure of the state, where power is thinly scattered among institutions, too much for one person to surmount?

Enter Jerry Brown for his second act as governor. After dispatching former eBay CEO and Republican gubernatorial candidate Meg Whitman in the 2010 race, the resurrected Jerry Brown and California faced one of the largest budget deficits in state history. As the previous governor, action-hero superstar Arnold Schwarzenegger demonstrated that he could only save the world in movies, not in real life, as he failed to turn around the state's financial death spiral and left office with some of the lowest job approval ratings of any California governor. Schwarzenegger's time in office only added fuel to the fire that the state was now ungovernable. Brown's first task was to address the state's dire fiscal situation. "It's a pretzel palace of incredible complexity," he mused in 2012.[2] To tackle the $26 billion deficit, he proposed a number of program cuts, accounting maneuvers, and, most important, a sales and income tax increase. After failing to secure enough Republican votes to pass the tax increase through the legislature, Brown sponsored his own initiative, Proposition 30. Its surprisingly strong support (55 percent) in the 2012 election, along with other steps to strengthen the state's finances (e.g., pension reforms), put the governor in a strong position to run for reelection in 2014. In the end, it was virtually no contest. Brown campaigned very little, spent less than his opponent ($6 million to $7 million), the little-known Republican Neel Kashkari, and cruised to a 20-point margin of victory.

In his second term, as the state's financial condition continued to improve, with the help of one of the longest economic recoveries in U.S. history, Brown turned his attention to other problems. Always a concern of his since his first time in the governor's office, Brown cemented his reputation as a staunch environmental advocate by extending the state's cap-and-trade system, the first in the nation, and pushing policies to increase the state's energy reliance on renewable resources. Both efforts sought to reduce carbon emissions and combat climate change when the federal government, under the Trump administration, was doing the opposite. Brown also moved the needle on several other fronts: he secured an ongoing funding source for the beleaguered high-speed rail system, advanced the twin-tunnels plan to address the San Joaquin–Sacramento delta, and promoted criminal justice reforms to lessen mandatory sentencing laws, begun under his first stint in office. By the end of his term, discussion turned to his legacy, but Brown would have nothing of it: "I don't have a legacy. I don't know what a legacy is. This is a media construct."[3] Although the assessment of his legacy will await the outcomes of the policies and projects alluded to above, Brown's second time in office did much to answer the question about governability. As Mark Baldassare of the Public Policy Institute of California put it, "Perhaps Gov. Jerry Brown's most important contribution . . . was to restore public confidence in state government . . . His tenure offers a successful model for governing the state in the future."[4]

Just when we thought California was done with Jerry Brown, somewhat ironically, his successor Governor Gavin Newsom has a long, and sometimes rocky, history with Brown. Their two families go back several generations. Newsom's grandfather helped lead the campaign of Pat Brown, Jerry's father, for district attorney in San Francisco. Later as governor, Jerry Brown appointed Newsom's father to two judgeships, and they remained lifelong friends.[5] In 2010, Gavin Newsom initially ran for governor and then exited the race when Jerry Brown declared his candidacy. After eight years of waiting in the wings as lieutenant governor, Newsom finally ascended to the governor's office in 2019. And Jerry Brown, unlike several recent predecessors, left Newsom with the best gift of all: a state with a strong financial foundation and a $20 billion surplus. Early indications are that Newsom plans to continue the fiscal prudence modeled by Brown and, at the same time, attempt to tackle some of the state's most intractable problems, such as homelessness, housing affordability, and early childhood education.

Brown's extensive time in office and Newsom's early months in office suggest that gubernatorial leadership depends on a fluid mix of many factors—actual job performance, electoral moods, the health of the economy, legislative friends and enemies, formal powers, structural constraints, partisanship, and one's own personality.

Executive branch politics is both fascinating to watch and complicated to study. State governors perform many of the same tasks American presidents do, but governors are out of the national spotlight—usually. The 1992 budget stalemate between Governor Pete Wilson and the legislature occupied the national media for weeks, as did Gray Davis's recall and Arnold Schwarzenegger's election. The state's budget rebound in recent years garnered Brown national attention as a turnaround artist and model of fiscal stewardship. The formal powers of governors, like those of presidents, are not exhaustive. Both must compete for influence in a system full of checks and balances. Political scientist James MacGregor Burns once described presidential power as "essentially the power to dicker and transact."[6] This is all the more true of American governors. Let's examine the political and administrative setting in which California governors operate.

HOW GOVERNORS LEAD

The governor operates in a complex pattern of executive leadership. On one hand, California's governor is at the apex of the political system—more powerful than any other individual. On the other hand, the entire executive branch exemplifies the themes of this book. It regulates and/or provides benefits to virtually every group or issue in the state, in effect mirroring the diversity that is California. As such, the executive branch (appointed officials, career civil servants, and other workers) represents the state's population. But given how the executive branch is organized and structured, it also exhibits its own form of hyperpluralism: diluted and shared power, politically independent offices and agencies, and many avenues for interest group influence. Legislators debate policy, help constituents, and collectively pass legislation. Although voters often consider their own legislators political leaders, the legislature's primary role is more to provide representation than to provide leadership. Even the legislative leaders discussed in chapter 7 provide institutional leadership, not statewide political leadership. This function necessarily resides in the governorship. But the state's diversity and fragmented political system present numerous roadblocks to leadership.

Experience with colonial governors on the East Coast taught the original colonies a lesson: to prevent autocratic governors, constitutionally weaken their offices. As newer states copied older state constitutions, they also limited gubernatorial power. California did so, too, even though it had experienced relatively weak colonial governors under Spain and Mexico.

Table 8.1 lists all California governors from the establishment of statehood to the present. Three observations are in order. First, few early governors are memorable to contemporary Californians. Strong executive leadership was neither valued nor experienced in those years. The most familiar 19-century governor, Leland Stanford, is better known for his membership in the Big Four and for the university he founded. Second, throughout most of its history, the California governorship has been a rapidly revolving door. Service of less than one term was common among early governors. In 1860, Milton Latham served all of five days! He quit to replace a U.S. senator who had been shot in a duel. Hiram Johnson was the first governor to serve more than four years. He took office in 1911, was reelected in 1914, and resigned to serve in the U.S. Senate in 1917.

Third, as table 8.1 shows, with few exceptions, two consecutive terms are now the norm. Keep in mind that Proposition 140 established term limits—two four-year terms for governors and other statewide executives even though that

Table 8.1 The Governors of California

Governor	Party	Years	Terms
Peter H. Burnett	D	1849–1851	<1
John McDougaf	D	1851–1852	<1
John Bigler	D	1852–1856	1
J. Neely Johnson	A†	1856–1858	<1
John B. Weller	D	1858–1860	<1
Milton S. Latham	D	1860	<1
John G. Downey*	D	1860–1862	<1
Leland Stanford	R	1862–1863	<1
Frederick F. Low	R	1863–1867	1
Henry H. Haight	D	1867–1871	1
Newton Booth	R	1871–1875	1
Romualdo Pacheco, Jr.*	R	1875	<1
William Irwin	D	1875–1880	>1
George C. Perkins	R	1880–1883	<1
George Stoneman	D	1883–1887	1
Washington Barlett	D	1887	<1
Robert H. Waterman*	R	1887–1891	1
Henry H. Markham	R	1891–1895	1
James H. Budd	D	1895–1899	1
Henry T. Gage	R	1899–1903	1
George C. Pardee	R	1903–1907	1
James N. Gillett	R	1907–1911	1
Hiram W. Johnson	R	1911–1917	>1
William D. Stephens*	R	1917–1923	>1
Friend W. Richardson	R	1923–1927	1
C. C. Young	R	1927–1931	1
James Rolph, Jr.	R	1931–1934	<1
Frank F. Merriam*	R	1934–1939	>1
Culbert L. Olson	D	1939–1943	1
Earl Warren	R	1943–1953	>2
Goodwin J. Knight*	R	1953–1959	<1
Edmund G. "Pat" Brown	D	1959–1967	2
Ronald Reagan	R	1967–1975	2
Edmund G. "Jerry" Brown	D	1975–1983	2
George Deukmejian	R	1983–1991	2
Pete Wilson	R	1991–1999	2
Gray Davis	D	1999–2003	>1

(Continued)

Table 8.1 *Continued*

Governor	Party	Years	Terms
Arnold Schwarzenegger	R	2003–2011	2
Edmund G. "Jerry" Brown	D	2011–2019	2
Gavin Newsom	D	2019–	

Question: To what extent and on what basis will recent governors be memorable a century from now?

† American Party.
* Lieutenant governor succeeded to governorship.

Newly elected governor Gavin Newsom speaks to an audience about immigration.

limit had become an informal custom. Earl Warren served more than two terms and governors from Pat Brown to Wilson each served two four-year terms. The 2003 recall prevented Davis from completing a second term to which he had been elected. Presumably, eight years gives a governor ample time to form an agenda, exercise leadership, and implement priorities. Ironically, the records of recent governors suggest that lengthy tenure alone does not necessarily guarantee effective leadership.

The governor's annual salary of $201,680 is among the nation's highest and would seemingly reflect the office's leadership role. In reality, several California public employees, including public health administrators, top public university administrators, and many local government managers, earn more.

Like other elected executives, California governors do not exercise power in a political vacuum. Borrowing heavily from research on the American presidency, Robert Crew identified five variables that affect gubernatorial leadership.[7] We will apply them to gubernatorial politics in California. They include the governor's personality, political skill, political resources, the overall political environment or context, and strategic considerations:

1. *Personality.* Highly personal factors such as motivation, behavior, and character affect how governors lead. California governors have possessed diverse personality traits. For instance, Hiram Johnson was tenacious and persuasive; Warren, competent and well liked; Pat Brown, confident and active; Reagan, gregarious and surprisingly flexible. During his first stint as governor, Jerry Brown was aloof and philosophical; George Deukmejian was persistent and stubborn; Wilson was tough yet pragmatic. Davis was called a "Lone Ranger," a governor short on people skills. Disavowing "politics as usual," Schwarzenegger brought to the office star power, a desire for action, and a willingness to challenge legislative opponents. He also did little to ingratiate legislators and cultivate their support. Naturally, the personalities of governors affect how they approach the job, relate to staff and legislators, and communicate with the public.

2. *Political Skill.* California governors need extraordinary political skill to push their priorities through the legislature and the state's bureaucracy. These skills involve working successfully with legislative leaders, political party operatives, the media, and interest groups. For instance, Warren sponsored nonpartisan "town halls"—inviting thousands of concerned citizens to Sacramento during a legislative session. Reagan mastered the art of sounding ultraconservative (to please his followers) while acting with moderation (in recognition of political reality). Schwarzenegger alternated between media-driven public confrontation and private negotiation (often in his cigar-smoking tent just outside his capitol office). Unlike his earlier experience, Jerry Brown engaged legislators and even testified at their hearings.

3. *Political Resources.* Such resources come from inside or outside the governor's office. Internal resources include the amount of time, information, expertise, and energy a governor has. External resources include party support in the legislature, public approval, electoral margins, and professional reputation. Johnson could attribute his success to a legislature controlled by fellow Progressives. Republican Wilson possessed the experience and largely moderate political views that historically have been valued by Californians. Public opinion itself is a political resource. Schwarzenegger's political strength ebbed and flowed largely in concert with his job approval ratings. Unlike Schwarzenegger, Brown left office with approval ratings above 50 percent, largely a reflection of his successful turnaround of the state's financial condition.

4. *Political Context.* The term **political context** refers to factors in the external environment that affect a governor's performance. California's economy is one such factor. After Depression-era governors battled anemic revenues, post—World War II governors (Warren, Goodwin Knight, and Brown) took advantage of a growing economy and the taxes it generated. A second external factor is the state's political environment. This includes the electorate's partisan and ideological leanings. It also includes the political era during which a governor serves. Each era witnesses its

own governing coalitions, expressions of political culture, and an overall political mood expressed by the public. Public confidence in the future of the state as measured in public opinion polls (see chapter 1) provides an upbeat political context in which governors can maneuver. The other side of that coin—when the public's mood sours and public confidence in the future fades—imparts a decidedly downbeat context in which to govern. Schwarzenegger reflected this mood in his unusually short 2009 State of the State speech when he declared, "I will not give the traditional state of the state address here today because the reality is that our state is incapacitated until we solve the budget crisis."

5. *Strategic Considerations.* Given the factors mentioned, each governor must craft a strategy to achieve desired goals. This involves a game plan to deal with the legislature and methods to gain interest group and popular support. Previous strategies in California have involved large-scale, ambitious programs such as water projects and the master plan for higher education. Wilson took office espousing "preventative government": programs to reduce the dependence of California's children on government. Schwarzenegger faced skeptical legislators and continuing budget deficits that narrowed to some extent his policy options. In 2011, Brown advocated a "tough love" approach—giving the voters a choice between cutting taxes and severely reducing government services.

Timing is an important strategic consideration for governors. Relatively few windows of opportunity exist—times when governors can pursue a policy agenda with some hope of success. These windows are determined by routine political cycles, such as the election calendar and the annual budget process. As with presidents, California governors normally experience brief "honeymoons" of popularity and support early in their administrations. Windows of opportunity often close during election years, especially if tax increases are contemplated. During recessions, when revenues cease to grow or even shrink, those windows might never fully open. Because so many policy issues depend on adequate funding, revenue levels themselves open and close windows of opportunity. For instance, Brown used the dire budget environment to restructure the state–local relationship through his "realignment" plan in 2011 and an improving revenue outlook in 2012 to propose a significant change in the state's school funding formula.

THE GOVERNOR'S DUTIES AND POWERS

Whether resources are in their favor or not, California governors possess a wide range of duties and powers. In terms of public expectations, their responsibilities to lead the state outstrip their actual formal powers. The range of powers that are discussed in this section are both formal and informal. They stem from both the constitution and political necessity. They are both visible and invisible to the public. The governor must share some powers with the legislature or other executive branch agencies. Others are relatively unchecked by competing forces. Compared to the institutional powers of all 50 governors (including shared executive power, tenure potential, party control, and the powers of appointment, budget, and veto), California's governor ranks just below the middle. But remember, that is an average. On a scale of 1 to 5 (where 1 represents gubernatorial weakness and 5 strength), California's governors have been assigned a "1" in terms of shared executive power and a "4" in terms of their budget power.[8]

Executive Powers

The governor is first and foremost the chief executive officer of the state. According to the California Constitution, the "supreme executive power" of the state is vested in the governor. "The Governor shall see that the law is faithfully executed."[9] Although this is much easier said than done, the governor possesses several powers to achieve this goal.

Organizing a Personal Staff. The governor's **inner circle** consists of a chief of staff and a variety of assistants called "secretaries," assigned to legislative matters, administration, the press, appointments and scheduling, and legal affairs. Top personal staff members often are veteran associates of the governor. *Their* staffers are often young, energetic, recent college graduates with workaholic schedules. The administrations of Reagan and Deukmejian were known for rather hierarchical staff relations (resembling a strict organization chart), whereas in his first stint in office, Jerry Brown had a relatively loose "spokes of the wheel" arrangement. In this latter style, numerous individuals had relatively free access to the governor. Given Schwarzenegger's lack of public-sector experience, his initial appointments included former Wilson aides and staffers from several business-oriented interest groups; later he even hired as chief of staff Susan P. Kennedy, a onetime Democratic party official and Davis appointee. Many observers noted that the greatest personal asset Jerry Brown brought to the governorship in 2011 was his closest confidant and wife, Ann Gust Brown.

Making Appointments. Although 99 percent of executive branch employees belong to a civil service system, the governor appoints several thousand individuals to various administrative, board, and commission posts (see figure 8.1). Many are "at pleasure" appointees who serve as long as the governor wishes them to. They include the governor's personal staff and high-level administrators. Some governors, including Schwarzenegger, borrow selected appointees from various departments to augment their own office staffs. Most appointees are "term" appointees, including board and commission members, who serve a fixed number of years. During a governor's term, still others will need to be appointed to fill vacancies and judicial retirements. What motivates these appointments in addition to administrative needs? First, governors can diversify their administrations. For instance, in a departure from previous practice, Brown named numerous ethnic minorities and women when he was first governor. Second, they can reward their friends and political allies. Schwarzenegger appointed a number of personal friends and political associates to various regulatory boards. Watchdog groups complained of cronyism, charging that many of his appointments favored the industries the boards were established to oversee on behalf of the public.[10]

Managing the Executive Branch. California governors have their own versions of presidential cabinets. Figure 8.1 shows an organization chart of the upper levels of the state's executive branch. Wary of the huge number of appointees reporting directly to him, Governor Pat Brown reorganized a plethora of departments into several **superagencies**. Subsequent governors have reorganized a bit, including Jerry Brown in 2012. These agencies include (1) Business, Consumer

Services, and Housing; (2) Environmental Protection; (3) Health and Human Services; (4) Natural Resources; (5) Transportation; (6) Labor and Workforce Development; and (7) Government Operations. All these people are part of the governor's *cabinet*, but they are less powerful than their "super" titles would suggest. For instance, within Business, Consumer Services, and Housing are Consumer Affairs, Fair Employment and Housing, Alcohol Beverage Control, and the Horse Racing Board. Each operates like a semiautonomous fiefdom, well outside the governor's routine attention span. These agency secretaries, joined by several other departments, such as Corrections and Rehabilitation, Food and Agriculture, Finance, and Veterans Affairs, make up the governor's 11-member cabinet. These various agency heads vary in importance. The director of finance is a crucial appointee, given the governor's budget responsibilities. As a group, the governor's cabinet is less a policy body than a collection of executive branch appointees.

Issuing Orders. The "executive power" of California's governor also includes the ability to take action independent of the legislature. A primary vehicle to do this is the **executive order.** Such orders usually involve a series of "whereas" statements detailing the reasons for the order followed by this language: "NOW, THEREFORE I, GAVIN NEWSOM Governor of the State of California, by virtue of the power and authority invested in me by the Constitution and the statutes of the State of California, do hereby issue this order to become effective immediately." Following that are the substantive actions the governor wishes to take. In one notable recent example, Brown issued an order for the first mandatory water-use cutbacks in state history that made international headlines.

Budget Leadership

Although the constitutional language "supreme executive power" sounds impressive, what requires the governor's constant attention is the state's budget (discussed further in chapter 11). The California Constitution requires the governor to submit a budget to the legislature within the first 10 days of each calendar year. A tremendous amount of preparation goes into the submission of that "budget bill." The state budget is the premier policy statement for California and governors want their priorities reflected in it. The process is twofold. The **internal budget process** (within the executive branch) begins the previous July when the governor, through the Department of Finance (DOF), submits a "budget letter/ price letter" to all executive agencies and departments. The budget letter relays the governor's policy priorities, whereas the price letter contains fiscal assumptions (such as the rate of inflation) used to determine budget baselines. During the rest of the year, departments and the DOF haggle over which figures will emerge in the governor's January budget.[11]

The **external budget process** pits the governor against the legislature. This part of the process is the most visible to the public and clearly the messiest from the governor's standpoint. At this stage, the governor shares budget power primarily with the Assembly Budget Committee, the Senate Budget and Fiscal Review Committee, and the Legislative Analyst's Office. Each has a staff that examines and often second-guesses the governor's figures.

When stalemates occurred in the past (they often did when revenues and expenditures did not easily match), a parallel group—the "Big Five"—usually

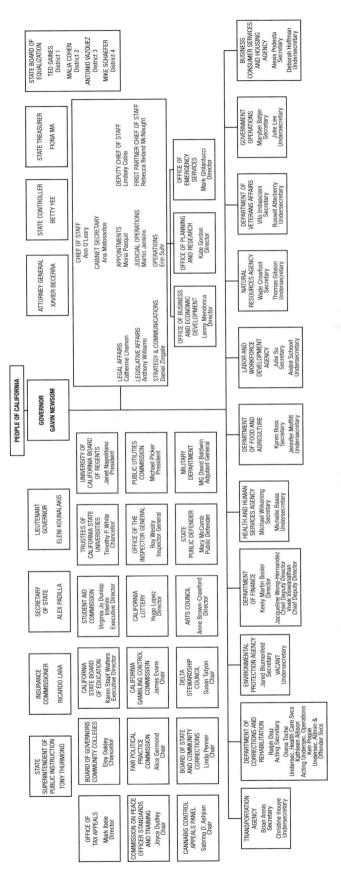

Figure 8.1 Executive Branch Organization Chart

Question: Which parts of the executive branch do you think cost the most? Compare your answer with budget data in Chapter 11.

Source: https://cold.govops.ca.gov/File/OrganizationalChart

emerged to further haggle over the budget bill. The governor and two caucus leaders each from the Assembly and Senate formed this group. With the change to a majority-vote budget, members of the minority party are no longer needed to adopt a budget. As a result, this group has shrunk to a "Big Three," consisting of the governor and majority leaders from each chamber. The constitution also requires that the legislature enact the budget bill by June 15 and for the governor to sign it by June 30, the last day of each fiscal year. It still takes a two-thirds vote to raise taxes and many fees—an important component of any budget process. Democratic supermajorities in the legislature make tax increases more feasible as what happened in 2017 when they voted to increase gas taxes and vehicle fees.

July 1 might pass without a budget as pundits declare the largest state in the Union "broke." On two occasions (1992 and 2009), creditors and employees were paid in registered warrants (called "IOUs") until a new budget was enacted. Less-publicized conflicts occur regularly. When revenues are down, budget makers argue over where to cut spending; when revenues are up, they argue over new spending ideas versus new tax cuts.

Once a budget is passed, additional spending requests plus new revenue projections require further adjustments during the fiscal year. Although the governor's budget power seems to dissipate during legislative debate on the budget bill, the governor's power over an approved budget is substantial. The most formidable tool the governor has at this point is the **line item veto**. This refers to the governor's ability to reduce or reject any item in an appropriations (spending) bill. Including California, 42 governors have this power in the United States. Box 8.1 displays a veto message attached to the 2015–16 budget bill. Here, Brown deleted $1 million to restore Clear Lake and suggested alternative funding sources. Attesting to the stronger budget conditions in his second term, Brown did not veto any budget provisions in his last term.

A final word on the governor's budget powers is in order. Many parts of the overall budget are difficult to control. They include separate spending decisions made by voters through initiatives (Proposition 98's funding requirements for education), particular revenues dedicated to certain uses (gas taxes for highway expenditures), or automatic spending increases called COLAs (cost-of-living adjustments). All these "uncontrollables," as political scientists call them, add up to a significant amount of the entire state budget. They substantially limit the ability of the governor to control spending and, therefore, policy.

Legislative Powers

California governors must deal constantly with the legislature and not just on the annual budget. They must exercise legislative leadership to achieve a host of other policy goals. California's most successful governors, legislatively speaking, were admired and respected by many legislators, used bipartisanship, and enjoyed high public approval ratings. But many California governors experienced significant political conflict because they brought profoundly different perspectives to their leadership role:

- *Party Differences.* The most telling source of conflict occurs when the governor is from a major political party and the legislature is controlled by another major party. In recent decades, Republican governors and

---

Box 8.1 ★ Item Veto Message

"I object to the following appropriations contained in Assembly Bill 93." With this simple declarative sentence, Governor Jerry Brown "blue penciled" 5 different spending items in the state's new 2015–16 budget. In this instance, he unilaterally deletes funding to restore Clear Lake and directs the Department of Fish and Wildlife to use other funding sources:

Item 3600-101-0200—For local assistance, Department of Fish and Wildlife. I delete this item. I am eliminating the $1,000,000 augmentation which would provide a grant to help restore Clear Lake. The Fish and Game Preservation Fund has a structural deficit and cannot absorb additional expenditures. There are existing grant programs that are available and appropriate to support the restoration of Clear Lake. I am directing my Administration to provide technical assistance to Lake County to assist them in identifying and applying for ecosystem restoration and drinking water grant funding.

Overall, Brown's actions cut a minuscule $1.3 million from a $250 billion budget. In subsequent years, he vetoed no line items. This is very atypical. Normally, item vetoes shave modest amounts off legislative appropriations as a way to control spending in a tight budget environment, reinforce the governor's own spending priorities, or make some other point to the legislature as a whole or one or more members who pushed the item.

Source: California Department of Finance, http://www.ebudget.ca.gov/2015-16/pdf/Enacted/BudgetSummary/FullBudgetSummary.pdf.

Democratic legislative majorities have clashed on taxes, welfare spending, and many other issues. In contrast, Davis and legislative Democrats had to temper efforts to impose an activist agenda the public might not support. In light of persistent budget problems, Schwarzenegger initially appeased both Republicans and Democrats—the former by opposing tax increases and the latter by postponing many deep program cuts. Subsequently, he became more aggressive and combative in pushing a variety of budget and political reforms. Unified party control does not necessarily connote smooth interbranch relations. For instance, fellow Democrats in the legislature overrode a number of Brown's vetoes in the late 1970s and, decades later, only reluctantly agreed to his proposed budget cuts.

- *Constituency Differences*. At times, differences in perspective between a governor and the legislature can be traced to constituency differences. Legislators represent individual, more homogeneous districts whereas the governor represents the entire state population, as diverse as it is. The needs of the whole state might not square with the constituent views of a particular Assembly or Senate district. For instance, a governor must balance the water needs of the entire state, not just those of farmers or city dwellers, as individual legislators might. Some parts of the state might hunger for economic development and growth; others might actively oppose it.
- *Interest Differences*. Legislators are particularly responsive to the views of individual interest groups, as noted in chapter 7. Governors try to represent the larger "general interest" of the state and, in doing so, seem more willing to step on interest group toes in the process. For example, Schwarzenegger

alienated some business and Republican allies by defending the state's global warming law. Brown received a great deal of electoral support (campaign contributions and votes) from public employee unions but was forced to advocate policies, such as state worker furloughs, that they opposed.

- *Responsibility Differences.* When California legislators want to diffuse blame, they can easily point their fingers to committee chairpersons, legislative leaders, or insensitive fellow legislators from elsewhere in the state. Governors cannot spread the blame for failure nearly as far. If they try, their own leadership ability is questioned. Furthermore, the public tends to lay singular responsibility on the governor. California's polling organizations measure the *governor's* popularity, not each legislator's.

Governors employ several resources in dealing with the California legislature: an overall legislative program, the general veto, calling special sessions, and personal relations. They work in the following ways:

- *Legislative Program.* Each January, the governor presents a "State of the State" speech, much like the president's "State of the Union" speech. This is an opportunity to fashion a coherent set of policy priorities by which legislation might be evaluated. California governors never command media attention comparable to that received by presidents, though. Many television stations rarely carry more than excerpts of the State of the State speech. In recognition of the media's short attention span and his proclivity to avoid excessive rhetoric, after his 2014 reelection, Brown combined his annual State of the State speech with his second inaugural address.
- *General Veto.* As noted earlier, the item veto allows the governor power to "blue pencil" a particular expenditure contained in an appropriations bill. A **general veto**, like the president's veto power, allows the governor to reject an entire nonspending or authorization bill. Box 8.2 features Brown's general veto of AB 725, a bill that would prohibit smoking on state beaches and parks.
- *Special Sessions.* In the past, when the legislature was not in session, governors would call **special sessions** to deal with pressing matters. Modern legislative sessions are virtually year-round, so fewer special sessions are needed. But governors still call them now and then, even when the legislature is in regular session to draw attention to a pressing problem. In 2015, Governor Brown announced two special sessions: one for health care and one for transportation funding to repair roads and highways. The former produced bills that restructured a tax on the health insurance industry, and the latter yielded no new legislation. The legislature later raised gas taxes and vehicle fees to repair roads and highways in 2017.
- *Personal Relations.* One of the governor's most potent but underrated legislative tools is good interpersonal relationships. For example, Reagan cultivated the press corps. Warren and Pat Brown were known for their warm relations with legislators, but Jerry Brown and Deukmejian were more distant and cool. Even members of his own party detested bachelor Brown's spartan lifestyle and unconventional tactics in the 1970s. Initially, Schwarzenegger capitalized on his larger-than-life persona by giving legislative leaders coveted

> **Box 8.2 ★ A General Veto Message**
>
> To the Members of the California State Assembly:
>   I am returning Assembly Bill 725 without my signature.
>   This bill prohibits smoking on state coastal beaches and throughout the State Park System, and requires the Department of Parks and Recreation to post signs to notify the public of the smoking ban.
>   Last year I vetoed Senate Bill 1333, a similar measure, because I believed that such a far-reaching prohibition in every state park and on every state beach was too broad. In addition, the fine prescribed in this bill for lighting one cigarette is excessive: over $250 dollars, after the mandatory assessments.
>   If people can't smoke even on a deserted beach, where can they? There must be some limit to the coercive power of government.
>
>   Sincerely,
>   Edmund G. Brown Jr.
>
> *Source:* California Legislative Counsel, http://leginfo.legislature.ca.gov.

personal attention but later preferred "going public" for cultivating personal relationships with legislators. Returning to the governor's office, now-married Jerry Brown was happy to host social events for both Republican and Democratic lawmakers, noting that "that's a very important part of how the Legislature works."[12]

Judicial Powers

Gubernatorial power also involves the judiciary or can be essentially judicial in nature. For instance, the governor's appointment power extends to the judicial branch, as explained in chapter 9. When a vacancy occurs on the California Supreme Court or the Courts of Appeal, the governor makes the appointment. Governors even appoint superior court judges when vacancies occur between elections. These appointments can add up. By the end of Jerry Brown's second stint in office, he had appointed four out of the seven justices on the state Supreme Court.

Like American presidents and appointments to the U.S. Supreme Court, governors can leave their imprints on state supreme courts. Deukmejian's appointments were moderate conservatives with pro-business credentials. Brown's appointments in the 1970s and early 1980s reflected his desire to create opportunities for minorities and to shake up the legal system. His selections included several firsts: Chief Justice Rose Bird (the first woman), Cruz Reynoso (the first Latino), and Wiley Manuel (the first African American). Once appointed, appellate justices must face the voters. Bird, Reynoso, and another justice, Joseph Grodin, were ousted in 1986, in part because they opposed the death penalty.

The governor's purely judicial powers involve **clemency** (or acts of mercy). First, the governor may *pardon* an individual convicted of a crime. This means releasing someone from the consequences of a criminal conviction. Second, the governor may *commute* or reduce a sentence. For example, just before leaving office in 2011, Schwarzenegger reduced the sentence of Esteban Nunez for voluntary manslaughter from 16 years in prison to 7. Nunez is the son of former Assembly Speaker Fabian Nunez, and the decision was criticized because of the Speaker's friendly relationship with Schwarzenegger. Third, the governor may issue a *reprieve* (the postponement of a sentence). Fourth, the governor may reverse parole decisions by the Board of Prison Terms, a power only three states grant their governors. For example, in 2018, Brown reversed a board decision that would have set free Gerardo Zavalo, one of seven people involved in the torture and killing of a black teenager in Delano. Fifth, the governor may *extradite* a fugitive to another state from which the fugitive has fled. Governor Brown once refused South Dakota's request in the 1970s to extradite Dennis Banks, a militant Native American, fearing he would not receive a fair trial.

A related task is more legal and political than judicial in nature. Along with the attorney general, the governor largely determines which court cases the state pursues at the appellate level. These cases involve appeals in which the state is a party or other cases on which the state wishes to take a stand. These top executives are not obligated to defend every state decision or policy, especially if they come from citizen initiatives. For instance, both Governor Schwarzenegger and then attorney general Jerry Brown refused to defend in court Proposition 8, the antigay marriage law.

Other Powers

During times of crisis and public disorder, the governor's role as *commander-in-chief* of the California National Guard (the state militia) comes into play. The scenario usually involves a local riot or disturbance, the inability of local police to restore order, a mayoral request for National Guard assistance, and the deployment of troops to restore order. In 1965, Pat Brown deployed 1,000 guard members during the Watts Riot. In 1992, Wilson sent 7,000 guard members to riot-torn Los Angeles, and in 1994, he sent a smaller number to Northridge to help with earthquake relief efforts. In 2018, at the request of President Trump, Brown sent 400 troops to the California–Mexico border to "combat criminal gangs, human traffickers and illegal firearm and drug smugglers" but stipulated that they would not enforce immigration laws.[13]

Last, governors are *chiefs of state*. As such, they greet foreign dignitaries, address interest group conventions, accompany presidents who are traveling in California, cut ribbons on public works projects, and process a huge volume of mail. Schoolchildren write governors, assuming they exercise far more power than we have discussed. Consider this one: "Dear Governor Reagan: I wrote you once before about having to go to school on my birthday—and nothing happened. My next birthday is a month away and I am wondering what your plans are. Let me hear from you soon. Jeff."[14]

THE PLURAL EXECUTIVE: COMPETING FOR POWER

As considerable as the governor's powers are, they are circumscribed in some profound ways. A significant limitation is called the **plural executive**—an array of executive officials with cabinet-sounding titles who are separately elected and politically independent of the governor. Cabinet members in Washington serve at the pleasure of the president and can be removed at any time. California governors (plus many other governors) can only wish they had that power. Many comparable state officeholders are elected directly by the people. This reflects a historic mistrust of gubernatorial power. Although competition for power understandably ensues, a plural executive does not necessarily hinder a governor's leadership role. The duties of some of these elected officials are largely administrative in nature; independent political power is neither feasible nor possible or consequential. That said, these executives may come from political parties other than the governor's and may publicly oppose the governor's agenda. Their own gubernatorial ambitions may color their relationship with the incumbent governor.

Lieutenant Governor

The least-threatening office of the group is lieutenant governor. California governor Friend W. Richardson (1923–27) never held the post but sized it up succinctly: "to preside over the senate and each morning to inquire solicitously after the governor's health." In 1998, former Assembly Speaker Cruz Bustamante won this office, the first Latino elected to statewide office since 1878. During 2003, he opposed the recall of Davis but also waged a losing campaign to replace him. Former San Francisco mayor Gavin Newsom served as lieutenant governor for eight years before becoming governor. He was followed by Elena Kounalakis, who became the first woman to serve in that position. Table 8.2 displays salaries for the lieutenant governor and other statewide officials.

Because lieutenant governors rarely preside over the California state senate and modern governors tend to be quite healthy, what do lieutenant governors do? First, they sit on various boards, including the Regents of the University of California, the Trustees of the State University System, the State Lands Commission, and the Commission for Economic Development. Politically ambitious lieutenant governors eke whatever publicity they can from these memberships and maximize (or exaggerate) their related policy accomplishments. Second, the lieutenant governor becomes acting governor the minute the governor leaves

Table 8.2 Salaries of Statewide Elected Officials

Office*	Salary†
Governor	$201,680
Lieutenant Governor	$151,260
Attorney General	$175,182
Secretary of State	$151,260
Controller	$161,342
Treasurer	$161,342
Superintendent of Public Instruction	$175,182
Insurance Commissioner	$161,342
Board of Equalization Member	$151,260

Source: California Citizens Compensation Commission, http://www.calhr.ca.gov/cccc/Pages/cccc-salaries.aspx.
* All statewide officers are limited to two terms.
† As of December 3, 2018.

the state, an obvious holdover from days of slower travel and communication. When Governor Brown was gone for a week on a trade mission to China in 2013, Lieutenant Governor Gavin Newsom used his new powers to name the artichoke the state's official vegetable and the avocado the official fruit. In the past, acting governors have taken more significant action by issuing executive orders and vetoing bills, raising the ire of the "real" governor.

Politically speaking, the lieutenant governor is in a "twilight zone" of sorts. The responsibilities assigned to the office rarely embrace the great issues facing California. The media all but ignore the office, giving its occupants few opportunities to communicate with the voters who elect them. Accordingly, the office is a slippery stepping stone at best. In California's history, only six lieutenant governors have become governors. Reformers would like to either abolish this post—five states seem to manage without it—or at least require the governor and the lieutenant governor to run on the same party ticket (a requirement in 25 other states). Yet, polls show that most Californians favor the status quo.

Attorney General

In contrast to the lieutenant governor, the state attorney general is quite powerful. Former attorney general Robert Kenny (1943–46) once quipped: "A smart A.G. could practically take over the state from a dumb governor—if he had a mind to." In fact, the attorney general is the second most powerful position in California's executive branch. This office oversees the state's Department of Justice, which employs 5,000 people, including 1,000 attorneys. Historically, the "A.G." has truly been a stepping stone to higher office. Attorneys General Earl Warren, Pat Brown, George Deukmejian and, most recently, Jerry Brown each became governor. Although some have come from legislative backgrounds (Dan Lungren was a congressman and Bill Lockyer state senator), others have been prominent, politically active district attorneys (Warren, Evelle Younger, John Van de Kamp, and Kamala Harris). Harris, a two-term San Francisco district attorney, succeeded Brown when he was elected governor in 2010. She became the first woman, the first African American, and the first South Asian in California to hold that office. She was elected to the U.S. Senate in 2016 and was succeeded by Democrat Xavier Becerra, the first Latino to hold that position.

In criminal matters, the department conducts investigations, argues all appeals above the trial court level, and nominally oversees local district attorneys and county sheriffs. On rare occasions, the department even prosecutes local crimes if a district attorney refuses to, as it did with the "Hillside Strangler" case in 1981. In civil matters, the attorney general and the army of department lawyers advise other state agencies and represent them in court either as prosecutor or defense counsel. The office also prepares titles and summaries for all ballot measures, which can become controversial. In 2018, some conservatives threatened to launch a recall campaign of Becerra in response to the language he used for the title and summary of Proposition 6, which would have repealed the 2017 gas taxes.

Secretary of State

In terms of discretionary power, the secretary of state stands in stark contrast to the attorney general. Whereas the nation's secretary of state is essentially a minister of foreign affairs, California's secretary of state is essentially a clerk of records and elections. As an archivist, this official maintains all current and historical records. This post also possesses many election-related duties (preparing and distributing statewide voter pamphlets, processing candidate papers, certifying initiative petitions, publishing election results, and tracking campaign donations and expenditures). Also, the secretary of state decides early on which candidates warrant a place on California's presidential primary ballot.

Historically, the position of secretary of state was so routine and devoid of controversy, it was held by a father–son team (Frank C. and Frank M. Jordan) for nearly all of the period between 1911 and 1970. Although Jerry Brown once occupied the office (1970–74), most secretaries of state rarely move up the political ladder, and most generate little controversy or fanfare. In one notable exception, Kevin Shelley gave the office unwelcome publicity when he was accused of fiscal irregularities and verbally abusing his staff. More recently, former state senator Alex Padilla became the first Latino secretary of state when he was elected in 2014.

Superintendent of Public Instruction

One of the most plural, indeed fragmented, arrangements in California's executive branch is the superintendent of public instruction. Several features of this office set it apart from other statewide elective offices. First, unlike other members of the plural executive, the position is officially nonpartisan, reflecting the notion that education and "politics" should not mix. Second, the superintendent does not "superintend" in the dictionary sense. Rather, the office shares responsibility for the 1,200-employee Department of Education with an 11-member Board of Education appointed by the governor. Furthermore, even though 80 percent of school funding flows through this department, the actual task of education takes place locally in more than 1,000 school districts. Although the recently enacted Every Student Succeeds Act delegated more responsibility to the states, the federal Department of Education still plays a role in local education policy. This governance structure has been a perfect formula for policy fragmentation and diffusion of educational responsibility.

Consequently, in hyperpluralistic fashion, governors, superintendents, the state board, legislators, local educators, and interest groups continually battle over education policy and funding (see chapter 13). In 2018, former assemblyman Tony Thurmond narrowly won the office, becoming the second African American to occupy the position.

Insurance Commissioner

In 1988, California voters "pluralized" still further the executive branch by approving Proposition 103. They authorized auto insurance rate reductions and joined eight other states that have an elected insurance commissioner. Prior to "103," the governor had appointed the commissioner. This is the only office in California's plural executive to have been created by the initiative process. The commissioner heads the state's Department of Insurance, which regulates the insurance industry in California. The insurance commissioner enforces the state's insurance code, approves industry mergers, pursues industry fraud, levies fines for insurance wrongdoing, and controls some types of insurance rates. As health insurance rates have increased in recent years, the commissioner's powers have drawn attention because they lack the ability to review and approve rate hikes for health insurance as occurs in 37 other states. In 2014, insurance companies spent $57 million to defeat Proposition 45, which would have given authority to the commissioner to approve insurance rates.

The goal of protecting insurance consumers is more problematic than one might think. Republican commissioner Chuck Quakenbush resigned in disgrace in 2002 after diverting and misspending insurance funds intended for Northridge earthquake victims. A deeper problem stems from the elective nature of the post itself. For years, consumer groups viewed the Department of Insurance as little more than a cheerleader for the politically powerful insurance industry. Making the post elective rather than appointive may have worsened the problem as candidates seek campaign contributions from the very industry they are seeking to regulate. Former state senator Ricardo Lara was elected to the post in 2018.

Fiscal Officers

Although all members of California's plural executive are elected and therefore require campaign funds, the job descriptions of some of them center around money: collecting it, investing it, and disbursing it to pay the state's bills. These offices are the controller, treasurer, and Board of Equalization:

- *Controller.* As the chief fiscal officer of the state, the controller pays all bills, monitors all state accounts, and audits various state and local programs. In addition to managing disbursements of over $200 billion annually, this official sits on nearly 80 boards, committees, and commissions, including the Franchise Tax Board (which collects the state's income tax) and the Board of Equalization (which collects other taxes). Controllers who have sought to run for governor have experienced victory and defeat. The Board of Equalization served as a training ground for two recent controllers, John Chiang (2006–14) and Betty Yee (elected in 2014), who were former members. Despite its mainly administrative tasks, Chiang attempted to extend the office's power in 2011. Claiming authority under the newly passed Proposition 25, Chiang determined that the state budget was not "balanced" and docked legislators' pay. A state court later ruled that only the legislature has the ability to determine whether a budget is balanced.
- *Treasurer.* If the controller writes the state's checks, the treasurer handles the money when it is in the checking account. Because there is a lag between when revenue is received and when it is spent, the treasurer invests it in the interim. Obviously, the goal is to obtain the highest possible interest rates for money on deposit. Another important responsibility is to sell state bonds (a form of borrowing discussed in chapter 11). Because this revenue funds major construction (such as water projects, school construction, and affordable housing) and must be paid back with interest to large financial institutions, the treasurer tries to obtain the lowest possible rates. The treasurer oversees the investment of nearly $100 billion in state and local money and sits on pension boards that invest the retirement assets of millions of public employees and schoolteachers. Because the treasurer decides who gets to

resell revenue bonds to investors, investment firms have been known to contribute to treasurers' election campaigns, a questionable practice given their economic stake in the office. Although Jesse Unruh enhanced the powers and clout of this office during his long tenure (1974–86), it also remains a rather slippery stepping-stone to higher office. A series of politically ambitious individuals including Kathleen Brown (Pat Brown's daughter and Jerry Brown's sister), Matt Fong, and former Democratic Party chair and businessman Philip Angelides have attempted to run for higher office from this precarious perch. Former vice chairwoman of the Board of Equalization, Fiona Ma, became treasurer in 2018.

- *Board of Equalization.* The last fiscal office in California's plural executive is the Board of Equalization, which consists of four elected individuals plus the state controller, who serves ex officio (without vote). Districts, representing more than 9 million people each, elect the four. These four are largely invisible to average Californians, even when campaigning. In 2017–18, the board underwent a major restructuring after it was revealed that the agency had mishandled close to $50 million that was owed to local governments and board members were found meddling in daily operations. Many of its functions were stripped from it and moved to two new agencies—one that would collect taxes (mainly sales) and one that would hear appeals. The board retained its responsibility over property taxes, the alcohol beverage tax, insurance taxes, and certain taxpayer appeals.[15]

CALIFORNIA'S BUREAUCRACY AND THE POLITICS OF DIVERSITY

Any large, diverse state with a complex economy and a comprehensive state government will possess a substantial bureaucracy. California boasts one of the nation's largest. Virtually every aspect of life in California is touched in some way by the state's executive branch and the people that work in it. Roughly 200,000 full-time employees work for a host of departments, agencies, boards, and commissions. Is this number high or even too high? It depends on one's perspective. If you consider the ratio of state employees to the state's overall population—a more realistic measure of bureaucratic size—that number has declined over time. In fact, the number of state employees per 1,000 Californians was consistently higher in the 1970s than it has been in recent years and currently ranks among the lowest of the 50 states.

Several hiring systems govern state employees. Over 130,000 are governed by the tenure and hiring practices of the University of California and State University systems. Most of the rest operate under **civil service**—the idea that permanent employees should be hired and evaluated based on merit not politics. This means competence and expertise rather than political connections and clout. California's civil service system, like those of other states, was modeled after the federal *Pendleton Act of 1883* and Progressive Era opposition to patronage. In 2011, Governor Brown spearheaded a move to restructure oversight of the vast civil service system. The Department of Personnel Administration was abolished and its functions, along with some of those under the State Personnel Board, were placed under the new California Department of Human Resources. The new department now administers the overall civil service system, hears appeals from aggrieved employees or job applicants, and handles all issues subject to collective bargaining including salaries, benefits, job classifications, and training.

Functions of Bureaucracy

Even the briefest survey of California's bureaucracy demonstrates the magnitude of government and the diversity of its work. A majority of all state employees work for the two university systems or in the area of public safety (prisons, highway patrol, the Department of Justice, and the courts). The primary purpose of California's bureaucracy is implementation—carrying out policies and laws approved by the legislature and even the voters (through initiatives). Most of the myriad day-to-day activities of bureaucracies are required to implement policy. The following sampling of various state agencies illustrates some of these activities. The Highway Patrol *patrols* state highways and *monitors* school bus transportation. The Department of Alcoholic Beverage Control *licenses and regulates* the manufacture, sale, purchases, possession, and transportation of alcoholic beverages. The Integrated Waste Management Board *promotes* recycling and composting. The California Department of Transportation *builds, maintains, and rehabilitates* the state's roads and bridges. The Department of Fair Employment and Housing *enforces* the state's civil rights laws that ban various forms of discrimination. The Department of Public Health *manages* numerous health programs. The Air Resources Board *establishes* clean air standards and *administers* the state's cap and trade program.

To the extent that the various layers of government in California contribute to hyperpluralism, the same can be said about California's bureaucracy. Excepting higher education, virtually all state agencies, departments, offices, and boards coordinate their activities with similar local government efforts, or they may actually direct those efforts. Consider just K–12 education. The State Board of Education selects textbooks for grade levels K–8, develops curricular frameworks like the Common Core standards, approves local waivers from state regulations, and oversees the credentialing of teachers. The Commission on Teacher Credentialing certifies teacher preparation programs in the state's colleges and universities. The Department of Education communicates education policy to school districts, approves instructional materials, and provides curriculum leadership. Local school districts receive and account for state funds, deliver education per state standards, administer state-designed tests, cope with enrollment growth, and innovate wherever they can.

All these functions have produced mountains of paperwork in the Golden State. No matter where one turns, there are regulations to follow, forms to fill out, and fine print to read. The title of a 1995 Little Hoover Commission report on California's bureaucracy summed it up—*Too Many Agencies, Too Many Rules.*[16] Critics often point to this red tape as a major factor behind the state's poor business climate ranking. But they would do well to remember this: given the state's size, complexity, and diversity, California's bureaucracy is bound to be large, complex, and diverse. Furthermore, as the editors of the *California Almanac* put it, "Wrapped in red tape they may be, but bureaucrats are the technicians that keep the machinery of state government humming."[17]

Power Sharing and Clout

California's bureaucracy also shares power with the federal government. Most federal aid destined for the state and even local governments passes through state agencies. Structurally, you can think of these relationships as a fiscal version of a picket fence. For example, the portion of federal gas taxes returned to the state funnel through the Department of Transportation (Caltrans) to various state or local transportation improvements (see figure 8.2). Certain state agencies rely on counties to channel the delivery of state services such as foster care, welfare, and public health.

The clout of California's public employees comes not only from what they do but also from their ability to organize. Borrowing labor practices from the private sector, most state employees are organized into more than 20 different bargaining units, represented by 12 unions. The largest is the California State Employees' Association, representing over 140,000 active and retired civil servants. There are also specific unions representing specific professions in state government. The largest is the Service Employees International Union that represents nearly 100,000 state workers from nurses to bus drivers. More than 30,000 prison guards belong to the California Correctional Peace Officers Association. As their website declares, this group represents "the men and women who walk the toughest beat in the state."[18] As union members, state employees deal with many personnel-related issues such as collective bargaining rights, and sexual harassment, plus the administration of pension plans. In 1992, they heavily supported the passage of Proposition 162, which gave public employee pension boards greater power to manage their own affairs. In the past, the legislature occasionally "borrowed" (some say "raided") assets from the pension plans to help balance state budgets. The two largest boards are CalPERS (the Public Employees Retirement System) and STRS (the State Teachers Retirement System).

As in other states, California's public employees have come under fire for the large unfunded liabilities that remain outstanding in the state's two pension systems. Critics have decried what they regard as overly generous public-sector salaries, fringe benefits, and retirement packages. Responding to increased public scrutiny and long-term funding threats, Brown and legislative Democrats passed

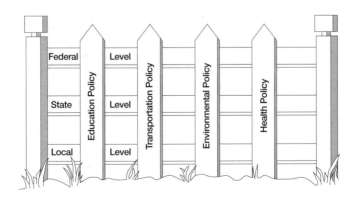

Figure 8.2 Picket-Fence Relationships in California

a comprehensive package of pension reforms in 2012. The package eliminated options that enhanced benefit levels for current employees, reduced benefit levels for future workers, and raised employee contribution amounts. Some observers argued that the reforms did not do enough to reduce long-term funding problems. State policymakers took a significant additional step to shore up funding for STRS in 2014, which was in worse shape than CalPERS. Contribution rates for teachers, school districts, and the state will gradually rise to help fill a projected funding hole near $75 billion.

Executive Branch Reform

When Schwarzenegger campaigned for governor, he vowed to "blow up the boxes," that is, reorganize the workings of state government. It made for colorful, *Terminator*-like election rhetoric, but one had to wonder at the time how much he knew about those boxes that constituted the executive branch. If not then, he would later learn that 339 separate boards and commissions shared power with executive branch agencies and departments. One such board, the Unemployment Insurance Appeals Board, paid each member over $128,000 per year for work easily managed by civil service workers and administrative law judges. Most board members were, in fact, termed-out legislators. Calling the state government a "mastodon frozen in time," Schwarzenegger appointed a 275-person team—the California Performance Review—to study the executive branch and make recommendations for reform. Their 2,700-page, six-inch-thick report contained more than 1,000 recommendations, including the elimination of more than 12,000 jobs, the abolition of 118 boards and commissions, and the streamlining of still other agencies where policy redundancy was routine.[19]

Schwarzenegger and reform proponents praised the report: "We cannot just chip away at the edges of our state's problems. Sometimes a surgeon has to cut in order to save the patient."[20] The governor later lost interest in that ambitious reform agenda and larger budget woes preempted it in his second term. By the time he left office, he had even appointed some former staffers to boards he once would have eliminated. Whereas Schwarzenegger failed to implement his vision for reform, Brown scaled the size of reform back and successfully pushed a reorganization plan through the legislature in 2012. The elimination of more than 50 boards, commissions, and other entities was estimated to save the state about $10 million annually. Although the amount is a drop in the bucket in a state budget of over $200 billion, this and other measures to reduce government expenditures, such as cutting the number of state vehicles, provided the governor with badly needed symbols of austerity in a time of fiscal crisis.

CONCLUSION

The themes of hyperpluralism and diversity emerge from a review of California's executive branch. Executive leadership in California is a diffused phenomenon. Power is shared among the governor, other statewide elected officials, and a huge bureaucracy. California governors, as elsewhere, can employ several resources to enhance their leadership potential. Historians regard Hiram Johnson, Earl Warren, Pat Brown, and Ronald Reagan as gubernatorial giants. They clearly made the most of the power they had. But they governed in a simpler time over a smaller and less-diverse California. Today's governors wield substantial formal powers, but even these are shared by the legislature, a plural executive system and, at times, the voters themselves. The office's most singular duties are constitutionally mandated, such as submitting a budget, exercising veto power, and performing various judicial roles.

The vastness of California's bureaucracy in some respects mirrors the diversity of the state itself. As figure 8.1 suggests, virtually every economic sector and demographic group is represented in and/or regulated by the executive branch. The state's bureaucrats can wield a great deal of power but commonly share it with the judiciary or legislature. In the past, reformers believed that the gridlock between the executive branch and the other branches was the source of California's governing problems. Calls for reform abated as the state's financial condition improved under the Brown administration. Future economic and fiscal challenges will truly test whether California is indeed governable in good times and bad.

KEY TERMS

political context (p. 165)

inner circle (p. 167)

superagencies (p. 167)

executive order (p. 168)

internal budget processes (p. 168)

external budget processes (p. 168)

line item veto (p. 170)

general veto (p. 172)

special session (p. 172)

clemency (p. 173)

plural executive (p. 174)

civil service (p. 179)

REVIEW QUESTIONS

1. Apply Crew's gubernatorial leadership variables to Governor Jerry Brown and other recent California governors. What did Brown discover about leadership since his first two terms as governor?
2. Of the governor's duties and powers, which do you think are the most and least important?
3. How have recent governors addressed the state's budget troubles? What letter grade would you give them?
4. In what ways does California's plural executive increase political fragmentation and encourage hyperpluralism?
5. If you wanted to use a statewide elective office as a stepping-stone to the governorship, which would you seek, not seek, and why?
6. In what ways can California's bureaucracy exercise power independent of the governor? Is the bureaucracy itself a function of hyperpluralism?

WEB RESOURCES

Governor's Office
https://www.gov.ca.gov

This site features biographical information, speeches, press releases, executive orders, video blogs, and volumes of other information related to the current governor.

State Agencies

https://www.ca.gov/agencysearch

This directory leads you to a stunningly long list of agencies, departments, divisions, boards, commissions, and other state entities with links to each one. The scope and diversity of California's executive branch are readily apparent.

Capitol Weekly

http://capitolweekly.net

This online newspaper includes many articles and features of interest to all Californians and public-sector workers in particular, including job postings, salary data, and policy decisions affecting those workers.

9

California's Judiciary

★ ★ ★

LEARNING OUTCOMES

Students will be able to:

★ Describe how California courts are organized, including the functions of each level.

★ Explain the steps and processes involved in selecting California judges.

★ Analyze the factors that go into decision-making by judges and juries.

★ Define court policymaking and explain how it differs between trial and appellate courts.

★ Describe how social trends, sentencing mandates, and prison reforms have affected criminal justice in California.

IN BRIEF

California's judiciary shares power with the legislative and executive branches. As in other states, it is divided into two levels: trial courts and appellate courts. Lower courts handle major disputes and offenses and hold preliminary hearings on more serious matters. Trial courts decide matters of fact; appellate courts, matters of law. All cases are either criminal (wrongs against society) or civil (disputes among individuals and/or organizations).

★ ★ ★

LAWYERS WHO WANT TO BE JUDGES must become politically involved. Although all judges in California must eventually face the voters, most assume the bench through gubernatorial appointment. In a representative democracy, judges need to be both independent and politically accountable—a difficult balance to achieve. Judges are also accountable to professional standards policed by the California Commission on Judicial Performance.

Judges make case-specific decisions in addition to public policy. At the trial court level, cases follow a predictable chronology, including various pretrial activities designed to avoid trial, the trial itself, and the sentence or judgment.

Appellate justices have the most leeway in making public policy, as recent state supreme courts demonstrate. The judiciary's most visible policy role involves criminal justice, especially cases involving the death penalty.

Although the legal profession does not reflect California's growing ethnicity, judicial policymaking in California is influenced by both the state's diversity and its population growth. In addition to carrying out its own policy role, California courts also share power with the legislative and executive branches.

INTRODUCTION

Fact: A parent in Granada Hills, California, sues a Little League executive after he is told to stop smoking during a game. The parent claims emotional distress.

Fact: Losing a citizen initiative campaign, an interest group sues the state to prevent its implementation.

Fact: One Californian files more than 1,000 claims against businesses and governments, alleging that they failed to comply with disability laws.

These examples illustrate some broad trends occurring in California and the nation. First, we are a litigious society. Americans increasingly view all manner of problems and even public policies in legal terms. Lawyers and laypersons alike assume that for every wrong there must be a legal remedy, usually determined in a court of law. Second, there has been an explosion in the number of lawyers in U.S. society. Of all U.S. lawyers, about one in seven practices in California. In 2019, there were more than 191,000 active attorneys in California; thousands more join the state bar each year.[1] More lawyers likely mean more lawsuits. Third, the crush of civil and criminal cases has bogged down California's busiest court systems. At any one time in Los Angeles County, there are more than 1 million small claims and civil cases in process; resolving many of them can take years.

Despite all the litigation, Californians' knowledge of the legal system is rather spotty. On one hand, surveys suggest that many cannot identify specifics in the national Bill of Rights, and nearly half are unaware that defendants are innocent until proved guilty. Yet, most are aware that it takes a .08 or higher blood alcohol level to be convicted of adult drunk driving and that both parents could be liable for child support.

Given the role of law in California's political system, what courts, judges, and juries do affects all Californians. The judiciary has always shared power with the legislative and executive branches. Conflict among them is increasingly common. At times, judges seem to have the final say; at other times, they seem only to contribute to the policy gridlock occurring in the nation's most populous and diverse state. This chapter examines California's legal system and its policymaking role, how it is organized, and what its participants do.

STATE COURTS IN OUR LEGAL "SYSTEM"

We use the term *legal system* advisedly. The federal *Judiciary Act of 1789* actually created a dual system of courts, national and state. The federal courts deal with matters arising from the U.S. Constitution, civil cases involving regulatory activity, plus a relatively small number of criminal offenses. Fifty separate state systems address matters arising from state constitutions, civil matters, and most criminal offenses. State courts handle the vast majority of all court activity in the nation.

California is only one of those 50 systems, but it is not simply a copy of the others. Each state's judiciary reflects, to some extent, its political culture and history. The independent spirit that characterized California's history was bound to be reflected in its legal system; in fact, its Supreme Court has developed a national reputation for independence from the federal judiciary. Unlike many Southern states that used a "states rights" philosophy to impede federal civil rights efforts, California's courts have viewed independence in progressive terms. The state's "independent-state grounds" doctrine assumed that when state and federal constitutional provisions are similar, California could interpret those provisions more expansively or liberally. This view, pioneered by the late state Supreme Court justice Stanley Mosk, expanded individual rights beyond those granted by the U.S. Supreme Court—a doctrine called "independent-state grounds."[2] In several celebrated cases, the California Supreme Court struck down the death penalty before its federal counterpart did, rejected the state's method of financing public education (a decision the U.S. Supreme Court has refused to make), and invalidated a citizen initiative that would have banned fair housing laws.[3] This exemplifies **judicial federalism**: the ability and willingness of different court systems to produce potentially diverse, fragmented, and contradictory policy.

California's independent-minded judiciary does not operate in a vacuum. Some people prefer to resolve their legal disputes at the federal level. California has four federal district courts located throughout the state. It is possible for state and federal courts to hear the same kinds of cases (civil rights and liberties), a phenomenon called "concurrent jurisdiction." As a result, Californians can "shop" for the level—federal or state—most likely to give them the desired result. Challenges to voter-approved initiatives are often filed in federal court. Examples include Propositions 187 (immigration), 209 (affirmative action), and 8 (same-sex marriage).

If decisions by the federal district courts in California are appealed, they go to the U.S. Court of Appeals for the Ninth Circuit. This court is famous for its own judicial independence. In fact, the U.S. Supreme Court has rebuked this circuit court for frustrating California's efforts to execute death row inmates. More than most federal appellate courts, the Ninth Circuit handles cases involving diverse populations and sweeping social changes. The judges themselves admit that California provides them with a variety of cutting-edge issues because of the state's size, diversity, and independence from federal policies. Occasionally, the U.S. Supreme Court itself overturns California law and policy. For example, in 2018, it struck down a California law that required crisis pregnancy centers, typically run by antiabortion activists, to disclose more information to the public, such as whether they are a licensed medical facility (some are not). The law was intended to ensure that women who walk through the doors were not misled, but in *National Institute of Family and Life Advocates v. Becerra*, the court ruled that the state law violated First Amendment provisions of free speech.

HOW CALIFORNIA'S COURTS ARE ORGANIZED

California's judicial system is the largest in the world, consisting of more than 2,000 judicial officers divided into three tiers of courts. These layers divide the judiciary's caseload within the system while allowing ample opportunity for

Box 9.1 ★ California Court System

California Supreme Court, 1 chief justice, 6 associate justices

- Hears oral arguments in San Francisco, Los Angeles, and Sacramento
- Has discretionary authority to review decisions of the Courts of Appeal and direct responsibility for automatic appeals after death penalty judgments

Courts of Appeal, 105 justices

- Six districts, 18 divisions, and 9 court locations
- Review the majority of appealable orders or judgments from the superior courts

Superior Courts, more than 2,000 judges, commissioners, and referees

- Fifty-eight courts, one in each county, with from 1 to 55 branches
- Provide a forum for the resolution of criminal and civil cases under state and local laws, which define crimes, specify punishments, and define civil duties and liabilities

Question: Should death penalty cases go directly to the Supreme Court or work their way through the courts of appeal like other cases?

Source: Judicial Council of California.

litigants to appeal unfavorable decisions (see box 9.1). Let's briefly look at each layer, beginning where most cases start—at the bottom.

Trial Courts

On the lowest rung of the judicial ladder are the state's trial courts. Called **superior courts** in California, they are triers of fact; they determine who is right or wrong in civil disputes and who is innocent or guilty in criminal cases. Until recently, there were both municipal courts and superior courts. The municipal courts handled minor criminal offenses (punishable by fines or jail time), infractions (fineable violations of state statutes or local ordinances), and civil claims of $25,000 or less. In 1998, the passage of Proposition 220 allowed municipal and superior court functions to merge into the superior courts.

All state trial courts are now organized in this manner. In recent years, roughly 1,700 authorized judges and 342 commissioners and referees have been authorized to act as judges. In addition to all felony and civil disputes, the superior courts serve as family, juvenile, and probate courts. Depending on the county's size, superior court judges either hear a wide variety of cases or specialize in a particular area of the law: juvenile, family, probate, or criminal. They are paid about $181,000 per year, plus benefits. Cases may be decided by juries or only judges (bench trials). Supporting the judges are professional court administrators who manage court personnel, budgets, and workloads. In addition to traditional courts are collaborative justice courts or "problem solving" courts that combine judicial supervision with rehabilitation services. Seeking to reduce recidivism and improve offender outcomes, these specialized courts address issues such as domestic violence, drug abuse, driving under the influence, elder abuse, the homeless, mental illness, and juvenile justice. The availability of these courts depends on where one lives. The largest counties can afford to provide most of these collaborative courts; the smallest can barely afford two judges and a part-time commissioner.

The volume of trial court cases in California is staggering. Superior courts handle more than 6 million filings annually, most of those criminal in nature.

In addition to court consolidation, California's judiciary has experienced other recent improvements. The *1997 Trial Court Funding Act* transferred financial responsibility for the trial courts to the state. The purpose of this reform was to stabilize and make more equitable judicial services across the state. Then chief justice Ronald M. George called it "without a doubt one of the most important reforms in the California justice system in the 20th century."[4] California has also increased court interpreter services and with good reason. Interpreters can be certified in 15 languages, although Spanish accounts for more than 80 percent of the demand.

Appellate Courts

District courts of appeal hear appeals from superior courts and quasi-judicial state agencies. They are geographically divided into six districts, serving nine locations. Unlike superior courts, they normally decide questions of law, not fact. For instance, instead of deciding guilt or innocence in a car theft case, California's 105 appellate justices typically sit on three-member panels to determine if legal procedures were applied properly in that case. (Was the suspect informed of his or her rights? Did the judge instruct the jury properly?) If legal errors did occur, they can order a new trial. At that level, there are no "trials" as such, no witnesses or juries. The justices read trial court transcripts and occasionally hear oral arguments by opposing attorneys. They spend hours in private legal research, not in the courtroom. When they hear cases, they usually sit as panels of three. Because the California Supreme Court also declines to hear most cases appealed to it, appellate court decisions are often final. Appeals rarely involve life-or-death, earth-shaking issues; one justice called most of them the equivalent of junk mail. The courts of appeal process more than 20,000 filings annually and dispose of fewer than 10,000 matters through written opinions. Fewer than 9 percent of those are deemed significant enough to warrant publication.[5] Appellate justices earn about $207,000 annually; presiding justices earn somewhat more.

Supreme Court

The **California Supreme Court** is at the pinnacle of the system. Its purpose is to raise important constitutional issues and to maintain legal uniformity throughout the state. When it speaks, other courts listen—not only in California but also in other states and throughout the federal judiciary. Because of heavy volume, this court must be selective in what it chooses to hear and what it chooses to say. The Supreme Court averages nearly 8,000 filings annually but issues only 80 to 90 written opinions per year. Its seven justices spend most of their time in legal research and opinion writing. They hear oral arguments for only one week of every month they are in session. The court consists of a chief justice and six associate justices. The associate justices earn about $221,000 a year; the chief justice earns about $232,000 a year.

If the Supreme Court is so selective, what kinds of cases is it willing to hear? First, much of its work is civil in nature, reflecting the legal problems of California businesses. Second, all death penalty cases are "automatic appeals"; they bypass the appellate courts and must be heard directly by the Supreme Court.

In its 2017–18 term, the court considered 37 new death penalty appeals and disposed of 33 such cases, usually backlogged ones. Most of these cases are over a decade old by the time they reach the court, and when they do, they consume huge amounts of the Court's time and resources. Lengthy records and numerous motions demand court time even before formal hearings occur. Third, as noted in chapter 4, the widespread use of initiatives fosters litigation and, ultimately, interpretation by the California Supreme Court. In a rare decision in 2018, the court removed Proposition 9 from the November ballot, which would have begun the process to split California into three states.

SO YOU WANT TO BE A JUDGE

A law school official once said that A-students become law professors, B-students become judges, and C-students become rich! A judgeship is a noble goal regardless of grade point average. Judges earn much less than senior corporate law partners, but the pay is reasonable; plus, a judgeship offers a level of prestige no law firm can match. Several steps are required to become a judge. Given the number of judicial officers and active attorneys in California (2,000 and 191,000, respectively), only a small percentage will ever achieve this elusive goal.

Courtesy of the Supreme Court of California, photograph by Bob Kapnik

The Supreme Court of California (left to right): Associate Justice Leondra R. Kruger, Associate Justice Ming W. Chin, Associate Justice Goodwin H. Liu, Chief Justice Tani G. Cantil-Sakauye, Associate Justice Mariano-Florentino Cuéllar, Associate Justice Carol A. Corrigan, Associate Justice Joshua P. Groban

Entering the Profession

To become a judge, one must first become a lawyer, but this was not always the case. In the past, nonlawyers could serve as justices of the peace. Today, virtually all California judges are law school graduates. To practice law, the state constitution requires all practicing lawyers to join the State Bar Association of California, a quasi-official group that oversees the admission and discipline of the state's attorneys. Applicants to the state bar must pass a 2-day state bar exam, considered one of the nation's toughest. It is common for nearly half of exam takers to fail, sometimes repeatedly. That badge of honor is shared by the likes of Governor Jerry Brown, former California Supreme Court justice William P. Clark, and a host of lesser knowns. The best overall preparation for the exam is law school. California boasts 21 American Bar Associations—accredited law schools and 22 schools accredited by the Committee of Bar Examiners, plus several unaccredited schools and distance-learning law courses.

Who employs California's lawyers? About three-fourths are in private practice. The rest work in government, private industry, education, or other contexts. The demographic makeup of both the California bar and bench does not mirror California as a whole. Although they are gradually becoming more diverse, both the bar and the courts, even more so, remain largely male and white. One of the most significant demographic changes is the influx of women in the legal profession. Nearly 41 percent of the state bar are women, and for those with 10 years or less since bar admittance, nearly 53 percent are female. For nonwhite groups, the trend is much slower. They constitute about 20 percent of the state bar and more than 30 percent of the state bench.[6]

A major challenge facing the legal profession in California is equal access to legal representation. As we have seen repeatedly, two Californias are evident—in this case, those who can afford legal representation and those who cannot. Although public defenders represent indigent defendants in criminal cases, civil cases are more problematic. There are relatively few legal aid lawyers compared to other private attorneys in California. The State Bar of California is addressing this by encouraging more attorneys to volunteer a portion of their time for the public good ("pro bono" work).

The Right Experience

Few California lawyers are situated to become judges. To be considered judgeship material, lawyers find they need a network of personal, legal, and political relationships. The right law school may help. Governor Jerry Brown's two appointees to the California Supreme Court in 2014, Leondra Kruger and Mariano-Florentine Cuéllar, had one thing in common with the governor: all were Yale Law School alumni. After law school, most lawyers settle into private practice or work for government. They become involved in a local bar association and may dabble in partisan politics. Attending political fund-raisers and contributing to a governor's campaign helps, as many judges can attest. One's legal specialty also affects one's chances of becoming a judge. Young lawyers grinding out billable hours for high-powered law firms may find little time, energy, or incentive for politics. Of those who practice criminal law, aspiring judicial candidates are likely to be district attorneys, not defense attorneys.

Selection Mechanics

The formal steps to becoming a judge vary, depending on the court level. All levels in California employ a version of the **Missouri Plan**, which combines both elections and appointments. This hybrid method is based on two assumptions: (1) fellow lawyers can best assess the attributes of judicial candidates, and (2) in a representative democracy, ultimate accountability to the voters is important, even for judges.

Trial Courts. At the local, trial court level, voters elect judges for six-year terms in officially nonpartisan elections (once again, thanks to the Progressives). Reelection is virtually guaranteed, even if there is an opponent—and opponents are rare. What lawyer wants to run against a judge, lose, and then face that judge in court? If judges leave office between elections, the governor appoints a replacement to fill out a term based on recommendations from the local bar and political allies. Judges themselves can fill some vacancies by appointing commissioners, lawyers who act as judges on a temporary basis. These lawyers gain invaluable experience they can tout if a permanent judgeship opportunity arises.

Although some political scientists refer to judges as "politicians who wear robes," local judicial elections have been staid affairs. Judges raise modest campaign support from fellow lawyers and the business community, but rarely wage the kind of combative election campaigns voters see in other branches of government. There is little or no precinct walking, television advertising, or direct mail flyers. Maybe a few yard signs or newspaper ads. In fact, the state's Code of Judicial Ethics proscribes judicial candidates from knowingly misrepresenting the identity, qualifications, and views of their election opponents. But times are changing. As more judicial candidates hire political consultants, their campaigns increasingly resemble those of other offices—more politicized, negative, and costly (see box 9.2).

Box 9.2 ★ California Voices: The Angst of a Judicial Candidate

I bought space on slate mailers, as suggested by my campaign consultant. Being a political naïf, I did not realize that my name might appear on highly partisan and/or issue-oriented slates—like on the candidate slate of the "Republicans Against Abortion" and on the slate for "Pro-Choice Democrats." Did I fail to sufficiently inform myself? (Who has time for that?) Given the mandatory disclaimers on slate mailers, does it matter? I was asked to respond to questionnaires. Although some were legitimate—requesting my background information and soliciting my views on how the administration of justice might be improved—others were blatantly political. They demanded to know whether I believed *Roe v. Wade* was incorrectly decided and whether prayer in the schools should be permitted. They said a refusal to answer would be construed as a negative response. I ignored them. Was there a better way?

Question: Should judges wage campaigns much like other officeholders? Why? Why not?

Source: Excerpted from Maria P. Rivera, "The Complexities—and Importance—of Running a Fair Campaign," *California Courts Review* (Fall 2007—Winter 2008): 16.

Note: Judicial candidate Maria P. Rivera won her Contra Costa judgeship and is now associate justice for the First District Court of Appeal.

Appellate and Supreme Courts. The process of becoming an appellate or Supreme Court justice is a combination of initial appointment and later election, but there are additional layers of evaluation. Although the governor makes the initial appointment, two other groups have substantial input. First, the state legislature requires the California State Bar's Commission on Judicial Nominees Evaluation to investigate nominee credentials and rate their fitness for office. Options are exceptionally well qualified, well qualified, qualified, unqualified, or "not qualified at this time." The most common rating is well qualified. Second, a nominee needs approval by a three-member Commission on Judicial Appointments, consisting of the chief justice of the Supreme Court, the attorney general, and the senior presiding justice of the court of appeals. Although this group normally approves a governor's choice, a split vote can embarrass the governor and spell future trouble for the nominee. Both Rose Bird and Cruz Reynoso were approved by a 2–1 vote, raising public doubts about their fitness. Once confirmed by this group, the appellate or Supreme Court justice takes the oath of office and begins work.

The voters have input at the next gubernatorial election. In these "retention" elections, the justices have no specific opponents and run solely on their records. For example, one ballot item would read "FOR ASSOCIATE JUSTICE OF THE SUPREME COURT Shall ASSOCIATE JUSTICE GOODWIN LIU be elected to the office for the term provided by law?" State Supreme Court justices face all California voters. Appellate justices face only the voters in their respective appellate districts. Once they win, they serve 12-year terms, after which they face another retention election. If they are filling an unexpired term, they serve only the remainder of the term and then face election. Usually, voters pay little attention to what judges do, but 1986 was different. In a historic election, California voters rejected Chief Justice Rose Bird and Associate Justices Joseph Grodin and Cruz Reynoso. The justices' support for defendant rights and consistent opposition to the death penalty, despite public support for it, fueled a successful "anti-Bird Court" campaign. A 1998 effort by antiabortion activists to unseat Chief Justice Ronald George and Justice Ming Chin was unsuccessful but forced them to raise money and actually campaign. The fall 2018 ballot was more typical. According to the National Institute on Money in State Politics, not one California appellate justice (out of 50 races) or Supreme Court justice (out of 2 races) raised or spent *anything* to be retained.[7]

Judicial Discipline

As we have seen, voters can, but rarely do, oust sitting judges. Does that mean lawyers and judges can do most anything they want? Not quite. The California Constitution provides for the impeachment of state judges "for misconduct in office."[8] This involves impeachment (an indictment of sorts) in the Assembly and a trial in the Senate. Aside from this rarely used method of judicial discipline, there is a complex system of judicial accountability involving not only the public but also the legal profession. Judges are held to professional norms and subject to peer review.

Professional Norms. Lawyers learn to think and behave like judges during law school, a process called **judicial socialization**. First, they learn about judicial ethics. For example, judges are not supposed to decide cases in which they have a personal stake. Yet some do. One trial court judge issued an order releasing from custody his own son who had been arrested for drunk driving, an action roundly criticized in the legal community. Second, they learn to appreciate the rule of precedent—*stare decisis*. Judges are expected to make new decisions by relying heavily on previous ones, especially those of higher courts. Third, judges render decisions within certain limits such as sentencing standards, jury instruction rules, and uniform legal procedures. Whereas the public cares primarily about verdicts, judges are equally concerned with procedures used to achieve verdicts. In a state and nation governed by the "rule of law," procedure is the all-important vehicle through which courts ascertain truth and determine justice.

Peer Review. Socrates once said, "Four things belong to a judge: to hear courteously, to answer wisely, to consider soberly, and to decide impartially." What happens when a judge does otherwise—yells at attorneys and their clients or calls two juvenile defendants "bitches" or gives preferential treatment to friends and family? These are the kinds of complaints handled by California's Commission on Judicial Performance. This independent state agency consists of 11 members, including judges, attorneys, and lay citizens.

Its primary duty is to investigate accusations of willful misconduct by judges, including offensive courtroom demeanor, disparaging the attorneys present, moral turpitude, sexual harassment, and using court resources for personal business.[9] The Code of Judicial Ethics lays out standards of conduct. Although some complaints are valid, most are filed by litigants upset they lost their cases. Only a few judges are disciplined in any way, and fewer still forfeit their posts.

The Ballot Box. Although few voters pay attention to disciplinary matters, they do react to well-publicized or controversial decisions they do not like. When judges consistently make decisions outside the broad political beliefs of Californians, they may pay a price on Election Day. In the 1986 election, three Supreme Court justices were defeated largely because of their adamant opposition to the death penalty; they had reversed 52 of 55 death penalties by early 1986. In some cases, they seemed to stretch reason, at least in the opinion of some Californians. For example, the court majority overturned one death sentence, finding the defendant lacked the intent to kill, even though the victim had been decapitated and was missing both hands.

At the local level, unpopular decisions can lead to recall efforts, even though they usually fail. However, one successful recall occurred in 2018 when a Santa Clara County judge sentenced a man to six months in jail for sexually assaulting an unconscious woman. It was the first time a judge had been recalled in California in more than 80 years.[10] One superior court judge echoed the paradox of judicial accountability: "We don't want judges who are totally immune and divorced from real life, and on the other hand we want them to be sufficiently independent so that they can make decisions based on principle."[11]

HOW COURTS MAKE DECISIONS

In previous chapters, we examined how legislators and executives make policy and share power. Judges do both as well. But court decisions are different from policy decisions made in other branches. They result from pretrial and trial activity. As elsewhere in the nation, trials in California are based on the concept of **adversarial justice**. Determining truth and justice involves a contest between two conflicting sides. Each presents only information favorable to its side. Judges and juries find the "truth" in and around conflicting claims.

In any California courtroom, the process one sees is rather generic. The steps may vary somewhat depending on whether the case is criminal or civil. Criminal cases involve alleged wrongs against society (murder, armed robbery, and so on). That is why such cases are titled "People" v. whomever the defendant might be. Civil cases involve disputes between individuals in society (usually involving financial transactions, real estate, personal property, business relationships, family relationships, and personal injuries).

The Criminal Process

According to the *California Penal Code*, criminal offenses can be infractions, misdemeanors, or felonies. **Infractions** (e.g., traffic tickets) involve no jail time. **Misdemeanors** are lesser crimes for which a person may be sentenced to time in county jail. **Felonies** are more serious crimes for which a person may be sentenced to state prison or to death. Many crimes may be misdemeanors on the first offense but become felonies if repeated. "Wobblers" are felonies that judges may reduce to misdemeanors under certain conditions.

Criminal cases feature numerous steps and decision points. We will examine what happens before, during, and after trials. Throughout the process, an enormous amount of discretion is available to virtually everyone but the defendant.

Pretrial Activity. The first decision is to arrest someone. Police exercise discretion at this point based on their own attitudes, the nature of the crime, the relationship between the suspect and the victim, and department policy. The second decision is the decision to prosecute. County district attorneys make those decisions based on the quality of evidence and witnesses, office policy, and the availability of alternatives such as alcohol education programs. Deciding which charges to file can vary depending on local prosecutorial policy. For example, minor offenses like shoplifting and walking an unleashed dog are rarely prosecuted in mega-counties such as Los Angeles. They may return undocumented defendants to their countries of origin rather than press charges. Overall, district attorneys play a dominant role compared to judges or defense attorneys.

Two conflicting values play out at this stage. On the one hand, courtroom work groups (prosecutors, defense attorneys, judges, and other court officers) often operate on an assumption of guilt. "If you are there, you are there for a reason," so the reasoning goes. According to judicial scholars and practitioners, this logic is based less on prejudice than on daily experience. Plea bargaining is the logical result of this value among court professionals. On the other hand, the concept of "innocent until proven guilty" is an essential ingredient of the American legal system. Judges constantly remind prospective jurors and juries that this value must undergird all they do.

After charging, several other steps occur. During an **arraignment**, a judge informs the accused of the charges and the legal options available. In a felony case, a **preliminary hearing** determines if there is probable cause to hold a trial. That decision is called an **indictment**. In addition to district attorneys, grand juries sometimes issue indictments. These bodies are citizen boards, selected from auto and voter registration lists. They tend to be used in complex or sensitive cases and when witnesses need protection. Most criminal arraignments are accomplished with dizzying speed given the volume of cases judges must face. When people talk of "assembly line justice," they usually mean the arraignment calendar.

As we noted, defendants and prosecutors often bypass trials using **plea bargaining**. A plea bargain is a negotiated agreement between the prosecutor and the defendant whereby the latter pleads guilty to a particular charge in exchange for some concession by the prosecution. Concessions include dropping weaker charges or agreeing to lighter sentences (reduced jail time or fines in lieu of jail time). A plea can be bargained at any step in the process.

Who wins and who loses? Actually, both sides benefit. With a trial looming, defendants can plead no contest or guilty to fewer or lesser charges, thereby avoiding unpredictable juries and uncertain sentences. Overworked prosecutors can avoid lengthy trials or submitting admittedly weak evidence to juries. According to one public defender, "A deal is a win for the prosecutors because they put someone away. That same deal can also be a win for the public defender, because we brought the client's [sentencing] exposure down dramatically."[12] Whatever the motivation, judges usually rubberstamp plea agreements negotiated by prosecutors and defense lawyers.

How often does plea bargaining occur? Well over 90 percent of criminal cases are disposed of before an actual trial. Laying aside the ideals of and rights to a jury trial, the criminal justice process would grind to a halt without this essential tool.

The Trial. In the small percentage of cases that go to trial, the first step is selecting a jury. Criminal trials can be heard before a judge only (bench trials) or a jury made up of one's peers. Sometimes a defendant can choose which type. Bench trials are common for less-serious offenses. Prosecutors and defense attorneys traditionally have played key roles in the selection of juries. Juries of less than 12 are possible in misdemeanor cases.

Because felony cases require 12-member juries and convictions require unanimous verdicts, picking the "right" jury is essential to both the prosecution and the defense. The process is both art and science, as jurors are asked about anything in their backgrounds that would tempt them to prejudge a case. Nowadays, there are even "apps" to aid attorneys as they question and sort potential jurors (e.g., *iJuror*). Although judges are in charge of this *voir dire* process, attorneys ask potential jurors questions and may request removal of a few without stating a reason (peremptory challenges). On occasion, judges grant change-of-venue motions if they find that pretrial publicity has tainted the local jury pool. If granted, the trial is moved to another county.

Misdemeanor trials must begin within 45 days of arraignment, or within 30 days if the defendant is in custody. Felony trials must begin 60 days after arraignment unless the defense requests a delay. Judges usually grant such requests. Based on the notion that "justice delayed is justice denied," criminal cases take priority, forcing lengthy delays for civil cases that have no such time constraints. In recent years, cuts in court funding have exacerbated this problem.

The steps of a trial are rather predictable. After opening statements by both sides, the prosecution presents evidence consisting of witnesses and various exhibits (direct examination). The defense cross-examines the witnesses. The defense makes its case in much the same fashion. As the trial ends, both sides give closing arguments, lawyerly interpretations of the case. The judge instructs the jury, if there is one; the jury deliberates and decides guilt or innocence.

The Verdict and Sentence. After the trial, the judge determines a sentence if the accused is found guilty using state-imposed guidelines. Generally, judges are guided by a determinate sentencing law that sets finite prison terms and gives judges less discretion than they once had. Within these bounds, judges do have discretion based on restitution to victims, the need to protect society, or other special conditions. For example, they may require juvenile offenders to clean up graffiti, participate in a forestry camp, or attend a drug rehabilitation program overseen by the state's Division of Juvenile Justice.

The Civil Process

Most courtroom time is devoted to civil cases—disputes involving individuals, businesses, and government agencies. As mentioned earlier, civil cases are constrained by mandated deadlines. When can a civil litigant expect justice? On the whole, more than 90 percent of limited and unlimited civil cases reach disposition within two years; the process may take longer in some metropolitan counties. Justice delayed may well be justice denied when evidence becomes stale or when potential witnesses become unreachable. There are distinctive stages to the civil processes including pretrial activity, the trial itself, and a judgment.

Pretrial Activity. First, an aggrieved party, the plaintiff, files a **complaint** against another party. It consists of a specific claim (e.g., a faulty auto repair leading to an accident and bodily injury) against a defendant and a proposed remedy (often a dollar amount to cover medical expenses and possibly pain and suffering). The defendant is informed of the claim and files an answer. The next step is called **discovery**, the gathering of information to prepare for a possible trial. This process can involve **depositions** (oral testimony under oath) conducted by the lawyers involved, **interrogatories** (written questions and answers), and research into various documents and materials.

Every effort is made to settle the case before a trial actually begins. Sometimes the process involves **alternative dispute resolution (ADR)**. It takes two forms. Generally, **mediation** is voluntary whereas **arbitration** is governed by law or by prior agreement. An arbitrator's decision is legally binding. California requires a "mandatory settlement conference" as the trial date approaches. As one court administrator puts it, "Show them an open courtroom and they settle." Out-of-court settlements can range from mutual apologies to millions of dollars. To avoid lengthy, costly, public, and unpredictable trials, some corporations and celebrities use retired judges who charge up to $10,000 per day to privately hear disputes and render decisions. This "rent-a-judge" trend is speedy and efficient but only for those who can afford it. It also lacks the transparency expected or at least hoped for in our political system. With or without private judging, the vast majority of California's civil cases are settled without a public trial.

The Trial. Trials are available for those who cannot or will not settle out of court. The process in court is similar to the process in criminal trials. In a civil jury trial, three-fourths of the jury must agree for a verdict to result.

The Judgment. At the conclusion of a trial, the judge or jury decides whether a wrong was committed, who was responsible, and what damages, if any, should be awarded. Lawyers for the losing side may file posttrial motions asking to set aside or reduce any damages awarded. Judges (trial and appellate) may reduce damages they think are excessive; this occurs most commonly with punitive damages intended to punish or make an example out of a defendant.

Juries and Popular Justice

More than 10,000 jury trials take place each year in California and, for many Californians, serving on a jury is their primary exposure to the legal system. In both criminal and civil cases, juries are charged with deciding questions of fact and reaching appropriate verdicts. One superior court judge calls his jurors "visiting judges" who determine the truthfulness of witnesses. Yet, jurors may not necessarily research decisions as judges would. Microcosms of the local community, juries have been known to weigh facts selectively or interpret them in light of their own experiences. Absent clear arguments at trial, they may conduct their own case investigations. Contrary to judges' instructions, they may "tweet" their opinions during a trial.

The practice of jurors substituting their own judgments contrary to judicial norms has been called **popular justice**. The extreme of this is the centuries-old doctrine of **jury nullification**—when individual jurors or entire juries follow their consciences rather than the law or the evidence before them. For example, many Californians believed that the jury in the 1994 O. J. Simpson murder trial ignored certain incriminating evidence in acquitting him. In civil cases, popular justice may result in huge, sometimes exorbitant, punitive damages to plaintiffs (e.g., victims of auto crashes, faulty products, or injurious medical treatments). Because nullification by even one juror in a criminal case could result in a hung jury and a mistrial, judges are allowed to remove jurors suspected of this behavior.

HOW COURTS MAKE POLICY

Courts not only make decisions; they also make policy. Public policy is what governments choose to do or not do. Individual policy decisions can be made by a host of public officials, including those in the judiciary. Individual court decisions might not seem like broad policy statements; it depends on which level—trial or appellate.

Trial Court Policymaking

Trial court judges in California, as anywhere else, are primarily finders of fact. They make public policy in less obvious ways. First, they reflect policy preferences over time in many cases. This is called **cumulative policymaking**. Years of decisions in comparable cases reveal certain patterns, which vary from judge to judge. As a trial court judge, former California chief justice Malcolm Lucas was labeled "Maximum Malcolm" because of his typically harsh sentences in criminal cases. Second, judges generally reflect community norms. These norms are part of a community's local legal culture. Because these cultures vary from place to place, a form of judicial diversity results. For instance, California's big city judges may decide certain cases differently than would their counterparts in rural communities. Charges of disturbing the peace, loitering, or obvious marijuana use may be treated differently in university towns than in wealthy residential enclaves. Third, trial judges' decisions may reflect their own ideological perspectives. For instance, legal norms aside, conservative judges tend to side with insurance companies in claims cases or with management in labor disputes; liberals with claimants and organized labor. Governors take these decision records into account when making judicial appointments.

Appellate Court Policymaking

Unlike trial courts, California appellate courts decide matters of law, not fact. They can confirm, reject, or alter public policy with a single decision. Although guided by *stare decisis* (the rule of precedent), they are not wedded to it. They can enter the "political thicket" of partisan conflict or avoid it. The choice is theirs. When Californians think of judicial policymaking, they usually think of the California Supreme Court and rightfully so. We will consider briefly this court as policymaker under the last four chief justices: Bird (1977–86), Lucas (1986–96), George (1996–2010), and Cartril-Sakauye (2011–).

The Bird Court. Rose Bird, a former public defender, presided over a court that viewed itself as a seeker of social justice, independent of the federal judiciary. The California Supreme Court has been a national trendsetter in this regard. In 1955, it ruled that illegally seized evidence could not be used in court. It took the U.S. Supreme Court six years to agree. The California court stipulated various rights of accused persons one year before the famous *Miranda* decision did the same nationally. The Bird court was independent, active, and viewed as very liberal. It overturned numerous death sentences, widened opportunities for liability suits, nullified several initiatives, and generally favored environmental protection and the rights of workers, renters, women, and the LGBT (lesbian, gay, bisexual, transgender) community. As one frustrated judge then put it, "Nothing is sacred anymore. It's difficult for trial judges to know what the law is. They change it every 10 minutes."[13]

The Lucas Court. The historic defeat of Bird, Reynoso, and Grodin in 1986 allowed Republican governor George Deukmejian not only to name their replacements but also to shape the court's future policy role. A succession of appointments by Deukmejian and his successor, fellow Republican Pete Wilson, left the court with only one liberal, Stanley Mosk, a 1964 appointee of Pat Brown. Under Lucas, the court became less activist, less assertive, and less willing to use the state constitution to establish new legal doctrines apart from those of the U.S. Supreme Court. Unlike the Bird court, the Lucas court found most trial errors too minor to overturn guilty verdicts. Most important, the Lucas court upheld more than 80 percent of death penalty convictions, in remarkable contrast to the 94 percent reversal rate of the Bird court. Lucas also made numerous legislative enemies when he upheld the most important elements of Proposition 140, the initiative that set term limits for statewide offices and the legislature.

The George Court. Associate Justice Ronald George became chief justice in 1996. Under his leadership, the California Supreme Court continued many of the trends and policies set by the Lucas court. Possibly because of greater diversity on the court (three women, one Asian American, and one Latino), it could not be neatly divided into ideological voting blocs. Different majorities emerged on a case-by-case basis. The court still retained its independent-mindedness relative to federal law and even state election trends. During George's years as chief justice, the court negotiated one legal minefield after another from abortion to civil rights to gay marriage. As we noted earlier, George oversaw the state's takeover of the entire court system, including county superior courts.

The Cantil-Sukauye Court. Replacing George in 2011 was Tani Cantil-Sakauye, a 20-year veteran of both trial and appellate courts. The Judicial Nominees Evaluation Committee rated her "exceptionally well qualified," the

Commission on Judicial Appointments confirmed her unanimously, and the voters elected her in the November 2010 general election. Appointed by Republican governor Arnold Schwarzenegger, she made national headlines in 2018 when she gave up her Republican registration. Cantil-Sakauye said the contentious U.S. Supreme Court nomination of Brett Kavanaugh, who was accused of sexual assault in college, prompted her to re-register as an independent. Under Cantil-Sakauye, the court has frequently rendered decisions that were unanimous or near-unanimous. This cohesion is expected to continue even though four of the seven justices have been appointed by Democratic governor Jerry Brown.[14] She has worked to make justice more accessible to its diverse population, including an initiative to improve self-representation since "4 million Californians come to court without an attorney."[15]

CRIMINAL JUSTICE AND PUNISHMENT

The policy role of California's courts is most visible in the area of criminal justice. Coping with endless waves of defendants is a challenge shared by other policymakers, the federal courts, and society in general. California's criminal justice system demonstrates both the diversity of the state and the hyperpluralistic nature of its political system. The state's judiciary has been affected by sweeping social trends, changing sentencing laws, the perennial issue of capital punishment, and the challenge of running one of the world's largest prison systems.

Social Trends

In many ways, court cases simply mirror broad social trends. They include changing demographics plus the widespread use of guns and drugs. First, population experts have noticed a rise of young, minority males who statistically contribute more than their fair share of street crime; prison populations reflect this. Experts attribute this to reduced employment opportunities, residential segregation, the presence of gangs, and the absence of positive role models in minority communities. Despite tough law-and-order, "build more prisons" rhetoric by elected officials, crime rates are largely dependent on these economic and demographic trends.

Second, the widespread availability of handguns and assault weapons also colors the crime picture in California. The statistics are sobering. Close to 900,000 guns are sold annually, with the number peaking at more than 1.3 million in 2016 (see figure 9.1). Sales tend to increase after high-profile mass shootings or after new gun control regulations are proposed. More than 800 handgun models are certified for sale in California.[16] Gun-related homicides are extraordinarily high among young, urban youth. Although handguns far outnumber assault weapons, the latter are increasingly used against the police, in drive-by shootings, and by California's gang culture. In short, the state is awash in weapons. In recent years, the state legislature and voters have responded by requiring background checks and 10-day waiting periods, limiting multiple purchases at one time, prohibiting certain assault weapons, and limiting high-capacity ammunition clips. The state may even confiscate firearms from people who once purchased them legally but who were later disqualified from owning them because of a subsequent criminal conviction or determination of serious mental illness.

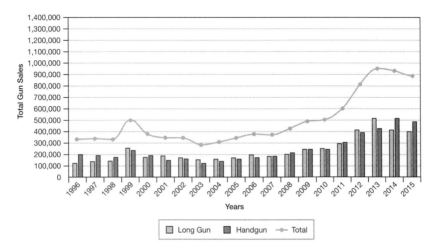

Figure 9.1 Gun Sales in California, 1996-2015

Question: What accounts for the rise in gun sales in recent years?

Note: From 1972 to 1990 the California Department of Justice tracked only handguns.

Source: California Department of Justice, https://openjustice.doj.ca.gov/firearms/overview#/sect2.

Third, drugs and alcohol figure in many of California's criminal cases. Because criminal cases take priority over civil cases, they have in effect swamped the courts. As we noted, the courts have responded by creating specialized drug courts that offer comprehensive supervision, drug testing, and treatment programs including sanctions and incentives.

Sentencing Mandates

California courts are not only affected by social trends, but they also must abide by the state's sentencing policies. Traditionally, the state legislature sets sentencing policy. For example, before 1977, California judges worked with an "indeterminate sentence" policy adopted by the legislature. Convicts would stay in prison until "rehabilitated" or until the completion of a broadly defined term (say, 1–5 or 1–10 years). The policy assumed that most convicts could and would be rehabilitated. The only problem was that "rehabilitated" convicts returned to prisons at alarming rates, a phenomenon called **recidivism**. In 1976, the legislature passed the *Uniform Sentencing Act*. This law narrowed sentencing ranges available to judges and added "enhancements" that added additional prison time (e.g., added years for using a gun in the commission of a crime). In 1994, California voters lengthened prison terms further bypassing the state's **Three Strikes Law**. Some scholars called this reform "the largest penal experiment in American history."[17] Three Strikes provided 25-years-to-life sentences for anyone convicted of a third felony, whether violent or not. Despite efforts by district attorneys to avoid some three-strike convictions, life terms began to mount. Even the public questioned the justice of third-strike sentences for minor felonies like stealing cigarettes or a slice of pizza. Eventually, voters modified the law in 2012 by approving Proposition 36. This measure reserved life sentences for new felonies deemed "serious or violent" and allowed the resentencing of third strike offenders whose felonies were not serious or violent.

Proposition 36 signaled the start of a trend that would see voters and policymakers ease some of the sentencing mandates that had begun decades earlier and contributed to jail and prison overcrowding (see the discussion later in the chapter). Ironically, the efforts to reverse these policies were led by Governor Jerry Brown, the same governor who originally instituted mandatory sentencing decades earlier. The reversal was driven by several factors, including an order from the U.S. Supreme Court to reduce the prison population, a $26 billion budget deficit, and a realization that the emphasis on punishment over rehabilitation was unsustainable.[18] In addition, it was widely recognized that mandatory sentencing laws disproportionately affect communities of color leading to high incarceration rates for minority groups. These sentencing reform policies reduced the penalties for certain lower-level drug and property offenses (Proposition 47), granted earlier releases to inmates for good behavior (Proposition 57), sent many lower-level offenders to county jails (realignment), and eliminated the cash bail system. Critics of these policies fear steep rises in crime, but the initial evidence does not support this. Although there has been a modest increase in property crimes, the rate of violent crime has remained the same.[19]

Capital Punishment

The ultimate sentence, of course, is death. Age-old arguments over both its morality and its effectiveness have characterized its history in California. The penalty has been a political football in recent decades. In 1972, both the U.S. and California Supreme Courts ruled the death penalty unconstitutional relative to their respective constitutions because of its capricious and arbitrary use. In the federal case *Furman v. Georgia* (1972), Justice Potter Stewart regarded the death penalty as cruel and unusual "in the same way that being struck by lightning is cruel and unusual." One year later, the California legislature reinstituted capital punishment by adding "special circumstances" under which it would be employed (such as killing during a robbery, multiple homicides, and murder of police officers). Like other states, it also established bifurcated trials; the first stage would determine guilt or innocence, and the second stage would determine the appropriate sentence.

In 1976, the U.S. Supreme Court ruled in *Gregg v. Georgia* that such efforts to reduce the penalty's arbitrariness were permissible and that capital punishment was allowable where such measures were employed. In 1977, the California legislature further amended its law by permitting mitigating evidence to be allowed at the sentencing stage, potentially avoiding the death penalty. In 1978, California voters passed an initiative extending the special circumstances noted earlier, but the Bird court usually found ways to overturn particular death sentences. Since that time, the California Supreme Court has hesitated to overrule death penalty verdicts. By 2018, 744 inmates were on death row—more by far than in any other state. In 1992, California resumed actual executions, and by 2006, executions had numbered 14. Because of lengthy appeals, far more have died as a result of suicide or natural causes, such as old age or illness.

Just as the idea of capital punishment has evolved in California, so has its implementation. The general goal has been this: state-imposed death should at least be as humane as possible. Accordingly, the gas chamber replaced hanging in 1938. A 1993 law allowed the condemned to request lethal injection and in 1994, a federal judge essentially mandated its use by ruling the gas chamber cruel and unusual punishment. With this presumably more humane method, those slated for execution are strapped to a gurney and injected with a cocktail of three chemicals. But lethal injection has faced its own hurdles. In 2006, a federal judge halted executions in California until the state could demonstrate that the poisons used did not inflict excruciating pain, as critics had claimed. In response, the California Department of Corrections and Rehabilitation sought to improve its lethal injection procedures. Then, the U.S. Supreme Court ruled in 2008 that lethal injections were constitutional if humanely administered. However, in July 2014, a federal judge ruled that California's entire death penalty system was unconstitutional because it was fraught with arbitrariness and plagued by systemic delay. The state was given the green light again for executions in 2018, but new regulations must be approved before they can take place.

Aside from the methodology of capital punishment, why are there so many death row inmates and so few executions? First, state and federal appeals may take decades to complete. Many appeals never proceed because qualified lawyers refuse to take them on. Decades of delay are commonplace. Second, there is no single capital punishment policy for the state. The death sentence continues, as always, to be dependent on local prosecutorial practice. Because district attorneys in each county decide who is charged with special circumstances offenses, California has, in effect, 58 death penalty policies.

What does the public think about capital punishment? In the past, Californians broadly supported it, but that support has been slipping. A 2012 effort to ban the death penalty (Proposition 34) failed by a relatively close 52–48 percent margin. Two years later, a Field Poll revealed that only 56 percent of voters favored the death penalty, the lowest level of support in nearly 50 years.[20] Despite the declining support, voters narrowly passed Proposition 66 in 2016, which seeks to speed up death penalty appeals.

Corrections Reform

Correctional policy in California is both exorbitantly expensive and arguably ineffective. If "You get what you pay for" is at all true, how can this be? The numbers tell only part of the story. In 2018, the California Department of Corrections and Rehabilitation (CDCR) held in custody about 129,000 felons. State prisons housed most of them; others were housed in contract facilities in and outside California. Another 47,000 were on parole. In addition, each of the 58 counties operates a jail system that houses those convicted of lesser crimes or who are awaiting trial. Most of these facilities are overcrowded but voters tend to reject the tax increases necessary to expand the jails or add new ones.

The pressures contributing to both costly and ineffective incarceration are several. First, as we noted earlier, the legislature devised longer, determinate sentences without expanding the prison space needed as a result. Second, high rates of recidivism have added to the prison population. True, some ex-cons commit new felonies but others have committed only minor parole violations (such as missed meetings with parole officers or failed drug tests). Violations aside, few parolees are trained or equipped for life outside prison. According to the CDCR,

California Department of Corrections and Rehabilitation

Prison guards handcuff an inmate at San Quentin State Prison after releasing him from a segregated enclosure. Inmates are disproportionately people of color.

nearly half of all California felons are convicted of a new crime within three years of their release.[21]

Third, the longer convicts remain in prison, the more expensive their care becomes. Housing a prisoner can average $81,000 per year. Two-thirds of those costs are for security and health care. Elderly, chronically sick, or gravely ill prisoners can cost much more, especially if they require corrections-funded hospital care. Medical parole is available to the most incapacitated prisoners who are no longer a threat to public safety.

As a result of these pressures, the federal courts found that prison overcrowding and inadequate medical care constituted cruel and unusual punishment in violation of the Eighth Amendment to the U.S. Constitution. One district court judge assigned control of the prison health care system to a federal receiver until various reforms were approved. In *Brown v. Plata* (2011), the U.S. Supreme Court ruled that, because of severe overcrowding, the state had to reduce its prison population by 33,000 inmates. Writing for a 5–4 majority, Justice Anthony M. Kennedy referred to suicidal prisoners being held in "telephone booth-sized cages without toilets," prison gymnasiums filled with bunk beds, and prisoners dying for lack of medical attention.

In response, Governor Brown proposed shifting the responsibility for custody, treatment, and supervision of nonviolent felons from state prisons to the counties. Called **realignment,** this policy required counties to augment jail capacity, devise penalties that avoided jail time, and treat parole violators locally rather than returning them to state prison. This policy change represented a significant shift in the state's approach to dealing with corrections. California has managed to drastically reduce its prison population by 44,000 inmates since its peak in 2006 with little effect on crime rates. However, should they begin to rise steadily again, the reforms adopted in recent years will be the key suspects.

CONCLUSION

California's judiciary manifests several trends in California politics. First, the legal profession in California certainly does not mirror the state's growing ethnic and cultural diversity. It remains largely white, middle class, and male in membership. To be sure, more women are seeking legal careers and gaining professional strength. Second, in terms of workload, the judiciary is clearly affected by the state's diversity. Criminal caseloads reflect population changes plus widespread use of alcohol, drugs, and guns. Civil caseloads reflect a large, increasingly complex, and regulated economy, plus an increasingly litigious society. Third, access to the judiciary is problematic, especially for the poor. Although public defenders, court-appointed attorneys, and legal aid clinics provide low- or no-cost legal help, the poor in California do not enjoy the quality and quantity of legal assistance available to the middle and upper classes.

Fourth, in terms of governance, the judiciary carries out some vital functions (such as dispensing case-by-case justice and reviewing legislative and executive actions), but it also contributes to "divided government" and to policy paralysis by extending political struggles for years or even decades. The history of capital punishment illustrates this point. That said, the judiciary can also break inter-branch gridlock as it has in areas such as reapportionment. Also playing a role are interest groups that use the courts to achieve policy victories they cannot obtain elsewhere in government.

California's judiciary also reflects political fragmentation and hyperpluralism. Judges themselves are relatively insulated from the electorate, rightly so in their view. Yet, they can occasionally feel the pressure and even the wrath of volatile voters. But holding judges accountable is no easy task for voters. Trial court judges share power with policing agencies, courtroom work groups, and juries. On occasion, juries define facts, the law, and justice on their own terms. In making decisions, all judges respond to professional norms, statutory laws, conflicting interest group demands, and their own sociological and political backgrounds.

Finally, the state's correctional system, the final step in the criminal justice process, has been the target of numerous reforms. These reforms have emphasized (1) reducing costs, (2) complying with constitutional standards for punishment, and (3) reversing some of the harsher incarceration policies adopted in recent decades.

KEY TERMS

judicial federalism (p. 187)

superior courts (p. 188)

district courts of appeal (p. 189)

California Supreme Court (p. 189)

Missouri Plan (p. 192)
judicial socialization (p. 193)
adversarial justice (p. 194)
infractions (p. 195)
misdemeanors (p. 195)
felonies (p. 195)
arraignment (p. 195)
preliminary hearing (p. 195)
indictment (p. 195)
plea bargaining (p. 196)
complaint (p. 197)
discovery (p. 197)

depositions (p. 197)
interrogatories (p. 197)
alternative dispute resolution (p. 197)
mediation (p. 197)
arbitration (p. 197)
popular justice (p. 198)
jury nullification (p. 198)
cumulative policymaking (p. 198)
recidivism (p. 201)
Three Strikes Law (p. 201)
realignment (p. 204)

REVIEW QUESTIONS

1. How does the dual judicial system help explain judicial independence in California?
2. How would the job descriptions vary between trial judges and appellate justices?
3. If you were a lawyer aspiring to become a judge, what would you do or not do to reach that goal? How would you be held accountable once you reached your goal?
4. Describe the various steps of the civil and criminal process.
5. How do both trial and appellate courts make policy? How "activist" should state courts be relative to other branches?
6. What factors explain who is charged and sentenced in California?
7. How has California changed its approach to crime and punishment in recent years?

WEB RESOURCES

The State Bar of California

http://www.calbar.ca.gov

This site includes law profession news, trends in legal education, bar exam information, efforts to diversify the profession, and expanding access to attorneys by low- and moderate-income Californians.

Judicial Branch of California

http://www.courts.ca.gov

This site contains a wealth of data on California courts, including opinions, procedures, administrative issues, latest developments, and links to other law- and court-related websites.

California Department of Corrections and Rehabilitation

https://www.cdcr.ca.gov

To learn more about capital punishment in California, prison populations, or specific prison facilities, this site is helpful.

10

Community Politics

★ ★ ★

LEARNING OUTCOMES

Students will be able to:

- ★ Describe how communities underscore the themes of this book.
- ★ Discuss the roles of and challenges faced by California counties.
- ★ Analyze the variety of cities in California and describe how they are governed.
- ★ Define special districts and discuss their advantages and disadvantages as a form of local government.
- ★ Compare and contrast California's school districts and special districts.
- ★ Describe how regional governments in California engage in coordination and regulation.

IN BRIEF

Chapter 10 surveys the most diverse set of institutions in California politics: local government. The thousands of local governments in California can be grouped into five types: counties, cities, special districts, school districts, and regional governments, plus privatized versions of local government such as urban villages and homeowner associations. This chapter considers the idea of community and the functions of local governments in the communities. Such governments are limited in their capacity and even in their willingness to govern effectively.

★ ★ ★

ALL SIX TYPES REPRESENT diversity and fragmentation in California politics. With each type, we examine how local governments are established and how local officials exercise power.

Also surveyed are the inherent limits of local government, the role of the state in local affairs, and the fiscal and policy problems that each type of government faces. In recent years, all local governments have faced revenue volatility because of voter-enacted tax cuts, reduced aid from the state, and the ups and downs of California's economy. In general, cities are fiscally healthier than counties.

California's numerous local governments represent a rich diversity of governing styles and institutions, allow ample opportunities for citizen participation in politics, and provide a wide assortment of options for living in a community. There is, however, a downside to this diversity. According to political scientists, the sheer numbers of local governments in California reduce political accountability and undermine the ability of local governments to manage problems, especially those that spill beyond their boundaries.

INTRODUCTION

The arithmetic of California's cities seems to include both addition and subtraction. As figure 10.1 suggests, Californians have been forming incorporated cities and towns ever since statehood. Although motivations for doing so vary, a common theme is a desire for self-government closer to the people than can be achieved at the county or higher levels.

In recent years, the urge to form new cities has been countered by an urge by state policymakers to subtract fiscal resources from those very cities. The state's newest cities (Riverside County's Jurupa Valley, Eastvale, Menifee, and Wildomar) know this arithmetic all too well. Shortly after they incorporated, the state legislature, in its own effort to balance the state budget, cut the very funds the fledgling cities depended on to balance their budgets. Jurupa Valley's budget was cut by a staggering 47 percent as a result. In response, some services were cut to levels below what they were *prior to* incorporation—not exactly what voters had in mind. City manager Stephen Harding mused that his city could be both the newest and shortest-lived in state history.[1] Indeed, a lengthy disincorporation process began in early 2015.

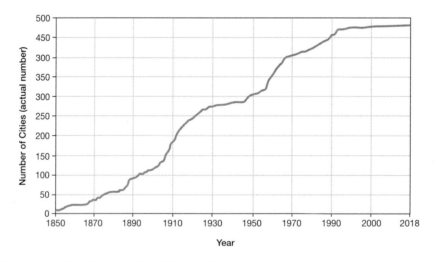

Figure 10.1 The Growth of California Cities

Question: What do you think is the local impetus to incorporate—to form cities?

Source: Paul G. Lewis, Deep Roots: Local Government Structure in California (San Francisco: Public Policy Institute of California, 1998).

Although cities receive a great deal of public attention in California, this chapter explores the entire spectrum of local governments in the state and the issues they face. If you could view the boundaries of these myriad governments from the air, they would resemble a stack of jigsaw puzzles. Cities, counties, special districts, school districts, and various regional governments are the official local governments of California. There are also various "urban forms"—places that look and behave like cities but most definitely are not governed like them.

The two broad themes of this book, diversity and hyperpluralism, are vividly represented in California's local politics. The state's profound diversity plays itself out at the community level. Communities are where people work, pursue various lifestyles, raise families, educate their children, and go about civic life. It is where neighbors do or do not get along, where California's polyglot of racial and ethnic groups live—in harmony or otherwise. From school board meetings to city hall hearings, it is in community that values collide and cultures clash. Communities are where the American notion of individual sovereignty (power in the hands of the individual) rubs up against the need for group norms, responsibility, and expectations. In short, California communities are vivid expressions of a culturally pluralistic, differentiated society. At this level, the struggle for power and control between individuals and groups is constant.

California communities also represent government at its most fragmented level and are one manifestation of what we call hyperpluralism. Fifty-eight counties, 482 cities, more than 1,000 school districts, and more than 2,000 other **independent special districts** all present diverse approaches to community governance. During most any weekend drive, a California motorist will encounter (unknowingly in most cases) dozens of governmental jurisdictions, and these do not even include a growing number of quasi-governments, such as neighborhood homeowner associations. Californians may complain that their local governments are ineffective; they can hardly object that there are too few of them. Los Angeles County alone has nearly 500 subdivisions of government. There are so many local governments across the state that citizens are often unsure which government provides which service and whom to call when a problem arises. As Kim Alexander put it, "I currently have twenty-two people I elect to represent me at all levels of government, and I can't name them—and I'm President of the California Voter Foundation."[2]

Hyperpluralism also suggests a host of public policy problems beyond the reach of governing institutions. Increasingly, problems facing local officials spill beyond their reach (e.g., air quality). And funding shortages, an absence of public support, and a lack of political will leave those public problems within their reach unaddressed—for years, decades, or longer. Local interest groups and regional forces, economic and demographic, usually dictate where growth occurs more than local government does. Furthermore, the growing dominance of the state in local matters has fostered both local dependence on the state and resistance to it.

The Role of Community

The late U.S. House Speaker Thomas P. "Tip" O'Neill once said, "All politics is local." A corollary could well be: "All politics begins at the community level." Local governments in California's communities perform three generic yet important functions: providing services, socializing community members, and managing conflict.

Providing Services. Local governments deliver various goods and services to their residents. These include education, garbage disposal, water, sanitation, building inspection, law enforcement, and fire protection. To some extent each community can determine the mix and quality of services to provide. But most services are either fully expected by local residents (law enforcement) or flatly required by the state (welfare). The question, "Which level of government, state or local, should pay for what services?" is a perennial issue in Sacramento. Those who believe the primary purpose of local government is to provide tangible services tend to think local government can and should operate as an efficient business.

Socializing Community Members. In addition to services, local governments provide varying degrees of personal attention to community residents. Most newcomers are assimilated into local society; they learn what behavior is acceptable and unacceptable. These norms can vary from community to community or even from neighborhood to neighborhood. For example, numerous conflicts (parking, noise, and partying) occur in college towns between students and permanent residents. Graffiti (or "tagging") may be grudgingly tolerated in some neighborhoods but quickly painted over in others. The presence of immigrant workers waiting curbside for day-labor jobs may be ignored in some communities but actively opposed in others. Regulation of behavior by local government is called the "police power." This fundamental power makes it possible for governments to regulate public health, safety, and morals.

Managing Conflict. One of the most important functions of local government is managing conflict among people and groups. Some conflicts are essentially arguments over policy such as service complaints, land-use controversies, and budget allocations. Others reflect deep-seated social and cultural divisions in a community—divisions among racial and ethnic groups, rich and poor, homeowners and renters, or newcomers and old-timers. The more heterogeneous a community population or the more a community values extensive political participation, the more visible conflict will be. Such conflicts become political because government is expected to intervene. Political conflict is common in cities of all sizes. The larger cities of California contain numerous and diverse ethnic and income groups. A growing number of California communities no longer contain a single ethnic or racial majority—they are "majority-minority" cities. As many of these groups have become more politically conscious, they have become more politically assertive. Small, relatively homogeneous, and presumably peaceful communities often experience high levels of political involvement, no matter how small the issue. Both settings require the management of conflict, at times intense conflict.

The Limits of Community Government

Despite expectations that local governments provide all three functions, California communities are limited in doing so. Three limits discussed here are the privatization of development, state power, and the myth of apolitical politics.

Privatization of Development. Historically, California's communities were regarded as economic entities. The growth of these places was dictated by a tradition of **privatism**—an ongoing succession of private economic transactions. The Big Four, land speculators, and private utility companies were the essence of early privatism in the Golden State. To be sure, local government had a role to play, usually accommodating, assisting, and, at times, subsidizing those private interests. Because many local governments have continued this traditional role, they have remained largely ineffective in controlling private interests when public and private interests clash. How this applies to land use politics is addressed in chapter 12.

State Power. In 1868, shortly after California's admission to the Union, an Iowa judge promulgated a judicial doctrine that to this day governs a great many state/local relationships. Judge John F. Dillon wrote, "Municipal corporations owe their origin to, and derive their powers and rights wholly from, the legislature. It breathes into them the breath of life, without which they cannot exist. As it creates, so it may also destroy. What it may destroy, it may . . . control."[3] The idea that states dominate local governments was adopted by the U.S. Supreme Court, other state courts, and, naturally, state legislatures. In California, "Dillon's Rule" underlies all state-local relationships. Granted, the state allows significant **home rule** (the ability of local governments to govern themselves on local matters as they see fit). But Article XI of the California Constitution stipulates local powers and even the very existence of local government. Although this legal doctrine is obscure to average Californians, local officials know it all too well. For example, California expressly preempts local governments from regulating certain aspects of gun ownership. California local officials also find they must defend their sources of revenue from being diverted by the state.[4]

Apolitical Politics. A final limit on local self-government in California is the enduring assumption that party politics corrupts governing. As noted in chapter 4, the Progressives wanted to take "politics" out of government,

Some cities allow graffiti in designated places as a form of "public art."

Question: To what extent can a city's police power truly curtail some forms of urban behavior?

meaning the corrupting influences of political parties and bosses. Their solutions included nonpartisan, at-large local elections, and professional city management. California political scientist Eugene Lee once described the nonpartisanship ideal: "City government is largely a matter of 'good business practice' or 'municipal housekeeping' . . . There is little room for 'politics.' Therefore, it is not necessary to establish organized political competition as suggested by the partisan ballot."[5] The Progressives believed good government meant the efficient provision of various municipal services. They underestimated government's role in reflecting and managing political conflict. Even today, some local officials sincerely believe that an entire constellation of social and political issues are beyond the scope of local government. Like it or not, local governments find that they are caldrons of California's diversity—expected to articulate, address, and even solve the pressing problems faced by various individuals and myriad groups.

California's local governments are both numerous and richly diverse. We now survey the most common local governments in California: counties, cities, special districts, school districts, and regional governments.

COUNTIES

One of the most diverse units of California local government is the *county*. California, as did other states, borrowed the county idea from British local government tradition. Originally, a county was a territory administered by a count. It was both a local government and a subdivision of a central government; counties retain this dual role today. In fact, unless prohibited by the state constitution, the legislature may delegate to counties any task belonging to the state itself. In addition to providing state-mandated services, counties provide to unincorporated areas an assortment of services typically provided by cities (law enforcement, transportation, etc.).

The Shape of California Counties

In many ways, California's 58 counties reflect a bygone era. Consider the map in figure 10.2. At the time of statehood, California had relatively few large counties. Southern California was one vast desert; much of it still is, as San Bernardino County's boundaries attest. The Sierra foothill counties are elongated and relatively small for a reason. During the Gold Rush, it was thought that miners should be no farther than a day's horseback ride from a county seat where mining claims were filed. Those boundaries remain today.

At the time of statehood in 1850, California had 27 counties. In the late 1800s and early 1900s, new counties were formed, reflecting population growth, power shifts, and emerging local rivalries. Giant Mariposa County (encompassing much of Southern California) was subdivided into 12 counties. San Mateo broke away from San Francisco. Farmers and ranchers, fearing the early growth of Los Angeles, helped form Orange County in 1889. The last breakaway, Imperial County, formed east of San Diego in 1907. Despite vast demographic and economic change, the shape of California's counties has remained fixed since 1907. The reasons are several. First, local political cultures developed and calcified in that span of time, giving each county its own identity. Second, because county split elections are countywide in scope, selling a split to an often skeptical voting

Figure 10.2 California's Counties
California's 58 counties come in all shapes and sizes; their boundaries have not changed in more than a century despite massive population growth and change.

Question: How would you redraw these boundaries if given the chance?

Source: California State Association of Counties

majority is problematic, if not impossible. Third, the start-up costs for a new county (infrastructure, personnel, and tax base) are so high, county splits seem financially unfeasible.

This static situation has resulted in tremendous differences between modern California counties. In area, San Bernardino is the nation's largest (20,000 square miles). It is 200 times larger than San Francisco County and embraces about 20 percent of the entire state. Los Angeles County is home to over 10 million residents (more than that of 43 other states); within its borders are 89 cities.

At the other end of the spectrum is tiny Alpine County, home to less than 1,200 people, not one of whom lives in an incorporated city. Some counties have experienced persistent growth whereas others have languished in California's economic backwaters.

The state expects all 58 counties to perform similarly as units of government but the resources for doing so vary widely.

The Shape of County Government

Legally speaking, there are only two types of counties: **general law counties** and **charter counties**. California's 44 general law counties follow state law relative to the number and duties of county elected officials. Fourteen charter counties are governed by a constitution-like document called a "charter" that replaces some general laws regarding elections, compensation, powers, and duties. Charters also provide a limited degree of home rule or authority over certain offices and governing structures and require voter approval initially and for subsequent amendments. California's urban counties usually have charters, and two-thirds of all Californians live in those counties. Both general law and charter counties are the primary units of local government in rural and some suburban areas.

Answering the classic question, "Who governs?" at the county level is no easy task. Authority and responsibility—in short, power—is widely dispersed and shared among the following decision makers.

Boards of Supervisors. In California, each county's legislative body is a five-member board of supervisors (San Francisco is both a county and a city with an 11-member board and one mayor). Board members serve for four-year staggered terms and are elected during June primary elections in even-numbered years. If they do not garner a majority of votes (50 percent plus one), a November general election runoff is necessary. Although the elections are technically nonpartisan, informed voters likely know the partisan leanings of better-known candidates, especially incumbents. Their names sometimes appear on those partisan slate mailers discussed in chapter 6. In the past, county supervisors were "good old boys"—older white men with business backgrounds. In recent years, more women have become supervisors, and in a few counties, they have constituted board majorities. Over the years, service on a board of supervisors has been a stepping-stone to the state legislature or other elective posts. Occasionally, the reverse occurs. Given the considerable powers of county boards, attractive salaries (in larger counties, supervisors may earn well over $100,000 annually plus benefits), and a fundamental desire to remain in public life, some termed-out state legislators welcome a run for county supervisor.

Boards adopt county budgets, determine some service levels, and make numerous decisions affecting unincorporated areas. The most contentious policy issues often surround land use. Although county planning commissions make many land-use decisions, supervisors hear various appeals and make final decisions. Where to locate shopping centers, housing projects, or unpopular industries (sometimes called LULUs—locally undesirable land uses) pit counties against cities, neighborhood against neighborhood, and occasionally neighbor against neighbor. Ironies abound. On one hand, a small but controversial land-use project might fill a room with surly citizens on both sides of the issue. On the other hand, discussion of a multimillion-dollar expenditure deep inside a county budget may attract little or no public interest whatsoever. Boards of supervisors hire *chief administrative officers* (CAOs; called county managers in some places) to carry out board policy and administer county routines. Preparing and monitoring annual budgets plus preparing board meeting agendas consume a lion's share of a CAO's time.

County services are also provided by a variety of other elected officials. Together, they are California's local version of the plural executive we described in chapter 8. The exact arrangement of these positions varies from county to county. The most common elected officers are district attorneys, sheriffs, various fiscal officers, clerks, and school superintendents. Typically, they serve four-year terms and are elected during statewide elections.

District Attorney. The "people's lawyer" in each county is an elected district attorney (DA). Although the DA's duties are not limited to criminal prosecutions, such prosecutions form their most essential function. As noted in chapter 9, DAs can exercise a great deal of discretion in setting prosecution policy in a county. Below the elected DA is a staff of deputy DAs and investigators. Some California DAs have become well known because of the occasional celebrities they have prosecuted (Los Angeles's Gil Garcetti and O. J. Simpson, and Santa Barbara's Tom Sneddon and Michael Jackson). Public defenders (who provide criminal defense counsel for the poor) are also county employees but not elected—making them potentially more dependent on a board of supervisors. Given their crime-fighting and "law and order" reputations, DAs usually have a competitive advantage over public defenders and private lawyers when judgeships become available. The post of DA can be a stepping-stone to a much higher office. Kamala Harris was San Francisco's DA before becoming state attorney general and then a U.S. Senator. Earl Warren, both governor and U.S. Supreme Court chief justice, was once DA for Alameda County.

Sheriff. The chief law enforcement and public safety officer for a county is an elected sheriff. This office is one of the oldest law enforcement positions in the common law tradition. Although anyone can run for this position, successful candidates are usually law enforcement professionals. Sheriffs administer an office, numerous deputy sheriffs, the county jail, and, in some cases, the coroner's office. The coroner conducts inquests of all questionable deaths. Through contractual arrangements, county sheriff departments often provide law enforcement to cities that cannot or will not provide their own. As chief jailers, sheriffs have had major roles in implementing the realignment reform discussed in chapter 9.[6]

Fiscal Officers. Several county officials focus on finances. Assessors determine the value of taxable real estate and personal property. Tax collectors/treasurers distribute tax bills and collect and deposit revenues. Auditors/controllers allocate revenues to all eligible local governments (county, cities, schools, and special districts). Because their tasks are largely ministerial (administrative in nature with little room for personal discretion), they usually generate little controversy and few political enemies or opponents. When they do, it is usually because they have taken undue risks in managing county assets, including retirement funds.

County Clerk/Recorder. These individuals wear several hats. First, they maintain county documents and records, such as real estate transactions and marriage licenses (they also can perform civil marriage ceremonies). Second, as a registrar, this office registers voters, maintains voter lists, verifies initiative signatures, and conducts all federal, state, and local elections in the county. Voters rarely hear from clerks and usually reelect incumbents.

County Superintendent of Schools. In some ways, this position is an oddity in county government. California's county school superintendents often respond to separately elected county boards of education, not boards of supervisors. They do not administer local schools because district-appointed superintendents do that. The offices headed by superintendents provide staff, payroll, training, and other operations support to local school districts. Because of economies of scale, they can provide those services more cheaply than many local school districts acting separately. Although the California Constitution Revision Commission recommended that this office be abolished, there is little public concern one way or the other.

Other departments vary in size depending on the size of the county. Commonly offered services include local transportation, land use planning, public health, welfare, personnel, and probation. In fact, California's counties play a critical role in administering CalWORKs—the state's version of the federal Temporary Assistance for Needy Families program (TANF), which is discussed in chapter 13.

California's Troubled Counties

Governing California's counties is particularly challenging today, but some of these challenges are inherent to county government in America. In the 1800s, British observer James Bryce perceived that American citizens are less attached to county government than other levels: "[The county] is too large for the personal interest of the citizens: that goes to the township. It is too small to have traditions which command the respect or touch the affections of its inhabitants: these belong to the state."[7] Lord Bryce considered counties artificial entities. He could well have been writing about California today. Several developments in recent decades have created substantial pressures for California counties, affecting their identity and their ability to govern at the local level.

Funding Pressures. Unlike cities, counties do not possess broad revenue generating authority. Proposition 13, which cut property taxes by half in 1978, also cut the counties' share of that tax. Some counties responded by closing libraries or delaying road improvements. Counties cannot cut just any program, however, because the state requires them to deliver a variety of services (welfare, environmental regulation, and public health). Some of these policy directives or mandates are fully funded; others are not.

Although county budgets have become healthier in recent years as a result of the economic recovery and stronger growth in property tax revenues, counties still face mounting fiscal pressures. Prior to the Great Recession in 2008, counties (and other local governments) promised higher salaries and retirement benefits than they could possibly afford over the long term. These legal commitments were not fully paid for, resulting in huge unfunded pension, retirement, and health care liabilities. In some counties, more than half of the budget is consumed by expenditures to meet pension obligations alone.

Issue Spillover. Modern policy problems in California ignore political boundaries. Smog readily moves across county lines, frustrating the ability of any single county to deal with the problem. Regionwide population growth has swamped some urban and "urbanizing" counties with traffic jams on obsolete road systems. Some welfare recipients, crushed by housing costs along coastal California, have moved to the state's more affordable interior. Ironically then, the poorest California counties—those with the fewest governmental resources—also attract the neediest Californians, including parolees, welfare recipients, at-risk children, and patients requiring publicly funded health care. The fact that one in five residents is poor in several Central Valley counties underscores the severity of this problem.[8]

Political Responsiveness. In a representative democracy, people expect elected bodies to be responsive to their wishes. This is problematic for county boards. In smaller counties, boards of supervisors are often ideologically conservative and pro-growth regarding development. Even in the face of desperate need, some boards champion a low-tax, low-spending ideology. Furthermore, with the possible exception of San Francisco, how can a five-member board possibly represent the diverse interests found in larger counties even if they are elected by district? The Los Angeles board has been called the "five little kings" by critics who believe it cannot possibly meet the needs of the county's 10 million–plus residents. Some reformers argue that larger boards in larger counties would allow greater opportunity for minority representation and political responsiveness.

For a variety of reasons, some communities seek to separate from counties, incorporate, and become municipalities. Often, they are dissatisfied with county services and/or want greater control over land-use development. In sprawling counties, government offices may be too distant to be of practical use. Many recent incorporations stem from a local desire for control, image, and identity—those same qualities Bryce considered missing from county government in the 1830s. The communities that manage to incorporate drain county budgets further by reducing the county's share of property and sales taxes.

CITIES

Although California has its share of open space, most of its residents are fundamentally urban. Today, more than 80 percent of the state's residents live in cities, and 71 of those cities have more than 100,000 residents. California's earliest cities (San Diego, Los Angeles, Monterey, and San Francisco) were located along the coast, when passage by ship was one of the few travel choices available. Subsequent cities developed along major land transportation routes: roads, railroad routes, and, later, freeways. Growing cities needed adequate water to develop and urban giants such as Los Angeles and the Bay Area channeled it from great distances. Smaller urban areas developed local reservoirs to capture runoff water, tapped into agricultural water projects (like the Central Valley Project), or even built desalinization plants (converting coastal saltwater into potable fresh water).

California's 482 cities have developed their own identities through economic specialization. Central Valley cities serve surrounding farm areas. Large central cities are home to banking, legal, corporate, and information services. Other cities are manufacturing centers that attract many commuters. Still others in scenic locations (including coastal cities, mountain communities, and California's wine-growing regions) attract tourists. Many suburbs are bedroom communities, offering housing, some shopping, and little else. Others have attracted "clean" industries, shopping malls, and opportunities for recreation.

California's cities and the communities that comprise them defy overgeneralization. Together, they now represent the state's economic and ethnic diversity. For example, table 10.1 depicts a considerable range in median household incomes among some of California's largest cities. In San Francisco, income in the top 95th percentile of households is 16 times more than that of the bottom 20 percent.[9] This trend is not limited to California. Rising income inequality has forced

Table 10.1 Income Inequality in California's Big Cities: Household Income in the Lowest 20 Percent and Highest 95 Percent of Households, 2016

City	20th Percentile ($)	95th Percentile ($)	95/20 Ratio
San Francisco	31,840	507,824	15.9
Los Angeles	20,152	258,144	12.8
Fresno	16,700	181,767	10.9
San Jose	38,087	347,618	9.1
San Diego	30,228	267,615	8.9
Sacramento	22,129	195,061	8.8

Source: Alan Berube, "City and Metropolitan Income Inequality Reveal Ups and Downs Through 2016," *Brookings*, February 5, 2018, https://www.brookings.edu.

some lower-income residents to flee cities where housing is unaffordable. It has also prompted cities themselves to consider "living wage" ordinances that would require employers to boost minimum pay above the statewide minimum wage. Ethnic diversity also characterizes California cities. In a growing number of them, no single racial or ethnic group constitutes a majority of a city's residents. These are California's majority-minority cities.

How Communities Become Municipalities

If voters in a locale wish to incorporate, they usually initiate such a proposal via a petition. A countywide **local agency formation commission** (LAFCO) studies the possible impacts of the new city. LAFCOs were established in 1963 to foster the orderly development of local government and to prevent urban sprawl. Usually consisting of two city council members, two county supervisors, and one public member, LAFCOs in recent years have been particularly sensitive to the revenue losses counties experience when new cities are formed. After a favorable LAFCO vote, the voters decide whether or not to incorporate. New cities with fewer than 3,500 people must be general law cities, operating under the general laws of the state. For example, a state general law requires every city to maintain a current general plan, a document that guides the city's future physical development, including design, land uses, expansion plans, and infrastructure goals. Larger ones can choose to be general law or to adopt their own voter-approved charters. Only 121 California cities have their own charters. Some are quite detailed—Los Angeles's newest charter contains 10 articles and more than 1,000 sections. Charter proponents believe these governing documents allow more flexibility for cities.

"Cities" without "Government"

In the early 1960s, Samuel Wood and Alfred Heller wrote about the **phantom cities** of California. According to the authors, such places are "thickly settled, urban in nature. But they are not cities in the traditional sense of being more or less self-contained settlements controlling their own destinies. They are phantom cities."[10] Included were unincorporated cities (generalized urban growth outside city boundaries), special interest cities ("cities" dedicated to one industry or land-use type, such as housing), contract cities (jurisdictions that buy some or all of their services often from counties), seasonal cities (recreation-oriented communities that become bustling "cities" only during the tourist season), legitimate cities (but with problems that extend well beyond their borders), and regional cities (entire metropolitan areas without effective governments to match). All these phantoms exist today.

In recent years, a newsworthy example has been the City of Vernon, five miles south of downtown Los Angeles. The city is home to not only 123 residents but also 1,800 businesses and 55,000 weekday commuters. Dominated by heavy industry, it contains no schools, libraries, privately owned housing, or grocery stores. In fact, one city manager called Vernon's status as a municipality a sham. Amid charges of political corruption (bloated salaries, rigged elections, and misappropriated funds), the state legislature nearly dissolved this "phantom" in 2010. In response, Vernon officials instituted a series of "good governance" reforms.

A variation on phantom cities has been so-called **urban villages** or **edge cities**—conglomerations of shopping malls, industrial parks, office "campuses," institutions, and residential housing. They are located outside of traditional downtowns or central business districts. Orange County's urban village—the Costa Mesa–Newport Beach–Irvine complex—is considered California's third-largest "downtown." In these "postsuburban" communities, a consumer culture predominates.[11] The development of such places may overlap several jurisdictions that would otherwise manage their growth. They also blur traditional relationships between central city downtowns and surrounding suburbs.

Even at the neighborhood level, a growing number of middle-class Californians live in housing developments governed not by city hall but by **homeowner associations** (HOAs). Today, an estimated 9 million Californians live in over 55,000 common interest developments (CIDs). Developers initially establish them and all homeowners become members. Elected boards of directors operate under assorted bylaws and documents called "CC&Rs" (covenants, conditions, and restrictions). In some respects, these documents are analogous to city charters. No wonder they have been called "shadow governments." Like cities, state law governs many aspects of HOA operations. The powers of HOA boards to enforce self-imposed regulations are both substantial and picayune— from maintaining private streets to dictating exterior paint colors. These powers are largely unregulated by the state; significant disputes are often taken to court. Many associations augment local law enforcement with security gates and alarm systems. Do such neighborhoods foster "cocoon citizens" who flee community life around them, as some critics suggest? Although research suggests that CIDs are less diverse than the larger communities that surround them, there is little evidence that these residents have seceded from public life generally. Nonetheless, these "privatopias" could be considered the newest phantom cities in contemporary California.[12]

How California Cities Are Run

As with counties, California cities are general law or charter; they are governed under the general laws of the state or operate under their own voter-approved charters. Exception for the City and County of San Francisco, city governments in California follow one of two forms—mayor–council or council–manager.

Mayor–Council. Nationally, the **mayor–council** form predates the Progressive movement and tends to have strong mayors with substantial legislative, budget, appointive, and administrative powers; full-time city councils with members elected by district; and substantial partisan influence on elections and personnel. California has its version of mayor–council cities, including San Francisco, Los Angeles, and San Diego (see figure 10.3). There are exceptions to the national norm, however. As you recall, California cities must be officially nonpartisan. Also, California mayors in mayor-council systems are less powerful than their national counterparts. For example, the mayor of Los Angeles shares administrative powers with numerous managers, boards, and commissions, although his appointive powers increased under a revised charter. He remains able to veto ordinances passed by the city council. California's big-city mayors maximize what powers they do have by becoming visionaries and seeking bold policy initiatives. During the recent recession, however, those bold ambitions were replaced by more modest "making do with less" strategies.

What do city councils do in strong-mayor systems? As with all councils, they pass ordinances (local legislation), approve budgets, confirm appointments, and decide land use projects. They also have the power to reject decisions by other city bodies, such as rejecting a proposed utility rate increase. Compared to their counterparts in some other states, city councils in California's larger cities are small. San Francisco has 11 members on its board of supervisors and Los Angeles has 15 council members. In contrast, New York has 51 and Chicago 50.

Council–Manager. A much more prevalent city government pattern in California is the **council–manager** form (see figure 10.4). In this form, typically part-time, modestly paid city councils hire professionally trained city managers or administrators who appoint most department heads and run the day-to-day affairs of their cities. Like their counterparts in larger cities, city councils adopt ordinances (local statutes), allocate revenue, determine the extent of public services offered, and make land use decisions. In smaller cities, council members are usually elected on an at-large (citywide) basis and often possess a volunteer ethic, a take-it-or-leave-it attitude toward their jobs. Many do little more than respond to city manager proposals. Some are elected on single issues such as a controversial land use project and remain singularly focused. All in all, the primary power of most city councils in this system is to veto or second-guess the recommendations of city managers. As with county supervisors, council members used to be white, male, and middle class, but political times have changed. City councils today are more diverse—representing a wider range of economic interests, more ethnic minorities, and many more women.

Most mayors in California council–manager cities are council members chosen by their colleagues to be mayor, although a growing number now have direct election of mayors. Although they preside over council meetings and grant more media interviews, they are, in many ways, equal to other council members. They rarely possess a mandate to lead in any meaningful sense. Their mayoral duties are largely ceremonial: cutting ribbons, presenting congratulatory resolutions, and speaking at various social functions. When their cities are successful, they rarely get the credit, but when community problems arise, they can easily become scapegoats.

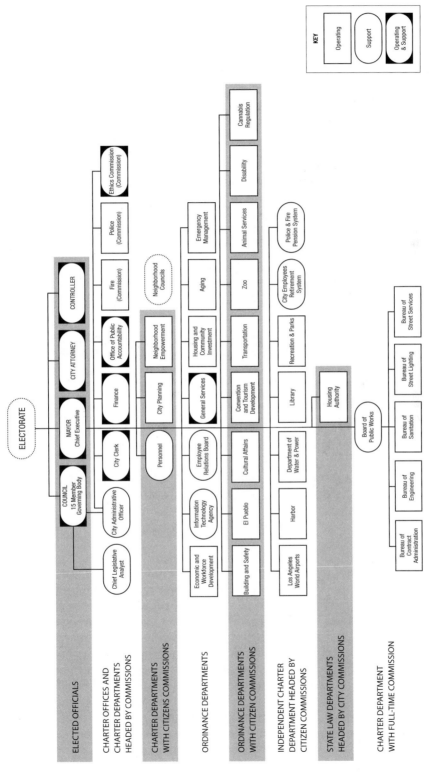

Figure 10.3 Los Angeles's Strong-Mayor Organization Chart

Source: City of Los Angeles Organization Chart, http://cao.lacity.org/misc/LAorgchart.pdf.

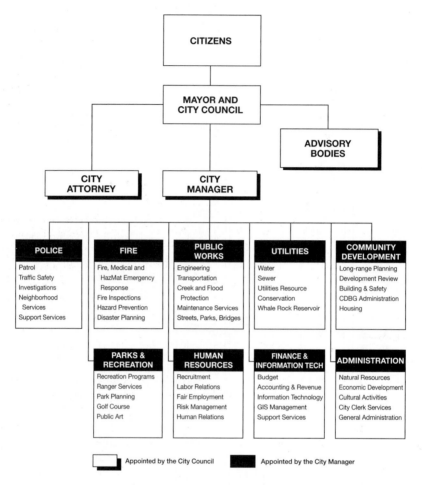

Figure 10.4 San Luis Obispo's Council–Manager Organization Chart

Source: City Organization Chart, http://www.slocity.org/home/showdocument?id=4991.

In council–manager systems, city managers play powerful roles. They represent the Progressive ideal that "politics" and "administration" can be separated. City managers are directly responsible to the council. Although a growing number have long-term contracts, their tenure still depends on a council majority. "Three votes on any Monday night and I am out of a job," said one. A primary responsibility of the manager is to build agendas for council meetings. Between meetings, managers hire and supervise department heads, provide budget leadership, study the city's long-range needs, and otherwise do the council's bidding. In recent years, they have had to devote growing chunks of time to finance. Some develop statewide reputations as fiscal wizards, able to generate revenue from unlikely sources. Contrary to Progressive thinking, good city managers *are* good politicians. As a general rule, they know how to credit their elected bosses and steer clear of scandal (see box 10.1).

In California, gated communities come in all varieties—from exclusive adult communities (as pictured) to middle-class condominiums to mobile home parks.

Box 10.1 ★ Case in Point: Bell, California

How on earth did a relatively poor, blue-collar city near Los Angeles with a population of 35,000 largely Latinx and Hispanic residents become a national symbol of local government run amok? A 2010 investigation by the *Los Angeles Times* revealed that Bell City manager Robert Rizzo earned an annual salary and benefits package totaling $1.5 million and, once retired, stood to become the highest-paid public pensioner in state history. Other city officials also earned substantially more than their counterparts elsewhere. All but one of the part-time city council members earned nearly $100,000 per year, well beyond the average $4,800 earned by members in similarly sized cities. The sheer weight of Bell's city hall payroll required continual tax increases and dubious fee hikes. All this occurred in a city where the annual per capita income was only $24,000.

The roots of the scandal dated to a 2005 state law that limited city council pay in general law cities like Bell. Ironically, the law was a reaction to high council salaries in neighboring South Gate. In response, the Bell City Council authorized a special election seeking to make Bell a charter city, thereby exempting it from those salary caps. The little-noticed election attracted a scant 390 voters.

Measure A's backers never revealed its true intent, cost, or consequences. After the vote and in quid pro quo fashion, the council raised Rizzo's own pay.

Now that Bell was a charter city and the council could set its own pay, how could it do so under the public's radar? The council's base pay would be only $1,800, but the council added to that amount about $19,000 annually for serving on *each* of several boards and commissions. Most of these bodies met concurrently with regular city council meetings if they met at all.

(continued)

Box 10.1 ★ *Continued*

After the scandal came to light, Bell voters recalled the entire city council, and most administrative officials resigned or were fired. Several were convicted on various corruption charges, and Risso himself was sentenced to 12 years in state prison and ordered to pay nearly $9 million in restitution. That was on top of a federal prison term for tax evasion.

In the years that followed, new administrators and a new city council moved to make city policies and records more open and transparent. The Bell case was sensational to be sure, but it illustrated the need for local government accountability to a citizenry informed by a vigilant media.

Source: Adapted from various *Los Angeles Times* news accounts, including Jeff Gottlieb, "Bell Council Found Loophole in Law to Allow Big Salaries," *Los Angeles Times*, July 22, 2010; and Corina Knoll and Jeff Gottlieb, "Risso Gets 12 Years in Prison, Marking End to Scandal That Rocked Bell," *Los Angeles Times*, April 16, 2014.

A city manager's ability to get along with a city council is paramount. Council factions often determine a city manager's success. A manager can be too entrepreneurial and dynamic (thereby competing with the mayor and council) or insufficiently dynamic (and therefore ineffective as city hall and community leader). In recent years, the biggest problem managers have faced is how to meet unrealistically high expectations such as proposing cuts in government services without inflicting the inevitable pain that ensues. As group diversity and conflict become commonplace in California cities, so does criticism of these career professionals. No wonder city manager turnover tends to be high.

Regardless of city size or system type, city governments depend on various commissions and boards to govern. Large cities have many of them whereas small cities might have only a few. Some commissions may actually operate harbors, airports, or public works enterprises. Others merely advise or make recommendations to elected policymakers. The most common are planning commissions that advise city councils on land use matters. They can exercise considerable power, as any developer can attest. Other boards provide advice on social services funding, libraries, the arts, and other matters. Service on these boards provides lessons in governing, and occasionally that first step toward elective office.

Cities and Counties: An Uneasy Relationship

California cities and counties invariably joust for influence and, more important, revenue. In general, California cities are in better fiscal shape than California counties. The reasons are clear. First, California cities have fewer policy responsibilities mandated by the state such as welfare, jails, and public health. As a result, they are unburdened by rising caseloads in those areas. Second, cities have more flexibility than counties. County boundaries are fixed, whereas cities can annex unincorporated land for future development. Furthermore, new cities can form, capturing revenue generated from suburban population growth. For instance, by the time Wildomar and Menifee incorporated, Wildomar's population was more than 20,000 and Menifee's more than 72,000—presumably providing a built-in revenue base from the first day of cityhood. Also, cities can pick and choose what services to provide and at what levels. If they want to provide police protection or garbage collection without maintaining expensive bureaucracies, they can "contract out" for those services. Third, cities have more opportunities to raise revenue than counties. When Proposition 13 cut California property taxes, cities sought other revenue sources. Because one cent of the state sales tax is returned to where it was collected, cities tend to favor revenue-rich commercial projects such as shopping malls, auto dealerships, and "big box" retailers like Costco and Walmart—the **fiscalization of land use**. Although counties are free to approve such developments, most shopper-friendly building sites tend to be within city boundaries.

Until recently, cities (and a few counties) also generated revenue by creating hundreds of **redevelopment agencies** (RDAs) intended to improve and revitalize depressed or blighted areas. These agencies invested in new, largely private-sector development and then captured the "tax increment," the amount of increased property taxes attributable to new development in order to plan future projects. Typical results included office complexes, in-town malls, entertainment facilities, convention centers, and other mixed-use projects. The cumulative impacts of these fiscal tools drew criticism. Over time, redevelopment agencies created ever-larger project areas, consumed ever-larger shares of local property taxes, and caused resentment in other local governments. In order to relieve pressure on the state's general fund, the 2011 Budget Act dissolved the RDAs. Since that time, general property taxes have been used to pay off agency obligations. What remains is supposed to be redistributed to cities, counties, special districts, and school districts—jurisdictions that were "shortchanged" by redevelopment. Numerous cities challenged the dissolutions, but the California Supreme Court upheld them.

SPECIAL DISTRICTS

They have been called America's "forgotten fiefdoms." There are nearly 30,000 of them across the country; they outnumber cities. California claims about 3,300, not including more than 1,000 school districts. Four counties have more than 200 of them; most counties have 50 to 200. They are special districts. Many of them were formed years ago to extend urban services to rural areas.

What Makes Them Special?
Although California's special districts together provide 50 different services, nearly 85 percent of them provide only one service such as water or fire protection. Other services include community services, reclamation, sanitation, recreation, and even cemeteries (we consider school districts separately). Special districts do what general purpose local governments (cities and counties) cannot or will not do. They can assess property taxes, issue bonds, and charge user fees tied directly to the service provided. Not only do they spend vast sums on these services; they also manage billions of dollars in budget reserves.

A San Joaquin irrigation district was California's first special district. Created in 1887, its purpose was to provide steady water supplies at predictable prices to area farmers. Since that time, special districts have multiplied in the Golden State. They became attractive to communities that desired a particular service and local control over its provision. Cities and counties rarely resisted because these districts did not threaten existing political structures or boundaries; they simply added new, noncompeting layers of local government.

California special districts are either **dependent** or **independent**. Dependent ones are actually subdivisions of cities and counties. They commonly fund parking lots or street lighting through separate assessments, which, in effect, insulate a particular service from the larger annual budget battles faced by general purpose governments. City councils and county boards of supervisors provide policy direction. Counties also maintain county service areas to provide one or more services in unincorporated communities. These districts sometimes give way to municipal incorporation efforts by residents who want more home rule than these districts can provide. California's 2,300 independent districts are separate legal entities with their own elected boards that provide and finance the particular services noted earlier.

Special districts epitomize the diversity of local government in California. Some are tiny slivers of government that quietly provide a specialized service at modest cost to relatively few people. Others are gargantuan. The Southern California Rapid Transit District and the Metropolitan Water District of Southern California are two of the nation's largest. The latter's jurisdictional tentacles reach to the Eastern Slope of the Sierra Nevada—channeling precious runoff water to nearly 19 million Californians in six counties. Acting as a giant water wholesaler, this district maintains water supplies, determines water rates, establishes mandatory conservation programs, and levies fines against noncomplying client agencies.

The Stealth Governments of California

The largest special districts are powerful indeed. But most of them are virtually invisible and in many ways unaccountable to average Californians. They are the stealth governments of California in that relatively anonymous elected boards govern them. Although their meetings are open to the public, the public rarely shows up and the media rarely report their actions. One cemetery district manager could not recall someone from the public ever attending a meeting. Special district elections are often the misnomers of democracy. Challengers are rare, and elections are sometimes canceled when no one steps forth. Voter turnout is typically low unless these elections are folded into California's primary or general elections. On occasion, lavish business-trip spending, exorbitant managerial salaries, or bloated cash reserves make news and inspire calls for reform. But special districts usually operate outside the limelight, much like private businesses. No wonder many citizens express a combination of ignorance and apathy regarding these stealth governments.[13]

Special District Politics and Problems

Political scientists are often critical of special districts. First, they represent the height of governmental fragmentation. Why should the Bay Area have two dozen separate transportation agencies? Why should a patchwork of neighboring water agencies trip over each other to provide a commonly scarce resource? Why shouldn't single purpose agencies have to weigh competing priorities like general purpose cities and counties do? Defenders of special districts disagree. To them, special districts foster home rule by providing particular services tailored to particular locales—customized or "boutique" government, if you will. According to the California Special Districts Association, "By focusing on a particular

Table 10.2 Special Districts Pros and Cons

Pros

1. They can tailor services to citizen demand.
"Special districts only provide the services that the community desires."
2. They can link costs to benefits.
"Only those who benefit from district services pay for them. Those who do not benefit do not pay."
3. They are responsive to their constituents.
"Small groups of citizens can be quite effective in influencing special districts' decisions."

Cons

1. Special districts can lead to inefficiency.
"Many special districts provide the same services that cities and counties provide. Overlapping jurisdictions can create competition and conflict . . . "
2. Special districts can hinder regional planning.
"It can be difficult to organize the various water, sewer, and fire services in one region to provide equitable services for all residents."
3. Special districts can decrease accountability.
"The multiplicity of limited purpose special districts can make harder for citizens to gather information. [They] have a hard time finding out who's in charge."

Source: What's So Special About Special Districts? A Citizen's Guide to Special Districts in California 4th ed. (Sacramento: State Senate Local Government Committee, October, 2010).

service—water delivery, fire protection, parks and recreation, etc.—districts pay greater attention than bigger bureaucracies to both long-term planning and everyday constituent and rate-payer feedback"[14] (see table 10.2).

Second, contrary to their association's claims, critics of special districts believe that many of them lack true accountability and transparency, two key ideals of representative democracy. Any government agency that is empowered to raise its own revenue but is largely ignored by voters and the media is apt to spend those revenues in potentially controversial ways. For example, one San Diego County water agency serving only 350 meters and employing only nine people paid its general manager nearly $300,000 in salary and benefits in 2010.

In spite of these concerns, most of California's special districts have successfully resisted elimination, consolidation, or other reforms. But, as journalist Peter Schrag observed, "As California's ever-more desperate leaders cast around for both savings and efficiency—and maybe for a little better government generally—special districts should make for fat, tempting targets."[15]

SCHOOL DISTRICTS

California's 1,000 plus school districts are different enough from other special districts to warrant separate consideration. As a group, they, too, exemplify both diversity and hyperpluralism—our continuing themes. They range in size from the mammoth Los Angeles Unified School District, with more than 600,000 students and a $6 billion-plus budget, to several hundred districts composed of single schools. As a group, these districts educate the state's children and youth, a growing segment of the state's population. Increasingly, they serve an ethnic rainbow in California—people groups from the four corners of the Earth.

Organizationally, school districts reflect the assumption that politics and education can and should be separate. With the exception of Los Angeles (which has a seven-member board), California's local school boards consist of five members. All board members run on nonpartisan ballots, and a growing percentage of them run in individual districts rather than on an at-large basis. Like other units of government, district-based boards must reapportion every 10 years and have been under pressure to better reflect California's minority groups. Boards typically meet several times a month. Most boards receive nominal pay or only minimal fringe benefits and have been common stepping-stones to higher office, especially for women. Increasingly, however, women reach higher office through a variety of local offices (city councils, county boards of supervisors) in addition to school board service.

Professionally trained superintendents head educational staffs—teachers, support personnel, and other administrators. Usually possessing advanced degrees in education, superintendents prepare board agendas, systemwide budgets, and various policy proposals. Whereas small districts may be "lean and mean," large districts employ huge numbers of administrators, often a bone of contention among lesser-paid teachers. Board members and administrators are destined to conflict. Elected board members represent accountability in a representative democracy. They bring to meetings the "commonsense" views of parents, taxpayers, and neighbors. By contrast, education professionals bring expertise, including educational practices, trends, and jargon that might be foreign to their boards.

Unlike most other special districts, school districts operate under close scrutiny—by parents, various interest groups, and the state government on which they depend heavily. The state's influence is pervasive. First, a majority of school funding comes from state aid, based on average daily attendance figures. Second, California's massive Education Code dictates in surprising detail what districts can and cannot do. Third, the state Department of Education also affects local districts by administering statewide testing of various grade levels in various subjects, influencing curricula, approving textbook lists, and inspecting district performance. The federal government once played a relatively modest role by funding or subsidizing certain programs (such as school lunches) and enforcing various civil rights laws. Since the passage of the No Child Left Behind law in 2001, the federal government has taken on a much bigger role in setting education policy, particularly when it comes to performance and accountability. The Every Study Succeeds Act, passed in 2015, is the latest example of this enhanced role. It requires states to identify the lowest-performing schools (the bottom 5 percent) receiving federal Title I funding for low-income students and fix them. However, California recently adopted new performance measures that conflict with the federal ones, leaving the path forward unclear.[16] Although federal policy requires heightened performance and accountability, the federal portion of the state's education budget is only about 9 percent.

Pressures on California school districts will increase in the future as enrollments grow and financial challenges mount. Education policy will continue to be a battleground involving ethnic, religious, and ideological groups—each demanding that their priorities be reflected in the curriculum and in education policy generally. At one level, they must cope with a host of social phenomena such as divorce, juvenile delinquency, drug abuse, and many inattentive parents.

At another level, they are supposed to respond to a growing school-age population, parent demands for greater choice, state expectations for reform, ethnic diversity, and the usual assortment of local conflict and controversy. We discuss education policy further in chapter 13.

REGIONAL GOVERNMENTS

A few years ago, a three-mile bike path from Burbank to Los Angeles became both a source of community pride and of intergovernmental frustration. Through the Burbank stretch, cyclists passed well-tended neighborhood gardens and white-picket fences. By the time they reached North Hollywood, riders faced waist-high weeds, discarded mattresses, and graffiti-marred industrial warehouse walls. As one reporter put it, "It's a tale of one bike path, two cities, and too many bureaucrats." It turns out that the Burbank portion was monitored and maintained by one city department. Accountability for the North Hollywood portion was spread over three Los Angeles city departments, one of which flatly refused to begin maintenance of the path until the project was fully complete.[17] This seemingly minor example demonstrates the potential challenges local governments encounter when working together toward a common goal. If a several mile bike path can become an interjurisdictional muddle, consider the mega-regional dilemmas of traffic gridlock, affordable housing, periodic water shortages, and climate change issues such as air pollution. Here we consider the role and importance of regional governance in California.

Because these policy challenges spill beyond jurisdictional boundaries, local governments acting alone will invariably be unprepared to deal with them. Thinking in regional terms would be a start, and California's regional governments already do that. But Californians rarely aspire for regional government. The proliferation of local governments in a region has allowed greater local identity, access to policymakers, opportunity for influence, and insulation from problems faced by nearby jurisdictions. Supporters of regional government point to two models in California: coordination and regulation.

Regional Coordination

The coordination model is best exemplified by the state's 35 regional planning agencies. Twenty-three of them are **councils of governments** (COGs). COGs are confederal—much like small United Nations—groups of autonomous counties and cities in a region coming together to deal with issues of common significance. The federal government designates them as *metropolitan planning organizations* (MPOs) and requires them to draw up long-range plans for transportation, growth management, hazardous waste management, and air quality. But they usually lack the legal authority to implement their plans. At minimum, COGs provide a forum for the member jurisdictions to communicate with each other. Although COGs continue to receive federal funding because of federally mandated tasks, they also rely on member dues, transportation planning funds, consulting fees charged to member agencies, and voter-approved sales tax "add-ons," notably for transportation improvements. In addition to the state's required regional councils are 13 regional commissions who focus exclusively on transportation planning and policy.

Of the nation's nearly 700 regional councils, the Southern California Association of Governments is the largest—its members include six counties and 191 cities, representing more than 18 million persons. The Association of Bay Area Governments does planning for a nine-county, 101-city region. In these large metropolitan areas, subregional councils enable more local governments to participate and allow more detailed planning than otherwise possible. Numerous other COGs cover only one county (such as Kern, Humboldt, Fresno, Merced, San Diego, Sacramento, and Santa Barbara). The members of these councils are city council members and county supervisors chosen by their peers and serve on a largely volunteer basis. Not only do COGs lack significant legislative authority, their voting members typically and understandably put local interests first. They resist giving a regional agency the power to dictate policy to member local governments. Yet, to the extent that knowledge is power, the COGs' ability to issue reports and studies often frames local policy debates.

Regional Regulation

Regional agencies that employ a regulation model have the power to both write and to enforce various rules and regulations, usually in the field of environmental pollution. For example, the San Francisco Bay Conservation and Development Commission can veto any waterfront construction that threatens the bay itself. The Tahoe Regional Planning Agency has similar powers relative to Lake Tahoe. Of the state's 35 air quality districts, the South Coast Air Quality Management District (SCAQMD) is one of the more active and controversial. Its rules either discourage, control, or ban polluting emissions from primarily stationary sources (power plants, factories, and corner gas stations) and consumer products (house paints, other solvent-based products, lawnmowers, etc.). These regionwide regulatory efforts usually involve complex trade-offs among various agendas, mandates, and organized interests.[18]

Regional government in California seems to be at a crossroads. Two contrary political forces explain the dilemma. On one hand, some government officials and business leaders would like to strengthen or require regional approaches to admittedly regional problems. There are even state regulatory agencies that impact regions and communities in areas such as toxic pollution, water resources, environment, and waste management. On the other hand, pressure has been growing to empower grassroots groups and strengthen home rule *below* the local government level. NIMBY (not in my backyard) and environmental groups have flourished by opposing land-use projects of both local and regional significance. These contrary goals lock horns profoundly in an increasingly diverse and hyperpluralist state.

CONCLUSION: DIVERSE COMMUNITIES, DIVERSE GOVERNMENTS

California's local governments mirror the profound diversity of the state. Cities and counties come in all shapes and sizes. Special districts, the stealth governments of California, provide single services controlled by unpublicized boards. School districts educate children and youth through high school whereas the state's 72 community college districts provide similar services to some high school students, college students, and adults. Regional governments face the permanent challenge of coordinating other local governments and educating them to think regionally. Private groups, such as homeowner associations, duplicate public governments but avoid (or think they do) the worst social, political, and economic problems at the local level.

Local government fragmentation mirrors a diverse state, but how problematic is fragmentation itself? Experts are not sure. Some governing problems are a function of size; some jurisdictions are simply too large or too small. The Los Angeles Unified School District might be too large to serve well its diverse school-age population. In recent years, reformers have discussed breaking up this behemoth into smaller, more manageable districts and downsizing its largest schools—an idea that has some popular appeal. Other districts, especially some rural counties, are so small that they cannot adequately control overhead costs or provide statistically accurate evidence of student outcomes. One study suggests consolidating the tiniest districts and making them more accountable.[19]

Is California overly fragmented? The layering of local governments across California's political landscape does seem to create voter confusion and the need for constant coordination. The state's regional governments help, but only help, in addressing local fragmentation. Nonetheless, local government fragmentation seems to be less of a problem in California than elsewhere (see figure 10.5).

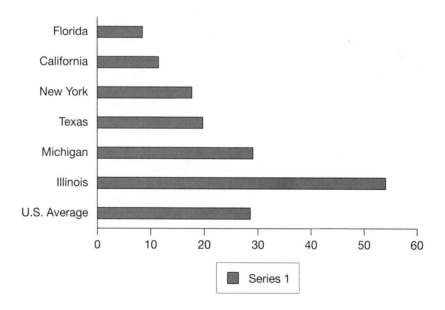

Figure 10.5 How California Compares: Number of Local Governments per 100,000 Population
The figure shows that local government in California is less fragmented than other states with large populations and the U.S. average.

Source: "Number of Local Governments by State," *Governing Magazine*, http://www.governing.com/gov-data/number-of-governments-by-state.html, accessed February 1, 2019. Based on 2012 Census of Government data and 2012 Census Population Estimates.

California has fewer cities, counties, and special districts per capita than the national average and other large states. The result has been jurisdictional stability in a sea of fiscal, political, and demographic change.[20]

That said, stable local governments do not necessarily mean governments that are accountable to California's diverse populations, or responsive to its modern policy challenges. Although the ideal of home rule is sacrosanct to local officials, it has caused woes of its own. With authority comes responsibility, and some local governments have lacked the latter. For example, in recent years, many cities and counties devised both generous salary packages and retirement pension formulas, especially for top-level employees. In retrospect, these decisions were unsustainable in the long term and unaffordable even in the short term, especially as the Great Recession reduced once-reliable local revenues like the property tax and assets like pension portfolios. A strong economy in recent years has boosted the financial health of local governments, but most observers think this is only temporary. The rising pension and health care benefit costs are expected to overwhelm local budgets in coming years and, with limited revenue streams to tap, may force local governments to adopt some significant reforms, not unlike what has occurred with the state budget, the subject of our next chapter.

KEY TERMS

privatism (p. 210)

home rule (p. 211)

general law counties (p. 214)

charter counties (p. 214)

Local Agency Formation
Commission (p. 218)

phantom cities (p. 218)

urban villages/edge cities (p. 219)

homeowner associations (p. 219)

mayor–council form (p. 220)

council–manager form (p. 220)

fiscalization of land use (p. 225)

redevelopment agencies (p. 225)

dependent special districts (p. 209)

independent special districts (p. 209)

councils of governments (p. 229)

REVIEW QUESTIONS

1. What are the purposes of and limits to government at the community level?
2. Survey the historical forces that shaped California counties.
3. Why are Californian counties more trouble-prone than cities?
4. If you wanted your community to incorporate, to become a city, what steps would you need to take?
5. Describe and illustrate "phantom cities" from the text and your own observations.
6. What do special districts do, and why are they the stealth governments of California? Which ones exist in your home county, and which ones could be combined?
7. Describe the two major approaches to regional governance in California.
8. How is local governance in California affected by home rule, diversity, and hyperpluralism?

WEB RESOURCES

California State Association of Counties

http://www.counties.org

Information here includes the counties' lobbying activity, issues of interest to counties, county profiles, maps, and links to all 58 county websites.

League of California Cities

http://www.cacities.org

The League of California Cities site features legislative bulletins, association news, and links to hundreds of city home pages. Look up yours.

California Special Districts Association

https://www.csda.net

In addition to members-only content, this website provides background information on special districts and links to related local government resources.

California School Boards Association

https://csba.org

The California School Boards Association is one of several education groups representing education policymakers and professionals. Its website contains helpful information on education governance in California.

11

Budget Policy: The Cost of Diversity

LEARNING OUTCOMES

Students will be able to:

★ Explain the importance of the state's economy to the budget.

★ Analyze the key steps of the budget process and the constraints on it.

★ Summarize the major revenue sources and issues affecting them.

★ Discuss how the state's expenditures are allocated.

★ Describe California's boom and bust history and factors that led to current fiscal conditions.

IN BRIEF

One of government's most important and contentious activities is to raise and spend money. The state of California and its local governments, like governments elsewhere, develop budgets to do so. These are government's premier policy statements, highly political documents that essentially represent contracts between policymakers and various sectors of society. As with the nation, the basis and context of California budgeting is the state's economy. The Golden State's economy historically has been diverse and continues to be. But economic upturns and downturns can significantly affect the dynamics of the budget process.

★ ★ ★

THE STATE BUDGET PROCESS in California is characterized by historic spending habits, significant input by various executive branch bureaucracies, and control by the governor and legislative leaders. At the local level, executive leadership and outside forces well beyond local control significantly affect budgeting.

Major California state revenues include the personal income tax, the sales tax, corporate taxes, excise taxes, and borrowing. Local revenues include the property tax, aid from other levels of government, and miscellaneous taxes and fees, plus borrowing. Where does all this money go? The state spends most of it on the Big Three: education, health and welfare, and corrections. California's counties spend most of their revenue on public assistance and public safety activities. Cities spend most of theirs on public safety (police and fire), utilities, community development, and transportation activities.

In recent years, budgets have been whipsawed both by volatile revenues and demands for spending increases. Stormy budget debates in recent years seem to illustrate an increasingly diverse state whose policymakers can no longer achieve consensus on its arguably most important public policy.

INTRODUCTION: BUDGETING AS PUBLIC POLICY

Proposed Cuts Show Depth of State Crisis (2009)
California's Next Budget Casualty—70 State Parks on Governor's
   Closure List (2011)
California's Budget Deficit Is Gone (2013)
California Has 'Extraordinary' Budget Surplus, Analysts Say (2018)

These actual newspaper headlines epitomize budgeting in California. Because of its dependence on the condition of the economy, the budget process has a yo-yo quality to it. In bad economic times, there is pessimistic debate over service cuts, denied pay increases, postponed projects, and possible tax increases. In good economic times, there is rosy talk of service expansion, restored funding, pay increases, new programs, and possible tax cuts. But even in the good years, budgeting itself is not easy. The process is cumbersome, party politics infuses deliberations, interest groups clash, and numerous external constraints limit budget options. In this chapter, we discuss how and why budgeting in California works the way it does. In the end, we find that budgeting in California increasingly reflects the state's hyperpluralistic character as increasingly diverse groups make claims on the public purse. How policymakers respond to those demands is characterized by conflicting interest group goals and a budget process often colored or even paralyzed by the competing demands placed on it.

Before proceeding to budgeting in the Golden State, we need to explain four basic characteristics of public budgets in American politics:

1. Any **budget** is simply a plan that specifies what monies will be spent (expenditures) and how those monies will be obtained (revenues). According to political scientist Aaron Wildavsky, "Budgeting is concerned with translating financial resources into human resources. A budget, therefore, may also be characterized as a series of goals with price tags attached. Because funds are limited and have to be divided in one way or another, the budget becomes a mechanism for making choices among alternative expenditures."[1]

2. A California legislator once told some college students, "The top three issues up here are budget, budget, and budget." Indeed, a government's budget is its premier public policy statement. **Public policy** is whatever government chooses to do or not do. What governments spend on these activities reflects societal priorities, what is important and unimportant. Where government obtains its money also represents the allocation of

political power—who pays, who benefits, who wins, and who loses where money is concerned.

3. Budgeting is profoundly political. The budget process is where the sentences and paragraphs of this premier policy statement are torn apart, analyzed, and reassembled. In this regard, the budget shapes government around various spending and taxing decisions, consuming policymakers' attention spans and often dictating what can and cannot be done. Politically speaking, it reflects the state itself. California's state budget, for instance, exemplifies an assortment of phenomena: past budget decisions by both policymakers and voters, legislative/gubernatorial relationships, population growth, interest group conflict, and the health of the state's economy.

4. Budgeting is, in essence, a contract. Contracts represent agreements and commitments between two or more parties. Budgets serve as short-term political contracts between various participants in the political process and between the voters and their government. At a deeper level, a budget represents a covenant or contract between a society's present and its future. For example, arguments over education spending, low-cost higher education, and new highways essentially are arguments over how best to invest in the state's future.

WHERE BUDGETING BEGINS: THE ECONOMY

To best understand the politics of budgeting in California, we need first to ask, "Where does the revenue come from?" In short, the basic source of public revenue is the economy. When Americans think of "the economy," they tend to think in national terms, yet there are 50 interdependent state economies that make up the whole. The health or vitality of California's economy is directly related to the revenues available both to the state government and to the state's local governments.

Economic Diversity

Historically, California's diverse and resilient economy has been one of its strengths, heralding the state as a place of opportunity for all comers. As we noted in chapter 1, modern California possesses a balanced economy that consists of numerous sectors: service occupations, retail, agriculture, tourism, manufacturing, and a plethora of "high-tech" activities such as computers, communications, and financial services. California's modern, $3 trillion economy is both industrial and postindustrial—noted for innovation, sophistication, new ideas, new products, and the new jobs that follow. Over the years, California's economy has been stimulated by discoveries of gold and oil, agricultural mass production, automobile manufacturing, defense spending, the aerospace industry, and, in recent decades, the revolution in technology. Also, international investment and foreign trade have contributed to making California the fifth-largest economy in the world.[2]

How California's Economy Affects Budgeting

Two aspects of California's economy ultimately affect the budget process. First, California's bad times and good times seem to be either very bad or very good. During California's early 1990s recession, its unemployment rate was twice the national rate. Several hundred thousand jobs disappeared or left the state. Given the number of military installations and defense contractors in California, cuts in federal defense and aerospace funding further eroded California's economic base. By the late 1990s, California's economy was booming—as was state budget revenue—but that was followed by another economic downturn in the early 2000s and the "Great Recession" of 2007–2009. More than earlier ones, the most recent recession resulted in increased unemployment, housing foreclosures, depressed state and local revenues, and heightened demands on state and local services. Economic volatility leads to budget volatility as policymakers agonize over ways to cut spending or raise revenue. Budget volatility also stems from the fact that, compared to other states, California has increasingly depended on the unstable income tax and less so on the more stable property tax.

Second, the state's economic trends (up or down) affect different Californians in different ways. We see it in a long-term trend toward economic inequality, especially between California's high-paid sectors (such as technology and professional services) and lower-paid sectors (such as agriculture and tourism). This is why California has higher household incomes *and* higher poverty rates than the national average. The gap is particularly acute between the wealthiest 1 percent of Californians and the other 99 percent.[3] Also, some differences are geographic in nature. As a rule, California's coastal economy is more varied, produces higher incomes, and is quicker to rebound from recessions than is California's inland economy where many jobs are agricultural in nature.[4]

Demographics help explain some of this. Compared to whites, California's Hispanic and African American workers earn lower wages because of lower levels of education and the poorer paying jobs that result. Immigration impacts the economy as well. Historically, immigrants relied on decent-paying manufacturing jobs to better their lives. Nowadays, they face the prospect of low-paying jobs in low-paying economic sectors with little opportunity for advancement. These economic variations have profound implications for budget making. Those who fall behind increasingly rely on tax-funded income support, medical care, and housing—the very programs that are jeopardized when the state's economy turns downward.

California's Local Economies

In chapter 10, we noted the rich diversity of communities and local governments in California. There is also a rich diversity of local economies, which constitute the generalized "California economy." Whereas some economic trends affect all communities in the state, these local economies vary enough to create their own opportunities and challenges for state and local policymakers. Some communities depend largely on only a few sources of income—tourism, agriculture, a dominant regional shopping mall, or even the spending generated by the presence of a single state prison. Others remain militarily dependent; for better or worse, their destiny is tied to federal defense spending. Logging communities in Northern California depend on the vagaries of the construction industry. Silicon Valley communities are home to both successful technology firms and boom-or-bust Internet firms. During the most recent recession, public-sector layoffs deeply affected communities where those workers lived (e.g., the Sacramento region). Large cities are so diverse that troubles in one economic sector may be compensated for by growth in other sectors. Consider Los Angeles. Today, the city's economic growth is fueled by small, minority-owned manufacturing concerns. Collectively, these companies have made the Los Angeles region the nation's largest manufacturing center.

THE BUDGET PROCESS

Whatever the state of the economy, California policymakers must agree to budgets every year. The budget process is the institutional framework within which budget decisions are made. We will discuss some basic features of the process in California, the various constraints on it, and on budgeting at the local level.

How California Budgeting Works

Although California's budget process is quite complicated, three features of it deserve special attention. It is incremental throughout, highly bureaucratic in the planning stages, and leadership-dominated in the later stages.

The Role of Incrementalism. California's budget process is **incremental**. In other words, specific agencies typically request increased funding for one **fiscal year** (July 1–June 30) based on whatever was allocated for the previous fiscal year. To look ahead, agencies look back. In the "fat" years, when revenues continually grow, incrementalism makes budgeting easy. There is little incentive to ask whether an agency, service, or program is still needed. From the early 1950s to the present, the state budget grew steadily from $1 billion to over $150 billion—a reflection of California's economic and population growth. In the "lean" years, when revenue growth declines, incrementalism no longer works, and the potential for political conflict and gridlock increases dramatically. When revenues do not match desired expenditures, agencies accustomed to incremental growth can face less money than in the past. At minimum, they must settle for status quo budgets.

The Role of the Executive. The governor and the bureaucracy dominate the planning stage, which takes about 18 months to complete. For example, the formal process to build the 2019–20 budget (July 1, 2019, to June 30, 2020) began early in 2018, as agency budget planners developed spending estimates. Negotiations between the governor's office, agency staff, department heads, the Department of Finance (DOF), and its director take nearly a year. According to political scientist Richard Krolak, this is when DOF "earns its reputation as the most powerful department in state service."[5] The end product is a budget the governor unveils at a press conference and submits to the legislature by January 10 each year (see figure 11.1). The state constitution requires that the budget be balanced; if expenditures exceed anticipated revenues, the governor must propose additional sources of revenue. Governors often balance their budgets by proposing severe cuts, confident that the legislature will never approve them.

Incrementalism dominates the bureaucratic process. Projecting revenue is largely a guessing game as DOF officials must estimate future growth based on current trends, such as job growth and economic productivity. They might be on target; maybe not. At this stage of the process, career administrators provide continuity, given the comings and goings of their appointed bosses and elected officials, and form alliances among California's many interest groups. Masters of incrementalism, they can provide the most plausible reasons for retaining or increasing any agency's funding base.

JANUARY
- Governor releases budget by January 10
- Identical budget bills are introduced in budget committees

FEBRUARY
- LAO releases analysis of the budget bill

MARCH
- Budget subcommittees review budget and hold hearings

APRIL
- Governor releases May revise budget with updated expenditures and revenue

MAY
- Full Assembly and Senate consider budget bills
- Conference committee reconciles differences between chambers
- Legislature, by majority vote, required to pass budget by June 15
- "Big 3" (Governor, Senate Pro Tem, Assembly Speaker) negotiate final budget

JUNE
- Governor signs budget and issues vetoes
- New fiscal year

Figure 11.1 The Budget Process

Note: LAO = Legislative Analyst's Office

The Role of Leadership. A third feature of California budgeting is that the external part of the process is leadership-dominated. When the governor submits the "budget" to the legislature, lawmakers actually receive several documents (all available online, http://www.ebudget.ca.gov): the *Governor's Budget Summary* (a document highlighting the governor's priorities), the actual *Governor's Budget* (a large phone-book-sized document), a *Salaries and Wages Supplement*, and the budget bill itself (listing each expenditure line by line). The process is leadership-dominated in that these bills are submitted only to the two fiscal committees—the Assembly Budget Committee and the Senate Budget and Fiscal Review Committee. Standing policy committees (e.g., Education) are not directly involved. The two fiscal committees divide into subcommittees (such as Education and Health and Welfare) to study in depth portions of the overall budget. The Legislative Analyst's Office issues a series of reports that analyzes the governor's budget and concludes with an assessment of the enacted budget. These reports sometimes challenge the governor's budget assumptions (e.g., what to expect in state revenues or federal aid). During legislative consideration, the governor proposes revisions, the most notable being the **May Revision**. Included may be new spending priorities and, more important, updated revenue estimates. Depending on the economy, these revenue updates can represent bad news (shortfalls where revenues drop more than anticipated) or good news (windfalls where revenues exceed previous estimates). Good news or bad, the May Revision affects budget deliberations greatly. In budget years when severe cuts appear necessary, the legislature has made few decisions until the release of the May Revise, hoping it may bring better news.

Although budget disagreements occur annually, some budget years move along more smoothly than others. In some years, the full fiscal committees vote on their respective budget bills and send them on to the floors of each house well before state-imposed deadlines. A conference committee is supposed to hammer out differences, allowing time for floor votes before the constitutional deadline of June 15. The governor is supposed to sign the budget before July 1, the first day of the new fiscal year. Once the *Budget Act* is passed, **trailer bills** follow. These bills make statutory language changes needed to implement the budget by specifying exact taxes, fee increases, and spending formulas in broad policy areas such as education or transportation.

When this process broke down prior to 2011, the Big Five (the governor, Assembly Speaker, Senate president pro tempore, and minority leaders in both houses) met behind closed doors to hammer out agreements that would garner a two-thirds vote in each chamber. Often these negotiations dragged on for months, which resulted in payment disruptions to state vendors and employees. With the change to a simple-majority-vote requirement to pass the budget (Proposition 25), the final stage has evolved into talks among the **Big Three**— the governor, Assembly Speaker, and Senate president pro tempore. Despite the fact that the Big Three were all Democrats in 2011, the first year with the lower vote threshold, the process did not move as smoothly as the Democrats hoped. After discussions with Republicans to place a tax measure on the ballot proved fruitless, Democrats in the legislature passed a budget that the governor vetoed in its entirety, for the first time in the state's history. In addition, the state controller determined the budget was not balanced, which meant that legislators would have to forfeit pay. The governor later signed a revised budget that included accounting maneuvers and unrealistic revenue assumptions. The process has gone much smoother since then, as the "Big Three" have overcome mostly small disagreements about spending, perhaps signaling a new era of budget cooperation.

Once a compromise is reached, the legislature sends the final budget along with the trailer bills to the governor to be signed. The constitution requires the governor to sign a balanced budget, but a state court ruled in 2011 that only the legislature can determine whether it is balanced.

Constraints on the Process

In 1987, *The Economist* carried an article titled "The State That Tied Its Own Hands,"[6] referring to the budget constraints faced by California policymakers. Other states face constraints as well, but California's tend to be the most severe and, when combined, create an extremely difficult budget environment. Here, we describe six of those constraints.

The Need for Supermajorities. In November 2010, voters approved Proposition 25, which lowered the legislative votes required to pass the annual budget from two-thirds to a simple majority (21 in the Senate, 41 in the Assembly). Prior to that change, California was one of only three states with a supermajority requirement, which was passed by voters back in 1933 with little regard for its long-term consequences.[7] Proposition 25 did not alter the **two-thirds requirement** to raise taxes and this can be a major impediment to on-time budgeting, if new revenue is sought. When recession-era budgets cannot be balanced through spending cuts alone, some taxes must be raised. Democratic supermajorities make the two-thirds threshold more attainable, but even moderate Democrats are reluctant to support tax increases. So, the very reasons it was difficult to pass a budget in the first place remain in place when it comes to raising revenue. In effect, two constitutional requirements clash: (1) the mandate to balance the annual budget and (2) the need for a two-thirds vote to raise the revenue that a balanced budget may require.

The Annual Budget Myth. California's Constitution also requires the governor to submit a budget each year, but there is nothing sacred about annual budgets. Long-term economic, social, and political trends (all of which affect budgeting) ignore arbitrary calendars. Economic and business cycles can last for many years. An approved budget on any July 1 is merely a primitive and temporary snapshot of the state's economy, its tax policy, and its expenditure choices. One-year budgets encourage California policymakers to "cook the books" through arcane budget maneuvers, lending the appearance of a balanced budget. When the state confronted deficits in the 2000s, the budgeting cycle became more semiannual than annual. The governor typically signed a budget in July or August, only to have it fall out of balance several months later. Special legislative sessions for fiscal emergencies were called, but legislators were usually reluctant to adopt any drastic actions to address the mismatch between revenues and expenditures. Some budget reformers have recommended that a two-year budget be adopted (four years in the case of capital outlays).[8] Some California cities and 20 other states already do so. As the state's financial condition has improved in recent years, policymakers have been able to return to the traditional one-year budget calendar.

Cruise Control Spending. One constraint, which we call **cruise control spending,** has to do with the relatively automatic nature of many spending decisions. For example, large portions of the budget are spent on **entitlements**—those payments to individuals who meet eligibility requirements established by law. CalWORKs (California's major welfare program) and Medi-Cal (California's version of federal Medicaid for the poor) are two of the largest entitlement programs. As caseloads grow, so does spending. Other increases are based on the growth of certain populations (school-aged children and prisoners). Cruise control spending is also evident in cost-of-living adjustments (COLAs). This spending technique gives eligible groups *automatic upward adjustments* in the funding they already receive, such as welfare or state employee pension payments. Yearly cost-of-living increases by policymakers easily become yearly expectations by recipients. During the fat years, the legislature routinely grants these increases. In lean years in the past, however, statutes authorizing some of these COLAs have been eliminated.

Third-Rail Issues. "Touch it, you die!" **Third-rail issues** refer to politically volatile issues that policymakers avoid, fearing voter wrath. Until recently, the federal Social Security and Medicare programs have illustrated this phenomenon. In California, Proposition 13 has been a third-rail issue. Because it has become such an antitax icon, California lawmakers usually hesitate to make even needed reforms. In one exception, Proposition 38 in 2000 lowered the threshold for local school bond approvals from two-thirds to 55 percent, making it easier to expand local campuses or meet other needs. In addition, one of the most discussed modifications to Proposition 13 is the idea of a **split-roll property tax**. This would use the market value for commercial and industrial properties to calculate the tax burden, rather than the property's purchase price, which is currently used for residential and commercial properties. Advocates of the split-roll argue that business owners often structure a change in ownership to avoid paying higher property taxes.

Ballot-Box Budgeting

An additional constraint of increasing importance is the phenomenon of **ballot-box budgeting**. This occurs when measures are placed on the ballot, either through the initiative process or by the legislature, that modify the budget process, change the tax system, or redirect spending.[9] The initiative process, in particular, has given voters greater control over controversial issues and, to the consternation of many Sacramento policymakers, control over budgeting as well. One estimate suggests that more than 30 percent of California's appropriations are governed or locked in by voter initiatives.[10] Some argue that voters, not elected officials, now make the most important budget decisions. Consider Proposition 13 (property taxes), Proposition 98 (education funding), Proposition 30 (tax increases), and Proposition 2 (rainy-day fund) as just a short list. Surprisingly, many of these measures are put on the ballot by the legislature and governor rather than by citizens. For instance, Governor Brown sponsored Proposition 30, just as several of his predecessors had for other budget-related initiatives.

This phenomenon has had a profound impact on the budget process. First, some propositions have fundamentally restructured state and local relationships. Proposition 13 cut property taxes so severely that the state government "bailed out" cities, counties, special districts, and schools with surplus revenues. Greater aid meant greater control, which local governments feel even today. As we noted in chapter 10, school districts are now heavily dependent on state support.

Second, propositions have also furthered the practice of **earmarking** (allocating or restricting certain revenues to certain purposes). The most notorious example is Proposition 98. This constitutional amendment established a complex formula for setting minimum annual funding levels for K–12 schools and community colleges. Although its intent was to stabilize education funding and better tie it to enrollment and income growth, it unrealistically assumed revenue would grow indefinitely.[11] Because of the significant funding territory carved out by Proposition 98, it encouraged other program areas to seek funding protections as well. This has resulted in a snowball effect, whereby each additional measure adopted enlarges the mound of restrictions. Some of these earmarks are accompanied with funding sources, which indicates that normally tax-averse voters are willing to support programs that they perceive as beneficial, but it also precludes the use of this new revenue for other purposes.

Third, ballot-box budgeting leads to piecemeal budgeting, where voters consider each decision in a vacuum and without broader consideration of the state's needs and priorities. Bond measures are but one example; they fund singularly worthy projects but encumber the state with cumulative long-term debt obligations. For instance, voters adopted a bond in 2004 to support stem cell research (Proposition 71) even though the federal government typically spearheads this type of research and, at the time, the state faced enormous deficits.

The result of all these constraints has been what one editorialist called a "fiscal pretzel." Policymakers find themselves negotiating merely at the margins of $100 billion budgets. Although antitax crusaders Howard Jarvis and Paul Gann are gone, the initiative process gives voters awesome powers to make complex taxation and spending decisions. They also tend to paint policymakers into a corner in terms of budget flexibility. Unlike other states, California's voter-passed initiatives become permanent fixtures—a kind of semi-constitutional law—that can only be altered by a subsequent popular vote. Thus, with the passage of each new initiative, it further tightens the vise around policymakers' hands.

Local Budget Processes

Given the diversity of local governments in California, we can make only broad generalizations about how they raise and spend money. First, as we noted, local revenues depend on a host of factors including the nature of the local economy. The more diverse the economy, the more stable will be a community's revenue base. Second, local budgeting parallels state budgeting in many respects. Departments and finance offices build their budget requests; the mayor, city manager, school district superintendent, or special district manager submits a formal budget to the elected governing body; that group takes input from the public during public hearings and, after revisions are made, adopts a final budget. California local governments normally use the same July 1–June 30 fiscal year timetable. With some exceptions, they, too, use annual budgets.

Third, the public is largely apathetic. Duly advertised budget hearings are often sparsely attended. Proposition 13 effectively eliminated the need for local governments to set property tax rates; as a result, most voters lost interest in the subject. Exceptions include local interest groups such as chambers of commerce, taxpayer groups, or recipients of local grants. Fourth, the local budget process is at the end of a "fiscal food chain." The federal and state governments respectively monopolize the income tax and the sales tax. What is left for California's local governments? The answer is the property tax, assorted "nickel and dime" taxes, fees, and aid from governments higher up the chain.

Because local governments are so dependent on state funding and spending decisions, local governing boards can only guess at what the final outcomes will be. Because state policymakers do not finalize the contents of the budget until just before the start of the fiscal year (and, in the past, much later), local governing boards are also forced to complete their budgets then, or even later as information and data pertaining to each jurisdiction are distributed. School districts are in a real bind. They must make midsummer budget decisions (and hiring decisions well before that) using the previous year's attendance figures and estimates regarding next fall's enrollment, all the while closely watching the state budget process.

TYPES OF REVENUE

California's state budget consists of a general fund (for ongoing operations), special funds (revenues and expenditures segregated for specific purposes), and bond funds (revenues and expenditures involving borrowed monies). Including all these funds, the entire 2019–2020 budget neared $210 billion. If we added funding the state receives from the federal government, the total budget would be over $300 billion. Here, where we examine particular revenues and expenditures, we focus on the general fund, the state's main account.

If a budget is the premier public policy statement, what can be said of the money raised to fund it? Revenues are by-products of spending desires and ultimately mirror society's values. In this section, we describe major revenue sources used by California state and local governments. Each has its defenders and critics based on the following criteria.

Equity. Fairness or equity generally refers to citizen ability to pay a particular tax. Not all taxes are alike in this regard. A **regressive tax** is one where the effective tax rate falls as taxable income rises; it imposes a greater burden on lower-income than upper-income groups. A flat sales tax disproportionately burdens the poor, who must spend a greater percentage of their incomes to pay it. That is why most groceries are exempt from the sales tax. A **progressive tax** rate increases according to one's ability to pay. The income tax is progressive in that rates climb (up to a point) as incomes climb. The property tax is regressive (based on real estate value, not household income), but the wealthy tend to pay plenty of it because they own higher valued properties. California's overall tax system is both progressive and regressive in that income, sales, and property taxes are all part of the revenue mix. In the end, tax equity depends on one's income level. According to a recent study, households in the lowest 20 percent (with incomes less than $23,200) pay 10.5 percent of their income in state and local taxes. This percentage is slightly higher than for all other income groups except those in the top 1 percent (with incomes over $714,000), who pay 12.4 percent of their income in taxes.[12] In recent years, the meaning of equity has come to include the "benefit principle" (those who receive benefits from government should pay for those benefits). State park campsite fees use the benefit principle.

Yield. Another criterion is yield, the amount of revenue collected given the effort required to collect it. From the government's perspective, the sales tax is the easiest to collect—retailers do it. The property tax is more cumbersome to collect, especially if people appeal their assessments or request lower valuations because of drops in home prices. The state income tax is much more cumbersome to collect for both government and taxpayers. Until recently, sales tax on online purchases has been one of the most difficult taxes to collect, but that is expected to change due to a recent U.S. Supreme Court ruling (see the following discussion on sales tax).

Certainty. Will revenues be steady, regardless of economic or other conditions? Or are they uncertain and unpredictable? Consumption taxes, such as the sales tax, are considered elastic, and therefore unstable. During a recession, people

> **Box 11.1 ★ Did You Know . . . ?**
>
> One of the reasons that California's revenue system is so volatile is that it relies on high-income households for a disproportionate share of personal income tax revenue. Those making $500,000 and above, or the top 1 percent of tax filers, generate more than half of the state's income tax revenue, while those making $50,000 or less represent nearly 60 percent of tax filers and account for just 2 percent of revenue. The top 1 percent receive some of their income from stock market investments, which contribute to revenue volatility.
>
> *Source*: Judy Lin, "The Open Secret about California Taxes," *CalMatters*, May 8, 2018, https://calmatters.org/articles/the-open-secret-about-california-taxes.

tend to spend less and therefore pay less sales tax. In recent years, California's income tax revenues have become quite volatile, reflecting the gyrations of the stock market (see box 11.1). On the other hand, the property tax is usually stable and dependable because it grows slowly and does not depend on the incomes of those who own taxable property. We say "usually." In the wake of the housing crisis of the late 2000s (risky real estate loans, subsequent bank foreclosures, and resultant drops in home sales and prices), local assessors were forced to reduce property values and, consequently, the taxes based on those values. Local budgets were hit hard in the process.

Accountability. In a representative democracy, this criterion suggests that taxes should be explicit or transparent, not hidden. California indexes the personal income tax to make it less hidden. That is, the tax is adjusted each year by the rate of inflation to prevent taxpayers from being pushed into higher tax brackets without a real increase in income. Prior to indexing, taxes "increased" without taxpayers realizing it. At the local level, many taxes such as special assessments appear only in the fine print on their property tax bills.

Acceptability. A final criterion asks whether a particular tax is generally acceptable to the citizenry. True, everyone complains about taxes, but some sources of revenue are more politically acceptable or tolerable than others. For example, many nonsmoking Californians readily support higher taxes on tobacco products. Obviously, smokers find those taxes less acceptable. Although 57 percent of Californians perceive that their overall taxes are too high,[13] information in box 11.2 suggests that assessment may depend on which tax we are talking about.

Major State Revenues

California's revenue system is a patchwork of taxes that were put into place during the 1930s. Experts regard the structure as complex and incomprehensible to average Californians. Indeed, most Californians themselves do not know how the state budget works and misperceive basic budget facts. Specific revenues described are found in the pie chart in figure 11.2.

Personal Income Tax. The largest source of state revenue is the personal income tax. Adopted in 1935, it largely parallels the federal income tax: Taxpayers pay at different rates based on wages, salaries, stock options, and other forms of

Box 11.2 ★ How California Compares: Are Californians' Taxes Too High?

Although many Californians think their taxes are much too high, compared with other states California ranks high on some taxes like the income tax and is more toward the middle on other taxes like property and sales/excise taxes. Overall, California has the 10th-largest tax burden.

Type of Tax	State Ranking	% of Personal Income
Property Tax	19	2.66
Income Tax	5	3.65
Sales & Excise Tax	22	3.26
Total Tax Burden	10	9.57

Note: Rankings represent taxes collected as a percentage of personal income in the 50 states, not including the District of Columbia.

Source: "2018's Tax Burden by State," *WalletHub*, April 9, 2018, https://wallethub.com/edu/states-with-highest-lowest-tax-burden/20494.

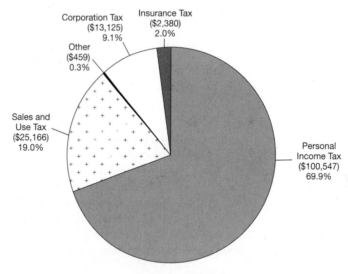

Excludes $1,767 million transfer to Rainy Day Fund

Figure 11.2 General Fund Revenues and Transfers, 2019–20

Question: If your intent as a legislator was to cut taxes in general or for specific groups, how might this chart inform you?

Note: Of a general fund of more than $140 billion for Fiscal Year 2019–20, the bulk of revenue came from the personal income tax and the sales tax. Some revenues, like bonds and motor fuel taxes, are restricted to certain types of spending and are not included in the general fund.

Source: California State Budget, 2019–20, California Department of Finance, http://www.ebudget.ca.gov/budget/2019-20/#/BudgetSummary.

income. For most Californians, the state's standard rates range from 1 to 9.3 percent. With the passage of Proposition 30 in 2012, the state imposed three new tax brackets with higher rates for high-income earners. The new rates (for single filers) are 10.3 percent for income over $250,000, 11.3 percent for income over $300,000, and 12.3 percent for income over $500,000. Proposition 55 (2016) extended these higher rates until 2030.

All in all, the income tax constituted close to 70 percent of the state's 2019–20 general fund. Yet, in one major survey, only one-third of California adults knew that the income tax is the state's top revenue source.[14]

Sales Tax. The second-largest source of state revenue is the sales tax. Constituting about 19 percent of the 2019–20 state general fund, it began in 1933 as a modest 2.5 percent tax on retail sales subject to the tax. The current statewide rate is 7.25 percent, including 2 percent for local government activities. Because it is inherently regressive, necessities of life, such as food, prescription drugs, and utilities, are not taxed. In addition, voters in numerous counties and cities have approved sales tax "add-ons" to fund local transportation or other projects. The actual effective sales tax can be as high as 9.25 percent (Alameda County), making those rates among the nation's highest.

Although the California sales tax seems high, it is limited to tangible goods, not services such as legal advice or medical examinations, the kinds of economic activity that compose a substantial portion of the California economy. What about tangible goods ordered online? Here confusion reigned until recently. When e-commerce emerged, Californians were supposed to keep track of their online purchases and remit a use tax (technically it is the sales and use tax), with their annual state income taxes. Few people complied with this tax. California and other states were prohibited from collecting sales taxes directly from online retailers unless the retailer had a physical presence in the state due to a 1992 U.S. Supreme Court ruling. In 2012, the governor struck a deal with Amazon to begin collecting sales tax on their transactions. In 2018, the court ruling was overturned, and California began collecting sales tax from online retailers who met certain sales volume. The imposition of the online sales tax is expected to generate more than $1 billion annually in state and local revenue.

The state's sales tax is fraught with other loopholes and dichotomies—a testimony to benevolence, good intentions, and interest group clout. Numerous exemptions provide "targeted tax relief" to a variety of sales ranging from animal feed and farm harvesting equipment to horse-racing breeding stock to meals for students and the elderly.

Corporate Taxes. California businesses pay a variety of taxes. The corporation tax is levied on all corporations doing business in the state. Nonprofit corporations are exempt. The flat rate is 8.84 percent of profits earned in California. There are two kinds. A franchise tax is imposed on corporations for the privilege of doing business in California. The corporate income tax is levied on those businesses outside California that derive income from California sources. In 2012, voters passed Proposition 39, which altered the tax calculation for out-of-state businesses and earmarked the new revenue, about $1 billion, for renewable energy projects. Financial institutions, including banks, pay an additional 2 percent of income in lieu of personal property and local business taxes. The politically powerful insurance companies pay only a 2.35 percent tax rate on insurance premiums sold. Insurance taxes constitute only 2 percent of the 2019–20 general fund; bank and corporation taxes, about 9 percent. Businesses and corporations claim this is too high but many of them can take advantage of deductions and credits not available to individuals. Corporations avoided an estimated $6.6 billion in taxes in 2018–19 through tax loopholes, such as the Hollywood film credit, research and development credit, and various hiring credits.

Excise Taxes. Numerous other taxes complement these larger sources of revenue. Excise taxes are assigned to particular items when they are made, sold, transported, or consumed. For example, California taxes tobacco products, alcoholic beverages, horse racing, and gasoline. They resemble sales taxes but are levied separately. Historically, California's "sin" taxes on tobacco and alcoholic beverages have been relatively low because of interest group pressure in Sacramento. Yet, voters have approved several propositions significantly increasing the tax on tobacco products. The tax on cigarettes now stands at $2.87 per pack. Taxes on alcohol depend on the beverage but are quite low. For example, although the sales tax on liquor is $3.30 per gallon, the tax on beer and wine is only 20 cents per gallon. Traditionally, "sin" taxes were considered a dependable, albeit small, source of revenue. Small indeed. They amount to less than 0.3 percent of the 2019–20 general fund. Because smoking has declined somewhat in recent years, analysts predict that this source of revenue will remain minimal.

The excise tax on motor fuels (mostly gasoline and diesel fuel) is added to federal excise taxes, both of which are included in the retail price at the pump. Gas stations collect it, and motorists rarely think about it. The tax on gasoline is currently 42 cents per gallon after policymakers increased it and other vehicle fees in 2017. The new revenue is expected to help pay for road repairs and more public transit. Gas tax revenue had not been keeping pace with needed repairs because hybrids and other fuel-efficient cars consume less gasoline than older "gas-guzzlers," sport utility vehicles, or trucks. Consequently, their owners pay less gas tax in the process. The gasoline tax is regressive, as are most excise taxes. Experts believe that the poor pay a greater share of their income in gasoline taxes than do the wealthy, even though fewer of them drive.

The Lottery. Joining many other states, Californians approved a statewide lottery in 1984. To sell voters on the idea, one-third of the proceeds were earmarked for education. In 2010, a bill changed the allocation formula so that no less than 87 percent of revenue goes toward prize money and to fund education. No more than 13 percent can be used for administration. Although participation in the lottery is purely voluntary, participant demographics roughly mirror those of the state population as a whole. As a source of public education revenue, lottery proceeds are small, unpredictable, and inefficient. It amounts to less than 2 percent of all K–12 spending in the state. Accordingly, critics complain that the lottery has not lived up to its potential. Of course, in some parts of the state, the California Lottery faces intense competition from Indian casinos. In recent years, the Lottery Commission, with the help of legislation, has significantly boosted revenue by adding new games, increasing the number of ticket sellers, and joining the interstate Powerball jackpot. Still, the funding support for education will likely never be the savior for education that some initially believed.

Debt. Some government policies require more money than current revenues can provide. Adding a new state park, prison, office building, or state university campus takes huge sums for land acquisition and construction costs. These capital improvements are normally funded through external borrowing. Although the state's Constitution limits the debt the legislature can incur, it places no such limits on the voters. Therefore, when policymakers need to borrow for capital improvements, they seek voter approval to issue bonds. Why borrow? The rationale is that long-term financing pays for projects used and enjoyed by future generations. When the state borrows money, it issues bonds that are purchased by investors. The wording of the bond tells the investor its worth, the interest rate to be earned, and when the bond can be redeemed.

Two types of bonds are used in California: **general obligation bonds** and **revenue bonds**. General obligation bonds are backed or secured by the "full faith and credit" of the state, meaning general revenues paid by taxpayers. They finance projects that do not produce revenue in and of themselves, such as schools, prisons, and freeways. Revenue bonds are backed by the future revenue generated by the facility being financed. "Lease purchase" bonds can be paid from any source—the general fund or project-generated revenue—and do not require voter approval. In recent years, several toll road projects in California have been financed through these bonds assuming that future tolls would pay back the bonds. Because revenue projections are only projections, interest rates on revenue bonds are typically higher than on general obligation bonds. In recent years, California voters have approved numerous general obligation bonds to fund rail transportation projects, school construction, prisons, and park acquisition. Backed by Governor Schwarzenegger and the legislature, they also borrowed $15 billion to close budget shortfalls in 2004. Although some voters resist such infrastructure borrowing, bond approvals are understandable. Voters can anticipate tangible results without paying directly for them.

Just as families can incur too much debt, so can governments. How much is too much? Proponents of borrowing claim that it is the only effective and politically feasible way to finance needed public improvements and that the mammoth size of California's economy makes such borrowing affordable. Furthermore, bond proceeds arguably create needed jobs, especially during economic downturns. Opponents of borrowing claim that interest paid to investors inflates the real cost of capital projects and gives voters the impression that they can get something for nothing. Borrowing for infrastructure improvements may be understandable. Borrowing in lieu of taxes to meet routine annual expenses is unacceptable even during economic downturns.

Who is right? One authoritative answer comes, not from Sacramento, but from bond-rating services in New York City. When Standard & Poor's Corporation or Moody Investor Services say the state of California is borrowing too much, California's credit rating suffers. This effectively makes California bonds riskier and harder to sell. This forces the state to offer higher interest rates, which, of course, increases borrowing costs. Depending on economic conditions, budget difficulties, and borrowing trends, these services have both upgraded and downgraded California's credit ratings. In recent years, the ratings have been rising as state budget conditions have improved.[15]

What happens when state revenues drop but current-year expenses and spending demands do not? In times like these, the governor and legislature may "balance" budgets by borrowing from (some say "raiding") other public assets such as special funds. This short-term borrowing may last only one day (to cover cash flow) or more than a fiscal year (during economic recessions). These funds are so huge that borrowing from them is tempting. To cover ongoing budget deficits in the 2000s, the state borrowed significant amounts from these funds. The accumulation of this borrowing and other spending deferrals was known as the "wall of debt," but it was expected to be eliminated under the Newsom administration.

Throughout the 2000s and until 2013, the state confronted a **structural deficit**, where ongoing revenues were insufficient to meet ongoing expenditures. This mismatch between revenues and expenditures was driven by a number of factors. On the revenue side, numerous tax cuts that were adopted reduced revenue, while caseload and population growth, spending formulas, state worker costs (pensions, etc.), court mandates, and debt service drove expenditures higher. With the help of a significant influx of revenue from Proposition 30 (sales and income tax increase) and a growing economy, Governor Brown and legislators were able to close the gap in 2013. Early in the Newsom administration, budget forecasts suggested that surpluses would occur for the foreseeable future unless a recession interrupted the growing economy.

Local Revenue

Traditionally, the property tax has been a distinctly local revenue source to pay for property-related expenditures. California's ad valorem (based-on-value) property tax is primarily governed by the provisions in Proposition 13. As we noted in chapter 4, it froze existing residential and commercial assessments at 1975 levels. Growth in that value, hence the tax, could not exceed 2 percent per year, no matter how high the actual value had risen. Over time, new construction and property sales would trigger new assessments based on updated, higher values.

The property tax is generally considered regressive in that it is not dependent on the ability to pay. Regressivity is most severe for renters, who pay the tax indirectly through their rents but enjoy none of the other financial benefits of homeownership. The revenue effect of Proposition 13 was a substantial cut in property tax revenue followed by increased aid from the state and higher local fees. Proposition 13 essentially restructured the fiscal relationship between local governments, notably counties and school districts, and the state.[16]

But Proposition 13 illustrates a more general axiom regarding revenue in California local government: Revenue strategies in California communities are first and foremost dependent on factors external to local decision making. These factors include the state of the overall economy, federal and state aid, voter initiatives, and interest rates. For instance, during periods of recession, people spend fewer dollars and therefore generate fewer sales taxes. Federal aid to local governments has dwindled in recent decades. Proposition 13 cut property tax revenue, leaving a multitude of local governments to divvy up what was left. When the Federal Reserve Board cuts interest rates, local revenues on deposit earn less interest.

Local governments have responded to these trends as best they can. As a group, California cities receive only 9 percent of their general revenues from local property taxes and 8 percent from sales and use taxes. Increasingly, they depend on assessments, service charges, and miscellaneous fees to balance their budgets. Many cities have attracted large shopping malls, which generate voluminous sales taxes. They have also aggressively pursued user fees associated with particular services (such as land-use permitting, swimming pool use, recreation programs, and bicycle licenses). Some fees serve no purpose but to raise additional income (such as cable television franchise fees and business licenses).

California counties have also raised fees considerably for public health and environmental inspections and processing land-use projects. In many counties, inspectors once seen only infrequently now show up like clockwork, in part because of their fee-generating potential. On the whole, however, counties have proved less nimble in recovering from the long-term impact of Proposition 13. Most revenue-rich shopping malls are within cities, not unincorporated areas served by counties. They are also heavily dependent on the vagaries of state budgeting to administer state programs, including occasional voter initiatives such as Propositions 218 and 26. In 1996, voters approved Proposition 218—*The Right to Vote on Taxes Act*. It required local governments that seek new or increased assessments to do three things: (1) specify how assessed properties will benefit, (2) assess rather than exempt other local government property, and (3) hold a "mail-in" election of all affected property owners. In 2001, the California Supreme Court allowed certain local fees to bypass 218 requirements. In November 2010, voters narrowly passed Proposition 26. This constitutional amendment classified some local fees as taxes, thereby subject to a two-thirds vote of local voters. The measure may not hamper local officials as much as they once feared. Preexisting fees were not subject to the initiative and potential new fees might well fall under several of the measure's exemptions.

These initiatives have caused a situation in which there are more severe limits on local revenues than state revenues. In response, the state has increased its own aid to California's local governments, enabling them to increase spending well beyond their own ability to pay for that spending with local-only revenues. According to one study, this system of state-local transfers encouraged excess local spending, clouded budget accountability, and contributed to past budget crises.[17]

Like the state, local governments may borrow money for needed projects. Voters may approve additions to the portion of sales tax that local governments receive. They may also approve various benefit assessments, parcel taxes, or special district charges that are added to their property taxes. **Parcel taxes** are usually modest charges levied per property type, not property value. For example, a single-family home might pay $49 per year for a school remodel or for library support. Historically, such levies have been difficult because Proposition 13 required a two-thirds vote of the people. As we noted, Proposition 39 lowered this threshold to 55 percent but only for school district bond issues. Since then, more school bond measures have passed than otherwise would have been the case. One method of financing has sidestepped Proposition 13. The *Mello-Roos Community Facilities Act of 1982* allows local governments to establish community development districts and then tax land slated for development within those districts. Future property owners who had no say in the matter pay the taxes that fund needed infrastructure improvements and public services.

WHERE THE MONEY GOES

As the state of California and its communities divide policy responsibilities, spending policies result not only from clear policy choices but also from incremental, historical decisions that develop their own political momentum. Because we devote the last two chapters of this book to public policy specifics in the Golden State, we only briefly survey state and local expenditures here.

State Expenditures

Occasionally, newspaper reporters uncover legislators' spending ideas: $2 million for a San Francisco aquarium, a $150,000 model curriculum on human rights and genocide, or $149,000 for a California trade office in Armenia. Although such projects might confirm voter suspicions about wasteful spending, they do not reflect where most state revenue actually goes. Note figure 11.3: a staggering 80 percent of the 2019–20 state general fund went to education, health and human services, and corrections—the "Big Three" of state budgeting. This spending trio in California is quite typical of spending patterns in other states. We should call this spending "state initiated" because about three-quarters of state revenues are actually spent by local governments (e.g., school districts, community colleges, police departments, sheriffs, and county health and human services departments). This may be why the perceptions of average Californians are so mistaken. The survey we cited earlier indicated that only 15 percent of adults thought that education was the top state spending item. Fully 43 percent thought it was corrections and prisons.

Education. Public education from kindergarten through 12th grade consumed about 41 percent of the 2019–20 general fund. Spending for education remains enrollment-driven. In recent decades, the rate of enrollment growth has been declining. Statewide, it is expected to decline, but the pattern will vary substantially by county. Where enrollments grow, so will the need for more classrooms and more teachers. Higher education (including the University of California and the California State University system) consumes 12 percent of the 2019–20 general fund. Because of the Great Recession, California's public university systems (University of California and California State University) have had to cut spending, raise fees, and seek greater productivity.

Health and Welfare. Addressing the health and welfare needs of California's poor, aged, blind, and disabled claimed 28 percent of the 2019–20 general fund. Caseloads have dropped somewhat in recent years because of job growth, welfare reform, and budget cuts. Expenditures in this area largely represent direct payments to individuals (such as CalWORKs) and to providers of particular services (medical doctors and hospitals). Within this portion of the budget, costs for Medi-Cal (California's version of federal medical care for the poor or Medicaid) have soared in recent decades because of rising medical care costs and federal requirements to serve more medically needy groups. As a result of new changes from the passage of the Affordable Care Act at the federal level (see chapter 13), enrollment in Medi-Cal surged to 13.2 million in 2018, which represents close to one-third of the state's population.

Corrections and Rehabilitation. California's correctional system consumed more than 9 percent of the 2019–20 general fund—up from 3 percent in 1969–70. This dramatic increase is the result of a combination of factors: rising crime rates,

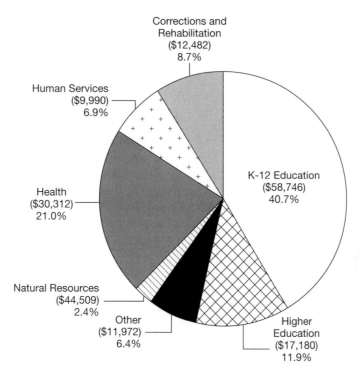

Figure 11.3 General Fund Expenditures, 2019–20
Percentages are based on general fund expenditures of $144 billion. Not included are bond-based expenditures and special fund expenditures including highways.

Questions:

1. How will some slices of the budget pie expand with population growth in California?

2. Does it surprise you how little money is spent on operating the major branches of government?

Source: California State Budget, 2019–20, California Department of Finance, http://www.ebudget .ca.gov/2019-20/pdf/BudgetSummary/SummaryCharts.pdf.

increases in crime-prone populations, and tougher sentencing policies (more prison time and less parole time). Increased sentences were partly mandated by Proposition 8, the 1982 "Victims' Bill of Rights." The state's *Three Strikes* law (see chapter 9) also incarcerated more felons for longer periods of time. As a result, California's prison population jumped from 35,000 in 1983 to 172,000 in 2007, at its peak. Under pressure from a federal court order to reduce its population, the state shifted responsibility for a significant number of inmates and parolees to the counties. In 2015, the state met the court-imposed maximum with a population of 112,000 inmates and 45,000 parolees.

What Is Left. Other state operations (such as environmental protection, resource management, business regulation, the state courts, the legislature, and a host of executive branch agencies) consume the remaining 10 to 11 percent of the general fund. Most of the executive branch agencies portrayed in chapter 8 spend little compared to the population-driven portions of the state budget. Efforts to balance state budgets by cutting these government operations will always have limited success because they constitute so little of the overall budget to begin with. The passage of Proposition 13 in 1978 marked the start of a long period of general voter resistance to tax increases that has begun to let up in recent years. California voters have twice supported major tax increases (Propositions 30 and 55) to maintain and increase funding support for its major programs, mainly education and health care. However, the "leftover" portion of the state budget is usually the first to go when tough budgetary times hit. Public opinion polls show that voters oppose cuts to the major spending programs, including schools, higher education, law enforcement, health care for the poor and disabled, and mental health.[18]

Local Expenditures

The two general purpose local government institutions in California are cities and counties. Although California cities vary greatly in size and spending patterns vary, on average they spend their revenues accordingly (excluding the City and County of San Francisco).

Individual cities can vary substantially from these averages primarily because of their size. Generally, the smaller the city, the less likely it will be to manage utilities, airports, museums, hospitals, and mass transit systems. Controlling for size, cities, unlike counties, can pick and choose many of the services they wish to provide.

California counties present a much different spending picture. For the most part, this is because counties deliver services on behalf of the state. As noted in figure 11.4, the two largest spending commitments are on health and sanitation and public protection. The counties' health and sanitation responsibilities include public health, medical care, mental health, drug and alcohol abuse services, and sanitation costs. Public protection includes the local courts, sheriffs' departments, jails, and fire protection. Public assistance includes welfare, social services, general relief, care of wards of the court, and veteran services. By far the largest expenditure in this area is the CalWORKs program. Other spending categories include general government (county boards of supervisors and administrative offices), roads, education administration, recreation programs, cultural facilities, veteran memorial buildings, and interest on county indebtedness.

THE CHANGING BUDGET ENVIRONMENT

In reviewing the politics of budgeting in California, we see diverse interests confronting rather rigid political structures and economic trends. As Richard Krolak has put it, "California's budget is a complex process with many nuances and intangibles."[19] That said, two patterns of budgeting in California emerge:

1. *California budgeting is both volatile and cyclical*—the state's reliance on the personal income tax and sales tax depends heavily on the health of the state's economy. When the economy is growing, those revenues grow, and so do public budgets. In these fat years, more revenue is available for all manner of policies and programs; those revenues can accommodate higher school and university enrollments, larger prison populations, and greater

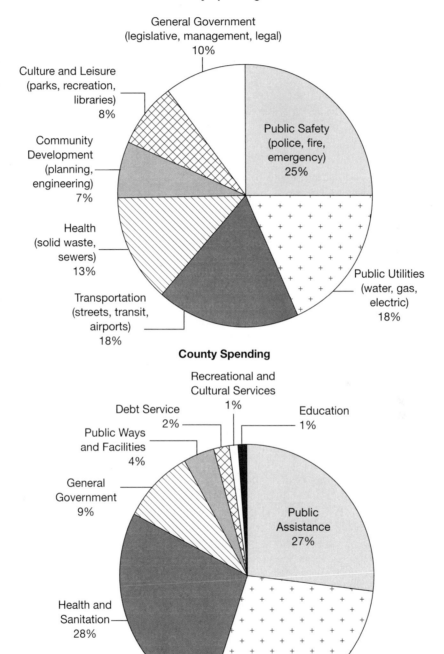

Figure 11.4 Local Government Spending by Category

Source: State Controller, "Cities and Counties Annual Report, Fiscal Year 2015–16," https://cities
.bythenumbers.sco.ca.gov/#!/year/default.

Medi-Cal caseloads. Tax cuts are even possible. When the economy is stagnant or in recession, the opposite occurs. In these lean years, programs and expectations must be cut or scaled back. This revenue volatility is challenging in the face of long-term spending commitments.

2. *California budgeting is group-differential*—that is, it treats different groups in different ways. Consider the combination of all California taxes. The total tax burden on Californians is a function of how progressive or regressive different taxes are. Income taxes are highly progressive; sales, excise taxes, and property taxes are regressive. In general, higher-income Californians benefit from the state's tax policies. Although they pay a large share of California's income tax, the wealthy can take advantage of numerous tax credits and deductions to offset their tax liabilities. Lower-income families pay lower income taxes or possibly none at all, but they are hit hard by regressive sales, excise, and property taxes. On the spending side of the equation, lower-income Californians benefit from many state expenditures, especially in the areas of health and human services. They also have access to relatively low-cost higher education at the state's community colleges.

BOOM AND BUST BUDGETING

The advent of the Newsom administration in 2019 represented a dramatic transformation in the state's budget environment. Instead of grappling with large budget deficits, as his two predecessors had, Governor Newsom presided over a budget surplus that the Legislative Analyst's Office called "extraordinary." With an estimated $20 billion surplus, Newsom's primary challenge was restraining legislators from a spending spree that would jeopardize the state's newfound fiscal health once the next economic recession hit. The price tag for the legislature's wish list was $40 billion.

To appreciate this turnaround in the state's financial condition, it is instructive to review the depths to which California had sunk. California experienced structural deficits in the 1980s and 1990s, and then severe and persistent deficits throughout the 2000s. Jerry Brown took office in 2011 with a $26 billion deficit (see figure 11.5). Budget gridlock, driven by partisanship and the state's two-thirds vote requirement to pass a budget, was the norm.[20] Under the two-thirds vote requirement, Democratic majorities in the legislature had to garner a few Republican votes to pass the budget each year. With Republicans vehemently against raising taxes and Democrats reluctant to cut spending for education and social programs, it was a recipe for stalemate. The passage of the majority vote requirement (Proposition 25) in 2010 has alleviated this gridlock.

Despite the recurring nature of the structural deficits, until recently, the state had never prepared itself adequately for the next economic downturn, even though economic recessions were nothing new. Historically, California had a recession about every seven years on average. Like all other states, California had a rainy-day fund during these budget crises, but it never reached a significant balance to stave off severe budget cuts. In 2014, at the urging of Governor Brown, voters adopted a new, stronger rainy-day fund (Proposition 2) to help prepare the state for the next economic downturn. Socking money away in this new "savings" account became Brown's clarion call: "We must build on rock, not sand, so that

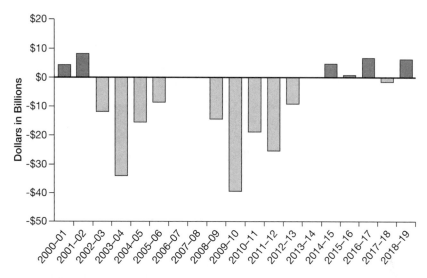

Figure 11.5 California Budget Surpluses and Deficits, 2000–19
The figure shows the governor's budget projection each year. Bars below the $0 line represent deficits and bars above it are surpluses. The figure shows deficits have been more frequent than surpluses.

Question: Given this history, how should policymakers plan for future ups and downs?

Source: "Governor's Budget, 2018–19," http://www.ebudget.ca.gov/budget/publication/#/p/2018-19/ BudgetSummary.

when the storms come, our house stands."[21] When Newsom took office in 2019, the balance in the rainy-day fund stood at $15 billion.

The relatively large balance in the state's rainy-day fund did not come easy for Brown. He consistently thwarted legislators' attempts to spend more on education and social welfare programs. By most accounts, the early days of the Newsom administration indicate that he plans to continue the fiscal course set by Governor Brown. This includes stashing more away in the rainy-day fund, paying down debt accumulated during the deficit years, and making down payments on the state's long-term financial liabilities (i.e., pension systems). The direction set by Brown and now Newsom appears to show that policymakers have learned from past mistakes. Still, like previous governors, Newsom ran for office espousing ambitious ideas, like universal health care and universal preschool, that carry large price tags. These ambitions may run into budget reality, like others before him, especially when the next recession comes.

Next Steps

Although the state's budget conditions have improved significantly in recent years, there are still steps that policymakers can take to further shore up California's finances. The biggest and perhaps most politically elusive is a tax structure overhaul. California's tax structure has not been overhauled since the income and sales taxes were adopted in the 1930s. Our current structure is not set up to deal with a modern economy driven by e-commerce and the transition to more service-based transactions (e.g., hiring lawn mowers and housekeepers). Because the sales tax is not imposed on these services, California has one of the highest sales tax rates among the 50 states. The budget volatility discussed earlier can also be attributed to an overreliance on unstable income tax revenue. Smoothing out the revenue fluctuations would mean transitioning toward revenue sources that are more stable, such as the property tax. Whatever form this tax overhaul takes, it will be a tough sell for the governor and legislative leaders. Tax reform is a third-rail issue that voters do not take lightly.

CONCLUSION: THE COST OF DIVERSITY

At the outset of this chapter, we noted that a budget is a government's premier policy statement. In a representative democracy, it seems to say, "These are the things that we, the people, want to do as a society—both today and on behalf of future Californians." The consensus assumed in that statement seems missing from contemporary budget politics. State and local budget makers might epitomize fiscal gridlock to many Californians, but they are not the root cause of the problem. The true cause of annual budget struggles stems from economic change, population growth, group competition, and partisan conflict.

In a sense, budgeting in California puts dollar signs on "the politics of diversity." To the extent that the tax system benefits the rich, it benefits only one segment of Californians. To the extent that state expenditures benefit the poor (public assistance, Medi-Cal), the middle class (higher education, highways), the wealthy (tax credits and low corporate taxes), or particular interests (farmers, renters), they divide 40 million Californians into groups. To the extent that the budget process itself divides power, fragments decision-making, encourages group competition, and incurs gridlock, it exhibits hyperpluralism. This is all the more true when California voters wrest budget decisions from elected budget makers—"ballot-box budgeting."

Budget experts have long regarded California's operating budget as relatively generous to those in need. But to what extent will that generosity continue, given other demands on state resources? The foremost budget question Californians and their policymakers will need to address is this: How can the state and its communities agree on budgets in an age when societal and therefore political consensus is lacking and quite possibly unachievable? The alternative is "every group for itself" in the nation's largest and most diverse state.

KEY TERMS

budget (p. 242)
public policy (p. 235)
incremental (p. 238)
fiscal year (p. 238)
May Revision (p. 240)
trailer bills (p. 240)
Big Three (p. 240)
two-thirds requirement (p. 241)
cruise control spending (p. 241)
entitlements (p. 241)

third-rail issues (p. 242)
split-roll property tax (p. 242)
ballot-box budgeting (p. 242)
earmarking (p. 242)
regressive taxes (p. 244)
progressive taxes (p. 244)
general obligation bonds (p. 249)
revenue bonds (p. 249)
structural deficits (p. 250)
parcel taxes (p. 251)

REVIEW QUESTIONS

1. Describe the general characteristics of public budgets.
2. How do state and local economies affect state and local budgets?
3. How does the California budget process work? What constrains the process?
4. Using various criteria to evaluate taxes, describe the major sources of state and local revenue in California.
5. Describe the Big Three of California spending. How do cities and counties spend their revenue?
6. How does budget policy in California describe the "cost of diversity" and reinforce the theme of hyperpluralism?
7. How have the state's budget conditions changed in recent years? What contributed to those changes?

WEB RESOURCES

California State Department of Finance

http://www.dof.ca.gov

This agency advises the governor on the annual budget and makes available numerous documents on past and current state budgets and the state's economy.

Legislative Analyst's Office

https://lao.ca.gov

This site provides nonpartisan, authoritative analyses of the state budget and other policy issues.

Advocacy Groups

California Budget and Policy Center

https://calbudgetcenter.org

This group conducts various budget studies and advocates fiscal equity and fairness in California.

California Taxpayers Association

https://www.caltax.org

This organization's mission is to "protect taxpayers from unnecessary taxes."

12

Policies Stemming from Growth

LEARNING OUTCOMES

Students will be able to:

★ Explain California's population growth patterns and policies to address that growth.

★ Discuss sources of water for residents and policy responses to deal with shortages.

★ Identify factors that contribute to the lack of housing affordability in California.

★ Explain how Californians' affinity for the automobile has impacted the state's approach to transportation policy.

★ Summarize the policy options the state employs to address environmental problems created by its energy policy.

IN BRIEF

Many state and local policies in California stem from the state's incessant population growth. Chapter 12 frames the issues of water, housing, transportation, and the environment in terms of the growth that makes them policy problems in the first place.

★ ★ ★

FOR DECADES, POLICYMAKERS not only accommodated existing growth but also "built" a California that would actually encourage future growth. A political division of labor made new development relatively painless. Local governments approved individual projects, while the state provided the infrastructure required. As growth continued, so did its negative effects. The result was reduced public support for the policies and taxes that had made growth possible. Political pressures in recent years have pitted Californian against Californian: farmers and city dwellers over water, new and old residents over housing, freeway drivers and mass transit advocates over traffic gridlock, and environmentalists and business over pollution.

Many of these policy problems stem from basic assumptions deeply ingrained in California and national politics: that water is "free," housing is a private-sector activity, widespread car ownership is a given, and government is responsible to clean up private-sector-generated pollution. Recent attempts to solve these policy problems have included market approaches to water availability and environmental pollution, plus modest public investment in rail transit. Affordable housing will likely remain an elusive goal. Policymakers have focused more on building the infrastructure needed to accommodate growth than on controlling the growth itself. In a diverse and hyperpluralistic state, this may be all policymakers can do or hope to do.

INTRODUCTION: GROWTH IN CALIFORNIA

In a public television documentary on the habitat of the bald eagle, narrator George Page declared, "California is where America meets its limit, a fitting place to realize that growth cannot extend itself forever. Growth itself has its limits." Many Californians would agree. In their view, the state's quality of life is gradually being undermined by the very growth that had sustained it for so many years. Ominous warning signs abound: air-quality improvements offset by still more cars, traffic gridlock in metropolitan areas, fertile farmland giving way to housing subdivisions and shopping malls, and pockets of smog throughout the Golden State. Furthermore, there is worrisome evidence that climate change is affecting California's environment, possibly resulting in chronic water shortages. The Great Recession added to these challenges. It slowed economic expansion, decimated jobs, and virtually halted housing construction—the raw fuels of growth—but it also hampered state and local government efforts to address past growth and what would assuredly be future growth, especially in inland California.

This chapter discusses growth and its ramifications in the Golden State. Numerous policy issues important to Californians, such as housing, transportation, water, and environmental pollution, are rooted in population growth. We look at the nature of California's growth, how specific growth-induced problems are addressed, and the efforts to manage growth itself. The central question is this: *How do California policymakers accommodate current and future growth without (1) degrading various qualities of life sought by diverse groups and (2) endangering the state's once-pristine environment?* This question brims with conflict ranging from the highest levels of state government down to interneighbor disputes over lifestyles, cars, noise, and fences. It also reflects the inability of a complex, fragmented, and hyperpluralistic political system to address, solve, or even keep pace with the problems that stem from growth.

An undercurrent in this chapter deals with evolving and diverse notions of what "quality of life" means. From the problematic neighbor who defines this term differently than the rest of the block to state and local debates on the subject, "quality of life" has come to represent alternative perspectives on what living in California was, is, and should be like. In the decades to come, as Californians become more numerous, culturally diverse, and politically divided, competing qualities of life will haunt, challenge, and elude policymakers.

Why California Grew
In California's history, population growth has resulted from several factors in and out of government. California boasted a favorable climate and scenic environment

in which to live, work, and play. Gold Rush miners inundated parts of California, and others were lured by savvy marketing efforts of the state's railroads, citrus growers, and real estate entrepreneurs. Local governments boosted their own locales while state government accommodated the pro-growth interests of the railroads and other industries. World War II brought increased federal spending and wartime employees to California. Growth-hungry city officials encouraged and enabled military-related growth.[1] After the war, military bases remained open and military spending continued.

California developed a de facto pro-growth policy in the postwar period. A statewide water system, new highways, and a complex master plan for higher education set the stage for future growth while accommodating growth pressures at the time. These bipartisan efforts, supported by business and labor, created not only a physical infrastructure to support more households but also a social infrastructure to support people's rising expectations. A new statewide political consensus viewed growth as positive and beneficial. In addition, national policies, in effect, subsidized growth in California by helping fund the Central Valley Project (a massive water project) and the state's intrastate highway system. During this pro-growth era, new housing kept pace with population growth. Much of it was suburban, low in density, and relatively cheap, considering the high demand for it. Necessary infrastructure (roads, highways, water projects, sewer systems, and schools) was funded through generous federal subsidies, state bonds, and growing general fund revenues. For decades, accommodating growth was relatively painless and uncontroversial.

The Drumbeat of Growth

Although rates of population growth in California fluctuate, this can be said: The state's long-term growth has been and will continue to climb. California's 2019 population of nearly 40 million is only one aspect of the state's growth challenge. The state's compound annual growth rate in the last 50 years has been more than twice the national rate. In 1940, California's population was 5.2 percent of the nation's; by 2010, it was 12 percent. Although the annual growth rate dropped to under 1 percent in recent years, the slowest growth period in state history, that still means projected growth of more than 300,000 per year—more than 800 per day (see figure 12.1).

Growth rates vary within California. In recent years, California's inland counties have experienced the highest population growth rates.[2] This is primarily due to natural increases and, to a lesser degree, immigration, mainly from Asia. The population, like the rest of the country, is also aging. The share of Californians at retirement age (65 and older) is expected to grow from 13 percent in 2013 to 19 percent by 2030.

The impacts of the state's historic growth have concerned many Californians. Beginning in the 1960s, some questioned how long rapid growth could continue without threatening the state's quality of life.[3] By the 1970s, the dominant growth consensus began to crumble. Why? First, California's political leaders sought to downsize government's role in fostering the state's growth. Governor Ronald Reagan (R, 1967–74), while not objecting to growth itself, opposed the "big government" that growth made possible. His successor, Jerry Brown (D, 1975–82), reduced infrastructure investment, especially in highway construction and large water projects.

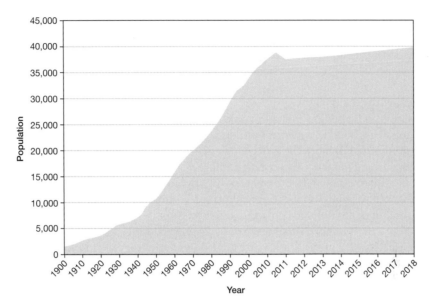

Figure 12.1 California's Drumbeat of Growth

Question: Are future growth rates destined to look like past growth rates? Why? Why not?

Source: California Department of Finance.

Second, economic restructuring altered the prospect of unlimited growth without apparent cost. California's heavy manufacturing base declined, as did growth in personal income. And so did taxpayer willingness to fund more public improvements. Proposition 13, which substantially cut property taxes in 1978, reinforced this unwillingness. It also cut funds local governments relied on to provide the infrastructure required by new development. Instead, developers were charged for infrastructure costs, which, of course, were passed on to new homeowners. The pressure to develop farmland near cities grew. As one Lompoc, California, farmer put it, "I could make a whole lot more money growin' condos than farming." As environmental public awareness increased, development in ecologically sensitive areas (such as waterfronts, flood plains, and estuaries) became politically unacceptable. By the 2000s, Californians were of two minds on growth. Many favored more commercial development while wishing to discourage the added growth that accompanies such development.[4]

Third, settlement patterns fed a popular desire to limit growth. Although California was not as densely populated as New Jersey (251 vs. 1,218 people per square mile in 2015), Californians *perceived* that they were overcrowded. This was because most of them lived in the state's coastal or near-coastal counties. Indeed, 69 percent of the state's population lives in coastal and bay counties. In recent years, the highly developed coastal strip has both lengthened and thickened. An urban corridor now extends from Santa Barbara to Ensenada, Mexico—arguably the nation's first binational megalopolis. Furthermore, development has moved inland in the three largest metropolitan areas (San Francisco, Los Angeles, and San Diego). Today, "edge cities" mix high-density commercial, professional, and residential uses while creating environmental impacts often beyond the control of any single government. The Los Angeles Basin boasts 26 such edge cities, the largest concentration of them in the nation.[5] These growth patterns result in some of the nation's costliest housing and busiest freeways.

Structuring Local Growth

Population increases are not the whole story. Californians equate "growth" with new housing projects, industrial parks, and shopping centers—decisions that are local in nature. How are these decisions made and who makes them?

Land-Use Planning. Cities and counties have planning or community development departments staffed by professional planners. They process various land use proposals, from simple room additions to massive multiuse projects. They make recommendations to a planning commission, which, in turn, advises a city council or county board of supervisors. The elected bodies then comment on the overall merits of a project, assess its environmental impact, and place conditions on approval to reduce those impacts. At both levels, public hearings allow citizens to comment on the project. After a project is approved, a developer must begin construction within a certain period. During construction, numerous inspections make sure a project conforms to the many building standards and conditions placed on it. Developers pay **impact fees** to "mitigate" the impacts of development—new roads, water systems, sewers, even schools—costs once borne by taxpayers.

Tools Planners Use. A wide variety of policies govern project approvals. For instance, each California community has a state-required **general plan** or overall blueprint for the physical development of the area. Such plans contain general goals for future development, zoning maps, and other maps projecting future development. These documents must contain various "elements" or chapters that address land-use types, traffic circulation, housing, conservation, open space, and safety. General plans do not determine or predict when growth will occur. Timing depends on economic conditions, developer initiative, and decisions by local governments.

Other planning tools abound. **Zoning ordinances** divide areas into districts to regulate the type and density of development. A typical zoning map will contain several residential zones (from low-density single-family homes to high-density condominiums or apartments) in addition to commercial areas, manufacturing areas, parks, open space, and other uses. These ordinances establish minimum lot sizes, setback rules (distances between a structure and a lot line or the street), maximum densities, height and bulk requirements for structures, and parking and landscaping requirements. **Subdivision regulations** dictate how a parcel of land can be divided into smaller lots including minimum lot sizes, street standards, and other public improvements required of developers. Planners also make use of statewide **uniform building codes**, which regulate the physical components of construction (roofing, heating, electric wiring, ventilation, sanitation, and earthquake resistance). **Planned unit developments** (PUDs) integrate many of these tools for housing developments or more complex projects. They allow developers to be more innovative and grant local officials more flexibility and control.

These policies do not necessarily appease residents who adamantly oppose specific projects or the overall momentum of growth in their communities. How do local officials address their concerns? First, they can control the timing of development by imposing temporary building moratoria or annual housing quotas. Sometimes, economic conditions play a role as well as we saw with a recession-era decline in construction activity. Second, zoning ordinances can also be modified through "down zoning" (reducing legally allowed building densities on undeveloped land). Because down zoning often spreads remaining development across more land, it can result in *more* traffic congestion, not less.

Slowing Growth in California

Opposition to development in California is common, especially along California's coast. It reflects a desire to improve the quality of life and a desire to slow down the pace of growth. These concerns ebb and flow with the relative health of the economy.

Quality-of-Life Concerns. Numerous public opinion surveys have documented this concern about development and its impacts. In a 2001 poll, 60 percent of Californian adults thought their communities were growing rapidly. They thought that the negative consequences of rapid growth included traffic congestion, high housing costs, urban sprawl, loss of open space, and pollution. Consequently, most respondents thought that the Golden State would be a less desirable place to live in the future.[6] In recent years, these quality-of-life concerns have extended to a variety of economic issues beyond the control of land-use policymakers, including heavy job losses, the crisis in home mortgages, and resulting bank foreclosures.

Slow-Growth Politics. Voicing these concerns, various groups and individuals across the state have advocated various growth control measures. They have included requiring developers to fund infrastructure improvements, limiting growth rates, reducing zoning densities, prohibiting development on agricultural and rural land, purchasing open space, and subjecting development decisions to city- or countywide voter approval. City councils and county boards of supervisors enact some of these controlled-growth or "smart growth" policies but upset voters initiate others, a practice dubbed "ballot-box planning." Some initiatives address growth in general (e.g., creating urban growth boundaries) or seek to veto particular projects (e.g., a new Walmart store). Although critics decry the shortcomings of citizen initiatives, they do give voice to local slow-growth sentiments and provide a check on local planners and developers.[7]

What explains this desire to limit growth? Several factors emerge. First, urban Californians indeed experience daily the impacts of growth; the freeways they ply daily seem more like parking lots. They view once-pristine open space now covered with housing tracts and shopping centers. Ironically, in some communities, no-growth views are shared even by newcomers. Second, many Californians seem ambivalent regarding growth. They may favor the idea of affordable housing but oppose its actual construction in their communities. In one survey, two-thirds of respondents believed low-density family housing should be encouraged yet also believed suburban sprawl is a very or somewhat important problem in their region.[8]

Third, opposition to growth often centers on specific projects close to home. Typical controversies involve **locally undesirable land uses** (LULUs) such as landfills, toxic cleanup sites, drug abuse centers, and many traffic-generating projects.

Even places of worship and schools may be opposed as LULUs. Downtown merchants may oppose the development of competing shopping malls, warehouse retailers, and factory outlet stores. Individual homeowners may fear the potential loss of property values. Common strategies used by **"not in my back yard"** (**NIMBY**) opponents may include circulating antidevelopment petitions, packing public hearings with project opponents, placing initiatives on the ballot, and filing lawsuits.

WATER: MAKING GROWTH POSSIBLE

One way or another, a variety of public policy issues can be traced to long-term population growth in California. Some policies have made growth feasible, such as the provision of water throughout the state. Other policies such as housing, transportation, and environmental protection address the impacts of growth. In this chapter, we explore several growth-related issues, but water comes first for a simple reason: increasing the supply of water and moving it around has been a necessary prerequisite for California's growth. Water drew people to the state and determined where they would settle.

California is really two states divided by water: Northern California has it, and Southern California wants it. Yet, in a sense, all of California is semiarid. In response, California policymakers have always assumed that water not used by people is water wasted—an assumption that defies the state's physical geography. Rain and snow are more frequent and plentiful in Northern California. As a result, the Sacramento–San Joaquin Delta region has been called "the great Central Valley mixing basin where a hundred rivers become one."[9] Once an inland sea, it now is a labyrinthine estuary of sloughs, waterways, and levees that channel drinking water to over half the state's population. In contrast, Southern California claims only 2 percent of the state's natural water supply. But that never stopped its impulse to grow. Southern California possessed an asset of its own: a pleasant climate. Several mountain ranges plus gentle coastal breezes protected Southern California from the heat and grit of the desert interior, creating a Mediterranean climate. The only resource missing was water. But as novelist Edward Abbey observed, "There is no lack of water [in the desert], unless you try to establish a city where no city should be."[10]

Storing Water

One marvel of California water is how it is stored for later use. California winters can be wet, but not all winters are equally wet. California endures cycles of wet years and droughts, which can be terrifying (see box 12.1). Winter precipitation is saved in three great storage systems, two of which are nature's own. First is the Sierra Nevada snowpack. Some of the world's heaviest snowfall can occur in the Sierras, creating a year-round source of runoff water. Second is the state's underground water basins or aquifers (the airspace in soil and geologic formations displaced by water). Groundwater accounts for one-third of California's water supply. A third storage system is artificial, consisting of numerous reservoirs—surface lakes created by damming rivers and capturing runoff from adjacent mountain ranges. Such reservoirs dot the California landscape. These three storage systems face dangers from both periodic drought and incessant population

Box 12.1 ★ California Voices: Steinbeck on California Water

The water came in a 30-year cycle. There would be five or six wet and won-
derful years when there might be 19 to 25 inches of rain, and the land would
shout with grass. Then would come six or seven pretty good years of 12 or
16 inches of rain. And then the dry years would come, and sometimes there
would be only 7 or 8 inches of rain. The land dried up and grasses headed out
miserably a few inches high and great bare scabby places appeared in the
valley. The live oaks got a crusty look and the sagebrush was gray. The land
cracked and the springs dried up and the cattle listlessly nibbled dry twigs.
Then the farmers and the ranchers would be filled with disgust for the Salinas
Valley. The cows would grow thin and sometimes starve to death. People
would have to haul water in barrels to their farms just for drinking. Some families would sell out for nearly nothing and move away. And it never failed that
during the dry years the people forgot about the rich years, and during the
wet years they lost all memory of the dry years. It was always that way.

Question: To what extent does Steinbeck's observation explain actual water
policy and politics in California?

Source: John Steinbeck, *East of Eden* (New York: Viking Press, 1952), 5–6.

growth. Due to less-frequent precipitation and warmer winters, scientists predict
that by 2050, the Sierra snowpack could shrink by 25 percent, thereby reducing flows to the reservoirs. Even with adequate inflows, reservoirs lose water to
evaporation and become choked with silt. Underground aquifers pose their own
challenges. When they are pumped excessively, "overdrafting" occurs. This not
only lowers the water table but also allows agricultural chemicals to invade rural
aquifers and saltwater to invade coastal aquifers.

Moving Water

Some say California water is never where you want it when you want it. But
Californians were never deterred by that fact. As water law developed, so did
various water rights. If you lived on top of or adjacent to a source of water, it
was yours (**riparian rights**). If you were the first to find or "create" a source of
water, it was yours (through **prior appropriation**). If you used someone else's
water with their knowledge, it was yours (**prescriptive rights**). Combined, these
rights encouraged the movement of water throughout the state. California's earliest water projects were localized irrigation systems consisting of earthen dams
and even hand-dug canals and ditches. In time, these efforts were dwarfed by four
immense projects that would forever change the face of California: the Owens
Valley and Colorado River Projects, the Central Valley Project, and the State
Water Project. The politics behind these projects reminds one of Mark Twain's
observation: "In the West, whiskey is for drinking, water is for fighting." As we
survey these projects, as portrayed in figure 12.2, remember that water is measured in acre-feet. An acre-foot is the amount of water needed to fill one acre to a
depth of one foot, enough to supply two urban households for a year.

Figure 12.2 California's Plumbing System

Water for Los Angeles. The City of Angels' unquenchable thirst began in the late 1880s. Through civic boosterism, Los Angeles's population was booming, but a lengthy drought left city officials and business interests desperate. Combining controversy and intrigue, Los Angeles's interests quietly purchased land in the Owens Valley east of the Sierra Nevada range. The goal? To divert the Owens River through 233 miles of aqueducts, tunnels, and pumping stations. In 1905, the *Los Angeles Times* audaciously announced the news: "Titanic Project to Give the City a River."[11] Drought-panicked Los Angelenos approved the bond measures required to build the Los Angeles Aqueduct. The project created one prerequisite to future growth—*surplus water* (more than people immediately needed). But tapping the Owens Valley was not enough, not for Los Angeles. Fueled by now-permanent growth, more bond issues, a cooperative federal government, and the belief that anything was possible, the city proceeded to harness the Colorado River. The Hoover Dam, completed in 1941, channeled the Colorado River to Los Angeles via a maze of dams, canals, tunnels, reservoirs, and pumping stations. In addition to water, this project created a second prerequisite to urban growth: *electrical power*. The Metropolitan Water District of Southern California was formed to build and operate the project. In concert with cities, counties, and other water districts, this giant water wholesaler "became and remains a Southern California growth machine." Northern Californians tend to criticize Los Angeles's thirst, but they have played the same game. In 1913, San Francisco dammed up the Tuolumne River inside Yosemite Park (over naturalist John Muir's objections), establishing its own permanent water supply. Because it "created" more water than it could ever use, the city was able to sell surplus water (60 percent of total supplies) to other Bay Area communities—spurring *their* growth.

Central Valley Project. In contrast to Southern California, the state's heartland is laced by two sizable river systems, the Sacramento and the San Joaquin, plus their tributaries. As crops replaced native grasses and national markets replaced local ones, valley farmers yearned for a steady, weatherproof water supply. As in Los Angeles, a lengthy drought forced political action. In the case of the valley, underground overpumping provided the impetus for the 1931 *State Water Plan.* The 1936 Central Valley Project (CVP) was an effort to implement the plan. The U.S. Bureau of Reclamation assumed control after the state failed to finance it, and the bureau has run it ever since. The largest federal water project in the country, the CVP, consists of an intricate network of rivers, dams, aqueducts, and power plants stretching nearly 500 miles from Shasta Dam in the north to Bakersfield in the south. It supplies about 20 percent of California's developed water and at heavily subsidized rates. According to one report, the average price for irrigation water from the CVP was less than 2 percent of what Southern Californians pay for drinking water.[12]

State Water Project. These projects did not end the political battles over water. California's postwar growth continued unchecked. Conflicts rose between urban and rural users, irrigation and flood control interests, and a confusing patchwork of water agencies. No single state agency had the power to referee this hyperpluralistic water anarchy. In the 1950s, a new Department of Water Resources published the *California Water Plan*, a visionary document that detailed the State Water Project. It clearly recognized Californians' penchant to live where water is scarce. A massive bond measure to fund the plan barely passed in 1960, thanks to overwhelming support in Southern California. Its first project was the Feather River Project, which "tamed" the flood-prone Feather River at Oroville and moved its water through the Delta and further south via the California Aqueduct. The project moves water a total of 700 miles through 19 reservoirs, 17 pumping stations, eight hydroelectric power plants, and about 660 miles of open canals and pipelines. Of the contracted water supply, 70 percent goes to urban users and 30 percent to agricultural users.

In the 1980s, another north–south water battle focused on the Sacramento–San Joaquin River Delta, the largest estuary in the western United States and an indispensable hub of California's water supply. The trick has always been to use and move Sacramento River water through the delta without allowing seawater from San Francisco Bay to intrude and endanger farmland. To solve this problem, the California Department of Water Resources proposed a "peripheral canal" to channel freshwater east of the delta and directly into the California Aqueduct. After years of study, the legislature approved the project in 1980. An anticanal referendum drive was launched by two strange political bedfellows: environmentalists concerned about the delta's fragile ecology and large-scale farmers upset at probable water price hikes. In 1982, California voters defeated the canal project by a 2–1 margin; Northern Californians by a 9–1 margin.

In the 1990s, a federal partnership (CALFED) was formed to coordinate efforts among the delta's constituencies. In 2009, the legislature updated these efforts with the passage of the Delta Reform Act. This law established the Delta Stewardship Council, a planning group charged with two coequal goals: (1) providing a more reliable water supply for California, and (2) protecting, restoring, and enhancing the delta ecosystem.[13] The council released a draft plan in 2012 to preserve the ecosystem and revive the proposal to divert water from the Sacramento River to users south of the delta. Instead of a "peripheral canal," however, twin tunnels, "30 miles long and 40 feet wide," would go under the delta. Dubbed the California WaterFix, the plan, with a price tag of $16.7 billion, ran into resistance from multiple stakeholders, including environmentalists and government officials from the region. Jerry Brown hoped to make progress on it before he left office, but the project lacked the necessary approvals and full financing upon his departure.

California's Water Crisis

More than a century of a hands-off approach to water management finally caught up to California policymakers in 2012. As mentioned earlier, periodic droughts in the state's past were not uncommon. However, by 2015, the third year of drought marked the driest stretch in the entire 120 years of record keeping. In some rural communities in the San Joaquin Valley, private wells dried up, forcing residents to stockpile bottled water to meet their basic needs. The drought's severity garnered national and international attention, leading one *New York Times* article to consider whether it was "The End of California."

The drought exposed several weaknesses in the state's management and use of water. First, California is one of the only states that does not regulate its groundwater. As such, it does not keep tabs on how much is underground (this is technologically difficult to do), nor does it track how much is withdrawn from over one million wells throughout the state. Second, the water shortage also shone a light on how water is used. Overall, the largest portion of available water, about 50 percent, is used for environmental purposes, such as maintaining ecosystems. Another 40 percent is used for agriculture, while the remaining 10 percent is for urban uses. These aggregate numbers mask what are believed to be wasteful practices by individuals and farmers. Some have pointed fingers at water-intensive crops, such as almonds and alfalfa. In what is known as the "nut rush," farmers tore up acreage dedicated to lower-value crops to plant hundreds of thousands of acres of almond orchards because of increasing demand *and* profits. As a result, it became common knowledge that each almond takes one gallon of water to produce. For homeowners use to lush, green lawns, the drought called into question whether these thirsty lawns should remain central components of suburban landscapes. Many homeowners replaced their lawns with drought-tolerant plants or converted to artificial turf.

Yet another shortcoming of the state's water policy is the arcane and convoluted patchwork of laws governing water rights. As but one example, a University of California study revealed that the state has granted five times more water rights than the system (e.g., reservoirs) can deliver in a *normal* year. This means that the promises made to water users, such as farmers, cannot be met even with average levels of rainfall and snowpack. During the drought, the State Water Resources Control Board shut off allocations for 10,000 water-rights holders.[14]

Cartoon 12.1 Saving Water in California Hotels

Question: What further steps will California need to take to ensure an adequate water supply?

The prolonged drought pressured lawmakers and the governor into taking unprecedented actions to conserve and better manage the state's water supply (see cartoon 12.1). In 2014, Governor Brown signed the Sustainable Groundwater Management Act, which required local water agencies to develop sustainable groundwater management plans by 2020. These plans are intended to address the problem of overdraft, where users have depleted underground aquifers through water pumping. The plans must specify how agencies will maintain a sustainable water supply through groundwater recharge (replacing water in underground aquifers) and pumping less. For the first time in the state's history, Brown also issued a mandatory executive order for local governments to cut their water use by 25 percent statewide. Local agencies eventually met that goal after they were assigned water-use reduction goals based on each agency's previous per capita water use.

In 2017, the vulnerabilities of the state's aging dam system were highlighted when the Oroville Dam broke and forced 200,000 residents to flee the region. The fracture cost more than $1 billion to repair and spurred efforts to evaluate the condition of dams statewide because more than half are 50 years old and not designed for the precipitation patterns brought by climate change.[15] Strengthening the state's dams and reservoirs is another key component to ensuring an adequate water supply for California's future.

In some respects, water is a highly contentious issue in California not only due to its variable supply but also the hyperpluralistic nature of California politics. Agricultural interests, urban users, and defenders of endangered fish populations (water's newest constituency) all have different perspectives on water and its provision. They also employ their own channels of influence at the state, regional, and local levels. Given the essential nature of water for urban and agricultural uses, political conflict over it is likely to continue.

HOUSING: FOR MANY, THE IMPOSSIBLE DREAM

If providing water to a growing and thirsty state seems challenging, consider the Golden State's version of the American Dream—owning a home. Here we consider the challenge of providing adequate, affordable housing for all Californians.

The California Dream

Although the American Dream has meant homeownership, it acquired a semirural dimension in California. According to California historian Kevin Starr, "At the core of the [California] dream was the hope for a special relationship to nature."[16] In terms of housing, this meant a single-family, detached home with landscaped front-, rear, and side yards and plenty of privacy. The ideal was a residential suburb, far from the congestion, filth, and heterogeneity of the central city.

With the blessings of local government, single-family developments spilled across the landscape. The gridiron plan (resembling a checkerboard), considered efficient by American developers, left little room for common community uses such as neighborhood parks. This dispersed, low-density pattern occurred in California just when the automobile industry itself was expanding. Affordable cars became necessities as Californians consumed one housing tract after another, well away from where they worked. Retail businesses and even factories followed homeowners to suburbia. For a time, the California middle-class "dream house" became ever larger—more and larger rooms, multiple baths, and roomy garages.

Housing Policy as "Filter Down"

Although the federal Housing Act of 1949 envisioned "a decent home and suitable living environment for every American family," governments (federal, state, and local) have not, nor ever will, build much housing. True, federally guaranteed mortgages have helped promote middle-class housing and some publicly owned rental housing exists. But for the most part, it is a private-sector activity. California's "policy" has largely mirrored the nation's: build housing for the haves, and their housing will filter down to the have-nots. A **filter-down policy** assumes that, as people on the upper rungs of the economic ladder move up to better homes, the ones they vacate will be made available to those on the lower rungs. Private builders propose and construct the housing, and private lenders finance its purchase. Local governments determine and enforce development standards. A smattering of government aid assists a small percentage of the have-nots in their quest for housing.

Does filter-down work? Yes, if there is equilibrium between the supply of housing and the demand for it. But this equilibrium has been rare in California due to several factors. First, developers gravitate to housing that local governments will approve. Communities often resist less costly starter housing or apartment buildings, and developers understandably prefer more-profitable higher-end housing. Second, California's constant population growth keeps demand for housing high, even when economic conditions retard construction or put home loans out of reach. This results in residential overcrowding, home sharing by both families and individuals, and an inability for some to move.

The Housing Crisis and Beyond

This private-sector-dominated system imploded in the late 2000s, dashing the American Dream, let alone the California Dream, for many. How did it happen? As more and more people sought homeownership, home prices increased. As prices rose, others thought they also needed to buy or homeownership would forever be out of reach. Californians stretched their own finances to enter the housing market.[17] This drove prices still higher, resulting in what experts believed to be an unsustainable housing "bubble." Lending practices made matters worse. Many lenders aggressively marketed subprime loans (adjustable rate mortgages with initially low interest rates) to many first-time home buyers who would not have qualified for traditional fixed-rate loans. As a consequence, homeowners in many places were spending upward of 50 percent of their incomes on housing. When these mortgage rates adjusted upward or when the inevitable balloon payments came due, some borrowers had to default on their loans. Lenders were forced to foreclose those properties, take title to them, and accept huge loan losses in the process. Thinking home values would rise indefinitely, other homeowners had borrowed from their home equity to finance second homes, cars, boats, college tuition—you name it. As the real estate market began to stagnate and home values dropped, some Californians found their loan balances were more than their homes were worth (known as "being underwater"). Eventually, this created a backlog of unsold homes and a precipitous drop in the production of new housing.

In the aftermath of this housing crisis, many homeowners became renters. They would sit out the California Dream at least for a while. Aghast by the miseries faced by homeowners, many renters vowed to continue renting, concluding that the California Dream was more of a nightmare. The one silver lining in this crisis was that it lowered home prices and interest rates, thereby putting homes within reach of many first-time homebuyers. Tightened loan requirements limited new borrowers to those better qualified to afford homeownership in the first place.

By most accounts, the long downward slide of the housing crisis began to turn around for California and the rest of the country in 2012. The ominous measures of the housing crisis—foreclosure rates and notices of default (homeowners unable to make mortgage payments on time)—began a retreat to more normal levels.

While the anticipated housing recovery was good news for homeowners, whose home values began to rise again, it also caused old housing issues to resurface: affordability and supply. If we use the U.S. Department of Housing and Urban Development definition of affordability—spending no more than 30 percent of household income on housing—much of California's housing remains unaffordable (see figure 12.3). This is especially true for renters, low-income residents, and first-time homebuyers. For first-time buyers, the percentage of households that could afford an entry-level home dipped to 45 percent in late 2018.[18] The minimum qualifying income for a first-time buyer was $81,120. It is no surprise then that only 54.8 percent of housing units in California were owner-occupied, among the lowest rates of any state in the nation.[19]

Why is California housing so expensive? First, there is a shortage of appropriately zoned land, especially along California's highly desirable coast. This has forced many who work in coastal cities to move inland, driving upward home

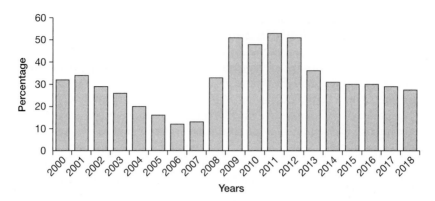

Figure 12.3 Housing Affordability, 2000–18
The figure shows the percentage of households that can afford a median-priced home.

Question: What can policymakers do to increase housing affordability?

Source: California Association of Realtors

prices in those areas. Second, many communities actually resist the construction of new housing, including "affordable" housing like rental units or "starter" housing. Opponents disfavor housing on flat land (because agricultural land needs preservation) *or* on hillsides (because of fire and flooding dangers). Third, many city officials believe housing does not generate enough property taxes to pay for the services it requires. They prefer sales tax-laden retail uses (such as auto malls and shopping centers) that require minimal public services. As noted earlier, this has been called the **fiscalization of land use**. This phenomenon spans the state and the consequences are dire, particularly for renters. Many are lower- or moderate-income individuals and families, whose incomes often do not keep pace with rising rents.[20]

TRANSPORTATION: STUCK IN TRAFFIC

California's legendary love affair with the automobile poses seemingly insurmountable challenges related to the state's growth. Consider this: a recent survey showed that the average daily commute time is 59 minutes in San Francisco, 54 minutes in Los Angeles, and 46 in San Diego, not to mention that they are also among the most stressful commutes.[21] Freeway speeds are slowing, and on many urban freeways, the "rush hour" itself has disappeared into a cloud of heavy traffic—all day, every day. A single accident can tie up traffic for hours more. Bus and rail transit riders are not exempt from traffic delays. In fact, simple door-to-door commute times are longer for bus riders than for automobile drivers. Smaller California communities also experience congestion as growing numbers of vehicles outpace narrow roads and surface streets. Throughout California, the number of vehicle miles traveled will continue to outpace both population growth and state highway capacity.

The Problem

Although traffic congestion is easy to see and experience, it is a complex policy problem. Three factors help explain why.

Personal Choice. True, Californians love their automobiles. Before widespread car ownership, streetcars and trolleys augmented walking, and living "in town" was actually desirable. The automobile essentially reversed those preferences. The automobile symbolized American individualism and personal choice. As a 1926 *Los Angeles Times* editorial put it, "How can one pursue happiness with any swifter and surer means than the automobile?" In modern times, acquiring one has become a rite of passage to adulthood. For many California college and university students, "wheels" are as fixed an expense as tuition, room, board, and books.

There is no escaping the congestion that results from these personal choices. Given the proliferation of car ownership, one household may claim at least one vehicle per driver. People can feel the effect. Lengthy commutes may be the logical extension of personal choice in individualistic California. In this view, the "jobs/housing imbalance" (as urban planners call it) is really a rational choice trade-off between relatively short commutes and affordable but distant housing. So is the choice of so many to avoid mass transit (buses and rail) as inconvenient. Compared to driving personal vehicles, buses are too slow, and rail stations often are too far from homes or places of employment.

Urban Development Patterns. Personal choice affects traffic, but so does the legacy of urban development in California. Cities dispersed as waves of newcomers arrived. Massive highway projects connected downtowns with the suburbs. These highways once accommodated the growth of suburban commuters, but no more. Even those who found jobs closer to home discovered local surface streets as clogged as the freeways. Urban and suburban sprawl has permeated California. Dispersed development has made the construction of rail-based mass transit systems exorbitantly expensive and often unfeasible.

Environmental Effects. California's motor vehicles do more than create congestion. Consider smog. The chief component of smog is ozone (which occurs when hydrocarbons and nitrogen oxides react to sunlight). Nitrogen oxide forms during the combustion of fossil fuels. California's combination of climate and terrain creates what the Air Resources Board calls "Mother Nature's perfect smog chamber." Long before statehood, Native Americans called the Los Angeles Basin the "Land of a Thousand Smokes." California smog reaches farther than most people realize. Central Valley smog can affect sequoia seedlings in the high Sierras, and Southern California smog can reach Arizona's Grand Canyon. Vehicle smog is acute for several reasons. First, while California is only average among the states in automobile ownership, the sheer volume of vehicles—gasoline and diesel—makes California's air among the nation's dirtiest. Second, California's older vehicles can emit twice the pollution of newer ones. The worst offenders nowadays are less regulated off-road and heavy-duty vehicles. They account for 80 percent of smog-forming emissions.[22]

Smog is only one vehicle-related culprit. Automobile contaminants (oil, grease, antifreeze, and small tire particles) wash into streams and waterways. Traffic noise, fumes, and toxic road dust are also major problems as ribbons of freeways snake through metropolitan areas. Asthma, heart disease, and cancer can result. According to University of Southern California researchers, the number of Californians who die each year from breathing sooty smog may be double or triple the official estimates of more than 9,000 per year.[23]

California's Transportation Policies

Transportation policies in California are supported by nearly $23 billion worth of federal, state, and local funds (gas tax revenues and bond funds). Those dollars largely reflect a broader policy that can be summarized in one sentence: *California's transportation policy has tended to favor and accommodate the automobile.* Local governments typically approved traffic-generating developments and provided the local streets that were required. Large-scale state and national highways and the interstate system were shared responsibilities, but the primary policymaker was the State of California. In 1923, a 2-cent-per-gallon gasoline tax was established to finance this policy of accommodation. In the late 1940s, a new building program began, to which was added the interstate system in the 1950s. Opposition to more freeways rose on occasion. In the 1970s, Governor Brown wanted to change the state's emphasis from highways to mass transit. Yet demand for highways continued and, by the 1990s, the renamed Department of Transportation (Caltrans) was understaffed, underfunded, and backlogged with unfinished projects. Although highway capacity increased by only 4 percent in the 1980s and 1990s, California's population grew by 50 percent. Why the disparity? Thirty states spend more per capita on highways than California.

Decades of California's underinvestment in its transportation infrastructure has led to concerns that population growth, albeit at lower levels than the past, will only exacerbate the state's transportation problems, namely congestion and air pollution. Commuters remain heavily reliant on the automobile: 76 percent drive to work alone, while 9 percent carpool. Only 5 percent use public transit.[24] The Department of Finance estimated that about $40 billion is needed to repair existing highways and roads. Traditionally, highway and road repairs were funded by the state's fuel taxes, but the revenue generated from those sources did not keep pace with needed repairs. Ironically, California's efforts to reduce carbon emissions through the use of more-fuel-efficient vehicles have meant that drivers spend less on fuel taxes.

In 2017, Governor Brown and the legislature adopted higher fuel taxes and vehicle fees to fund mass transit and repairs for the transportation network. This includes a flat fee of $100 for the increasing number of zero-emission vehicles that would otherwise avoid fuel taxes. The funding sources are expected to generate about $5 billion annually for maintenance and repairs. While some funding mechanisms may be less popular than others, the new "gas taxes" survived an initiative by opponents to eliminate them and require future fuel taxes to be approved by voters. Proposition 6 was defeated by 57 percent of voters in 2018, suggesting that the public is more willing to shoulder the financial burden as roadway conditions have deteriorated. California has ranked in the top 10 for *worst* highway conditions since 2000.

High-Speed Rail. State policymakers have realized that California's transportation woes cannot be solved only by an updated and expanded highway system. As other countries have done, policymakers have also looked to high-speed rail to relieve some of the congestion and pollution problems afflicting vehicle and air travel. With the help of a $9 billion bond passed by voters in 2008, plans are underway to build a high-speed train system that travels more than 200 miles per hour and links Los Angeles to San Francisco, and eventually to San Diego and Sacramento. Such a system would reduce the estimated 70 million passenger trips made each year now by vehicles and air travel. As one of the largest infrastructure projects in U.S. history, it has run into opposition from property owners and businesses in its path and questions pertaining to its affordability. Its total cost was originally projected to be $100 billion, but the High-Speed Rail Commission has modified the total cost several times. As of 2018, it stood at $77.3 billion. Governor Brown and other advocates believed that the federal government would chip in with more funding support, but Republicans in Congress, including those from California, have been staunch opponents of it. In 2013, Brown and the legislature reached an agreement to allocate 25 percent of the revenue from the state's cap-and-trade system (discussed more in the next section), which is providing a major source of funding for the project.

This controversial project has also generated a number of lawsuits challenging the environmental review process and the system requirements outlined in the 2008 bond measure. Some of the lawsuits have been resolved, but others from property owners in the train's path remain pending. Advocates contend that alternatives, such as increasing highway miles, to accommodate some 20 million additional people in the next several decades are just as, if not more, problematic. Building highways and expanding airports also displace residents and lead to more pollution. Construction of the first segment of the rail line from Fresno to Madera began in 2015 and the extension of it to northern Kern County is targeted for completion in 2027. In his first State of the State address, Governor Newsom shocked high-speed rail advocates when he proposed an initial rail line that would only run from Merced to Bakersfield until financing for the remaining phases of the system could be secured. This announcement left the envisioned statewide system in limbo.

All these strategies aim to alter the fundamental behavior of Californians regarding transportation. The challenge in doing so is monumental. The public resists pricing tools to discourage driving (higher gas taxes and toll roads) and moving jobs, not just housing, closer to transit stations requires a daunting mix of public- and private-sector commitments.[25]

ENERGY, ENVIRONMENT, AND CLIMATE CHANGE

California's population growth has severely affected the state's quality of life in two broad areas: energy and environment. Energy policies address the oil, natural gas, and electricity demands of a complex, energy-hungry economy and the lifestyles of nearly 40 million residents. Environmental policies address the impacts of economic and population growth on the quality of the state's water, air, land, and natural resources. In recent years, climate change, also known as global warming, has emerged as the paramount environmental concern.

Energy

The electricity crisis of the early 2000s highlighted a host of energy-related concerns. Californians suffered both spiraling electricity prices and infuriating gaps in service—brownouts and blackouts. At the time, the British journal *The Economist* declared, "One of the wealthiest regions in the world is on the brink of an energy crisis of third-world proportions. How did California come to this?"[23] The answer to that question lies in a confluence of public policies and events—electricity's version of the perfect storm. The key decision was the passage of AB 1890, a 100-page law that sought to replace a patchwork of regulatory practices with an open-market approach. Electricity generation did become more competitive, but other developments worsened the situation:

- Wholesale energy prices floated freely while policymakers froze retail prices.
- No new power plants were built to replace old plants and meet increased demand.
- Energy generators and traders (like the infamous Enron Corporation) "gamed" the system by withholding capacity to spike short-term prices.

In short, California's approach to deregulation failed. To many, the outcome was a bitter lesson in how *not* to deregulate. Governor Gray Davis and the legislature were slow to respond, but eventually offered more reforms, including (1) using public funds to bail out financially strapped public utilities, (2) selling energy bonds to repay state costs, (3) renegotiating costly energy contracts, (4) streamlining the construction of new power plants, and (5) encouraging consumer conservation. Ultimately, Davis's response to the crisis was not enough. Along with poor budget management, it contributed to his recall in 2003.

Environment and Climate Change

Continued efforts are also underway to address environmental pollution in the Golden State. The sheer size of California magnifies the scope of the problem. California is the 19th largest emitter of carbon in the world. But population is only one part of the equation. The development of new technologies (silicon chips, synthetic materials, and industrial processes) also adds new toxins to the environment. The long-range impact of environmental pollution has been called **climate change** or global warming. This is caused by a buildup of gases that allow the heat of the sun to penetrate the atmosphere but prevent it from escaping—the greenhouse effect. California's share of the contribution is 1 percent of the world's greenhouse gases and 6 percent of the U.S. total. The largest human sources come from transportation, electricity production, and industrial uses (see figure 12.4). The United States and the world are coming to the realization that some of the long-term effects of climate change are already beginning to appear. California experienced its four warmest years on record between 2014 and 2018. Scientists had anticipated that California would have more frequent droughts and that the Sierra snowpack, a vital source of water for the state, would diminish. The 2012–16 drought was evidence of the former, while snowpack levels in recent years have shown signs of the latter.

One of the most visible effects of global warming in California has been the surge in wildfires in recent years. The warming temperatures and lack of rainfall dry out plants and vegetation in the forested areas of the state. Once sparked, they spread quickly. The Camp Fire in Butte County in 2018 was the deadliest wildfire ever (88 died) in California and 2018 set the record for the most

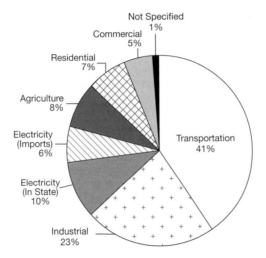

Figure 12.4 California Greenhouse Gas Emissions by Source

Question: In what ways do you contribute to climate change?

Source: California Air Resources Board, https://www.arb.ca.gov/cc/inventory/data/data.htm.

Wildfires increasingly pose risks for housing developments near forests and vegetation. Climate change has contributed to these risks by drying out vegetation and making it more flammable.

acres burned. The entire city of Paradise in northeastern California burned to the ground in the Camp Fire (14,000 residences were lost). Fire victims are not the only ones affected. The smoke and ashes from these wildfires drift into urban areas hundreds of miles away causing respiratory problems and forcing people indoors.

One of the major electricity providers in the state, Pacific Gas and Electric (PG&E), which serves the central and northern parts of the state (16 million people), became a victim of the wildfires as well. Investigations of the causes of many of these wildfires in recent years have been linked to downed power lines or neglected maintenance issues, creating financial claims for electric utilities from fire victims. Already reeling from the claims from the 2017 wildfires (17 were linked to PG&E), the claims from the 2018 fires led PG&E to file for bankruptcy. It faced an estimated $30 billion in damage liabilities. The announcement sparked discussions about the potential sell-off of its assets, such as its natural gas division, and a potential state takeover.

Policy Options

Increased media coverage and continued population growth give environmental and global warming issues a sense of urgency. Public opinion polls illustrate the public's concern with these issues. According to a recent survey, "two in three Californians believe the effects of global warming are already happening, and a similar proportion favor the state's emission reduction goals."[26] In what seems like an uphill battle, California policymakers now rely on five separate but interrelated approaches based on a fundamental truth: The private sector largely creates pollution, but it is the government's responsibility to eliminate it.

Monitor It. Understanding the scope and components of any problem is necessary for finding a solution. For example, the California Air Resources Board (ARB) is responsible for tracking and reporting the state's carbon emission levels to determine whether California is meeting the reduction goals (the Greenhouse Gas Emission Inventory can be found here: https://www.arb.ca.gov/cc/inventory/data/data.htm).

Regulate It. A second approach has been to issue regulations, set standards, and order offenders to comply. Sometimes called **command and control**, this approach has been implemented by numerous state agencies. For example, the legislature periodically authorizes the Air Resources Board to set emission standards for various types of vehicles and to establish deadlines for compliance. Recent governors have also pushed for more stringent limitations on carbon emissions. Schwarzenegger set a target to reduce emissions to 1990 levels by 2020. After the state met that goal, Brown set the bar even higher on his departure in 2018 when he committed the state to be carbon neutral by 2045. Opponents are concerned that the new targets are too ambitious and will harm the state's business environment.

Although the command-and-control approach seems heavy-handed, it has fostered new recycling techniques and some new products (unleaded gasoline, low-emission equipment, alternative fuels, and recyclable plastic).

Move It. Another "solution" to pollution in California has been to send the more solid forms of it somewhere else. Indeed, by the late 1980s, more than 30 other states were receiving toxic waste from California. In recent years, such exports have slowed considerably, but the state still generates 500,000 tons of hazardous waste each year. Ironically, strong environmental laws in California make intrastate waste disposal difficult and costly. Where it is feasible, large amounts of waste have been stored near poor, ethnic minority communities, a practice sometimes called "environmental racism." NIMBYism has discouraged the siting of new toxic waste facilities almost anywhere. With nowhere to go, many toxins are simply stored in garages, warehouses, and industrial facilities.

Price It. A recent development in environmental protection has been a market-based approach. Pricing incentives assume a partnership between the private and public sectors, but this is just beginning in California. The state's global warming law requires the ARB to implement a **cap-and-trade** approach. With cap and trade, the government sets pollution caps and issues allowances, or carbon credits, to polluting businesses. These credits allow businesses to pollute as long as they meet their individual limits and aggregate pollution is under the cap. Companies that successfully reduce emissions below their limit can sell their credits to less successful businesses to offset the excess carbon they produce. The "carbon market" kicked off in November 2012 when the state conducted its first auction of carbon credits for large emitters, such as utilities. In 2015, gas and diesel fuel suppliers were added to the program, raising fears that gas prices could rise as much as 75 cents a gallon. However, these fears were not realized when prices only increased around 10 cents a gallon. In 2017, policymakers extended the life of the cap-and-trade program to 2030. The revenue from the program is targeted for energy efficiency programs, the weatherization of state buildings, and clean energy projects. Governor Brown also secured one-quarter of annual revenues for the construction of high-speed rail.

Cap-and-trade proponents believe that this approach is the most effective way to fight global warming at the least cost to taxpayers. Using the idiom of the "carrot and stick," they think rewards are more effective than punishments. Opponents, including many environmentalists, believe that the state should never subsidize chronic polluters. They prefer the stick of fees and fines to force compliance.

Replace It. One last policy option in California has been to replace fossil fuels and hydroelectric power with renewable sources of energy such as solar, wind, geothermal, biomass, and small-scale hydropower. In the past, "green power" was not attractive to utility companies because it costs more to produce and was less predictable (due to cloudy days and sporadic winds). In recent decades, the state has offered tax credits and incentives to develop some renewables (e.g., solar power). Under the California Solar Initiative, utility companies offered their customers rebates to install solar electricity systems, causing a surge in demand for them. The California Energy Commission took the "replace it" strategy to another level in 2018 when it required all new houses to be powered by solar energy. The new requirement would add thousands of dollars to the price of new homes in an already-high-priced market, but the higher costs would be offset by lower energy bills.

CONCLUSION: A NEW GROWTH POLICY FOR CALIFORNIA

California has experienced phenomenal growth throughout its history. A generalized pro-growth consensus among policy leaders aided post–World War II growth. Population growth continued unchecked, local governments readily approved commercial and residential development, and the state provided the necessary infrastructure. Notable were vast water projects, highways, and a comprehensive education system. By the 1960s and 1970s, concerns about too much growth were raised. Development sprawled across the landscape, an automobile-dominated transportation system seemed to choke on itself, smog was a permanent reality in much of California, and news of environmental damage was commonplace.

Growth as a potent issue has an ebb-and-flow quality to it. By the late 1980s, concern over growth in California entered the mainstream of California politics. But California's economic recession in the early 1990s consumed political attention in Sacramento; in later years, education, energy, immigration, and climate change seemed to supplant growth as dominant issues. Yet the drumbeat of population growth fuels most other issues in the state.

To the extent that policymakers consider various "solutions" to the problem, they will need to include the following ideas.

A Statewide Growth Strategy. You may have been impressed with the number of agencies at all levels that address land use, water, housing, transportation, and environmental protection. This jurisdictional fragmentation can and does result in policy conflict. For example, some policies (such as building more freeways) encourage automobile use at the expense of mass transit. Building more housing might conflict with the protection of open space. One solution would be a comprehensive, future-oriented statewide growth strategy. Such a strategy would both control growth itself and accommodate growth that cannot be controlled.

Controlling California's population growth itself is a much more difficult challenge. It seems to be treated as a given that policymakers can do little about. After all, in a diverse, representative democracy that values freedom, how does government tell families to have fewer children? How can a state on its own barricade an international border? In light of private property rights, how do local officials tell people they cannot build houses on land zoned for that use? No wonder policymakers are at best ambivalent about population growth control.

Sustainable Infrastructure Planning. Infrastructure is an essential component of several of the policy areas covered in this chapter. Dams, aqueducts, and canals all help store and move water around the state for agricultural and urban uses. Roads and highways help move people and goods around the state for pleasure and business. At one time, California was considered a model of long-term planning to accommodate its expected population growth. Now, the lack of planning and investment in recent decades is highlighted by the deteriorating conditions of our roads and highways and concerns about an adequate water supply. The antitax movement has contributed to this underinvestment, but hyperpluralism plays a significant role as well. Californians, and the groups that represent them, have different ideas about what modes of transportation (e.g., car vs. rail) should be prioritized or what approaches (e.g., conservation or storage) will best help secure an adequate water supply. These disagreements are perhaps more intense and fragmented than they once were when the state embarked on a building spree in the 1950s and 1960s, but this conflict will have to be overcome to facilitate the prosperity of the next generation.

Rethink Home Rule. Under the ingrained doctrine of home rule, local governments can and should make their own decisions about growth. Yet this approach ignores the impact that decisions in one community might have on its neighbors. Interjurisdictional turf battles may result, but managing regional growth does not. Proposed solutions to the home rule "problem" include giving greater land-use authority to existing councils of governments, establishing still-larger superagencies to manage regional growth, and reducing the power of single-purpose, single-minded agencies that focus exclusively on water, air quality, or transportation. Progress on this front is slow.

Defiscalize Development. In recent decades, local governments have depended less on the state and federal governments to subsidize local growth and its infrastructure. This trend, coupled with Proposition 13, compelled local officials to approve projects that pay more in taxes than they consume in services (e.g., shopping centers). In turn, communities compete to attract such projects while shunning less lucrative ones (e.g., low-income housing). Numerous reform groups now seek "smart growth" strategies that manage, steer, and coordinate land-use decisions while decoupling them from their revenue impacts.

KEY TERMS

impact fees (p. 264)
general plan (p. 264)
zoning ordinances (p. 264)
subdivision regulations (p. 264)
uniform building codes (p. 264)
planned unit developments
  (PUDs) (p. 264)
locally undesirable land uses
  (LULUs) (p. 265)

not in my back yard (NIMBY) (p. 266)
riparian rights (p. 267)
prior appropriation (p. 267)
prescriptive rights (p. 267)
filter-down policy (p. 272)
climate change (p. 278)
command and control (p. 280)
cap and trade (p. 281)

REVIEW QUESTIONS

1. Why did California grow, and why does it continue to?
2. Describe land-use politics at the local level.
3. Explain the rise and meaning of California's no-growth movement.
4. Delineate the major components of California's plumbing system.
5. What is the California Dream, and to what extent do filter-down policies fulfill it? How did the housing crisis help or hinder the fulfillment of the dream for many Californians?
6. How have California's transportation policies emphasized the use of the automobile? Is this likely to continue in the future?
7. In what ways is California already seeing the effects of climate change?
8. To control the impacts of growth in California, what has been recommended, and what do you recommend?

WEB RESOURCES

Business, Consumer Services, and Housing Agency
https://www.bcsh.ca.gov

This state mega-agency provides links to a number of data-rich agencies dealing with housing and business, such as the Department of Alcoholic Beverage Control.

California State Transportation Agency

https://calsta.ca.gov

This agency oversees all the transportation departments, including the California Highway Patrol, the Department of Motor Vehicles, and the High-Speed Rail Authority.

California Environmental Protection Agency

https://calepa.ca.gov

This is a similar umbrella agency with links to boards dealing with air, water, and solid-waste pollution.

Realtor.com

https://www.realtor.com

To appreciate the challenge of homeownership in California as portrayed in this chapter, go to realtor.com, locate homes for sale in various California communities, and determine how much income you would realistically need to afford typical monthly payments. What, if anything, should the state do to make homeownership more affordable?

13

Policies Stemming from Diversity

★ ★ ★

LEARNING OUTCOMES

Students will be able to:

★ Explain the evolution of state policies toward abortion and LGBT rights.

★ Analyze the significant issues faced by the K–12 education system.

★ Discuss segments of the higher education system and the extent to which they are meeting their goals.

★ Summarize the policies California has adopted to address the higher education needs of undocumented students.

★ Identify the programs available to meet the welfare and health care needs of Californians, especially the low-income population.

IN BRIEF

In chapter 13, we consider the cultural diversity of California and its impact on five policy areas: abortion, LGBT (lesbian, gay, bisexual, transgender) rights, education, higher education, and social programs. Policy conflicts in these areas are struggles among competing groups—cultural hyperpluralism and ensuing political conflict seem best for describe this state of affairs.

★ ★ ★

IN CALIFORNIA, AS ELSEWHERE, the issues of abortion and gay rights mirror a diversity of values and fundamental disagreements over what constitutes personhood and marriage. Public education (K–12) must deal with population growth, ethnic diversity, social change, and variable funding. Education reforms are frequent, and they vary in effectiveness. Multicultural politics is evident even in textbook adoptions and testing. California's Master Plan for Higher Education promises affordable access to colleges and universities for all qualified Californians, yet observers wonder if it will be able to handle future demands.

California's array of social programs serves a growing, diverse population, many of whom do not fully participate in the political process. Programs to alleviate poverty involve all levels of government and are aimed primarily at the "deserving poor." In terms of medical care, the state health care system is undergoing significant changes as a result of the implementation of the federal Affordable Care Act. State-regulated private insurance and Medi-Cal cover an increasing number of Californians, at dramatically rising costs. The worst-off seem to be the deinstitutionalized mentally ill, some of whom are homeless. These are the challenges facing an emerging multicultural democracy—one depicted by population growth, cultural diversity, and group conflict.

INTRODUCTION: THE CHALLENGE OF DIVERSITY

To Californians, neighborhood conflicts are commonplace. African Americans may complain about the *ranchera* music of their Hispanic neighbors. One neighbor's redwood trees may block another's rooftop solar panels. One increasingly Asian community in Southern California found that Asians were avoiding homes with "4" in the house number, thereby flattening sales. The city council had to consider allowing people to change their own house numbers—for a fee. These actual incidents illustrate the most profound, long-term challenge facing the Golden State: building a diverse, multicultural society that is at peace with itself. In terms of the nation's motto, *E Pluribus Unum* (out of many, one), the likelihood of California's political system forging the *unum* out of a *pluribus* is an open question. There never has been one monolithic culture in California, but even the myth of one is diminishing. Politically speaking, the notion of an overarching public interest—what founder James Madison called "the good of the whole"— seems increasingly elusive in California.

California is at a major juncture in its political development, a time when the broad forces of growth and diversity are colliding and will likely change how politics is done. In chapter 12, the policy issues of water, housing, transportation, and pollution were used to explain the larger question of population growth and its consequences. This chapter examines the issues of abortion, gay rights, education, welfare, and health to emphasize the larger view of cultural diversity and its consequences. Cultural diversity is nothing new in California's political development. Historically, minority cultures were either extinguished or separated from the larger society. In the 1500s, a Spanish culture largely replaced California's Native American culture through disease and conquest. Mexicans subsequently dominated the region of California until the mid-1800s. The discovery of gold brought white settlers from other U.S. states and Europe to California. Historians refer to this influx of non-Hispanic whites as the "Americanization" of California. These settlers intermarried widely, creating a dominant culture—a process sociologists call **cultural amalgamation**. For much of California's history as a state, Euro-Americans have been the dominant cultural group. At times, they discriminated against Chinese and Japanese immigrants, and against African Americans and Latinos, enforcing a **cultural separatism**, often through housing segregation. The dominant pattern in modern times has been **cultural assimilation**; to "succeed," minority groups need to adopt the practices and characteristics of the "host" society.[1]

As the percentage of whites in California continues to shrink in size and no ethnic group constitutes a majority (see figure 13.1), the traditional idea of

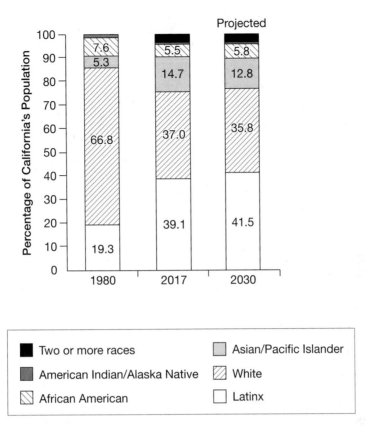

Figure 13.1 The Ethnic Composition of California: Past, Present, and Future

Source: Public Policy Institute of California, https://www.ppic.org/wp-content/uploads/californias
-future-population-january-2019.pdf.

assimilation into a "majority" culture loses its meaning. Some observers believe that California now faces **cultural hyperpluralism**: various ethnic, racial, religious, and other groups balancing the ideal of "one people" with the reality of group identity.

Cultural hyperpluralism goes beyond ethnicity. It is also evident in a variety of policy conflicts involving educational and lifestyle issues. Sociologist James Davison Hunter describes these conflicts as "political and social hostility rooted in different systems of moral understanding."[2]

According to this perspective, several policy debates in California and the nation (such as abortion, gay rights, and certain educational policies) can ultimately be traced to differing views of moral authority. The goal of opposing groups is not peaceful coexistence but winning a war of values. As you consider the policy topics in this final chapter, ask yourself this question: In California, are there "permanent and aggregate interests of the community," as Madison put it in the *Federalist*, No. 10, or simply an unending parade of policy clashes between conflicting groups or factions?

SOCIAL ISSUES: ABORTION AND LGBT RIGHTS

Some public policy issues do not involve large expenditures of public funds. They cannot be viewed as government programs, run by permanent state agencies. Unlike the annual state budget, they do not consume vast amounts of policymaker time. Yet they stir human emotions, produce conflict, and divide Californians unlike most other public policies. We call these policies **social issues**. Here we focus on the two most familiar ones—abortion and gay rights, now known as LGBT rights.

Abortion

Abortion is one of the most controversial political issues for both the nation and California. In the Golden State, the controversy actually preceded the U.S. Supreme Court's famous decision in *Roe v. Wade* (1973), which established a woman's right of privacy relative to giving birth. Before the 1960s, abortion in California was relatively rare and largely illegal. Prosecutions were rarer still because it was assumed physicians knew best what to do. During the 1960s, legislation was introduced to legalize what many doctors were already doing—performing abortions to protect the life and health of the mother. As medical procedures improved, the woman's health became a less important justification for abortion. In 1962, publicity surrounding a pregnant woman who had taken the drug thalidomide, plus a rubella epidemic, heightened public awareness of the philosophical issues involved. Was a damaged life still worth living? Few Californians had bothered to ask that question before. Physicians no longer controlled the abortion issue when the general public began asking what being a "person" really means.

In 1967, Governor Ronald Reagan signed the *Therapeutic Abortion Act* (the "Beilenson Bill") that clarified abortion practice in the Golden State. Allowable reasons to seek an abortion were expanded to include rape and incest, the mental health of the mother, and whether the infant would likely be deformed. There were restrictions: only licensed physicians could perform abortions and only in accredited hospitals. Although many factors explain abortion rates, many observers conclude that Beilenson, coupled with *Roe* a few years later, increased dramatically the number of abortions in California. According to state statistics, only 518 legal abortions were performed in 1967. In 1980, the year Reagan was elected president, there were 199,089 abortions performed. The total from 1968 to 1980 was 1,444,778.[3]

The California law and the *Roe* decision also unleashed two grassroots movements, each supporting a conflicting fundamental right—the right to terminate a pregnancy versus a right to be born.[4] The political divide between these two movements is deep and wide. One group calls the unborn "fetuses;" the other, "babies." Even group labels are politicized. According to one side, those calling themselves "pro-choice" are actually pro-abortion. According to the other side, self-described "pro-life" groups are not only antiabortion; they are also antichoice. Granted the conflict, where do Californians stand on abortion? A majority has been consistently pro-choice over the last 20 years. See figure 13.2 for a recent snapshot of voters' opinions on abortion in the Golden State. Much is at stake for both sides. Although accurate statistics are elusive, abortion rates

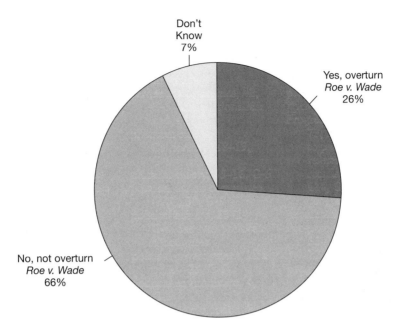

Figure 13.2 Californians and Abortion

Note: The question asks, "As you may know, the 1973 Supreme Court case *Roe v. Wade* established a women's constitutional right to have an abortion. Would you like to see the Supreme Court overturn its *Roe v. Wade* decision, or not?"

Source: PPIC Statewide Survey: Californians and Their Government, Public Policy Institute of California, September 2018.

in the United States and California have been declining since the early 1990s. In recent decades, several U.S. Supreme Court cases, *Webster v. Reproductive Health Services* (1989), and *Planned Parenthood v. Casey* (1992), although not overturning the right to an abortion, upheld several state restrictions on its use. In effect, this moved the political war over abortion to the states.

In California, the battle is waged on several fronts. The first is among policymakers and the interest groups that influence them. In Sacramento, interest groups such as the California Pro-Life Council and the California Abortion Rights League have lined up predictably for or against Medi-Cal funding of abortions for the indigent. As the state's Medicaid program for poor families, Medi-Cal funds more than 80,000 induced abortions per year. A second front has been in state courts. For example, in 1997, the California Supreme Court on a 4–3 vote struck down a never-enforced law requiring teenage girls to obtain parental or judicial approval for an abortion (*American Academy of Pediatrics v. Lungren*).

A third front has involved occasional protest activity. In the 1990s, antiabortion and pro-choice groups faced off outside clinics that performed abortions, but several court cases limited the ability of pro-life groups to block clinic access. Abortion protests have become less frequent as antiabortion activists focus more on counseling and abstinence education.

A fourth front has been the court of public opinion. In recent years, a majority of California voters have reflected a pro-choice sentiment, as figure 13.2 suggests.

Other polling data suggest that support for abortion rights declines the longer a woman is pregnant. A majority not only favors parental consent for teenage abortions but also supports late-term abortions if the mother's life is in danger.[5] A fifth front now includes the ballot box. Across the nation, several state legislatures have passed laws that restrict access to abortions, especially for minors. In the face of legislative inaction, abortion foes in California have opted for the initiative process. If nothing else, they have been persistent. Voters narrowly rejected both Proposition 73 in 2005 and Proposition 85 in 2006. Both would have required parental notification before a minor could terminate a pregnancy. Encouraged by these close votes, they submitted Proposition 4 that qualified for the November 2008 ballot. Proposition 4 was a constitutional amendment that would have prohibited abortions for dependent minors until 48 hours after a physician notified a minor's parents, legal guardian, or if necessary, another adult relative. Once again, voters rejected this measure, this time by a 52 to 48 percent margin.

To sum up, California's political climate today is largely pro-choice but with qualifications. California Democrats, who are more pro-choice than Republicans, control the legislature. Recent governors (Pete Wilson, Gray Davis, Arnold Schwarzenegger, and Jerry Brown) have been pro-choice. Even pro-life Republicans prefer discussing other issues such as taxes when running for office. This climate is supported by the state constitution's explicit right to privacy (Article I, Section 1). Although this provision was not passed with abortion in mind, it does provide a vehicle to defend abortion rights in California courts.

LGBT Rights

As with abortion rights, advancing the rights of California's LGBT community has been waged in several political arenas and over several issues. The most visible and controversial issue has been same-sex marriage, discussed in chapter 4. Here, we emphasize the less visible efforts to limit discrimination against LGBT people and provide equal access to public facilities.

These less visible efforts have occurred primarily within the formal legislative process and have focused on civil rights short of same-sex marriage. In 2011, Governor Brown became the first governor in the nation to sign legislation requiring school textbooks and history lessons to include the contributions of LGBT Americans. California became the first state to pass a law allowing transgender students to choose the restrooms they use and which sports teams they join based on their gender identity. More recently, the state required all public restrooms to have a gender-neutral option and added "x" as a third gender option on state-issued identity documents, such as birth certificates and driver's licenses.

The third arena has been local government. A growing number of counties and cities have passed ordinances barring discrimination against gays and lesbians. These rights vary from place to place, but they include public and private employment, public accommodations, education, housing, and lending practices. In order to do business with them, several cities now require private contractors to provide domestic partner benefits. On all these fronts, the overall issue continues to reflect fundamental cultural divisions in the state.

EDUCATION: COPING WITH GROWTH AND DIVERSITY

Unlike abortion and LGBT rights, education is a public service deeply rooted in California's political history. Yet the state's educational system faces unprecedented challenges. In chapter 10, we discussed school districts and how they are organized to implement education policies in California. Here, we analyze the challenges districts face in doing so. They include enrollment growth, ethnic diversity, and social change.

Pressures on Education

Pressures, many of which are external to the educational system itself, buffet California educators and students alike. Here we consider enrollment growth, ethnic hyperpluralism, social conflict, and funding challenges.

Enrollment Growth. In recent decades, the most significant challenge has been the sheer growth of California's school-age population. Historically, education enrollments have reflected a boom-or-bust pattern. Enrollments surge and slow based on birth rates and immigration. For example, some classrooms that were jammed with baby boomers in the 1960s stood empty in the 1970s, only to be filled again in the 1990s. In recent years, birth rates have declined so enrollment is expected to decline as well. The ebbs and flows of school enrollments vary across the state. Some school districts face school closures and teacher layoffs although others face the dire need for more classrooms, schools, and teachers. One would think that slowing enrollments should make it possible for school districts to catch up on infrastructure and other needs, but recent budget crises have prevented that. One school district in Riverside County was poised to open a new state-of-the-art high school in 2011 only to postpone the opening for lack of funding.

Ethnic Hyperpluralism. The ethnic composition in California's public schools has been shifting for years and will continue to do so well into the 21st century. Ethnic and cultural hyperpluralism are increasingly the norm. Consider figure 13.3: Latinxs constitute a slight but growing public school majority. These percentages vary dramatically throughout California. Diversity is more than ethnicity, as language differences illustrate. According to the California Department of Education, about a quarter of the state's K–12 students are English learners (EL). That is, they are not proficient enough in English to succeed academically in mainstream English programs. Of Hispanic K–12 students, nearly half are EL; that number can be much higher in some districts. Although Spanish is the most common first language for many students, it is by no means the only one. Students come from families where nearly 50 major languages are spoken. For many years, educators dealt with this language diversity by offering bilingual education. EL students were taught in both their first languages and in English, with the goal of making them eventually proficient in English. Many non-English speakers enter California schools at all grade levels, bringing a variety of language "readiness" with them. Growing frustration with the results of bilingual education resulted in the passage of Proposition 227 in 1998, which required all instruction to be in English. However, Proposition 58 (2016) repealed it and gave discretion over bilingual programs to local school districts.

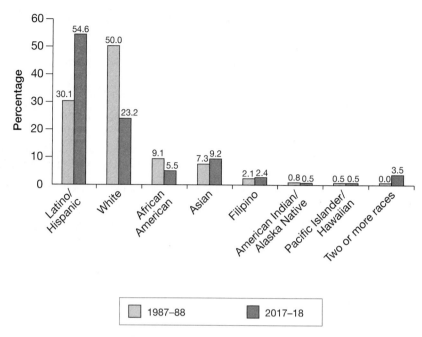

Figure 13.3 Public School Diversity in California

Question: To what extent are these trends evident in your community?

Source: California Department of Education

Social Conflict. Broader social changes affecting all segments of society have introduced new levels of conflict in California schools. Two-income parents, single parents, child abuse, parental neglect, and poverty have changed the very mission of public schools. Teachers are not only educators but also disciplinarians, surrogate parents, counselors, social workers, detectives, and nurses. Problems stemming from gangs, gang attire, graffiti, guns on campus, and drug use are increasingly routine. Student behavior often reflects differences based on race, ethnicity, income, gender, sexual orientation, and religious faith. Some students have even formed their own ethnic clubs. A few high schools have experienced a countertrend, the creation of "gay/ straight" alliances—clubs designed to discuss matters of sexual orientation with tolerance and acceptance in mind.

The Funding Challenge. In absolute numbers, California spends far more on education than any other state, over $80 billion in 2019–20. This translates to over $17,000 per pupil from all funding sources. The amount has grown quickly in recent years due to strong revenue growth, but California has ranked near the bottom of states in the last few decades. More recent state comparisons place California somewhere between 20th and 46th among the 50 states, depending on the methodology.[6] Although its teachers are relatively well paid, California ranks among the worst states in numbers of administrators, counselors, and librarians per student (i.e., too few).[7] Education spending in California results from numerous pressures involving court decisions, statewide propositions, enrollment growth, and substantive education policymaking:

1. In one court decision, *Serrano v. Priest* (1971), the California Supreme Court ruled that California's education finance system based on local property values created spending disparities between districts, in violation of equal protection provisions of the state constitution. Proposition 13 centralized education funding and that funding is largely equal between districts. Yet, spending differences remain. Federal aid and the state's new Local Control Funding Formula (LCFF) compensate for some of the differences. Basic-aid districts (often in wealthy communities) depend solely on property taxes to fund schools. As a result, their annual per-pupil expenditures can be considerably higher than if they received state funding.[8] Although local superintendents, principals, and school boards may be tempted to raise fees for after-school activities and other expenses, state law prohibits them from doing so. These limits do not apply to fund-raising. Accordingly, affluent districts often receive contributions from parents, booster clubs, and foundations—sources not realistically available to poorer districts.

2. California voters have made numerous decisions directly relating to state-wide education funding at the ballot box. These actions have ranged from tax cuts to funding guarantees and massive bond measures.

3. Enrollment change can whipsaw education spending. Because the state provides to most districts per-pupil funding based on average daily attendance, each new student triggers another $17,000 annually in education spending from all sources. But enrollment decreases have the opposite effect, resulting in personnel layoffs and program cuts.

4. In 2013, policymakers adopted the LCFF, which allocates a significant portion (about 87 percent) of education funding based on the percentage of EL and low-income students in a district. Those districts and charter schools with higher concentrations of EL and low-income students receive higher per-pupil funding. The goal is to provide lower performing schools, who usually have more EL and low-income students, with additional resources to improve their performance. The formula eliminated many of the categorical programs that provided targeted funding to meet specific goals and gives school districts more flexibility to meet their needs.

Education Reform

The challenges of enrollment growth, diversity issues, and funding pressures have led to several education reforms in California. In recent years, reform efforts have taken on a sense of urgency. Three areas of education reform reflect both current education trends and the politics of diversity in the state.

Improving Quality. Given the diversity of California students, educational performance is a constant challenge. Although student scores on California assessments have been rising over the last decade, California students still rank near the bottom when compared to their peers in other states. For example, California's fourth-grade students rank 43rd in reading and 46th in math on the National Assessment of Educational Progress. Achievement gaps between low-income (usually minority) and high-income students fare no better (see figure 13.4).[9] Complicating matters is the high number of California students who do not meet state criteria for language proficiency.

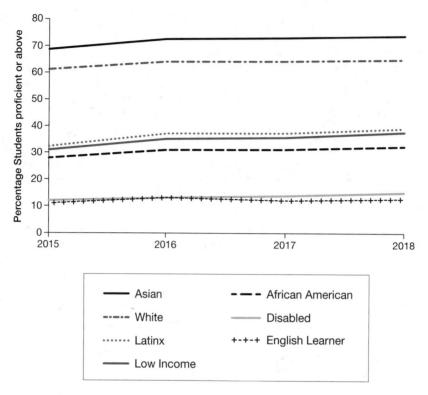

Figure 13.4 K–12 Student Performance Gaps

Question: What factors account for these gaps?

Note: The figures are based on the Smarter Balanced Assessment System, which uses computer tests and performance skills for English language arts and mathematics from the Common Core State Standards.

Source: K-12 Education: California's Future (San Francisco: Public Policy Institute of California, January, 2019).

Efforts to improve educational quality in California are nothing new. The 1983 *Hart Hughes Educational Reform Act* increased high school graduation requirements and provided for longer school days and school years. The 1992 *Charter Schools Act* allowed the creation of parent-, teacher-, or community-established schools that would operate independently of many state and local regulations. In 1996, after experiencing some of the highest student–teacher ratios in the nation, California launched a dramatic class size reduction program. In kindergarten through third grade, class sizes would be limited to 20 students. The results were immediate and mixed. Whereas teacher morale and classroom manageability increased, so did local costs and shortages of classroom space and credentialed teachers. In the late 1990s, new reforms included the monitoring of individual school performance, a mandatory high school exit exam, peer assistance for teachers, various awards and incentives, and new reading programs.

Dissatisfied with state-level reforms, Congress passed the *No Child Left Behind Act* in 2001. This was U.S. President George W. Bush's signature education policy aimed at improving educational quality and represented a significantly expanded role for the federal government. The law required schools to (1) give standardized English and math tests annually from third through eighth grades, (2) increase the number of students scoring high enough to be labeled proficient (100 percent by 2015), and (3) face sanctions for failure to do so. The ambitious performance targets, many thought unrealistic to begin with, were not met by the deadline. The Obama administration waived the performance requirements if states modified their teaching evaluation methods. New legislation adopted in 2015, the Every Student Succeeds Act, granted states more flexibility in designing assessments, measuring student performance, and improving problematic areas. The state is tasked with identifying the bottom 5 percent of schools and assisting districts with improvement plans. The new strategy was deployed in the fall of 2018.[10]

Improving Accountability. The politics of diversity is not limited to funding and reform issues. It also includes how students, schools, and even textbook publishers are held accountable for educational success. Textbook publishers must heed California's massive *Education Code* and work within a variety of frameworks (general curricular goals) and content standards (detailed subject specifications for each grade level). These standards guide local school districts on what to teach and publishers on what to write. For each grade level and subject area, the California Department of Education approves lists of textbooks from which local school districts can choose. Publishers must address questions like these: Should textbooks reflect America's European heritage versus the experience of "marginalized" groups—Latinos, African Americans, LGBT people, and women? Should reading texts be literature-based, phonics-based, or both?

State content standards underwent significant changes as California and 43 other states adapted to and integrated **Common Core** standards. The Common Core is a set of curriculum standards that all participating states have agreed to follow. Most of the content in core subjects is the same across all states, but they are given some flexibility on a small portion of the content. The Common Core began its rollout in the classroom in 2014.

Student and school accountability centers around testing. As educators well know, testing itself can raise as many problems as it purports to solve, leading some to conclude that "the perfect test" is an oxymoron. Accordingly, dissatisfied policymakers move from one statewide test to another or from one testing approach to another. For many years, California relied on the STAR program for testing in grades 2 through 11. In 2015, it began reading and math tests based on the Common Core. Like many states, California also moved to an online testing format.

The effort of schools to comply with frameworks, standards, and tests is never-ending. One problem stems from educational policy fragmentation, frequent policy changes, and lack of policy coordination. Local educators often complain that the state adopts new standards and employs new tests without aligning new textbook and curricula materials accordingly. The Common Core standards are expected to help address this problem. Critics also argue that a greater emphasis on testing skews academic objectives and fosters a "teach-to-the-test" mentality in the schools. California previously relied on an Academic Performance Index, or API, to evaluate performance in schools, but it was criticized for too much emphasis on testing. In 2016, state policymakers adopted a new accountability system, the California School Dashboard, which incorporates more indicators of a school's climate and conditions rather than mainly relying on testing. The dashboard still includes testing in its overall color-coded assessment (blue is for the highest-performing schools), but it also includes nontesting areas like graduation rates, suspension rates, textbook availability, college/career readiness, and parental engagement. The new accountability system is intended to assess a school's overall environment so that deficient areas can be identified and improved. A statewide summary of California's performance under the new system can be found here: https://www.caschooldashboard.org/reports/ca/2018.

Improving Choice. One approach to improving education policy in California is to improve educational choice. Many parents desire choice as a matter of principle; some school reformers claim it would encourage competition between schools resulting in educational improvement statewide. The most radical proposals have involved school vouchers, certificates issued by the state that parents could apply toward private school tuition. Proponents argue that, because public schools are wasteful and overly bureaucratic, parents deserve a choice of schools. Competition from voucher-funded private schools would also force public schools to improve. Opponents have feared that vouchers would drain public education budgets and allow private schools to deny access to poor families and "problem" students—the physically impaired, EL students, or low academic achievers. California voters overwhelmingly rejected two such voucher plans in 1993 and 2000.

Short of vouchers, less radical "managed choice" options are available. Charter schools—public schools that operate with fewer state regulations—have provided educational alternatives for a relatively small, but rapidly growing, number of Californians. More than 1,300 charter schools now serve 660,000 students, or 10 percent of the total student population. Compared to traditional schools, charter schools in California have a smaller percentage of Latinx students, low-income families, and EL students, but the gap is narrowing. Are they academically superior? Results are mixed. Traditional public schools outperform charter schools at the elementary level and lag charter schools at the middle and high school levels. Other choices are available. State law now allows intra- and interdistrict transfers. Once tied to their neighborhood school, space permitting, students may attend public schools within their districts or in other districts where their commuting parents work. These options allow parents to seek out more successful schools, but this choice is problematic if other schools are also underperforming or, due to budget cuts, cannot accommodate additional students.

In one sense, these choice-oriented policies reflect the popularity of "market" approaches to public services generally. But in another sense, they reflect a disintegration of majoritarian policymaking in education—where all Californians contribute and from which all equally benefit. General taxes still fund education, but the product itself is increasingly differentiated or fragmented. Educational choice seems a ready option for California's middle class and wealthy families. That is less the case for disadvantaged families and poorer school districts. Again, many challenges facing education in California find roots in social, economic, and demographic trends well beyond the control of educators.

HIGHER EDUCATION: AN UNCERTAIN FUTURE

Historically, Californians have taken pride in their institutions of higher education. But population growth, increased cultural diversity, and chronic underfunding have raised some profound issues for the state's colleges and universities. Students and faculty know the symptoms of the problem only too well. Fees are raised, courses are canceled, graduation plans are delayed, and needs outpace revenues. For many public university students, a four-year baccalaureate degree is largely a myth. How have these pressures come about?

The Majoritarian Ideal

Like other western states, California lacked a significant private college sector in the decades following statehood. In its place, the state developed a comprehensive public system of higher education, featuring high quality and open access. Initially, the *Organic Act of 1868* created the University of California. Later, state teachers' colleges and junior (or two-year) colleges were added. Concurrently, numerous private colleges and universities were established with little state attention or help. Anticipating an enrollment surge by baby boomers in the 1960s, the legislature passed the *Donahoe Higher Education Act of 1960*—commonly called the **Master Plan for Higher Education**. According to a legislative report, what began as a modest agreement between educational institutions evolved into a "world-renowned social compact" that articulated a bold vision for the future.[11]

The plan did three things. First, it prescribed enrollment parameters for each level. The University of California (UC) campuses would admit students from the top 12.5 percent of high school seniors, California State University (CSU) campuses (formerly the teachers' colleges) would admit the top one-third, and the community college system (formerly the junior colleges) would admit any student capable of benefiting from instruction. Low fees and no tuition would provide ready access to the academically qualified at UC and CSU, although admission to any particular campus was not guaranteed. Second, the Master Plan assigned different missions to each level. UC would emphasize research, graduate programs, and offer doctoral degrees. CSU would focus on liberal arts teaching and professional education through the master's degree. Community colleges would provide standard college courses for transfer to four-year institutions, plus vocational and technical training. The transfer function was to be paramount. Third, the Master Plan created governance structures to operate each sector and to resolve the inevitable turf battles that would occur.

The entire system grew beyond all projections in the decades that followed. Today, the overall system encompasses a huge complex of campuses throughout California. UC consists of 10 general campuses and one health science campus, enrolling about 280,000 undergraduate and graduate students. CSU consists of 23 campuses and six off-campus centers, enrolling 480,000 students, making it the largest university system in the nation. The state's 114 community college campuses and other sites enroll 2.1 million students. California's 76 accredited independent colleges, universities, professional schools, and other specialized campuses enroll another 330,000 students. Although the "privates" produce only a quarter of the state's baccalaureate degrees, they produce more than half of the master's and doctoral degrees and most of the professional degrees. Widely perceived as less diverse than public universities, 60 percent of students at private institutions have ethnic backgrounds that are not white.[12]

Rethinking the Plan

In recent years, revenue shortfalls and ensuing budget deficits have hit higher education's share of the state budget. University and college administrators have responded by authorizing significant budget cuts and sizable fee increases. Students have grumbled, protested, and transferred to community colleges, private colleges, or even to out-of-state public universities. Community college fees have also increased during this period. The students least able to absorb these increases have dropped out of college altogether. How much longer can these systems tolerate both enrollment and funding pressures?

Policy discussions in recent years have focused on three interlocking issues: access, performance, and pricing. First, how can California's colleges and universities provide access to growing numbers of students when resources are finite? Access is an especially sensitive matter for California's college-bound minorities and lower-income families. Responding to this issue, a Legislative Analyst's report recommended that the CSU campuses (where access is so crucial) work to better accommodate students from their immediate regions.[12]

Second, the performance of the higher education segments has come under fire as a result of low graduation and completion rates. At one time, it was expected that students would graduate within four years, but six-year periods are routinely used to measure performance at "four-year" universities and three-year periods are used at community colleges (see figure 13.5). Although UC's six-year

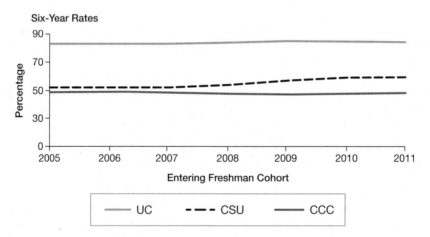

Figure 13.5 Higher Education Performance

Question: What can the higher education segments do to increase their graduation and completion rates?

Note: UC and CSU figures represent six-year graduation rates. The CCC figure represents the six-year completion rate, which includes students who attain a degree or certificate, transfer to a four-year institution, or become transfer-prepared. The years represent the year a freshman cohort entered the institutions and the rates for that cohort.

Source: "CalFacts" (Sacramento: Legislative Analyst's Office, 2018).

graduation rate is above 80 percent, CSU's has been growing more quickly in recent years, reaching over 60 percent. California Community Colleges' (CCC)'s six-year completion rate is about 50 percent. A number of reasons have been cited for this low performance: course availability, the lack of student support services, job demands, unmet financial needs, and academic choices. In order to track this problem, the legislature now requires the higher education segments to report annually on a set of performance measures, including graduation and completion rates.

Third, the era of ultra-low fees appears to have ended. Fees at UC campuses now exceed $13,000 per year; at CSU, fees are about half that. (UC officials now admit that their fees are actually "tuition." CSU officials maintain the "fee" terminology; only out-of-state students pay tuition.) CCC fees are still a relative bargain at under $1,000. State funding support for higher education has declined dramatically in recent decades, forcing students to shoulder a much larger share of the burden than earlier generations of students. State funding support, however, may level out temporarily with the passage of Propositions 30 and 55 and may even begin to increase again. Even with renewed state support and more stable tuition rates, the cost of higher education is much higher than just a few years ago. The Master Plan's promise of broad access to quality and affordable higher education seems strained at best. Former governor Jerry Brown put it this way: "It used to be four years and free. Now in many cases it's six years and expensive."[13]

Higher Education for Undocumented Students

One intriguing issue combines access, pricing, and federal/state conflict. Should undocumented immigrant students be charged in-state or out-of-state tuition at California's public colleges and universities? Being allowed to pay in-state tuition saves California residents as much as $23,000 a year. Federal law (the *Illegal Immigration Reform and Immigrant Responsibility Act of 1996*) prohibits undocumented persons from receiving in-state tuition at public institutions of higher education. It also denies them various kinds of federal financial aid. In contrast, several states with high immigrant populations, including California, have passed laws allowing in-state tuition for the undocumented, if they have attended high school in the state for three or more years. California's law, AB 540, includes that high school exemption. It also requires students to file an affidavit (a written declaration under oath) stating that they are seeking to legalize their status or will do so when eligible.

Policy action and inaction surrounding this issue involve the courts, the U.S. Congress, and the California legislature. In 2010, the California Supreme Court unanimously ruled that undocumented students are eligible for the same tuition as legal residents of the state. The justices reasoned that because the high school attendance exemption was available to all students regardless of immigration status, it applied to qualified undocumented students as well.[14] This ruling was likely to benefit an estimated 40,000 California students, the vast majority of whom attend the state's community colleges. Opponents of the decision vowed to appeal.

In recent years, Congress has considered legislation to allow states to charge undocumented students in-state tuition. The Development, Relief, and Education for Alien Minors Act, known as the **DREAM Act**, would also provide a multistep path toward citizenship for those students who were brought to the United States as children. In 2011, after Congress failed to pass the DREAM Act, the California legislature enacted the state's version. The legislation allows undocumented students to qualify for in-state tuition as well as private and state-funded financial aid.

More recently, as the Trump administration ramped up efforts to deport undocumented immigrants, undocumented students encountered more trouble returning to the United States after traveling abroad and some faced deportation. State and education leaders vowed to protect students from possible deportation. The 2018 budget included more than $20 million that went to public universities and colleges to provide legal services to undocumented students and their family members.

SOCIAL PROGRAMS

The Golden State has a long history of social programs that cushion the impact of life's slings and arrows. For example, California's workers' compensation system (to assist injured employees) dates back to the Progressive era. Still other programs are a legacy of the New Deal in the 1930s and the War on Poverty in the 1960s. Like other states, social programs in California are a jerry-built arrangement of multiple agencies and financial partnerships that span every layer of the federal system. In child care services alone, nearly 50 programs are administered by 13 California agencies. A patchwork of social programs reflects the different times in which they were enacted, mixed priorities, and approaches, plus some measure of ambivalence toward those in need. In fact, the history of social policy typifies **ambivalent benevolence**—on one hand, a caring concern for California's "truly needy" and, on the other, a reluctance to support overreliance on public assistance.

Taken together, California's social programs consumed nearly 30 percent of the state's general fund for 2019–20. In recent decades, this share of the budget has grown due to rising unemployment, high birth rates among the poor, continued immigration, high divorce rates, federal mandates, and a rising number of seniors. These programs received significant funding cuts in the wake of the Great Recession, but some of the support has been restored in recent years.

Who are California's poor? Over 13 percent of all Californians fall below official poverty guidelines. In 2018, the threshold for a family of four was $25,100 (and somewhat higher in Alaska and Hawaii). When a more comprehensive poverty measure is used, one that incorporates regional cost of living, government assistance, and other household expenses, California's poverty level jumps another 6 percent to 19 percent. Poverty rates are especially high for children overall (21 percent), Latinxs (26 percent), and African Americans (19 percent). Another 20 percent of Californians are near poverty, but just above the income thresholds. Contrary to popular impressions, nearly half of poor families have at least one person working full-time. Where do they live? The highest rates of poverty occur in Los Angeles County (about 24 percent), and the lowest rate was in El Dorado County (about 12 percent).[15]

Welfare Policy
Programs to help the poor are deeply rooted in perceptions about the poor. Americans perceive the poor as either deserving or undeserving. The **deserving**

poor or truly needy are poor presumably through no fault of their own. Children, the blind and disabled, the laid-off unemployed, and the elderly fall into this category. The **undeserving poor** include unemployed able-bodied adults, especially men; the "lifestyle" poor or unemployed; and abusers of drugs and alcohol. Presumably, these individuals have chosen their lot in life, and the personal consequences are not society's fault or responsibility. California's policies toward those in need combine these two perceptions. The largest programs target needy families, children, those who are elderly or disabled, and other adults. Although the dollar amounts and numbers served seem high, costs have actually been shaved in recent budgets in response to lower tax revenues.

1. *Families.* California's major program to aid needy families is **CalWORKs** (California Work Opportunity and Responsibility to Kids). This program implements the federal Temporary Assistance for Needy Families program that, under welfare reform, replaced the old Aid to Families with Dependent Children. It provides time-limited cash assistance to eligible families in times of crisis. The state's 58 counties administer the program. In 2019, the maximum monthly cash grant for a family was $785. For families that dip in and out of poverty, the cumulative limit on aid has been reduced from five to four years. Recipients must participate in job skills training and various work activities with the goal of becoming permanently self-sufficient. In 2013, the cumulative time limit for adults was further reduced to two years if these work requirements were not met. In 2017, the average number of CalWORKs recipients was 1.1 million, more than 80 percent of which were children. Is the program working? If the goal is to reduce poverty, then the answer is yes. According to the Public Policy Institute of California, more than 400,000 Californians would be in poverty if it weren't for CalWORKs support and another 190,000 would be in deep poverty.[16]

   Supplementing CalWORKs is CalFresh, the former federal food stamp program that provides nutritional assistance to eligible low-income families. Recipients receive bank-like debit cards to pay for food at participating grocery stores. In recent years, more than 4 million Californians, or 10 percent of the population, received food aid worth about $150 per recipient per month. Less than half of eligible California families participated in the program at one time, but that rate has increased to 70 percent.[17] Experts attribute under-enrollment to insufficient knowledge of the benefit, laborious paperwork, and fear among Spanish-dominant Latinxs that food stamps will negatively affect their employment or immigration status.[18]

2. *Children.* Obviously, children benefit if a parent qualifies under CalWORKs. Benefits include not only monthly cash assistance but also publicly funded child care while parents work or receive training. But there are many other programs to help California's high-risk children. The Child Protective Services program intervenes when there is evidence or suspicion of in-home child abuse or neglect. The state's foster care program places more than 60,000 such children with relatives, foster families, or group homes. The Cal-Learn program assists pregnant and parenting teenagers

to obtain high school diplomas or the equivalent. The Child Support Enforcement Program locates and requires noncustodial parents to pay court-ordered child support.

3. *Seniors and Disabled.* A variety of programs also assist the elderly and disabled. Some of them are separated from the largest federal programs, Social Security, and Medicare. People 60 years or older may receive continuing care at state-approved facilities. In-Home Supportive Services provides a variety of services to help seniors, the disabled, or blind remain in their homes. The federal Supplemental Security Income (SSI) program is part of Social Security. It provides monthly cash aid to 1.3 million aged, blind, and disabled Californians who meet the program's income and resource requirements. California augments the SSI payment with a State Supplemental Payment grant. Maximum individual grants from both the federal and state programs are about $930 per month. With a rapidly growing senior population, these programs are among the fastest growing in the state.

Health Policy

As Americans grow in number and live longer, medical care becomes a major policy issue at both the state and federal levels. Unlike welfare policy, health policy commingles the public and private sectors, both in terms of care and funding. The "medical industrial complex," consisting of medical professionals, hospitals, and insurance companies, dominates the system. Two simple truths govern the politics of health care. First, costly medical care does not necessarily equal good health; being healthy has a great deal to do with heredity, lifestyle, social conditions, and physical environment. Second, health services (both public and private) involve a vast transfer of wealth. In the public sector, this means in effect transferring resources from (less-needy) higher-income to lower-income (more-needy) Americans. In private-sector health care, it means transferring resources from the healthy to the sick and those who care for them. Although taxes and insurance premiums fund medical care in these two sectors, people rarely receive in care exactly what they have "paid" in taxes or premiums. Redistributing health dollars in both the private and public sector is a fact of life. California's approach to aiding the sick is multifaceted and increasingly expensive. It includes three broad approaches: private insurance, Medi-Cal, and deinstitutionalization. In 2010, Congress adopted major health care reform—the **Affordable Care Act (ACA)**—to address major health care challenges that have dramatically changed the landscape in our system. Later, we describe that landscape both before and after the adoption of the ACA.

Private Insurance. In the United States, our health care system depends heavily on private insurance. Traditionally, state-regulated insurance companies paid doctors on a **fee-for-service** basis. Each medical procedure had a price, and insurance companies unquestioningly paid whatever it was at the time it was rendered. Increasingly, insurance companies and doctors have been moving to **managed care**: networks of doctors and hospitals providing comprehensive services for a predetermined price. In recent years, 60 percent of California's nonelderly have been covered by employer-provided or privately purchased health insurance. What about the rest? Prior to the ACA, more than 7 million Californians lacked health insurance of any kind, ranking the state near the bottom in the percentage of residents without health care. Up to 75 percent of uninsured children, or about 771,000, qualified for Medi-Cal or Healthy Families, two major state programs, but were not enrolled. The rest were workers and their dependents whose employers provided no private health insurance (a common practice in agriculture, construction, retail, and small businesses) but who earned too much money to qualify for publicly funded care. They included the "working poor," but one-third were families with incomes over $50,000. Lack of health insurance disproportionately affected Latinxs and foreign-born adults.[19]

For years, people would lose their insurance if they switched jobs, were laid off, or a new insurance carrier discovered a "preexisting condition" such as AIDS or cancer. Although Congress passed legislation in 1996 guaranteeing the portability of health insurance coverage for those who lose or leave their jobs, that law does not help those who lacked insurance in the first place.

The ACA sought to address the uninsured problem in several ways. First, it expanded eligibility for the state's Medi-Cal program by increasing income limits, which will be discussed in more detail. Second, for private insurance, it imposed a number of changes. For those not eligible for Medi-Cal or an employer-sponsored plan, California established a state-run insurance exchange (some states use a federally run exchange) that allows individuals to use federal subsidies to purchase plans with varying levels of coverage. The exchange, called Covered California, launched in 2013 and enrolls about 1.2 million people, with nearly 90 percent of them qualifying for a federal subsidy. It is unknown how many of the new enrollees previously lacked insurance altogether. Provisions of the ACA also prohibited denials for preexisting conditions and required insurance companies to cover dependents up to 26 years of age. To avoid the incentive for only sick people to sign up for coverage, the ACA required everyone to purchase a plan, known as the individual mandate, or face a tax penalty. Congress repealed the individual mandate in 2017 and more than 260,000 Californians are expected to drop their coverage. Other provisions require employers to offer an insurance plan if they have more than 50 employees or also pay a penalty.[20]

Medi-Cal. California's version of the federal Medicaid program for low-income individuals is called **Medi-Cal**. Medi-Cal pays for two types of care—core and optional services. Federally required core services include access to physicians and nurses, hospital care, laboratory tests, home care, and preventative services for children. Federal matching funds are available for any of 34 optional services such as hospice care, adult dentistry, and chiropractic services. CalWORKs and SSI/SSP recipients, qualified expectant mothers, and poor children automatically receive Medi-Cal benefits. Other low-income people qualify but pay for a portion of their medical care.

Prior to the ACA, Medi-Cal spending generally increased or decreased in response to economic trends, various eligibility expansions, and state-imposed cost controls on health care providers. In 2011, about 7.5 million Californians participated in Medi-Cal. Since the ACA, Medi-Cal enrollment surged to 13.2 million, accounting for much of the reduction in the uninsured population (see figure 13.6). This huge influx of enrollees was the result of two changes brought by the ACA. First, the income limit for eligibility was increased to 138 percent of the federal poverty level and, for the first time, childless adults could qualify.

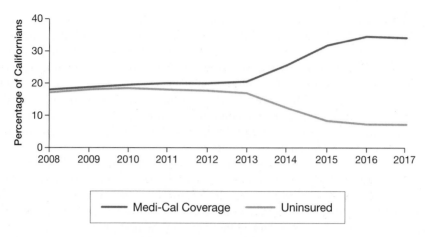

Figure 13.6 Medi-Cal and the Uninsured Population

Question: What else can California do to reduce the uninsured population?

Source: Health Care: California's Future (San Francisco: Public Policy Institute of California, January 2019).

For these new enrollees, the federal government picked up 100 percent of the cost in the initial years, but that is decreasing to 90 percent after 2020. Second, state outreach efforts also targeted those individuals who were previously eligible for Medi-Cal prior to the ACA, notifying them of simpler eligibility and enrollment rules. As was previous practice, California only receives a 50 percent match from the federal government for these enrollees. Despite federal funding support for certain enrollees, the state's share of costs is expected to significantly increase in the coming years.

What about health care for California's large immigrant population? Are they deserving or undeserving of Medi-Cal support? This has been the subject of protracted policy debate, political hyperbole, and numerous legal challenges. The result has been public confusion over coverage and frustration over perceived costs. This we know: (1) compared to the native-born, immigrants in California are less likely (and in some counties far less likely) to have health insurance; (2) undocumented immigrants do not qualify for publicly funded or subsidized health insurance programs, *including the ACA* (their citizen children do); (3) immigrants are less likely to seek out regular health care, thereby incurring lower health care costs; and (4) when seeking medical care, immigrant families are more likely to pay out-of-pocket for such care.[21]

What does this discussion tell you? California's health care system has undergone significant changes in recent years. Although the implementation of the ACA significantly reduced the uninsured population, an estimated 3 million Californians remain uninsured, of which two-thirds are Latinx and more than 40 percent are noncitizens.[22] Those uninsured will continue to turn to emergency rooms for routine care because emergency rooms cannot refuse service. Some state funding is allocated to local hospitals and health care networks to address this population, but it remains inadequate. Even with the federal government covering most of the costs of Medi-Cal expansion, experts believe the newly eligible population, along with those purchasing individual policies on the exchange, will strain a system that already has trouble keeping pace with demand for health care. In 2019, Governor Gavin Newsom and other policymakers began to discuss options to further expand insurance to those uninsured, including the possibility of a single-payer system, where the state government would be the sole funder of health care (with federal assistance). Such an ambitious proposal would be quite costly and is one that California's budget is unlikely to absorb anytime soon.

Deinstitutionalization. A much-less discussed health care approach in California has been the **deinstitutionalization** of the mentally ill. Historically, psychiatric patients were placed in institutions, apart from society and family. Prior to the 1960s, California had a reasonably progressive and balanced approach, including prevention and early intervention in mental cases. But in the 1960s, two trends merged. First, Governor Reagan persuaded the legislature to reduce funding for mental health programs and shift them to the counties. Second, mental health professionals embraced a new treatment philosophy that placed mental patients in communities, not institutions. Neighborhoods and families would help "mainstream" the mentally ill. In California, these forces converged in the *Lanterman–Petris–Short Act of 1968.* In effect a civil rights law, it made the confinement of unwilling mental patients exceedingly difficult.

Ironically and even tragically, many mental patients were victimized by this "reform." A decade later, Proposition 13 cut revenue for just the mental health programs these people needed. Anticipated community-based mental health centers never materialized. Many former mental patients did not return to families or live in group homes—they became homeless. Indeed, thousands of California's homeless population have disabilities, mental illness, or other health problems. Many call jail home because without close supervision or daily medication they lose control and commit crimes.

We should be clear that the homeless population in California, around 135,000 people, is not limited to the mentally ill and the chronically homeless. Even if they are employed, many Californians live from paycheck to paycheck. A layoff, catastrophic illness, or bank foreclosure could quickly result in life on the streets. Advocacy groups and those who serve the homeless report an increase in the homeless population due to the state's housing foreclosure crisis in the late 2000s. The state's chronic housing shortage and high housing costs also contribute to the problem.

How do the state and local governments respond to this issue? Shelters (some are open only in winter months), low-cost hotels, parking lots set aside for those who live out of their vehicles, and other "transitional housing" provide at least temporary accommodation but cannot meet the need entirely. Recognizing the severity of the problem, Newsom proposed $600 million in spending to care for the homeless and a new commission to tackle the issue in 2019. The new state approach stands in contrast to how some local officials have clashed with the homeless and their supporters over the use of property for their encampments. In 2007, a federal court ruled that the City of Fresno violated the constitutional rights of the homeless when sanitation crews bulldozed their shelters and belongings. At a deeper level, in California this represents a clash of civic values—authentic compassion for those in need versus the impulse to protect property values, tourism, and business interests.

CONCLUSION

California's size, diverse population, and cultural hyperpluralism affect its politics and policies in some profound ways. Many policies mirror the pushing and pulling of various interest groups based on ethnic, gender, class, lifestyle, or religious differences.

Examples abound in California. Abortion policy is essentially a continuing struggle among diverse values and contrary views over the right of privacy, moral authority, and the meaning of personhood. Education policy struggles to address enrollment growth, ethnic diversity, social change, a parade of education reforms, and funding shortfalls. Higher education faces a crossroad as the grand social compact called the Master Plan seems less venerable and more vulnerable. Even immigration impacts higher education as undocumented students seek the same benefits as residents of the state. The sheer magnitude of California's social programs reflects a subtle rivalry between California's taxpayers and tax spenders, a contest exacerbated in recent years by economic inequality. Today, the broad forces of economic volatility, growth, and diversity promise to challenge California's political system as never before. Forging a new multicultural democracy will be painful and controversial, straining both government institutions and policymakers at the state, regional, and local levels. Given demographic and economic trends, multicultural democracy in California will also strain public budgets to their limits as demands for more spending by some groups confront demands for less spending by others. The old Chinese curse "May you live in interesting times" seems particularly suited to modern California politics.

KEY TERMS

cultural amalgamation (p. 286)
cultural separatism (p. 286)
cultural assimilation (p. 286)
cultural hyperpluralism (p. 287)
social issues (p. 288)
Common Core (p. 295)
Master Plan for Higher Education
  (p. 297)
DREAM Act (p. 300)

ambivalent benevolence (p. 300)
deserving poor (p. 300)
undeserving poor (p. 301)
CalWORKs (p. 301)
Affordable Care Act (ACA) (p. 302)
fee-for-service (p. 302)
managed care (p. 302)
Medi-Cal (p. 303)
deinstitutionalization (p. 305)

REVIEW QUESTIONS

1. Why is there so little common ground among foes on abortion and LGBT rights? What might common ground look like?
2. Describe the pressures facing K–12 education in California.

3. To what extent and why is the Master Plan in trouble? How might that be evident in your own experience?
4. What are the pros and cons of undocumented students receiving in-state tuition?
5. Survey California's array of social welfare programs and analyze the pressures on each of them. Which Californians are easiest and hardest to help and why? In your view, does ambivalent benevolence describe California social policy?
6. Describe some of the recent changes in the California health care system. How has the ACA affected health insurance coverage for Californians?
7. What factors contribute to California's homeless population?

WEB RESOURCES

California Department of Education
https://www.cde.ca.gov
This site contains a wealth of data on virtually every aspect of K–12 education policy in California.

California Department of Social Services
https://www.cdss.ca.gov

Provides complete descriptions of most major social service programs offered or funded by the state.

Legislative Analyst's Office
https://lao.ca.gov
The Legislative Analyst's Office provides nonpartisan fiscal and policy advice on, among other topics, K–12 education, higher education, health care, and social services.

Glossary

A

adversarial justice The basis of judicial decision making whereby the process and result involves a contest between two conflicting sides. Judges and juries find the "truth" in and around these conflicting claims.

Affordable Care Act (ACA) The federal health care reform law that sought to expand health insurance coverage through an individual mandate, health insurance exchanges, and Medicaid expansion; individuals are required to sign up for health insurance coverage with the help of federal subsidies or pay a tax penalty; employers with more than 50 employees are also required to provide coverage for their workers or pay a penalty.

alternative dispute resolution (ADR) An effort to settle a civil case before a trial actually begins.

ambivalent benevolence An approach to welfare policy where, on one hand, the public demonstrates a caring concern for the truly needy and, on the other, shows a reluctance to support an overreliance on public assistance.

appropriation process The ability of the legislature to create spending authority, which allows agencies to implement their responsibilities.

arbitration A form of alternative dispute resolution where both sides must accept, by law or prior agreement, a decision by an arbitrator.

Arraignment The first step in a criminal trial where a judge informs the accused of the charges and the legal options available.

Assembly Speaker The top leadership post in the lower chamber that retains broad powers to appoint committee members, manage floor action, and assign office space and staff.

authorization process The ability of the legislature to give authority for an agency program to exist.

B

ballot-box budgeting Occurs when measures are placed on the ballot, either through the initiative process or by the legislature, that modify the budget process, change the tax system, or redirect spending.

Big Four Four post–Gold Rush era businessmen who built the Southern Pacific Railroad and exerted wide-ranging political influence.

Big Three The group of state policymakers that meets toward the end of the budget process to resolve outstanding issues between the executive and legislative branches; consists of the governor, the Assembly Speaker, and the Senate president pro tempore.

bills proposed state statutes.

black gold The discovery and production of oil, as well as the resulting growth and diversification of the state's economy.

budget A plan that specifies what monies will be spent (expenditures) and how those monies will be obtained (revenue).

C

California Progressivism Refers to the movement's experience in California as individualistic, moralistic, white, middle class, urban, nonradical, and dependent on entrepreneurial leadership.

California Supreme Court The pinnacle of California's judicial system, the Supreme Court decides important constitutional issues and maintains legal uniformity across the state. It chooses cases selectively but must hear all death penalty appeals.

CalWORKS California's version of the federal welfare program, Temporary Assistance for Needy Families, that provides time-limited cash assistance to eligible families.

cap and trade A program to reduce carbon emissions where the government sets pollution caps and issues allowances, or carbon credits, to polluting businesses; the credits allow businesses to pollute as long as they meet their individual limits and aggregate pollution is under the cap; companies that successfully reduce emissions below their limit can sell their credits to less successful businesses to offset the excess carbon they produce.

centralized federalism The federal government takes on greater roles and authority in domestic policymaking, even preempting states on occasion.

charter counties Those California counties that have constitution-like documents replacing some general laws regarding elections, compensation, powers, and duties.

civil service The idea that permanent government employees should be hired and evaluated based on merit, not politics.

clemency Judicial powers that allow the governor to grant acts of mercy, including a pardon, which allows the governor to release a convicted criminal; a commutation, which allows a sentence reduction; and a reprieve, which postpones a sentence.

climate change The long-range environmental impact of the buildup of gases that allow the sun to penetrate the atmosphere but prevent it from escaping, which is also known as the greenhouse effect; also used interchangeably with global warming.

command and control A policy approach that relies on issuing regulations, setting standards, and ordering offenders to comply with legal requirements.

Common Core A set of curriculum standards adopted by California and other states that brings uniformity to subject content across states.

complaint The first step in a civil case wherein the aggrieved party, the plaintiff, files a specific claim against a defendant and proposes a remedy.

components of California hyperpluralism (1) constancy of individualism: the tendency of Californians to depend on self rather than on society to fulfill both needs and wants; (2) diversity of interests and cultures: civic participation that is characterized by groups that advocate relatively narrow agendas that decrease the potential for intergroup consensus; (3) fading majoritarianism: decision-making on public policy that is either subject to supermajoritarian votes or based on participation from a small percentage of eligible voters; (4) structural conflict: a system characterized by horizontal power struggles between the executive legislative and judicial branches and vertical power struggles between state and local government.

Compulsory Referendum In this commonly used referendum, voters must approve a legislative action for it to take effect, such as ratifying constitutional amendments or approving bond measures.

conference committees Committees formed to iron out the differences between two versions of the same bill adopted in each house; the unified bill is sent back to both houses for final passage.

Constitution of 1849 Established by a constitutional convention, California's first constitution blended several theories of governing, provided the basic structure of the state's government, and created a declaration of rights.

Constitution of 1879 The state's revised constitution, much longer and detailed than the first, and containing numerous flaws.

constitutional amendments Modifications to the constitution that require a two-thirds vote in the legislature and approval from a majority of voters at a subsequent election.

constitutional convention One method of constitutional change whereby the legislature calls for a constitutional convention to meet and write a new constitution; used only once in California in 1878.

constitutionalism The idea of limited government or government operating within certain rules.

cooperative federalism Here, the roles between federal and state government become blurred and intermingled, making both levels active policy partners.

councils of governments (COGs) These regional governments encompass one or more counties and provide a forum for regional concerns, perform long-range planning, and administer a mix of regional transportation funds and projects.

county central committee The lowest level in the structure of the state party organization and consists elected party members who compete for influence with other elected officials and unofficial party clubs.

crowd lobbying Interest group members who gather in Sacramento for briefings to "play lobbyist for a day" as they roam capitol hallways.

cruise control spending State expenditures that are automatically determined each year by previous legislation and decisions.

cultural amalgamation The process of diverse peoples and cultures intermingling to form one, dominant culture.

cultural assimilation The belief that minority groups must adopt the practices and characteristics of the host society in order to succeed.

cultural hyperpluralism A society characterized by various ethnic, racial, religious, and other groups balancing the ideal of "one people" with the reality of group identity.

cultural separatism The unintentional and intentional division of races, ethnicities, and cultures, often through discrimination or housing segregation.

cumulative policymaking The decision patterns of trial court judges that reveal policy preferences over years of deciding comparable cases.

D

deinstitutionalization The process of releasing mentally ill patients to the community from institutions under the assumption that neighborhoods and families will mainstream them and improve their condition.

delegates Representatives who base their decisions on the wishes of their constituents and seek out their input.

democratic theory A model of how a political system ruled by "the people" should ideally work based on five criteria: (1) equality in voting; (2) effective citizen participation; (3) enlightened understanding; (4) final control over the government agenda; and (5) inclusion.

depositions During discovery, opposing lawyers themselves may seek oral testimony under oath from the other side.

deserving poor A view that the truly needy are poor through no fault of their own.

discovery Following an initial complaint in a civil case, discovery involves the gathering of information by both sides in preparation for trial.

district courts of appeal These appellate courts hear appeals from superior courts and quasi-judicial state agencies and decide questions of law, not fact.

DREAM Act A federal legislative proposal that provides a multistep path toward citizenship for those students who were brought to the United States as children. California's Dream Act (2011) allows eligible students to apply for and receive certain forms of financial aid.

dual federalism An early form of federalism featuring a clear division of labor between the federal government and assuming the states would make most domestic policy decisions.

E

earmarking Allocating or restricting certain revenues to certain purposes.

elite and class politics A perspective on how government works that assumes society naturally divides into two classes: the few who rule, usually wealthy individuals and corporations, and the many who do not.

elite media News and information outlets that cater to influential, select groups with relatively small numbers of readers or viewers.

entitlements Programs that rely on eligibility criteria to determine who receives benefits, usually in the area of social welfare.

era of limits Governor Jerry Brown's declaration that California should have lowered expectations for the future.

executive branch oversight The power of the legislative branch to oversee and approve decisions made by the governor, such as appointments and budget appropriations.

executive order A directive issued by the governor that has the force of law, but does not need legislative approval; subsequent governors can overturn them.

exit option A form of political participation wherein people opt out of a political system or public policy due to policy dissatisfaction.

external budget process The period when the legislature reviews the governor's budget through committee and floor consideration; it is open to public and interest group input.

F

Fair Political Practices Commission (FPPC) The commission established by the Political Reform Act of 1974 to administer the Act's provisions, including the monitoring of nonfederal elections, issuing advisory opinions, conducting random audits, and levying fines on wrongdoers.

federal gold The rapid growth of and dependence on federal expenditures in California, especially during World War II.

federal plan A bicameral legislature with representation in the Assembly based on population and, in the Senate, each county has no more than one representative.

fee-for-service A health care payment system where each medical procedure has a price and is paid by insurance companies and the patient.

felonies The most serious crimes for which the punishment is time in state prison or the death penalty.

filter-down policy Assumes that as people on the upper rungs of the income ladder move up to better homes, the ones they vacate will be made available to those on the lower rungs.

fiscal committees Committees that handle bills that spend money.

fiscal year The time period for California and many local governments that starts July 1 and ends June 30 that is used for budgeting and accounting purposes.

fiscalization of land use In reaction to Proposition 13, the tendency on the part of local governments to favor sales tax-generating commercial projects such as shopping malls, auto dealerships, and "big box" retailers.

flower petal policy A historical approach to immigration where immigrants are welcome or unwelcome depending on workforce needs at the time.

G

gender gap The margin of difference between the opinions and votes of men and women.

general elections Scheduled on the Tuesday after the first Monday in November, this is where the electorate votes for candidates chosen in the primary, local offices, and on propositions.

general law counties Those California counties that must follow state law relative to the number and duties of county elected officials.

general obligation bonds Loans to government that are backed or secured by the "full faith and credit" of the state; taxes can be raised to support them.

general plan Overall blueprints for the physical development of local communities that are required by the state; they contain general goals for future development, zoning maps, and other projections for future development.

general veto The ability of the governor to reject an entire nonspending or authorization bill.

gerrymandering Reapportioning legislative districts for partisan or other advantages.

Gold Rush The 1848 discovery of gold in California and the subsequent rush of miners and others, resulting in the state's rapid growth and transformation.

grassroots pressure A technique used by interest groups to mobilize and connect constituents with their representatives on specific policy issues in order to persuade legislators to act in a certain way.

Great Depression A national economic crisis that resulted in the New Deal and a variety of spending projects in California.

H

home rule A principle of state-local relationships where states allow local governments to govern themselves on local matters as they see fit.

homeowner associations A form of privatized governance in planned developments featuring elected boards, bylaws analogous to city charters, and the ability to enforce various self-imposed regulations.

hyperpluralism This view of government suggests that power is thinly scattered among institutions, policymakers, political parties, interest groups, and voters—often leading to ineffective government.

I

ideological bias Media outlets that favor Republicans or Democrats, or conservatives or liberals.

Illegal Immigration Reform and Immigrant Responsibility Act (1996) This law increased criminal penalties for immigration-related offenses and authorized greater border enforcement.

Immigration Reform and Control Act (1986) The law creating an amnesty program leading to legal residency for millions of foreigners, half of them California residents.

impact fees Charges to developers to mitigate the costs of development such as for new roads, sewers, water systems, and schools.

incrementalism An approach to budgeting where the proposed amount for the budget is based on last year's amount.

incumbent gerrymandering Drawing district lines in a way that gives an advantage to incumbents already in office and regardless of party.

independent groups Political organizations that tend to favor Democrats or Republicans and seek to influence election outcomes with campaign spending that is largely unregulated.

indictment A decision to hold a trial resulting from a preliminary hearing in a criminal case.

individualistic subculture Emphasizes the goals, aspirations, and initiative of private individuals or groups.

infractions Minor legal offenses that, if one is found guilty, involve no jail time (such as traffic tickets).

initiative entrepreneurs Those individual activists and policy zealots who qualify initiatives for voters to decide and the specialized, for-profit firms that enable them to do so.

initiative statutes Allows groups and voters to gather enough signatures to place their own statutory proposals on the ballot.

inner circle A set of advisors close to the governor that consists of a chief of staff and a variety of assistants called "secretaries," assigned to legislative matters, administration, the press, appointments and scheduling, and legal affairs.

interest group A body of individuals who share similar goals and organize to influence public policy around those goals.

internal budget process The budget development that occurs in the executive branch by the Department of Finance and all executive agencies and departments prior to the release of the governor's budget in January.

interrogatories During discovery, each side may seek from the other written answers to a series of written questions.

ironies of diversity The contradictions that are often reflected in California's political system, including the following: the state can be both a policy innovator and laggard; its policy generosity is cyclical, contested, and occasionally ambivalent; and while state government often encounters policy paralysis, local governments make policy progress.

J

joint committees Cers.

judicial federalism The ability and willingness of different court systems to produce potentially diverse, fragmented, and contradictory decisions and policy.

judicial socialization The process whereby lawyers learn to think and behave like judges, a process that inculcates judicial norms, fosters ethics, and attention to procedure.

juice committees Legislative committees where members frequently receive campaign contributions from industry groups they regulate.

jury nullification An extreme form of popular justice where individual jurors or entire juries follow their own consciences rather than the law or evidence set before them.

L

legislative proposal A form of constitutional change where legislature passes constitutional amendments as bills and places them before the electorate for approval.

line item veto The ability of the governor to reduce or reject any item in an appropriations (spending) bill.

lobbying The activities that interest groups undertake to influence the policy process.

lobbyists Individuals who represent interest groups in the policy process.

local Agency Formation Commission (LAFCO) A countywide agency that fosters orderly development of local government and studies the possible impacts, especially financial, of proposed incorporations (new cities).

locally undesirable land uses (LULUs) Specific projects, such as landfills or toxic cleanup sites, that are often opposed by nearby property owners.

M

managed care Health care plans where patients seek care from a network of doctors and hospitals providing comprehensive services for a predetermine price.

manager–council cities A city government pattern common in smaller cities that includes a part-time city council and professionally trained city managers or administrators that run the day-to-day affairs of their cities.

mass media The print (newspapers and magazines), electronic (radio and television), and new media (Internet) that funnels information, opinion, and user-friendly analysis to large numbers of people without direct, face-to-face contact.

Master Plan for Higher Education Legislation that established an agreement between California's educational institutions (California State University, University of California, and community colleges) and featured three overarching characteristics: (1) it prescribed enrollment parameters for each segment of the system; (2) it assigned different missions to each segment; for example, UCs would emphasize research, graduate programs, and offer doctoral degrees; and (3) it established governance structures to oversee each segment.

May Revision The modified state budget that the governor releases in mid-May that takes into account updated revenue and expenditure projections.

mayor–council cities A city governing pattern that includes separately elected mayors with relatively strong executive powers relative to an often full-time, elected city council. In these cities, California mayors tend to be less powerful than their national counterparts.

mediation A voluntary version of alternative dispute resolution where both sides agree to a mediator's decision.

Medi-Cal California's version of the federal Medicaid program that provides health insurance coverage for low-income individuals; it pays for two types of care: core, which includes access to physicians and nurses, hospital care, laboratory tests, and other services, and optional services, such as hospice care, dentistry, and chiropractic services.

minor or third parties Political parties that provide alternatives to voters from the two major political parties, the Democrats and Republicans.

misdemeanors More serious than infractions, misdemeanors are lesser crimes that may involve time in a county jail.

Missouri Plan A method of selecting judges, especially at the appellate level, using a combination of initial appointments and subsequent elections. California uses a hybrid of this method.

moralistic subculture Emphasizes a public-spirited citizenry dedicated to the common betterment of all its members.

multitiered workforce A labor pool divided into multiple levels based on employment status and income; the upper tiers include highly educated, well-paid employees in high technology, knowledge-intensive businesses and organizations, while the lower tiers include low-paid, low-status service jobs in retail, agriculture, tourism, and other industries.

N

new federalism A reaction to centralized federalism noted for returning some power to the states and offering revenue sharing between the federal and state governments.

North American Free Trade Agreement (NAFTA) A 1993 law to lower trade barriers between the United States and its neighbors, Mexico and Canada; the effects have been largely regarded as both positive and negative.

moralistic subculture Emphasizes a public-spirited citizenry dedicated to the common betterment of all its members.

not in my backyard (NIMBY) A mentality of opposing undesirable projects that are close to one's property; tactics include circulating antidevelopment petitions, packing public hearings with project opponents, placing initiatives on the ballot, and filing lawsuits.

P

parcel taxes Voter-approved charges to fund government programs or projects that are determined by property type (e.g., residential or commercial), rather than by property value.

partisan gap The sizeable gap between the views of Republicans and Democrats, reflected in the legislature and in the overall electorate.

partisan gerrymander Drawing districts in a way that favors one party or the other; it is usually done by "splintering" a district to dilute one party's strength or packing a district to concentrate one party's voters in that district.

party caucus A party's total membership gathered to conduct business.

party identification The extent to which citizens affiliate with, relate to, or support a specified political party.

party in the electorate Voters who hold partisan affiliations.

party in government Partisan elected officials and institutions, such as the legislature, which organize around party labels.

party organization The formal party apparatus including its structure, staff, budget, rules and processes for achieving its goals.

perimeters of politics The outer limits that in effect contain the scope of political power, including constitutional limits and jurisdictional boundaries.

phantom cities Clusters of populated local development which may be incorporated or unincorporated, but lack the ability to control their own destinies.

planned unit developments (PUDs) Communities that integrate planning tools for housing developments or more complex projects.

plea bargaining A negotiated agreement between a prosecutor and a defendant whereby the latter pleads guilty to a particular charge in exchange for some concession by the prosecution.

plural executive An array of statewide elected officials with cabinet-sounding titles who are separately elected and politically independent of the governor.

pluralist theory An explanation for how government works that is based on how groups share and compete for power to influence public policy with no single group dominating all the time.

political action committees (PACs) The political arms of interest groups, organized to support legislative candidates, statewide campaigns, and ballot measures.

political context Factors in the external environment, such as the economy and political environment, that influence a governor's performance.

political culture The shared beliefs, values, customs, and symbols of a society that affect how the society governs itself.

political development The growth and change that occurs over time within political systems.

political environment The set of social, cultural, economic, and physical attributes that informs and limits how politics is done.

political participation Individual or group activity intended to exercise influence in the political system.

political parties Organized groups that (1) possess certain labels; (2) espouse policy preferences; (3) both nominate and work to elect candidates for public office; and (4) help frame government's postelection policy agenda.

Political Reform Act of 1974 (Proposition 9) The California law that requires disclosure of campaign contributions and expenditures, regulates campaign committees and lobbying activity, and prohibits conflicts of interest by local officials.

political system The structure and process where public policy is made and involves control, influence, power, and authority; in the United States, this includes the 50 states and the federal government.

politicos Representatives who utilize both the trustee and delegate models of representation in their decision-making depending on how controversial specific topics are to their districts.

politics The authoritative allocation of values for a society as a whole.

politics of abundance An extension of the politics of welfare, where California's growing wealth made feasible a social welfare state and a plethora of expected public services.

politics of modernization A time when new political leaders emerge, a statewide economy is forged, and the political masses become the polity of the state.

politics of unification Where the primary function of government is to make a society into a state.

politics of welfare The stage of political development wherein government's role is to manage a well-functioning economy, improve standards of living, and assist the less fortunate.

popular justice The practice of jurors substituting their own judgments contrary to judicial norms.

postindustrial economy An economic system characterized by a large and growing service sector, economic interdependence, rapid change, innovation, and advanced technology.

pragmatic federalism An evolving form of federalism where pragmatic solutions to problems come about through top-down coercion and cost shifting.

preferential nonvoting Nonparticipation in voting based on personal alienation or choice including attitudes, interest, and life style.

preliminary hearing In a felony case, a preliminary hearing determines if there is probable cause to hold a trial.

prescriptive rights Legal access to someone else's source of water with their knowledge.

president pro tempore The top leadership post in the legislature's upper chamber that retains broad powers to appoint committee members, manage floor action, and assign office space and staff.

primary elections Where a state's voters choose party nominees and other candidates for congressional, state, or local offices.

prior appropriation Legal access to a water source claimed by whomever was the first to find or create it.

privatism A view that the development of communities is an ongoing succession of private economic transactions.

progressive reforms Reformers of this era claim credit for direct primaries, at-large elections, nonpartisan elections, merit systems coupled with short ballots, and professional management. They are also responsible for the initiative, referendum, and recall.

progressive taxes A tax rate that increases as income rises; it imposes a heavier burden on upper-income groups.

progressivism An early twentieth-century political movement seeking to rid politics of corrupting influences, return power to "the people," and make government more businesslike.

Proposition 8 This 2008 initiative constitutional amendment placed the prohibition of same-sex marriage in the state constitution but various legal challenges halted that result.

Proposition 11 An initiative constitutional amendment and statute that granted remapping authority over legislative districts and the Board of Equalization to a 14-member independent Citizen Redistricting Commission.

Proposition 13 This 1978 initiative cut local property taxes in half, resulting in service cuts, fee increases, dependence on other sources of revenue, and altered state/local relationships.

Proposition 22 This 2000 initiative statute defined only marriage between and man and a woman as valid or recognized in California. The political aftermath led to Proposition 8.

Proposition 64 This 2018 initiative statute legalized the possession, cultivation, and transport of marijuana for recreational or personal use.

Proposition 215 This 1996 initiative statute legalized the possession and use of marijuana for medical purposes, including serious illnesses and pain relief. It also spawned a new medical marijuana industry and subsequent regulation of it.

protest option A form of political participation wherein people express extreme policy dissatisfaction via public marches, civil disobedience, or even violence.

public opinion The collective beliefs, attitudes, and values held by the citizenry; what people think about politics, public policy, and those aspects of life that affect politics and policy.

public policy Whatever government chooses to do or not to do.

R

race/ethnicity gap The gap in voter turnout between various racial and ethnic groups, resulting in likely voters who are disproportionately white.

racial gerrymandering Historically, this involves drawing district lines so as to disadvantage minority groups and make unlikely the election of minority candidates; more recently, it refers to the opposite—drawing lines to increase the likelihood that a district will elect a minority candidate.

realignment A corrections reform that involves shifting the responsibility for the custody, treatment, and supervision of nonviolent felons from state prisons to the counties.

reapportionment The process of redrawing district lines for the U.S. House of Representatives, the state Assembly, the state Senate, and the Board of Equalization to reflect population growth and movement within the state.

recall (local level) An occasionally used method whereby voters seek to remove one or more members of city councils, county boards of supervisors, special districts, and especially school boards.

recall (state-level) A rarely used method whereby California voters are able to remove a state-level elected official between regular elections. The most famous instance was the removal of Governor Gray Davis in 2003.

recall Permits the electorate to remove state or local elected officials between elections.

recidivism The common pattern of former convicts returning to prison, often for the same or similar felonies.

redevelopment agencies Local agencies that once fostered economic renewal through development incentives and the ability to capture property taxes generated by that development. RDAs were curtailed by the state as a budget reform.

referendum Allows voters to approve or reject statutes already passed by the legislature.

regressive taxes A tax where the effective rate falls as income rises; it imposes a greater burden on lower- rather than on upper-income groups.

resolutions Statements representing the collective opinion of one house or both on miscellaneous topics.

revenue bonds Loans to government that are backed by the future revenue generated by the facility being financed.

riparian rights Legal access to a water source because one lives on or adjacent to the source.

S

scientific polls The various survey techniques used to increase the likelihood that polling samples more nearly reflect the actual views of the larger population.

select committees Legislative committees formed, usually temporarily, to study various issues facing California with long-term solutions in mind.

slate mailers Large postcards sent to voters by campaign-oriented businesses that list "endorsed" candidates and propositions; often candidates and proposition supporters and opponents pay for the endorsements.

social issues Problems that stir human emotions, produce conflict, and divide people unlike most other public policies.

Southern Pacific Railroad The train company owned by the Big Four that included 85 percent of the state's rails.

special districts (dependent) Special districts that are subdivisions of cities and counties formed to fund local activities like parking lots and street lighting.

special districts (independent) Special districts that are separate legal entities with their own elected boards; typically, they provide and finance one particular service, like water or fire protection.

special session A time designated for legislative consideration of pressing issues typically called by the governor when the legislature is not in regular session; concurrent regular and special sessions are infrequent but possible.

split-roll property tax Separates the method for determining the tax burden on commercial and residential properties; uses market value for commercial and industrial properties instead of purchase price.

standing committees Permanent committees in the legislature that have policy jurisdiction over certain subjects and amend, reject, and/or approve bills.

state central committee The key organizational unit for both Republicans and Democrats that consists of hundreds of party leaders, elected officials, and appointees that meet annually to discuss policy issues, select party leaders, hear elected officials and major candidates speak, network with each other, and rally the party faithful.

straw polls Educated but unscientific guesses as to what the public in general or one particular group of people is thinking (e.g., Internet polls).

structural bias Media outlets that structure news to minimize coverage of government and politics and focus more on human-interest stories concerning entertainment, crime, or sports.

structural deficit Occurs when ongoing revenue is insufficient to support ongoing spending; usually lasts at least several years.

structural nonvoting Nonparticipation in voting due to election rules or barriers to voting, such as age or residency restrictions.

subdivision regulations Policies that dictate how a parcel of land can be divided into smaller lots including minimum lot sizes, street standards, and other public improvements required of developers.

superagencies Offices in the executive branch that oversee a plethora of departments and are usually organized around common policy areas, such as transportation or natural resources.

superior courts On the lowest rung of the judicial ladder, these trial courts determine case facts and thereby who is right or wrong in civil cases, and who is innocent or guilty in criminal cases.

T

third-rail issues Politically volatile issues that policymakers avoid, fearing voter wrath.

Three Strikes Law A 1994 law, since amended, that provided 25-years-to-life sentences for those committing a third felony.

top-two primary A nomination system where the top two vote-getters, regardless of party, advance to the general election.

traditionalistic subculture Characterized by the dominance of a small, self-perpetuating, paternalistic ruling elite and a large, compliant nonelite.

trailer bills Legislation that follows and supports the budget bill specifying exact taxes, fee increases, and spending formulas in broad policy areas such as education or transportation.

trustees Representatives who base their voting decisions on their own best judgment rather than the wishes of their constituents who elected them.

two-thirds requirement Refers to the votes necessary (2/3) to pass certain bills in the legislature, such as tax increases; in the Assembly, 54 votes are needed, while 27 are in the Senate.

U

undeserving poor A view that the poor have chosen their lot in life and whose condition is not the fault or responsibility of society; includes unemployed able-bodied adults, especially men, the "lifestyle" poor or unemployed, and abusers of drugs and alcohol.

uniform building codes Policies that regulate the physical components of construction, such as roofing, heating, electric wiring, ventilation, sanitation, and earthquake resistance.

urban villages/edge cities Conglomerations of development (shopping centers, industrial parks, office "campuses," institutions, and residential development) located outside traditional downtowns or central business districts.

V

voter turnout The percentage of those registered voters who actually vote in any particular election.

voter/nonvoter gap Refers to the persistent gap in voter turnout between likely or regular voters and typical nonvoters.

voting age population (VAP) Those in the general population that are eligible to vote, sometimes called the electorate.

Z

zoning ordinances Policies that divide areas of land into districts or zones in order to permit and regulate the type and density of development.

Notes

CHAPTER 1: EXPLAINING CALIFORNIA POLITICS

1. Gavin Newsom, "A California for All," accessed January 9, 2019, https://www.gov.ca.gov/2019/01/07/newsom-inaugural-address.

2. Quoted in Andrew F. Rolle, *California: A History* (New York: Crowell, 1969), 34.

3. David Easton, *The Political System* (New York: Alfred A. Knopf), chapter 5.

4. Harold D. Lasswell, *Politics: Who Gets What, When and How* (New York: McGraw-Hill, 1938).

5. Hans P. Johnson, "A State of Diversity in California Regions: Demographic Trends," *California Counts* (San Francisco: Public Policy Institute of California, May 2002).

6. Frederick Douzet and Kenneth P. Miller, "California's East-West Divide," in *The New Political Geography of California*, eds. Frederick Douzet, Thad Kousser, and Kenneth P. Miller (Berkeley: Berkeley Public Policy Press, 2008).

7. Mark Baldassare, *PPIC Statewide Survey: Californians and Their Government* (San Francisco: Public Policy Institute of California, July 2001), 13.

8. Carey McWilliams, *Southern California: An Island on the Land* (Santa Barbara: Peregrine Smith, 1946, 1973), 183.

9. Quoted in Joseph S. O'Flaherty, *Those Powerful Years: The South Coast and Los Angeles, 1887–1917* (Hicksville, NY: Exposition Press, 1978), 23.

10. Baldassare, *A California State of Mind*, particularly chapter 6, "The Latino Century Begins."

11. Zoltan Hajnal and Mark Baldassare, *Finding Common Ground: Racial and Ethnic Attitudes in California* (San Francisco: Public Policy Institute of California, 2001).

12. Quoted in Stephen Birmingham, *California Rich* (New York: Simon & Schuster, 1980), 13.

13. Neil Fligstein and Ofer Sharone, "Work in the Postindustrial Economy of California," *The State of Labor in California, 2002* (Berkeley: University of California Institute for Labor and Employment, 2002).

14. Robert A. Dahl, *Preface to Democratic Theory* (Chicago: University of Chicago Press, 1956), 124.

15. Dan Walters, *The New California: Facing the 21st Century*, 2nd ed. (Sacramento: California Journal Press, 1992), 20.

16. Harold Lasswell and Daniel Lerner, *The Comparative Study of Elites* (Stanford, CA: Stanford University Press, 1952), 7.

17. See Mark Arax and Rich Wartzman, *The King of California: J. G. Boswell and the Making of a Secret Empire* (Cambridge, MA: PublicAffairs, 2003).

18. PPIC Statewide Survey, *Californians and the Future* (San Francisco: Public Policy Institute of California, May 2015).

19. Dahl, *Preface to Democratic Theory*, 124, 27.

20. Dahl, *Preface to Democratic Theory*, chapter 5.

21. Alexis de Tocqueville, *Democracy in America*, Vol. II, eds. J. P. Mayer and Max Lerner (New York: Harper & Row, 1966), 477.

22. See Herbert J. Gans, *Middle American Individualism :The Future of Liberal Democracy* (New York: Free Press, 1988); Robert N. Bellah et al., *Habits of the Heart: Individualism and Commitment in American Life* (Berkeley: University of California Press, 1985).

23. Joan Didion, *Where I Was From* (New York: Alfred A. Knopf, 2003), 23.

24. Karthick Ramakrishnan and Mark Baldassare, *The Ties That Bind: Changing Demographics and Civic Engagement in California* (San Francisco: Public Policy Institute of California, 2004).

25. Peter Schrag, *Paradise Lost: California's Experience, America's Future* (New York: New Press, 1998), 12.

26. Kevin Starr, *California: A History* (New York: Modern Library, 2005), 344.

CHAPTER 2: CALIFORNIA'S POLITICAL DEVELOPMENT

1. Daniel Elazar, *American Federalism: A View from the States*, 3rd ed. (New York: Harper & Row, 1984), 122–23.

2. Carey McWilliams, *California: The Great Exception* (Berkeley: University of California Press), 17.

3. Elazar, *American Federalism*, chapter 4.

4. For further discussion of development, see Karen Orren and Stephen Skowronek, *The Search for American Political Development* (Cambridge, UK: Cambridge University Press, 2004).

5. F. K. Organski, *The Stages of Political Development* (New York: Alfred A. Knopf, 1965).

6. *Secularization* in this context meant converting the missions into parish churches (some remain so to this day), reducing the power of the friars, and releasing mission land for nonmission uses.

7. J. S. Holliday, *The World Rushed In: The California Gold Rush Experience* (New York: Simon & Schuster, 1981), 48.

8. James Polk, "Fourth Annual Message, December 5, 1848," in *Messages and Papers of the Presidents*, Vol. V (New York: Bureau of National Literature, 1897), 2487.

9. Paul Mason, "Constitutional History of California," *Constitution of the State of California (1879) and Related Documents* (Sacramento: California State Senate, 1973), 75–105.

10. John W. Caughey, *California: A Remarkable State's Life History* (Englewood Cliffs, NJ: Prentice Hall, 1970), 215.

11. Holliday, *The World Rushed In*, 26.

12. Ward McAfee, *California's Railroad Era: 1850–1911* (San Marino, CA: Golden West Books, 1973), 157.

13. Carl Brent Swisher, *Motivation and Political Technique in the California Constitutional Convention, 1878–79* (New York: Da Capo Press, 1969), 12.

14. Article XIX, "Chinese," 1879 Constitution.

15. Donald Worster, *Rivers of Empire* (New York: Pantheon Books, 1985).

16. For an extensive analysis of the "metropolitan-military complex" in California, see Roger W. Lotchin, *Fortress California, 1910–1961: From Warfare to Welfare* (New York: Oxford University Press, 1992).

17. See Robert E. Burke, *Olson's New Deal for California* (Berkeley: University of California Press, 1953).

18. Kevin Starr, *Endangered Dreams: The Great Depression in California* (New York: Oxford University Press, 1996), especially part IV.

19. Quoted in David Lavender, *California: Land of New Beginnings* (New York: Harper & Row, 1972), 397.

20. Quoted in Gladwin Hill, *Dancing Bear: An Inside Look at California Politics* (New York: World Publishing Company), 100.

21. Robert Glass Cleland, *From Wilderness to Empire: A History of California* (New York: Alfred A. Knopf, 1959), 419.

22. For more on Brown's record see, Ethan Rarick, *California Rising: The Life and Times of Pat Brown* (Berkeley: University of California Press, 2006).

23. Lou Cannon, *Governor Reagan: His Rise to Power* (Cambridge, MA: PublicAffairs, 2003), 9.

24. Quoted in James J. Rawls and Walton Bean, *California: An Interpretive History* (New York: McGraw Hill, 2003), 458–59.

25. Gavin Newsom, "A California For All," accessed January 9, 2019, https://www.gov.ca.gov/2019/01/07/newsom-inaugural-address.

CHAPTER 3: CONSTITUTIONALISM AND FEDERALISM

1. Hinten Helper, *The Land of Gold* (1855), quoted in Joe Mathews and Mark Paul, *California Crackup: How Reform Broke the Golden State and How We Can Fix It* (Berkeley: University of California Press, 2010), 21.

2. Mathews and Paul, *California Crackup*, 24.

3. See Article IX, Section 6, adopted November 4, 1952.

4. *Roe v. Wade*, 410 U.S. 113 (1973).

5. California Constitution, 1849, Article I, Section 1.

6. California Constitution, 1849, Article XI, Section 21.

7. See Susan B. Hansen, *The Politics of Taxation* (New York: Praeger, 1983), 233.

8. "The Federalist No. 45," in *The Federalist*, ed. Jacob E. Cooke (Middletown, CT: Wesleyan University Press, 1961), 311.

9. Morton Grodzins, *The American System* (Chicago: Rand McNally, 1966), 8–9.

10. Parris N. Glendening and Mavis Mann Reeves, *Pragmatic Federalism: An Intergovernmental View of American Government,* 2nd ed. (Pacific Palisades, CA: Palisades Publishers, 1984), 27–28.

11. For more background on this phenomenon, see Richard P. Nathan, "There Will Always Be a New Federalism," *Journal of Public Administration Research and Theory* 16 (October, 2006), 499–510.

12. 2018 California Election Overview, *FollowTheMoney.org*, accessed January 14, 2019, https://www.followthemoney.org/tools/election-overview?s=CA&y=2018.

13. Beacon Economics, *2014 California Tribal Gaming Impact Study,* http://www.yourtribaleconomy.com.

14. Kitty Felde and Viveca Novak, "The Politics of Drought: California Water Interests Prime the Pump in Washington," *Open Secrets Blog,* April 10, 2014, http://www.opensecrets.org.

15. Robert M. Hertzberg, "Global California: Greater Legislative Participation in International Affairs," *Spectrum: The Journal of State Government* 76 (Fall 2003): 22.

16. California Immigrant Policy Center, *Looking Forward: Immigrant Contributions to the Golden State, 2014* (Sacramento, CA: California Immigrant Policy Center), scribd.com.

17. Daniel Levy and Gabriel Szekely, *Mexico: Paradoxes of Stability and Change* (Boulder, CO: Westview Press, 1987), 213.

18. Hans P. Johnson and Sergio Sanchez, *Just the Facts: Immigrants in California* (San Francisco: Public Policy Institute of California, May 2018), https://www.ppic.org.

19. Jerry Brown, *2017 State of the State Address,* http://governors.library.ca.gov/39-Jbrown.html.

20. Taryn Luna, "Federal Judge Rejects Trump Lawsuit Against California's Sanctuary State Law," *Sacramento Bee,* July 10, 2018.

21. *Martinez v. Regents of the University of California,* 50 Cal. 4th 1277 (2010).

22. Harley Shaiken, "The NAFTA Paradox," *Berkeley Review of Latin American Studies* (Spring 2014): 36–43.

23. Jen Kirby, USMCA, "Trump's New NAFTA Deal, Explained in 500 Words," *Vox*, November 30, 2018.

CHAPTER 4: DIRECT DEMOCRACY IN A HYPERPLURALISTIC AGE

1. James Weinstein, *The Corporate Ideal in the Liberal State: 1900–1918* (Boston: Beacon Press, 1968), 3.

2. George E. Mowry, *The California Progressives* (Berkeley: University of California Press, 1951), 101.

3. Mowry, *The California Progressives*, 97.

4. For a historical treatment of direct democracy in California, see John M. Allswang, *The Initiative and Referendum in California, 1898–1998* (Stanford, CA: Stanford University Press, 2000).

5. For more on this proposition's legacy, see Jack Citrin and Isaac William Martin, eds. *After the Tax Revolt: California's Proposition 13 Turns Thirty* (Berkeley: Institute of Governmental Studies, 2009).

6. Jennifer Warren, "Gays Gaining Acceptance, Poll Finds," *Los Angeles Times*, June 14, 2000.

7. *In Re. Marriage Cases*, 43 Cal. 4th 757 (2008).

8. *Strauss v. Horton*, 46 Cal. 4th 364 (2009).

9. *Hollingsworth v. Perry*, 569 U.S. 2652 (2013).

10. *Obergefell et al. v. Hodges*, 574 U.S. ___ (2015).

11. *U.S. v. Oakland Cannabis Buyer's Cooperative*, 532 U.S. 483 (2001) and *Gonzales v. Raich*, 545 U.S. 1 (2005).

12. See campaign information at Proposition 64, Marijuana Legalization (2016), *Ballotpedia*, https://ballotpedia.org/California_Proposition_64,_Marijuana_Legalization_(2016).

13. Thomas Fuller, "Recreational Pot Is Officially Legal in California," *New York Times*, January 1, 2018.

14. Katy Steinmetz, "What to Know About Marijuana Legalization in California," *Time*, November 9, 2016, accessed January 14, 2019, http://time.com/4565438/california-marijuana-faq-rules-prop-64.

15. Peter Schrag, *Paradise Lost: California's Experience, America's Future* (New York: New Press, 1998), 189.

16. Political scientists regard legislators as *trustees* if they are primarily guided by personal conscience and as *delegates* if they are primarily guided by the wishes of the constituents who elect them.

17. Lester Milbrath, *Political Participation* (Chicago: Rand McNally, 1965), 144–45.

18. Thomas E. Cronin, *Direct Democracy: The Politics of Initiative, Referendum and Recall* (Cambridge, MA: Harvard University Press, 1989), 84–89, 210.

19. Joe Mathews and Mark Paul, *California Crackup: How Reform Broke the Golden State and How We Can Fix It* (Berkeley: University of California Press, 2010), 30–34.

20. Carey McWilliams, *California: The Great Exception* (New York: Current Books, 1949), 213.

21. Elizabeth R. Gerber, *The Populist Paradox: Interest Group Influence and the Promise of Direct Legislation* (Princeton, NJ: Princeton University Press, 1999).

22. Daniel Smith and Caroline Tolbert, "The Initiative to Party: Partisanship and Ballot Initiatives in California," *Party Politics* 7 (2001): 739–57.

23. Campaign spending data can be searched at the California Secretary of State's website: http://powersearch.sos.ca.gov/quick-search.php.

24. Michael Arno, email communication, March 1, 2013.

25. Elizabeth Gerber, *Stealing the Initiative: How State Government Responds to Direct Democracy* (Ann Arbor: University of Michigan Press, 2001).

26. *Strauss v. Horton*, 46 Cal. 4th 364 (2009).

27. *Ewing v. California*, 538 U.S. 11 (2003).

28. Mark Baldassare et al., *Just the Facts: California's Initiative Process: 100 Years Old* (San Francisco: Public Policy Institute of California, 2011); and subsequent PPIC and Field polls.

29. For more on the Davis recall, see Larry N. Gerston and Terry Christensen, *Recall: California's Political Earthquake* (Armonk, NY: M.E. Sharpe, 2004), and David G. Lawrence, *The California Governor Recall Election* (Belmont, CA: Wadsworth, 2004).

30. Ryan Holeywell, "The Rise of the Recall Election," *Governing*, April 2011, accessed at https://www.governing.com.

31. Mark Baldasarre and Cheryl Katz, *The Coming of Direct Democracy: California's Recall and Beyond* (Lanham, MD: Rowman & Littlefield, 2007).

CHAPTER 5: HOW CALIFORNIANS PARTICIPATE

1. "The Public, the Political System and American Democracy," Pew Research Center, April 26, 2018, https://www.people-press.org/2018/04/26/10-political-engagement-knowledge-and-the-midterms.

2. National Conference on Citizenship, *California Civic Health Index—2010* (Washington, DC: National Conference on Citizenship, 2011), https://ncoc.org.

3. James E. Prieger and Kelly M. Faltis, "Non-Electoral Civic Engagement in California," *California Journal of Politics and Policy* 5, no. 4 (October 2013): 671–710.

4. For an early analysis of the exit option and other responses to civic dissatisfaction, see William E. Lyons and David Lowry, "The Organization of Political Space and Citizen Responses to Dissatisfaction in Urban Communities: An Integrative Model," *The Journal of Politics* 49 (May 1986): 321–46.

5. David O. Sears and John B. McConahay, *The Politics of Violence: The New Urban Blacks and the Watts Riot* (Boston: Houghton Mifflin, 1973), 199.

6. V. O. Key, *Public Opinion and Democracy* (New York: Alfred A. Knopf, 1961), 14.

7. Public Policy Institute of California, *PPIC Statewide Survey: Californians and Their Government, January 2015* (San Francisco: Public Policy Institute of California, 2015), https://www.ppic.org/content/pubs/survey/S_115MBS.pdf.

8. U.S. Government Accountability Office, *Issues Related to State Voter Identification Laws* (Washington, DC: U.S. Government Accountability Office, 2014), https://www.gao.gov/products/GAO-14-634.

9. Public Policy Institute of California, *PPIC Statewide Survey: Californians and Their Government, March 2015* (San Francisco: Public Policy Institute of California, March 2015), https://www.ppic.org/content/pubs/survey/S_315MBS.pdf.

10. California Secretary of State, https://www.sos.ca.gov/elections/voter-registration/voter-registration-statistics.

11. Public Policy Institute of California, *Just the Facts: The Age Gap in California Politics* (San Francisco: Public Policy Institute of California, August 2012), https://www.ppic.org.

12. In the March 2015 election, Los Angeles voters chose to combine city elections with higher-turnout state elections beginning in 2020.

13. Claudine Gay, *The Effect of Minority Districts and Minority Representation on Political Participation in California* (San Francisco: Public Policy Institute of California, 2001).

14. Greg Mitchell, *The Campaign of the Century: Upton Sinclair's Race for Governor of California and the Birth of Media Politics* (New York: Random House, 1992).

15. Jim Miller, "Ho-Hum California Election Cycle Paid Off for Political World," *Sacramento Bee*, March 15, 2015.

16. Open Secrets, accessed January 17, 2019, https://www.opensecrets.org/pres16.

17. Mark Baldassare, *At Issue: California's Exclusive Electorate* (San Francisco: Public Policy Institute of California, 2006).

18. CNN Exit Polls, "California Governor," https://www.cnn.com/election/2018/results/california/governor.

19. Mark DiCamillo and Mervin Field, "2014 TCWF-Field Health Policy Poll—Part 2," *The Field Poll,* #2478 (August 20, 2014), http://www.field.com/fieldpollonline.

20. CNN Exit Poll, "California Governor."

21. Mark Baldassare, Dean Bonner, Alyssa Dykman, and Lunna Lopes, *Just the Facts: Race and Voting in California* (San Francisco: Public Institute of California, August 2018).

CHAPTER 6: LINKING PEOPLE AND POLICYMAKERS

1. *Linkage* was first coined by V. O. Key, *Public Opinion and American Democracy* (New York: Knopf, 1961), chapter 16, and developed further by Kay Lawson in *Political Parties and Linkage: A Comparative Perspective* (New Haven, CT: Yale University Press, 1980).

2. "Mr. Speaker: A California Journal Interview," *California Journal* 17 (January 1986): 13.

3. Public Policy Institute of California, *Just the Facts: Californians' News and Information Sources* (San Francisco: Public Policy Institute of California, October 2014).

4. Steve Scott, "Tube Dreams," *California Journal* 30 (May 1999): 29.

5. Beth A. Rosenson, "Media Coverage of State Legislatures: Negative, Neutral, or Positive?" *Social Science Quarterly* 96, no. 5 (2015).

6. Quoted in Lou Cannon, "Bleeders Sweeping Leaders Off California TV," *Washington Post,* May 23, 1998, A6.

7. Franklin D. Gilliam Jr. and Shanto Iyengar, "Prime Suspects: The Influence of Local Television News on the Viewing Public," *American Journal of Political Science* 44 (July 2000): 560–73.

8. Lori Dorfman et al., "Youth and Violence on Local Television News in California," *American Journal of Public Health* 87 (August 1997): 1131–37.

9. Jennifer Dorroh, "Statehouse Exodus," *American Journalism Review* (April/May 2010), http://ajr.org.

10. Mark Baldassare, *California in the New Millennium: The Changing Social and Political Landscape* (Berkeley: University of California Press, 2000), 40–42.

11. Christopher Cadelago, "On Talk Radio, Recovering Politicians Seek Second Act," *Sacramento Bee,* August 23, 2015.

12. "California Voter Consumption of Media on Government and Politics: An Analysis of Key Findings from Statewide Survey Research," *Fairbank, Maslin, Maullin, Metz & Associates (FM3) and Mercury Public Affairs* (August 2013), https://irvine-dot-org.s3.amazonaws.com/documents/2/attachments/camediaconsumptionsurvey_fullreport%281%29.pdf?1412656192.

13. "Digest of Education Statistics," *National Center for Education Statistics* (Washington, DC: National Center for Education Statistics, February 2018), https://nces.ed.gov/programs/digest/d16/index.asp.

14. "California's Political Elite Relying on Internet More, TV Less," *Government Technology* (February 17, 2006), http://www.govtech.net/magazine.

15. Quoted in Sandy Harrison, "Online Campaigning Comes of Age," *California Journal* 35 (May 2004): 29.

16. Public Policy Institute of California, *Just the Facts: California's Digital Divide* (San Francisco: Public Policy Institute of California, June 2013).

17. Quoted in Harrison, "Online Campaigning Comes of Age."

18. California Department of Technology, *California Promotes Secure, Appropriate Use of Social Media Sites for State Government, Issues Policy* (Sacramento: Department of Technology, February, 2010), http://www.ocio.ca.gov/Public/Newsletters/technology_update022610.html.

19. Meredith Conroy, Jessica T. Feezell, and Mario Guerrero, "Facebook and Political Engagement: A Study of Online Political Group Membership and Offline Political Engagement," *Computers in Human Behavior* 28 (2012): 1535–46.

20. Lauren Rosenhall, "FPPC Approves New Rules for Political Bloggers," *Sacramento Bee*, September 19, 2013.

21. Frank J. Sorauf and Paul Allen Back, *Party Politics in America*, 6th ed. (Boston: Scott Foresman/Little Brown, 1988), 10.

22. Mark Baldassare, "Purple Vote Is Growing," *Riverside Press-Enterprise*, April 9, 2006.

23. Adrian D. Pantoja, Ricardo Ramirez, and Gary M. Segura, "Citizens by Choice, Voters by Necessity: Patterns in Political Mobilization by Naturalized Latinos," *Political Research Quarterly* 54 (December 2001): 729–50.

24. Jack Citron and Benjamin Highton, "When the Sleeping Giant Is Awake," *California Journal* 33 (December 2002): 42–46.

25. Frederick Douzet and Kenneth P. Miller, "California's East-West Divide" in *The New Political Geography of California*, eds. Frederick Douzet, Thad Kousser, and Kenneth P. Miller (Berkeley: Berkeley Public Policy Press, 2008), 36.

26. *California Democratic Party, et al. v. Jones, Bill, CA Secretary of State 99–0401* (2000).

27. Public Policy Institute of California, *Just the Facts: California's New Electoral Reforms: The Fall Election* (San Francisco: Public Policy Institute of California, November 2012); Daniel Krimm and Eric McGhee, "Three Lessons About California's Election Reforms," *PPIC Blog* (November 5, 2014), http://www.ppic.org/main/blog_detail.asp?i=1625.

28. Betsy Sinclair, "Introduction: The California Top Two Primary," *California Journal of Politics and Policy* 7 (2015): 1–6.

29. See Thomas M. Holbrock and Ray Lajara, "Parties and Elections," in *Politics in the American States: A Comparative Analysis*, 9th ed., eds. Virginia Gray and Russell L. Hanson (Washington, DC: CQ Press, 2007).

30. Kristin Olsen, "GOP Is Dead in California: A New Way Must Rise," *CalMatters*, November 13, 2018, https://calmatters.org.

31. Jim Miller, "Independent Money Washes Over California's Contests on Tuesday's Ballot," *Sacramento Bee*, October 31, 2014.

32. *Eu v. San Francisco County Democratic Central Committee, 489 U.S. 214* (1989).

33. Krimm and McGhee, "Three Lessons About."

34. Dan Walters, "Slate Mail Is Just Junk, But Costly," *Sacramento Bee*, October 24, 2010.

35. Alexis de Tocqueville, *Democracy in America* (New York: Alfred A. Knopf, 1945), 191.

36. John Howard, "What's Good for Business Is Good for California," *California Journal* 35 (December 2004): 46–50; and John Howard, "California Labor's Big Shift" *California Journal* 35 (November 2004): 7–13.

37. Perry Communications, https://perrycom.com/services.

38. Quoted in Fair Political Practices Commission, *Independent Expenditures: The Giant Gorilla in Campaign Finance* (Sacramento: FPPC, 2008).

39. Quoted in Peter Schrag, *Paradise Lost: California's Experience, America's Future* (New York: New Press, 1998), 211.

40. Kathy Mulcahy, "Q&A with Higher Education Lobbying Expert," *LobbyingFirms.com*, September 14, 2010.

41. Theodore Lowi, *The End of Liberalism: The Second Republic of the United States*, 2nd ed. (New York: Norton, 1979), 51.

CHAPTER 7: LEGISLATIVE POLITICS

1. James Bryce, *The American Commonwealth*, Vol. 1, 2nd ed. (New York: Macmillan, 1891), 536.

2. For more analysis, see Alan Rosenthal, *The Decline of Representative Democracy: Process, Participation, and Power in State Legislatures* (Washington, DC: CQ Press, 1998).

3. For more on this period, see William Buchanan, *Legislative Partisanship: The Deviant Case of California* (Berkeley: University of California Press, 1963).

4. *Reynolds v. Sims 377 U.S. 533* (1964).

5. The 50 legislatures were judged on how functional, accountable, informed, independent, and representative they were. See Citizen's Conference on State Legislatures, *The Sometime Governments: A Critical Study of the 50 American Legislatures*, 2nd ed. (Kansas City, MO: CCSL, 1973).

6. See Richard A. Clucas, *The Speaker's Electoral Connection: Willie Brown and the California Assembly* (Berkeley: University of California Press, 1995).

7. See A. G. Block and Stephanie Carniello, "Putting on the Squeeze," *California Journal* 18 (April 1987): 178–80; and Delia M. Rios, "Squeezing the Juice from Committee Assignments," *California Journal* 12 (March 1981): 109–10.

8. "New California Laws 2019," *Capital Public Radio*, http://www.capradio.org.

9. This "author system" is described in William K. Muir Jr., *Legislature: California's School for Politics* (Chicago: University of Chicago Press, 1982), chapter 3.

10. "Women in State Legislatures for 2019," National Conference of State Legislatures, http://www.ncsl.org.

11. For extensive research on this topic, see Sue Thomas, *How Women Legislate* (New York: Oxford University Press, 1994); relative to California, see the "Women in Politics" issue of the *California Journal* 32 (December 2001).

12. A classic study of legislative roles can be found in John C. Wahlke et al., *The Legislative System: Exploration in Legislative behavior* (New York: Wiley, 1962).

13. Kent C. Price, "Instability in Representational Role Orientation in a State Legislature: A Research Note," *Western Political Quarterly* 38 (March 1985): 162–71.

14. In 2009, the California Citizens Compensation Commission cut base legislative salaries from $116,291 to $95,291 in the wake of a severe recession. Later, they cut the per diem from $173 to $142. Base pay was further reduced to $90,526 in 2012.

15. Joseph A. Schlesinger developed this classic division in *Ambition and Politics: Political Careers in the United States* (Chicago: Rand McNally, 1966), 10.

16. Bruce E. Cain, *The Reapportionment Puzzle* (Berkeley: University of California Press, 1984), 166–68.

17. Mark Dunkelman, *Gerrymandering the Vote: How a Dirty Dozen States Suppress as Many as 9 Million Votes* (Washington, DC: Democratic Leadership Council, June, 2008), http://www.dlc.org.

18. Eric McGhee, *Legislative Reform* (San Francisco: Public Policy Institute of California, 2007).

19. *Just the Facts: California's 2011 Redistricting: The Commission's Final Plans* (San Francisco: Public Policy Institute of California, August 2011).

20. Rosenthal, *The Decline of Representative Democracy*, 162–77.

21. Although gender differences are not dramatic, men and women do have different policy priorities including committee preferences, according to a multistate study that included the California legislature. See Sue Thomas and Susan Welch, "The Impact of Gender on Activities and Priorities of State Legislators," *Western Political Quarterly* 44 (June 1991): 445–56.

22. See Anthony York, "Capitol Whispers," *Political Pulse*, January 30, 2004.

23. Elizabeth Hill, "California Legislative Analyst's Office: An Isle of Independence," *Spectrum: The Journal of State Government* 76 (Fall, 2003): 26–29.

24. Legislative salaries can be browsed here: https://www.sacbee.com/site-services/databases/state-pay/article2642161.html.

25. Quoted in Shane Goldmacher, "While Budget Waits, California Legislators Collect Campaign Contributions," *Sacramento Bee*, August 12, 2008.

26. Ali Winston, "Green Firms Balk at Coalition's Lobbying Effort," *San Francisco Chronicle*, January 18, 2010, https://www.sfgate.com.

27. Quoted in Laureen Lazarovici, "The Rise of the Wind-Makers," *California Journal* 26 (June 1995): 18.

28. For more on legislative strategies of interest groups, see Jay Michaels and Dan Walters, *The Third House: Lobbyists, Money, and Power in Sacramento* (Berkeley: Berkeley Public Policy Press, 2002).

29. Peverill Squire and Gary Moncrief, *State Legislatures Today: Politics under the Domes* (Boston: Longman, 2010), 79.

CHAPTER 8: EXECUTIVE POLITICS

1. Amy Chance, "Cracked Bolts, Climate Change and Chipotle: Things Jerry Brown Said Over the Years," *Sacramento Bee*, December 23, 2018.

2. Chance, "Cracked Bolts."

3. Adam Ashton, Sam Stanton, Ryan Sabalow, and Dale Kasler, "Jerry Brown Wanted to Save the Planet and the California Budget. How Did He Do?" *Sacramento Bee*, December 18, 2018.

4. Mark Baldassare, "What Approval Ratings Say About Jerry Brown's Legacy," *CalMatters*, December 17, 2018.

5. Kathleen Ronayne, "From Brown to Newsom, State to Get New Style, Substance," *Fresno Bee*, January 7, 2019.

6. James MacGregor Burns, *Leadership* (New York: Harper & Row, 1978), 388.

7. See Robert E. Crew Jr., "Understanding Gubernatorial Behavior: A Framework for Analysis," in *Governors and Hard Times*, ed. Thad Beyle (Washington, DC: CQ Press, 1992), 15–27.

8. Margaret Ferguson, "Governors and the Executive Branch," in *Politics in the American States*, eds. Virginia Gray, Russell L. Hanson, and Thad Kousser (Washington, DC: CQ Press, 2013), 225.

9. California State Constitution, Article V, Section 1.

10. Peter Nicholas, "Governor's State Board Choices Raise Charges of Cronyism," *Los Angeles Times*, April 2, 2007.

11. For more on the budget process, see Jeff Cummins, *Boom and Bust: The Politics of the California Budget* (Berkeley: Institute of Governmental Studies, 2015) and Richard Krolak, *California's Budget Dance: Issues and Process*, 2nd ed. (Sacramento: California Journal Press, 1994).

12. Jack Chang, "Jerry Brown's Wife Is Vital Campaign Partner," *Sacramento Bee*, September 22, 2010.

13. Quoted in John Wildermuth, "Jerry Brown Sends National Guard to the Border, But on His Terms, Not Trump's," *San Francisco Chronicle*, April 18, 2018.

14. Quoted in Helene Von Damm, *Sincerely, Ronald Reagan* (Ottawa, IL: Green Hill, 1976), 162–63.

15. Adam Ashton, "How Can California Possibly Make a New Tax Department in Two Weeks?" *Sacramento Bee*, June 16, 2017.

16. This report and other reform-oriented reports on California's executive branch can be found at https://lhc.ca.gov.

17. A. G. Block and Gerald C. Lubenow, eds. *California Political Almanac, 2007–2008* (Washington, DC: CQ Press, 2007), 75.

18. California Correctional Peace Officers Association, http://www.ccpoa.org.

19. For an overview of the California Performance Review report, see the Legislative Analyst's Office, https://lao.ca.gov/2004/cpr/082704_cpr_review_ov.htm.

20. Quoted in Peter Nicholas, "Schwarzenegger Vows to 'Make Every Use' of Overhaul Plan," *Los Angeles Times*, August 4, 2004.

CHAPTER 9: CALIFORNIA'S JUDICIARY

1. See http://www.calbar.ca.gov. The total number of California attorneys, including inactives, judges, and those not eligible to practice law in the state, swells to over 270,000, by far the nation's largest bar.

2. For an account of both Mosk's career and this doctrine, see Bob Egelko, "Justice Stanley Mosk," *California Journal* 32 (August 2001): 26–31.

3. The relevant cases were *People v. Anderson* (1972), *Serrano v. Priest* (1971), and *Mukley v. Reitman* (1966).

4. Ronald M. George, *1997 State of the Judiciary Address*, http://www.courts.ca.gov/7858.htm.

5. An appellate opinion is published only if it establishes a new rule of law, involves a publicly visible issue, or contributes significantly to legal literature.

6. Judicial Council of California, *2015 Demographic Data Reports*, http://www.courts.ca.gov, and "Predominantly White Male State Bar Changing . . . Slowly," *California Bar Journal* (January 2012).

7. For details, go to https://www.followthemoney.org.

8. Article IV, Section 18b.

9. Data on specific cases, especially removal of judges, can be found at the Commission on Judicial Performance website, https://cjp.ca.gov.

10. Maggie Astor, "California Voters Remove Judge Aaron Persky, Who Gave a 6-Month Sentence for Sexual Assault," *New York Times*, June 6, 2018.

11. Sheryl Stolberg, "Politics and the Judiciary Coexist, But Often Uneasily," *Los Angeles Times*, March 21, 1992.

12. Quoted in Michael Estrin, "Pleading for Justice," *California Lawyer* (April 2014): 18.

13. Quoted in K. Connie Kang, "Brown's Court Legacy: Crusaders against Social Injustice," *California Journal* 13 (September 1982): 311.

14. Dan Morain, "Chief Justice of the California Supreme Court Leaves the Republican Party, Citing Kavanaugh," *CalMatters*, December 13, 2018.

15. Tani G. Cantil-Sakauye, *2018 State of the Judiciary Address*, https://newsroom.courts.ca.gov/news/2018-state-of-the-judiciary-address.

16. Bureau of Firearms, California Department of Justice, https://oag.ca.gov/firearms.

17. Franklin E. Zimring, Gordon Hawkins, and Sam Kamin, *Punishment and Democracy: Three Strikes and You're Out in California* (New York: Oxford University Press, 2001).

18. John Myers and Jazmine Ulloa, "With Brown, Justice System Shifted Focus to Redemption; Governor Used Data to Update Old Approaches to Crime," *Los Angeles Times*, January 4, 2019.

19. Mia Bird, Magnus Lofstrom, Brandon Martin, Steven Raphael, and Viet Nguyen, *The Impact of Proposition 47 on Crime and Recidivism* (San Francisco: Public Policy Institute of California, June 2018).

20. Mark DiCamillo and Mervin Field, "Voter Support for the Death Penalty Declines in California," *The Field Poll Release #2486* (September 12, 2014).

21. California Department of Corrections and Rehabilitation, "2018 Recidivism Report," https://sites.cdcr.ca.gov/research/wp-content/uploads/sites/9/2019/01/2018-Recidivism-Report.pdf.

CHAPTER 10: COMMUNITY POLITICS

1. Stephan G. Harding, "Jurupa Valley: The Last City in California?" *Western City* (August 2012).

2. Quoted in Joe Mathews and Mark Paul, *California Crackup: How Reform Broke the Golden State and How We Can Fix It* (Berkeley: University of California Press, 2010), 161.

3. Quoted in *City of Clinton v. Cedar Rapids and Missouri River Railroad Co.*, 24 Iowa 455, 475 (1868).

4. A stellar defense of home rule can be found in Chris McKensie, "Why Home Rule Is a Birthright of California Cities," *Western City* (July 2014).

5. Eugene C. Lee, *The Politics of Nonpartisanship: A Study of California City Elections* (Berkeley: University of California Press, 1960), 173.

6. See *Just the Facts: California's County Jails* (San Francisco: Public Policy Institute of California, April 2015).

7. James Bryce, *The American Commonwealth* (London: Macmillan, 1891), 586.

8. Sarah Bohn and Matt Levin, *Just the Facts: Poverty in California* (San Francisco: Public Policy Institute of California, August 2013).

9. Alan Berube, "City and Metropolitan Income Inequality Reveal Ups and Downs Through 2016," *Brookings*, February 5, 2018, https://www.brookings.edu.

10. Samuel E. Wood and Alfred E. Heller, *The Phantom Cities of California* (Sacramento: California Tomorrow, 1963), 43.

11. For a thorough analysis of this phenomenon, see Rob Kling, Spencer Olin, and Mark Poster, eds., *Postsuburban California: The Transformation of Orange County since World War II* (Berkeley: University of California Press, 1991); and Thomas Tseng et al., *Growing Urban Villages: Cultivating a New Paradigm for Growth and Development in California* (Malibu, CA: The Davenport Institute, Pepperdine University, 2006).

12. Tracy M. Gordon, *Planned Developments in California: Private Communities and Public Life* (San Francisco: Public Policy Institute of California, 2004).

13. Little Hoover Commission, *Special Districts: Relics of the Past or Resources for the Future?* (Sacramento: Little Hoover Commission, 2000), https://lhc.ca.gov.

14. California Special Districts Association, https://www.csda.net.

15. Peter Shrag, "Can't We Dump Some of Our 3,300 Special Districts?" *California Progress Report*, May 9, 2011, http://www.californiaprogressreport.com.

16. John Fensterwald, "Federal, State Visions for Improving Schools Collide in California," *EdSource*, January 30, 2018, https://edsource.org/2018/federal-state-visions-for-improving-schools-collide-in-california/593053.

17. Connie Llanoz, "Bike Paths Tell Tale of Two Cities," *Los Angeles Daily News*, September 13, 2007.

18. For more on the SCAQMD, go to http://www.aqmd.gov. For links to other agencies, go to the California Air Resources Board website, https://www.arb.ca.gov/capcoa/roster.htm.

19. Legislative Analyst's Office, "How Small Is Too Small? An Analysis of School District Consolidation? (Sacramento: Legislative Analyst's Office, May 2, 2011), https://lao.ca.gov.

20. Paul G. Lewis, *Deep Roots: Local Government Structure in California* (San Francisco: Public Policy Institute of California, 1998).

CHAPTER 11: BUDGET POLICY: THE COST OF DIVERSITY

1. Aaron Wildavsky, *The New Politics of the Budgetary Process* (Glenview, IL: Scott, Foresman, 1988), 2.

2. Legislative Analyst's Office, *CAL Facts: 2014* (Sacramento: Legislative Analyst's Office, 2014); and *CAL Facts: California's Economy and Budget in Perspective* (Sacramento: Legislative Analyst's Office, 2006).

3. Luke Reidenbach, *The Growth of Top Incomes across California* (Sacramento: California Budget & Policy Center, February 2016), https://calbudgetcenter.org/resources/the-growth-of-top-incomes-across-california.

4. *Numbers in the News: The California Economy in 2010* (Palo Alto: Center for the Continuing Study of the California Economy, March 2011).

5. Richard Krolak, *California's Budget Dance: Issues and Process*, 2nd ed. (Sacramento: California Journal Press, 1994), 49.

6. "The State That Tied Its Own Hands," *The Economist* 304 (July 11, 1987): 30.

7. Tony Quinn, "Origins of a Stalemate," *California Journal of Politics and Public Policy* 1 (2009), https://escholarship.org/uc/cjpp.

8. California Constitution Revision Commission, *Final Report and Recommendations to the Governor and the Legislature* (Sacramento: California Constitution Revision Commission, 1996), 10.

9. For a detailed analysis of ballot-box budgeting, see Jeff Cummins, *Boom and Bust: The Politics of the California Budget* (Berkeley: Institute of Governmental Studies, 2015), chapter 5.

10. John G. Matsusaka, "Direct Democracy and Fiscal Gridlock: Have Voter Initiatives Paralyzed the California Budget?" *State Politics and Policy Quarterly* 5 (Fall 2005): 248–64.

11. Legislative Analyst's Office, *Proposition 98 Primer* (Sacramento: Legislative Analyst's Office, February 2005), https://lao.ca.gov/2005_98_primer.

12. "California: Who Pays? 6th Edition," *Institute on Taxation and Economic Policy*, October 17, 2018, https://itep.org/whopays/california.

13. *PPIC Statewide Survey: Californians and Their Government* (San Francisco: Public Policy Institute of California, March 2015).

14. *PPIC Statewide Survey: Californians and Their Government* (San Francisco: Public Policy Institute of California, January 2015).

15. To locate current ratings, go to https://www.treasurer.ca.gov/ratings/current.asp.

16. Isaac William Martin and Jack Citrin, eds. *After the Tax Revolt: California's Proposition 13 Turns 30* (Berkeley: Institute of Governmental Studies Press, 2009).

17. Bruce E. Cain and Roger Noll, "Institutional Causes of California's Budget Problem," *California Journal of Politics and Public Policy* 2, no. 3 (2010), https://doi.org/10.5070/P2088T.

18. Mark D. Camillo and Mervin Field, "Voters Express Views on Dealing with the State's Huge Budget Deficit," *Field Poll Release #2368* (San Francisco: Field Corporation, March 16, 2011).

19. Krolak, *California's Budget Dance*, 111, 24.

20. Jeff Cummins, "An Empirical Analysis of California Budget Gridlock," *State Politics and Policy Quarterly* 12, no. 1 (2012): 23–42.

21. Quoted in Amy Chance, "Cracked Bolts, Climate Change and Chipotle: Things Jerry Brown Said Over the Years," *Sacramento Bee*, December 18, 2018.

CHAPTER 12: POLICIES STEMMING FROM GROWTH

1. Roger W. Lotchin, *Fortress California, 1910–1961: From Warfare to Welfare* (New York: Oxford University Press, 1992).

2. Hans Johnson and Laura Hill, *Population: California's Future* (San Francisco: Public Policy Institute of California, February 2015).

3. Examples include Raymond Dasman, *The Destruction of California* (New York: Macmillan, 1965); and Samuel E. Wood and Alfred E. Heller, *California Going, Going. . .* (Sacramento: California Tomorrow, 1962).

4. California Opinion Index, *A Compilation of California Public Opinion on Growth and Development* (San Francisco: The Field Institute, May 2002).

5. Joel Garreau, *Edge City: Life on the New Frontier* (New York: Doubleday, 1991), especially chapters 8 and 9 on Southern California and the Bay Area, respectively.

6. Mark Baldassare, *PPIC Statewide Survey: Special Survey on Growth* (San Francisco: Public Policy Institute of California, May 2001).

7. To understand the scope of this practice, see Tracy M. Gordon, *The Local Initiative in California* (San Francisco: Public Policy Institute of California, 2004).

8. Mark DiCamillo and Mervin Field, *The Field Poll, Release #2045* (May 15, 2002).

9. Erwin Cooper, *Aqueduct Empire* (Glendale, CA: The Arthur H. Clark Company, 1968), 202.

10. Edward Abbey, *Desert Solitaire* (New York: Simon & Schuster, 1968), 126.

11. Quoted in Norris Hundley Jr., *The Great Thirst: Californians and Water, 1770s—1990s* (Berkeley: University of California Press, 1992), 148.

12. *California Water Subsidies* (Washington, DC: Environmental Working Group, 2004).

13. Jay Lund et al., *Comparing Futures for the Sacramento-San Joaquin Delta* (San Francisco: Public Policy Institute of California, July 2008). See also the Delta Stewardship Council website for extensive background and updates (http://deltacouncil.ca.gov).

14. Matt Weiser, "California Allocates Vastly More Water Than Supplies Allow, Study Shows," *Sacramento Bee*, August 19, 2014.

15. *Water: California's Future* (San Francisco: Public Policy Institute of California, January 2019).

Page, George. Nature: Land of the Eagle: The Great Encounter (Public Broadcasting System, November 1991).

16. Kevin Starr, *Americans and the California Dream, 1850–1915* (New York: Oxford University Press, 1973), 417.

17. Hans Johnson and Amanda Bailey, *California's Newest Homeowners: Affording the Unaffordable* (San Francisco: Public Policy Institute of California, 2005).

18. These data are maintained by the California Association of Realtors. For updates, go to https://www.car.org/marketdata.

19. *Housing: California's Future* (San Francisco: Public Policy Institute of California, January 2019).

20. For more on this rental dilemma, see *Locked Out 2008: The Housing Boom and Beyond* (Sacramento: California Budget Project, 2008), https://calbudgetcenter.org.

21. Robert Half, "Ahead of Halloween Robert Half Reveals US Cities with Spookiest and Most Stressful Commutes," October 17, 2017, http://rh-us.mediaroom.com/2017-10-23-Ahead-Of-Halloween-Robert-Half-Reveals-U-S-Cities-With-Spookiest-And-Most-Stressful-Commutes.

22. Louise Bedsworth and Ellen Hanak, *California Transportation: Planning for a Better Future* (San Francisco: Public Policy Institute of California, June 2010).

23. Janet Wilson, "Study Doubles Estimate of Smog Deaths," *Los Angeles Times*, March 25, 2006.

24. Brian Mckenzie, *Who Drives to Work, Commuting by Automobile in the United States, 2013* (Washington, DC: U.S. Census Bureau, August 2015), https://www.census.gov/content/dam/Census/library/publications/2015/acs/acs-32.pdf.

25. Louise Bedworth, Ellen Hanak, and Jed Kolko, *Driving Change: Reducing Vehicle Miles Traveled in California* (San Francisco: Public Policy Institute of California, 2011).

26. *Climate Change: California's Future* (San Francisco: Public Policy Institute of California, January 2019).

CHAPTER 13: POLICIES STEMMING FROM DIVERSITY

1. These terms were used by Milton M. Gordon in his seminal work *Assimilation in American Life: The Role of Race, Religion and National Origins* (New York: Oxford University Press, 1964).

2. James Davison Hunter, *Culture Wars: The Struggle to Define America* (New York: Basic Books, 1991), 42.

3. These data are cited in Lou Cannon, *Governor Reagan: His Rise to Power* (New York: PublicAffairs, 2003), 213. California no longer formally collects such statistics outside the Medi-Cal program.

4. James Davison Hunter, *Culture Wars: The Struggle to Define America* (New York: Basic Books, 1991), 42.

5. *PPIC Statewide Survey: Californians and Their Government* (San Francisco: Public Policy Institute of California, March 2010), and *The Field Poll, Release #2187*, March 14, 2006.

6. John Fensterwald, "How Does California Rank in per-Pupil Spending? It All Depends," *EdSource*, February 28, 2017, https://edsource.org/2017/how-does-california-rank-in-per-pupil-spending-it-all-depends/577405.

7. EdSource, "How California Ranks" (Mountain View, CA: EdSource, September 2010), https://edsource.org/wp-content/publications/pub-2010-09-CaliforniaRanks.pdf.

8. Louis Freedberg and Stephen K. Doig, "Spending Far from Equal among State's School Districts, Analysis Finds," *California Watch*, June 2, 2011, http://www.californiawatch.org.

9. Legislative Analyst's Office, *The 2015–16 Budget Proposal: Proposition 98 Education Analysis* (Sacramento: Legislative Analyst's Office, 2015), https://lao.ca.gov.

10. *K–12 Education: California's Future* (San Francisco: Public Institute of California, January 2019).

11. *Master Plan for Higher Education in Focus: Draft Report* (Sacramento: Assembly Committee on Higher Education, April, 1993), 2.

12. Legislative Analyst's Office, The *Master Plan at 50: Guaranteed Regional Access Needed for State Universities* (Sacramento: Legislative Analyst's Office, 2011).

13. Amy Chance, "Cracked Bolts, Climate Change and Chipotle: Things Jerry Brown Said Over the Years," *Sacramento Bee*, December 18, 2018.

14. *Martinez v. Regents of the University of California*, Ct. App. 3 C054124 (2010).

15. Sarah Bohn, Caroline Danielson, and Tess Thorman, *Just the Facts: Poverty in California* (San Francisco: Public Policy Institute of California, July 2018). For a discussion of the Census Bureau's Supplemental Poverty Measure, view their website at https://www.census.gov/topics/income-poverty/supplemental-poverty-measure.html.

16. Caroline Danielson and Tess Thorman, *Just the Facts: The CalWORKs Program* (San Francisco: Public Policy Institute of California, January 2018).

17. Caroline Danielson, *Just the Facts: The CalFresh Food Assistance Program* (San Francisco: Public Policy Institute of California, February 2018).

18. *California's Food Stamp Program Participation Rate: Trends, Implications and Suggested Actions* (Sacramento: California Department of Health Services, February 2006), https://www.dhcs.ca.gov.

19. Paul Fronstin, "California's Uninsured," *California Health Care Almanac* (Sacramento: California Health Care Foundation, December 2010), https://www.chcf.org.

20. *Just the Facts: The Affordable Care Act in California* (San Francisco: Public Policy Institute of California, May 2014).

21. *Just the Facts: Immigrants and Health* (San Francisco: Public Policy Institute of California, June, 2008).

22. *Health Care: California's Future* (San Francisco: Public Policy Institute of California, January 2019).

Index

Note: Page references for figures are *italicized*.